THE FAMILY BOOK OF
HOME
REMEDIES

THE FAMILY BOOK OF
HOME
REMEDIES

A Practical Guide to Common Ailments

Safely Treated at Home using

Conventional and Complementary Medicines

Consultant Editor:
MICHAEL VAN STRATEN

BARNES
&NOBLE
BOOKS
NEW YORK

Contributors

Consultant Editor: **Michael van Straten**
(Introductions, Acupressure, Exercise, Kitchen Medicine,
Nutrition, Preventative Measures)
Alexander Technique: **Katarina Diss**
Aromatherapy: **Josie Drake**
Conventional Medicine: **Naomi Craft**
Herbal Remedies: **Penelope Ody**
Homeopathic Remedies: **Fiona Dry**
Reflexology: **Kristine Walker**
Yoga: **Sarah Ryan**

This edition published by Barnes & Noble Inc.,
by arrangement with
THE IVY PRESS LIMITED

1998 BARNES & NOBLE BOOKS

ISBN 0-7607-1066-X
M 10 9 8 7 6 5 4 3 2 1

Note from the Publisher
Information given in this book is not intended to be taken as a
replacement for medical advice. Any person with a condition
requiring medical attention should consult a qualified medical
practitioner or therapist.

This book was conceived, designed and produced by
THE IVY PRESS LIMITED
2/3 St Andrews Place
Lewes, East Sussex BN7 1UP

Art Director: Terry Jeavons
Designer: Ron Bryant-Funnell
Editorial Director: Sophie Collins
Commissioning Editor: Viv Croot
Managing Editor: Anne Townley
Text Editor: Mandy Greenfield
Captions: Fiona Corbridge
Picture Research: Liz Moore
Photography Coordinator: Kay Macmullan
Studio Photography: Mike Hemsley, Walter Gardiner Photography;
Ian Parsons; Guy Ryecart
Illustrations: Jerry Fowler, Andrew Milne

Printed and bound in China

Dedication

This book is dedicated to two great English Dames who could not be more
different, although both have one enduring passion—the health of the nation.
Dame Barbara Cartland, world famous for her romantic novels and pink frocks, is
one of the early pioneers of nutritional therapy and was talking about the
dangers of food additives, pesticides, and insecticides long before most people
had heard of them. She was also one of the earliest advocates of vitamin
supplements and it was on this topic that I made my first radio broadcast
together with Dame Barbara, who has remained a friend and a constant spur to
my work and research for 35 years.

Dame Kathleen Raven is not a household name, but she is the most important
and influential nurse since Florence Nightingale and was born in the year she died
—1910. She devoted her entire life to the care of others and to the training of
nurses, not just in England but throughout the world. As a Sister at Bart's Hospital
(St Bartholomew's), London, she served throughout the war years, sleeping on
the floor and tending the casualties while the bombs rained down. In 1948 she
was appointed Matron of that great hospital, the Leeds General Infirmary, and 10
years later became the British Government's Chief Nursing Officer at the
Ministry of Health. In "retirement" this remarkable woman helped establish
hospitals throughout the UK and the Middle East, setting standards of nursing to
which only she could aspire. Dame Kathleen has always understood the
importance of a "hands-on" approach to patients, to which end she has now
endowed a Chair of Practical Nursing. In common with every medical student
who passed through her wards—many going on to reach the peaks of eminence
—I have learned more about real medicine from my regular chats with "Matron"
during the past 20 years than it is possible to learn in a lecture room.

As I write this, Dame Barbara approaches her 98th birthday and Dame Kathleen
her 88th. I can only hope that these home remedies, which they both know so
well, will enable me to be half as energetic when I get to their age. Knowing these
two women and working with them has been a joy, a privilege, and an education.
Michael van Straten

The publishers wish to thank the following for the use of pictures:
Heather Angel p.165t; Bruce Coleman pp.35t, 51b, 59t, 125t, 204b; Bridgeman Art
Library 201t; Garden Picture Library pp.29b, 43r, 49b, 58b, 68b, 71tl, 77bl, 85l, 89l,
93tl, 111t, 121tl, 129t, 171, 173t, 180r, 182r, 207t; image bank pp.20b, 21r, 29t, 34b,
52b, 60b, 70l, 79t, 80l, 96b, 112b, 115l, 118b, 125b, 133t, 147b, 153b, 161t, 177b,
185t; John Glover 198–9; NHPA pp.21l, 33l, 39c, 41r, 63, 74b, 83t, 86b, 113b, 116b,
119c, 132b, 137c, 164b, 175tl, 179l, 181, 183c, 185br, 204t, 205t; Science Photo
Library p.139tr; Wildlife Matters pp.107c; Zefa 206.

Acknowledgments

Without the help of lots of other people, this book would never have seen the
light of day. My thanks are due to my secretary Janet, to my ever-patient editor
Mandy Greenfield and all her colleagues at the Ivy Press, and, above all, to my
partner Sally, who has not only put up with lots of midnight-oil burning and very
little socializing, but also spent most of our Spanish holiday slaving over
her laptop computer.
Michael van Straten

Abbreviations used in the book

BRAT diet	Bananas, Rice, Apples, and (dry) Toast diet
IU	International Units
mcg/µg	Microgram
NSAIDs	Non-Steroidal Anti-Inflammatory Drugs
TAT	Tired All the Time syndrome

CONTENTS

INTRODUCTION   6

PART ONE: A–Z DIRECTORY   9

PART TWO: THE AILMENTS   19
Immune System   20
Nervous System   48
The Senses   64
Bones and Muscles   96
Circulatory System   112
Respiratory System   120
Digestive System   134
Reproductive System   164
Excretory System   174
First Aid   180

PART THREE: A PRACTICAL HOME PHARMACY   193
Herbal remedies   194
Basic methods   194
List of herbs mentioned, with botanical names   196
The 20 most useful herbal remedies and the ailments they can help   198

Kitchen medicine   200

Conventional medicine   202
The 20 most useful conventional-medicine remedies
and the ailments they can help   202
Doses for adults, children, and pregnant women   203
Symptoms that require urgent medical attention   203

Homeopathy   204
The 20 most useful homeopathic remedies
and the ailments they can help   205

Aromatherapy   206
The 20 most useful aromatherapeutic oils
and the ailments they can help   207
Additional remedies   207

Nutrition   208
The 20 most useful healing foods and the ailments they can help   208
Food combining (the Hay diet)   210
The exclusion diet   211

Outside help   212
Acupressure   212
The Alexander Technique   213
Reflexology   214
Yoga   215

Home medicine chest   216
Kitchen, conventional, herbal, and homeopathic remedies,
and aromatherapy oils   216

Useful addresses   218
Further reading   220
Index   221

Introduction

There is nothing new about home remedies. Since the time of man's most primitive homes—in caves and mud huts, the tree-houses of the tropical rainforest and the igloos of the frozen wastes, the farmer's cottage and the native North American wigwam, the monastery and the medieval castle—people have used home remedies to treat their everyday ailments.

Home remedies have been passed down from generation to generation—in the Western world, usually from mother to daughter—and, until quite recently, featured strongly in every cookbook, in which there was always a section on food for people who are ill. In fact, it was not so long ago that nurses had to take an examination in the preparation of appropriate healing foods for their patients.

For the first time, this book brings together the ancient wisdoms of herbal medicine, traditional Chinese acupressure, the more modern applications of homeopathy, the expertise of conventional medicine, the gentle effectiveness of aromatherapy, and the age-old practices of kitchen medicine. The information you will find in these pages tells you not only how to deal with minor health problems that affect every family, but also how to utilize home remedies to hasten the healing of more serious illnesses and relieve some of the discomforts of complex diseases.

From homeopathic pilules for sinusitis to cabbage poultices for arthritic knees, from acupressure for headaches to a mustard poultice for backache, from lavender for insomnia to dandelions for cystitis, there are answers for dozens of everyday health problems. What is more, these are gentle answers, to which more and more people are turning in order to avoid unnecessary medication with powerful drugs—many now available "over the counter"—and endless prescriptions for sleeping pills, tranquillizers, painkillers, and antibiotics.

Many "alternative practitioners" talk about the good old days before we had a pharmaceutical industry, but this is simply living in fantasy land. All treatments and medicines must be viewed in the light of both risk and benefit, and it is doubtless true that the majority of natural therapies represent minimal risk and valuable benefit. However, the advances of modern medicine and surgery, together with the life-saving benefits of sophisticated pharmaceuticals, cannot be dismissed.

Though many of the home remedies in this book are an alternative to other treatments, there is really no such thing as "alternative medicine"—only good and bad medicine. In serious illness the patient is best served by a combination of the most suitable therapies for their particular problem, and this is why I always use the term "complementary medicine." When physicians and other practitioners work together, and their treatments are complementary to each other, the patient reaps the greatest benefit.

This book is not meant as a substitute for your physician, though in many instances the safe, simple treatments suggested will help prevent unnecessary trips to the doctor's office. Remember, though, that first aid is just what it says, and if you are in any doubt as to the seriousness of a symptom—especially when it involves children—then see your physician. Most parents have a natural instinct about the health of their children, and if your gut instinct is worrying you, then do not delay in seeking medical help.

Most accidents occur in the home—more than half of us have an accident each year requiring some sort of treatment, and one-fifth of us suffer an injury that requires medical treatment. Common sense and care can help to make accidents less likely, but it takes a bit more effort to prevent many of the other ailments described in this book. However, making the effort is well worthwhile and you will find detailed advice on how improving your nutrition can help you avoid recurring problems; how taking appropriate exercise can protect your joints; and how, using many of the other home remedies, you can boost your resistance to everyday infections.

In today's overcomplicated, technological, and stressful world many of us are anxious to take more control of our own lives. Using the home remedies in this book is one step in that direction, and my colleagues and I hope that the information we have provided will give you the self-confidence and the knowledge that you need to tackle many common ailments. Most of the remedies have stood the test of time and, like many other aspects of complementary therapy, can now claim scientific validation. Others are included on the basis of centuries of use and a vast body of anecdotal evidence. Although scientists may scoff, modern medicine has been built on the observations and anecdotes of great practitioners of the healing arts, and some of the most powerful modern drugs were in common use long before clinical trials were invented.

I hope that you will quickly discover the benefits of these simple remedies and, by passing them on to your relatives and your friends, will add to that vast body of anecdotal evidence and old wives' tales that really work.

MICHAEL VAN STRATEN

1998

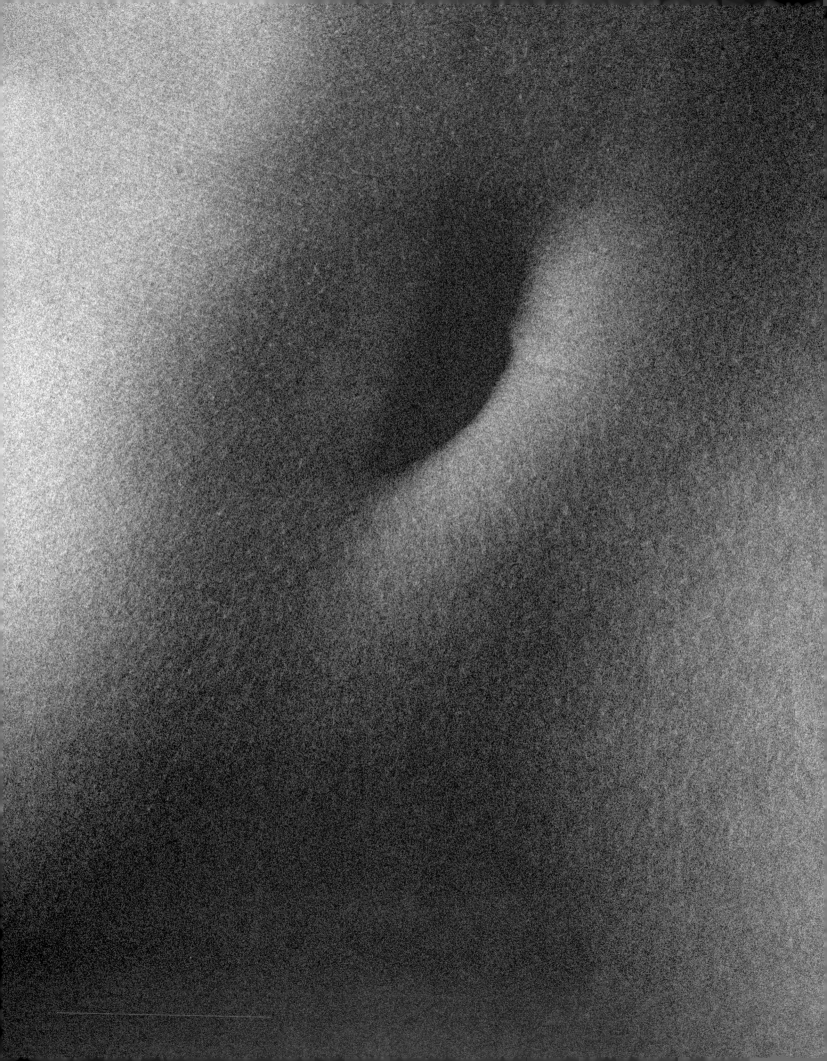

Part One

A–Z
DIRECTORY

A-Z
DIRECTORY *of* AILMENTS

THE DIRECTORY *is designed to give you quick, efficient access to The Ailments. Each ailment is entered independently and its page number indicated. The body system it affects is listed below the heading, and a short summary of symptoms and causes is given to enable you to pinpoint the ailment in question. A checklist of main therapies indicates which will help and a cross-reference directs you to similar or related ailments.*

Charts showing the acupressure and reflexology points mentioned throughout the text can be found on pp.212–15.

ABDOMINAL PAIN
STOMACH ACHE
page 140
DIGESTIVE SYSTEM
Abdominal pain, or stomach ache, can be triggered by stress and anxiety or by dietary indiscretion. Severe pain may herald serious disease.
- Aromatherapy
- Conventional medicine
- Herbal remedies
- Homeopathic remedies
- Kitchen medicine
- Nutrition
- Preventative measures

See also Constipation ❖ Diarrhea ❖ Flatulence ❖ Gallbladder problems ❖ Gastroenteritis ❖ Irritable bowel syndrome ❖ Peptic ulcers

ACNE
page 64
THE SENSES
Acne is a distressing skin problem characterized by angry red pustular spots and triggered by the fluctuating levels of hormones during adolescence.
- Aromatherapy
- Conventional medicine
- Herbal remedies
- Homeopathic remedies
- Nutrition
- Preventative measures

ALLERGIES
page 22
IMMUNE SYSTEM
An allergy is an abnormal response by the body's natural defense mechanisms, very often to something that would not normally be a hazard.
- Aromatherapy
- Conventional medicine
- Herbal remedies
- Homeopathic remedies
- Nutrition
- Preventative measures

See also Asthma ❖ Dermatitis ❖ Eczema ❖ Hay fever ❖ Hives

ANEMIA
page 118
CIRCULATORY SYSTEM
Anemia is a condition in which the blood has a reduced ability to absorb oxygen and transport it around the body, usually as a result of iron deficiency.
- Conventional medicine
- Herbal remedies
- Homeopathic remedies
- Kitchen medicine
- Nutrition
- Preventative measures

See also ❖ Fatigue ❖ Restless legs

ARTHRITIS
page 104
BONES AND MUSCLES
There are more than 200 different forms of arthritis that cause problems with the joints, although pain, stiffness, swelling, and inflammation are usually present.
- Aromatherapy
- Conventional medicine
- Herbal remedies
- Homeopathic remedies
- Kitchen medicine
- Nutrition
- Preventative measures

See also ❖ Rheumatism ❖ Osteoarthritis

ASTHMA
page 132
RESPIRATORY SYSTEM
In children, asthma is nearly always an allergic response to inhaled allergens; in adults it is triggered by changes in the body.
- Aromatherapy
- Conventional medicine
- Herbal remedies
- Homeopathic remedies
- Nutrition
- Preventative measures

See also ❖ Allergies ❖ Hay fever

BACK PAIN
page 100
BONES AND MUSCLES
Back pain has a number of causes, and may come on gradually or suddenly stab you in the back without warning, but most people will suffer from it at some time.
- Aromatherapy
- Conventional medicine
- Herbal remedies
- Homeopathic remedies
- Kitchen medicine
- Nutrition
- Preventative measures

BACTERIAL INFECTIONS
page 20
IMMUNE SYSTEM
See ❖ Infection (bacterial/viral)

BAD BREATH HALITOSIS
page 88
THE SENSES
Bad breath is nearly always the result of poor dental hygiene —a build-up of plaque, infected gums, a tooth abscess, a rotten filling, or lazy brushing techniques.
- Aromatherapy
- Conventional medicine
- Herbal remedies
- Homeopathic remedies
- Kitchen medicine
- Nutrition
- Preventative measures

See also ❖ Catarrh ❖ Constipation ❖ Gingivitis ❖ Sinusitis

BEDWETTING ENURESIS
page 174
EXCRETORY SYSTEM
Bedwetting is seldom the result of underlying disease or physical problems, but is usually one of those things that "just happen" and most children will grow out of it.
- Aromatherapy
- Conventional medicine
- Herbal remedies
- Homeopathic remedies
- Preventative measures

See also ❖ Stress

BITES
page 182

FIRST AID

Bites, by animals, insects, and marine species, vary in strength and seriousness, but often result in localized pain, reddening, and swelling, and sometimes in nausea, fainting, and breathing problems.

- Aromatherapy
- Conventional medicine
- Herbal remedies
- Homeopathic remedies
- Kitchen medicine

BLACK EYES
page 181

FIRST AID

See ❖ Bruises

BOILS
page 66

THE SENSES

A boil is characterized by a red, raised lump with pus in the middle, which is very tender to touch. It may be a sign of underlying illness or lowered resistance.

- Aromatherapy
- Conventional medicine
- Herbal remedies
- Homeopathic remedies
- Kitchen medicine
- Nutrition

See also ❖ Chilblains ❖ Herpes simplex

BRUISES & BLACK EYES
page 181

FIRST AID

Bruises are the visible sign of bleeding beneath the skin, resulting from pressure or a blow. They generally change color over a period of days.

A black eye is the result of severe bruising of the eye socket and lids. It is internal bleeding that results in the swelling and the skin turning black or dark blue.

- Aromatherapy
- Conventional medicine
- Herbal remedies
- Homeopathic remedies
- Kitchen medicine

BURNS
page 184

FIRST AID

Burns may be caused by dry heat, such as fire, friction, sun, chemicals, or electricity, and are often accompanied by shock.

- Aromatherapy
- Conventional medicine
- Herbal remedies
- Homeopathic remedies
- Kitchen medicine
- Nutrition

CANDIDA
page 166

REPRODUCTIVE SYSTEM

See ❖ Thrush

CATARRH
page 122

RESPIRATORY SYSTEM

Irritation of the mucous membranes in the nose and throat, or allergic reactions, can cause the blocked nasal passages that are characteristic of catarrh.

- Aromatherapy
- Conventional medicine
- Herbal remedies
- Homeopathic remedies
- Kitchen medicine
- Nutrition
- Preventative measures

See also ❖ Allergies ❖ Hay fever ❖ Sinusitis

CELLULITE
page 70

THE SENSES

The orange-peel-like skin that characterizes cellulite is not an illness, but is caused by a combination of hormone changes, skin structure, and fat deposits.

- Aromatherapy
- Conventional medicine
- Herbal remedies
- Nutrition
- Preventative measures

See also ❖ Weight problems

CHICKEN POX
page 40

IMMUNE SYSTEM

This highly infectious illness, characterized by a rash of small spots all over the body, is caused by the *Herpes zoster* virus and is most common in children.

- Aromatherapy
- Conventional medicine
- Herbal remedies
- Homeopathic remedies
- Nutrition
- Preventative measures

See also ❖ German measles ❖ Measles ❖ Mumps ❖ Scarlet fever ❖ Shingles

CHILBLAINS
page 112

CIRCULATORY SYSTEM

Chilblains are sore, itching, inflamed patches of skin, occurring most commonly on the backs of the fingers or tops of the toes, caused by restriction of the blood supply to the extremities.

- Aromatherapy
- Conventional medicine
- Herbal remedies
- Homeopathic remedies
- Kitchen medicine
- Nutrition
- Preventative measures

See also ❖ Boils ❖ Herpes simplex

CHRONIC FATIGUE SYNDROME ME
page 56

NERVOUS SYSTEM

This ailment is typified by grinding fatigue and exhaustion, an inability to stay awake, muscle pains, mood swings, and loss of concentration, enthusiasm, and appetite.

- Aromatherapy
- Conventional medicine
- Herbal remedies
- Homeopathic remedies
- Nutrition
- Preventative measures

See also ❖ Fatigue ❖ Stress

COLD SORES
page 28

IMMUNE SYSTEM

See ❖ Herpes simplex

COMMON COLD
page 124

RESPIRATORY SYSTEM

Colds, characterized by a sore throat, runny, sore, or blocked nose, headache, and general aches and pains, are caused by viruses, caught from other people.

- Aromatherapy
- Conventional medicine
- Herbal remedies
- Homeopathic remedies
- Kitchen medicine
- Nutrition
- Preventative measures

See also ❖ Catarrh ❖ Coughs and bronchitis ❖ Influenza

CONJUNCTIVITIS
page 86

THE SENSES

Conjunctivitis is an acute inflammatory condition of the mucous membrane covering the surface of the eye and lining the eyelids, caused by viral or bacterial infection.

- Aromatherapy
- Conventional medicine
- Herbal remedies
- Homeopathic remedies
- Kitchen medicine
- Nutrition

See also ❖ Styes

CONSTIPATION
page 156

DIGESTIVE SYSTEM

Constipation, or infrequent passing of stool, is one of the most common digestive problems, often caused by insufficient soluble fiber or fluid, or by bad toilet habits.

- Aromatherapy
- Conventional medicine
- Herbal remedies
- Homeopathic remedies
- Kitchen medicine
- Nutrition
- Preventative measures

See also ❖ Flatulence ❖ Hemorrhoids ❖ Irritable bowel syndrome

CORNS AND CALLUSES
page **68**

THE SENSES

These are hardened, thickened areas of skin occurring on parts of the body that are subject to constant friction, usually the hands and feet.

- Aromatherapy
- Conventional medicine
- Herbal remedies
- Homeopathic remedies
- Kitchen medicine
- Preventative measures

See also ✣ Warts

COUGHS AND BRONCHITIS
page **126**

RESPIRATORY SYSTEM

A cough may be caused by inhaled irritants, or it may be the sign of underlying illness; bronchitis, characterized by persistent coughing and copious phlegm, is caused by an infection, often following a cold or flu.

- Aromatherapy
- Conventional medicine
- Herbal remedies
- Homeopathic remedies
- Kitchen medicine
- Nutrition
- Preventative measures

See also ✣ Common cold ✣ Influenza ✣ Whooping cough

CRAMP
page **96**

BONES AND MUSCLES

Cramp is a sudden and severely painful contraction of the muscles, often in the calves, and can be due to a potassium deficiency.

- Aromatherapy
- Conventional medicine
- Herbal remedies
- Homeopathic remedies
- Kitchen medicine
- Nutrition
- Preventative measures

CUTS
page **180**

FIRST AID

Minor cuts do not usually require medical attention, because blood clots should quickly form and seal them, but they should be carefully cleaned and dressed.

- Aromatherapy
- Conventional medicine
- Herbal remedies
- Homeopathic remedies
- Kitchen medicine

CYSTITIS
page **178**

EXCRETORY SYSTEM

Cystitis is characterized by a stinging, burning sensation and increased frequency when passing urine, caused by infection of the bladder or urethra.

- Aromatherapy
- Conventional medicine
- Herbal remedies
- Homeopathic remedies
- Kitchen medicine
- Nutrition
- Preventative measures

DANDRUFF
page **82**

THE SENSES

See ✣ Hair problems

DERMATITIS
page **72**

THE SENSES

Dermatitis is an allergic reaction of the skin, producing an acute local inflammation, caused by contact with irritant substances or being part of a general allergic condition.

- Aromatherapy
- Conventional medicine
- Herbal remedies
- Homeopathic remedies
- Kitchen medicine
- Nutrition
- Preventative measures

See also ✣ Asthma ✣ Eczema ✣ Hay fever ✣ Psoriasis

DIARRHEA
page **158**

DIGESTIVE SYSTEM

The passing of frequent, loose, or even liquid stool is the result of irritation or inflammation of the gut, due to overindulgence or an infection.

- Aromatherapy
- Conventional medicine
- Herbal remedies
- Homeopathic remedies
- Kitchen medicine
- Nutrition
- Preventative measures

See also ✣ Gastroenteritis ✣ Irritable bowel syndrome

EARACHE
page **84**

THE SENSES

Pain in the ear is generally caused by an infection and is very common, especially in young children.

- Aromatherapy
- Conventional medicine
- Herbal remedies
- Homeopathic remedies
- Kitchen medicine
- Nutrition
- Preventative measures

ECZEMA
page **74**

THE SENSES

Eczema is inflammation of the skin, accompanied by redness, flaking, and tiny blisters, and often runs in families, sometimes accompanied by other allergies.

- Aromatherapy
- Conventional medicine
- Herbal remedies
- Homeopathic remedies
- Kitchen medicine
- Nutrition
- Preventative measures

See also ✣ Asthma ✣ Dermatitis ✣ Psoriasis

ENURESIS
page **174**

EXCRETORY SYSTEM

See ✣ Bedwetting

FAINTING
page **191**

FIRST AID

Fainting is caused by a temporary reduction in the supply of blood to the brain. It may be caused by a shock, fear, or exhaustion, missed meals, an over-hot atmosphere, or by standing still for too long.

- Aromatherapy
- Conventional medicine
- Herbal remedies
- Homeopathic remedies
- Kitchen medicine

FATIGUE
page **54**

NERVOUS SYSTEM

Fatigue is characterized by tiredness, irritability, stress, and anxiety; unless there is a specific diagnosis, it may be due to poor nutrition, insomnia, snoring, or even depression.

- Aromatherapy
- Conventional medicine
- Herbal remedies
- Homeopathic remedies
- Kitchen medicine
- Nutrition
- Preventative measures

See also ✣ Anemia ✣ Chronic fatigue syndrome ✣ Stress

FEVER
page **24**

IMMUNE SYSTEM

A fever or high temperature is the body's way of reacting to an attack by invading bacteria or viruses, and it is usually self-limiting.

- Aromatherapy
- Conventional medicine
- Herbal remedies
- Homeopathic remedies
- Kitchen medicine
- Nutrition
- Preventative measures

See also ✣ Gastroenteritis ✣ Infection ✣ Influenza ✣ Nausea

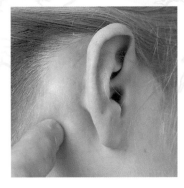

FIBROIDS
page 164
REPRODUCTIVE SYSTEM

Fibroids are benign tumors in the smooth muscles of the uterus and often cause heavy menstrual bleeding or menstrual pain.

- Aromatherapy
- Conventional medicine
- Herbal remedies
- Homeopathic remedies
- Kitchen medicine
- Nutrition
- Preventative measures

See also ❖ Anemia

FLATULENCE
page 142
DIGESTIVE SYSTEM

Flatulence, or excessive wind, often accompanied by a sensation of uncomfortable fullness, is the normal by-product of digestion and fermentation that takes place in the gut.

- Aromatherapy
- Conventional medicine
- Herbal remedies
- Homeopathic remedies
- Kitchen medicine
- Nutrition
- Preventative measures

See also ❖ Abdominal pain

FOOD POISONING
page 148
DIGESTIVE SYSTEM

See ❖ Gastroenteritis

FRACTURES
page 187
FIRST AID

A fracture is a broken or cracked bone, caused either by direct force (e.g. a blow or kick) or by indirect force, when the bone breaks at some distance from the point of force.

- Aromatherapy
- Conventional medicine
- Herbal remedies
- Homeopathic remedies
- Kitchen medicine

GALLBLADDER PROBLEMS
page 144
DIGESTIVE SYSTEM

Gallstones, characterized by discomfort or pain in the upper abdomen, and nausea and vomiting, are the main gallbladder problems, caused when a stone blocks bile flow to the stomach.

- Aromatherapy
- Conventional medicine
- Herbal remedies
- Homeopathic remedies
- Kitchen medicine
- Nutrition
- Preventative measures

See also ❖ Abdominal pain

GASTRITIS
page 146
DIGESTIVE SYSTEM

Gastritis is characterized by heartburn, vomiting, and flatulence, often with a burning sensation at the top of the stomach, and is nearly always self-inflicted.

- Aromatherapy
- Conventional medicine
- Herbal remedies
- Homeopathic remedies
- Kitchen medicine
- Nutrition
- Preventative measures

See also ❖ Abdominal pain ❖ Flatulence ❖ Nausea

GASTROENTERITIS
page 148
DIGESTIVE SYSTEM

The acute and violent diarrhea and vomiting that are a feature of gastroenteritis are most commonly caused by viral or bacterial infection.

- Aromatherapy
- Conventional medicine
- Herbal remedies
- Homeopathic remedies
- Kitchen medicine
- Nutrition
- Preventative measures

See also ❖ Abdominal pain ❖ Diarrhea ❖ Fever ❖ Nausea

GERMAN MEASLES
RUBELLA
page 32
IMMUNE SYSTEM

German measles is a mild, infectious disease typified by a rash that starts on the face and spreads down the trunk, sometimes accompanied by swollen glands.

- Aromatherapy
- Conventional medicine
- Herbal remedies
- Homeopathic remedies
- Kitchen medicine
- Nutrition
- Preventative measures

See also ❖ Chicken pox ❖ Measles ❖ Mumps ❖ Scarlet fever

GINGIVITIS
page 92
THE SENSES

Gingivitis, when the gums bleed very easily and dental plaque and tartar accumulate around the gum line, is by far the most common cause of gum disease.

- Aromatherapy
- Conventional medicine
- Herbal remedies
- Homeopathic remedies
- Kitchen medicine
- Nutrition
- Preventative measures

See also ❖ Bad breath

HAIR PROBLEMS
page 82
THE SENSES

Hair problems range from dandruff and damaged hair to hair loss and deterioration in hair or scalp condition, and are often a sign of underlying illness.

- Aromatherapy
- Conventional medicine
- Herbal remedies
- Homeopathic remedies
- Kitchen medicine
- Nutrition
- Preventative measures

HALITOSIS
page 88
THE SENSES

See ❖ Bad breath

HAY FEVER
page 128
RESPIRATORY SYSTEM

True hay fever is an allergic reaction to the pollen produced by grasses, characterized by sore, puffy eyes, streaming nose, and violent bouts of sneezing, but it may also describe allergic reactions to other airborne irritants.

- Aromatherapy
- Conventional medicine
- Herbal remedies
- Homeopathic remedies
- Kitchen medicine
- Nutrition
- Preventative measures

See also ❖ Allergies ❖ Asthma ❖ Sinusitis

HEADACHES
page 50
NERVOUS SYSTEM

A throbbing pain in the head, accompanied by tension in the neck and shoulders, is rarely a symptom of underlying disease, but is usually caused by stress, anxiety, or poor posture.

- Aromatherapy
- Conventional medicine
- Herbal remedies
- Homeopathic remedies
- Kitchen medicine
- Nutrition
- Preventative measures

See also ❖ Migraine

HEARTBURN
page 134
DIGESTIVE SYSTEM

Heartburn, or acid indigestion, in which there is a burning sensation behind the breastbone, is usually the result of too much of the wrong kind of food.

- Aromatherapy
- Conventional medicine
- Herbal remedies
- Homeopathic remedies
- Kitchen medicine
- Nutrition
- Preventative measures

See also ❖ Indigestion

HEMORRHOIDS
page **176**

EXCRETORY SYSTEM

Hemorrhoids, or piles, are varicose veins (either external or internal) in the soft lining of the anus, caused by constipation and straining, pregnancy, and childbirth.

- Aromatherapy
- Conventional medicine
- Herbal remedies
- Homeopathic remedies
- Kitchen medicine
- Nutrition
- Preventative measures

See also ❖ Constipation

HERPES SIMPLEX
COLD SORES
page **28**

IMMUNE SYSTEM

These unsightly and uncomfortable skin eruptions are sometimes the result of a cold, but are always triggered by stress—either physical or emotional.

- Aromatherapy
- Conventional medicine
- Herbal remedies
- Homeopathic remedies
- Kitchen medicine
- Nutrition
- Preventative measures

See also ❖ Boils ❖ Chilblains ❖ Shingles

HICCUPS
page **120**

RESPIRATORY SYSTEM

Hiccups are caused by a sudden spasm of the diaphragm and are nearly always the result of indigestion, overeating, rushing a meal, or having too many carbonated drinks.

- Aromatherapy
- Conventional medicine
- Herbal remedies
- Homeopathic remedies
- Kitchen medicine
- Nutrition
- Preventative measures

HIVES URTICARIA
page **76**

THE SENSES

Hives, also known as urticaria or nettle rash, is an allergic reaction to foods, plants, cosmetics or cleaning materials, alcohol, sudden cold or hot air, or sunlight.

- Aromatherapy
- Conventional medicine
- Herbal remedies
- Homeopathic remedies
- Kitchen medicine
- Nutrition
- Preventative measures

See also ❖ Allergies

INDIGESTION
page **136**

DIGESTIVE SYSTEM

Indigestion, typified by heartburn and severe discomfort around the breastbone, is often caused by the acid contents of the stomach getting back into the esophagus.

- Aromatherapy
- Conventional medicine
- Herbal remedies
- Homeopathic remedies
- Kitchen medicine
- Nutrition
- Preventative measures

See also ❖ Heartburn

INFECTIONS
BACTERIAL/ VIRAL
page **20**

IMMUNE SYSTEM

Infection occurs when the body's natural defense mechanism is not strong enough to withstand attack from one of the many billions of bacteria and viruses.

- Aromatherapy
- Conventional medicine
- Herbal remedies
- Homeopathic remedies
- Kitchen medicine
- Nutrition
- Preventative measures

See also ❖ Fever ❖ Nausea

INFESTATION
WORMS AND PARASITES
page **150**

DIGESTIVE SYSTEM

The term infestation covers a wide range of conditions, from head lice to a variety of intestinal worms.

- Aromatherapy
- Conventional medicine
- Herbal remedies
- Homeopathic remedies
- Kitchen medicine
- Preventative measures

INFLUENZA
page **26**

IMMUNE SYSTEM

Influenza is an acute viral infection, characterized by headache, fever and chills, muscle pain, loss of appetite, and a rapid pulse.

- Aromatherapy
- Conventional medicine
- Herbal remedies
- Homeopathic remedies
- Kitchen medicine
- Nutrition
- Preventative measures

See also ❖ Fever ❖ Nausea

INSOMNIA
page **62**

NERVOUS SYSTEM

Insomnia is a state of habitual sleeplessness, which may be caused by many different factors, although anxiety and stress often play a part.

- Aromatherapy
- Conventional medicine
- Herbal remedies
- Homeopathic remedies
- Kitchen medicine
- Nutrition
- Preventative measures

IRRITABLE BOWEL SYNDROME IBS
page **154**

DIGESTIVE SYSTEM

IBS is typified by severe abdominal pain, alternating diarrhea and constipation and bloating of the abdomen.

- Aromatherapy
- Conventional medicine
- Herbal remedies
- Homeopathic remedies
- Kitchen medicine
- Nutrition
- Preventative measures

See also ❖ Abdominal pain ❖ Constipation ❖ Diarrhea

LARYNGITIS
page **44**

IMMUNE SYSTEM

See ❖ Sore throat

ME MYALGIC ENCEPHALOMYELITIS
page **56**

NERVOUS SYSTEM

See ❖ Chronic fatigue syndrome

MEASLES
page **30**

IMMUNE SYSTEM

A highly infectious viral infection that attacks the respiratory system, usually accompanied by a red rash on the face, which spreads to the lower limbs.

- Aromatherapy
- Conventional medicine
- Herbal remedies
- Homeopathic remedies
- Kitchen medicine
- Nutrition
- Preventative measures

See also ❖ Chicken pox ❖ German measles ❖ Mumps ❖ Scarlet fever

MENOPAUSE
page **172**

REPRODUCTIVE SYSTEM

Menopause occurs when a woman's periods stop and there is a radical change in the balance of hormones circulating within the body.

- Aromatherapy
- Conventional medicine
- Herbal remedies
- Homeopathic remedies
- Kitchen medicine
- Nutrition

See also ❖ Menstrual problems

MENSTRUAL PROBLEMS
page 168

REPRODUCTIVE SYSTEM

Menstrual problems range from irregular or painful periods to heavy periods and lack of them, sometimes caused by an upset to the natural balance of hormones in the body.

- Aromatherapy
- Conventional medicine
- Herbal remedies
- Homeopathic remedies
- Kitchen medicine
- Nutrition
- Preventative measures

See also ❖ Menopause ❖ PMS

MIGRAINE
page 52

NERVOUS SYSTEM

There is no mistaking a real migraine; its visual disturbances, nausea, violent vomiting, neuralgia, and blinding pain.

- Aromatherapy
- Conventional medicine
- Herbal remedies
- Homeopathic remedies
- Kitchen medicine
- Nutrition
- Preventative measures

See also ❖ Headache

MOTION SICKNESS
page 190

FIRST AID

Any form of motion can cause the nausea, vomiting, headache, and dizziness or travel sickness.

- Aromatherapy
- Conventional medicine
- Herbal remedies
- Homeopathic remedies
- Kitchen medicine

See also ❖ Nausea

MOUTH ULCERS
page 90

THE SENSES

Mouth ulcers are painful, irritating, sore patches inside the mouth, generally on the lips and cheeks.

- Aromatherapy
- Conventional medicine
- Herbal remedies
- Homeopathic remedies
- Kitchen medicine
- Nutrition
- Preventative measures

See also ❖ Stress

MUMPS
page 34

IMMUNE SYSTEM

Mumps is a highly contagious viral infection, which starts with general malaise and fever, followed by painful swelling of one or both salivary glands on the side of the face.

- Aromatherapy
- Conventional medicine
- Herbal remedies
- Homeopathic remedies
- Kitchen medicine
- Nutrition
- Preventative measures

See also ❖ Chicken pox ❖ German measles ❖ Measles ❖ Scarlet fever

NASAL CONGESTION
page 122

RESPIRATORY SYSTEM

- Catarrh

NAUSEA
page 138

DIGESTIVE SYSTEM

Nausea is a feeling of sickness, often followed by actual vomiting, and may be due to overindulgence, ingestion of a toxic substance, food poisoning, or some other form of viral or bacterial infection.

- Aromatherapy
- Conventional medicine
- Herbal remedies
- Homeopathic remedies
- Kitchen medicine
- Nutrition
- Preventative measures

See also ❖ Motion sickness

NEURALGIA
page 48

NERVOUS SYSTEM

Neuralgia is pain in the nervous tissue, usually felt near the surface of the skin as a severe, piercing pain, which may settle down to a continual ache.

- Aromatherapy
- Conventional medicine
- Herbal remedies
- Homeopathic remedies
- Kitchen medicine
- Nutrition
- Preventative measures

See also ❖ Shingles

NOSEBLEEDS
page 188

FIRST AID

Nosebleeds may be caused by illness, a blow, by rupturing the nasal blood vessels, or may occur for no apparent reason.

- Conventional medicine
- Herbal remedies
- Homeopathic remedies
- Kitchen medicine

OSTEOARTHRITIS
page 106

BONES AND MUSCLES

Osteoarthritis is a degenerative joint disease, affecting mainly the hip, knee, spine, and fingers, and is often the result of wear and tear on weight-bearing joints.

- Aromatherapy
- Conventional medicine
- Herbal remedies
- Homeopathic remedies
- Kitchen medicine
- Nutrition
- Preventative measures

See also ❖ Arthritis ❖ Rheumatism

OSTEOPOROSIS
page 108

BONES AND MUSCLES

Osteoporosis is a condition in which the bones become weak and brittle, resulting in fracture, most commonly in women after menopause.

- Aromatherapy
- Conventional medicine
- Herbal remedies
- Homeopathic remedies
- Nutrition
- Preventative measures

PARASITES
page 150

DIGESTIVE SYSTEM

See ❖ Infestation

PEPTIC ULCERS
page 152

DIGESTIVE SYSTEM

Peptic ulcers are caused by erosion of the lining of the stomach, and are accompanied by abdominal pain, heartburn, cramp, and burning sensations.

- Aromatherapy
- Conventional medicine
- Herbal remedies
- Homeopathic remedies
- Kitchen medicine
- Nutrition
- Preventative measures

See also ❖ Abdominal pain ❖ Heartburn

PREMENSTRUAL SYNDROME PMS
page 170

REPRODUCTIVE SYSTEM

PMS, including bloating, mood swings, food cravings, and weight gain in the few days before the onset of a period, is the most common of all menstrual problems.

- Aromatherapy
- Conventional medicine
- Herbal remedies
- Homeopathic remedies
- Kitchen medicine
- Nutrition
- Preventative measures

See also ❖ Menstrual problems

PSORIASIS
page **78**

THE SENSES

Psoriasis is a chronic skin condition, characterized by a unique, silvery, scaly eruption of the skin, most commonly on the knees and backs of the elbows.

- Aromatherapy
- Conventional medicine
- Herbal remedies
- Homeopathic remedies
- Kitchen medicine
- Nutrition
- Preventative measures

See also ❖ Dermatitis ❖ Eczema ❖ Hives

REPETITIVE STRAIN INJURY **RSI**
page **98**

BONES AND MUSCLES

RSI is a result of overuse of the upper body at work and nearly always involves pain in the wrist, forearm, shoulder, and neck.

- Aromatherapy
- Conventional medicine
- Herbal remedies
- Homeopathic remedies
- Kitchen medicine
- Nutrition
- Preventative measures

RESTLESS LEGS
page **116**

CIRCULATORY SYSTEM

Restless legs are typified by an uncontrollable need to move the legs, pins and needles, and jerky spasms of the leg muscles, often caused by iron-deficiency anemia or circulation problems.

- Aromatherapy
- Conventional medicine
- Herbal remedies
- Homeopathic remedies
- Kitchen medicine
- Nutrition
- Preventative measures

RHEUMATISM
page **110**

BONES AND MUSCLES

Rheumatism is a general term used to describe painful problems affecting muscles, tendons, and connective tissue often (but not always) surrounding joints.

- Aromatherapy
- Conventional medicine
- Herbal remedies
- Homeopathic remedies
- Kitchen medicine
- Nutrition
- Preventative measures

See also ❖ Arthritis ❖ Osteoarthritis

RINGWORM
page **80**

THE SENSES

Ringworm is an inflammatory infection of the skin caused by mold or fungi and typified by red circular patches with a raised outside edge.

- Aromatherapy
- Conventional medicine
- Herbal remedies
- Homeopathic remedies
- Kitchen medicine
- Nutrition
- Preventative measures

See also ❖ Hives ❖ Psoriasis

RUBELLA
page **32**

IMMUNE SYSTEM

See ❖ German measles

SCARLET FEVER
page **36**

IMMUNE SYSTEM

Scarlet fever is an infectious illness that is nearly always the sequel of a bout of tonsillitis in children, characterized by a sore throat, fever, inflamed tonsils, and a scarlet rash.

- Conventional medicine
- Herbal remedies
- Homeopathic remedies
- Kitchen medicine
- Nutrition
- Preventative measures

See also ❖ Chicken pox ❖ German measles ❖ Measles ❖ Mumps

SEASONAL AFFECTIVE DISORDER **SAD**
page **58**

NERVOUS SYSTEM

SAD is much more than just the winter blues, involving episodes of depression, lethargy, mood swings, and weight gain, caused by lack of daylight.

- Aromatherapy
- Conventional medicine
- Herbal remedies
- Homeopathic remedies
- Kitchen medicine
- Nutrition
- Preventative measures

See also ❖ Chronic fatigue syndrome ❖ Fatigue

SHINGLES
page **42**

IMMUNE SYSTEM

Shingles is caused by the same virus that is responsible for chicken pox, and creates a burning sensation and blisters on the skin, which may be very sensitive.

- Aromatherapy
- Conventional medicine
- Herbal remedies
- Homeopathic remedies
- Kitchen medicine
- Nutrition
- Preventative measures

See also ❖ Chicken pox

SINUSITIS
page **130**

RESPIRATORY SYSTEM

Sinusitis is inflammation of the mucous membranes lining the sinuses, caused by a cold or upper respiratory infection, allergies, irritant smells, smoking, or adverse food reactions.

- Aromatherapy
- Conventional medicine
- Herbal remedies
- Homeopathic remedies
- Kitchen medicine
- Nutrition
- Preventative measures

See also ❖ Allergies ❖ Asthma ❖ Catarrh ❖ Hay fever

SORE THROAT
page **44**

IMMUNE SYSTEM

A sore throat may be caused by a viral or bacterial infection, dehydration, overuse of the voice, or by other infectious diseases.

- Aromatherapy
- Conventional medicine
- Herbal remedies
- Homeopathic remedies
- Kitchen medicine
- Nutrition
- Preventative measures

See also ❖ Common cold ❖ Fever ❖ Influenza ❖ Tonsillitis

SPLINTERS
page **189**

FIRST AID

Splinters are generally small pieces of wood or thorn that become embedded in the skin and may cause infection if not removed.

- Aromatherapy
- Conventional medicine
- Herbal remedies
- Homeopathic remedies
- Kitchen medicine

SPRAINS
page **186**

FIRST AID

A sprain occurs when the ligaments surrounding and supporting a joint are overstretched or torn, most commonly in the ankle or wrist.

- Aromatherapy
- Conventional medicine
- Herbal remedies
- Homeopathic remedies
- Kitchen medicine

STINGS
page **183**

FIRST AID

Stings, by insects and marine animals, vary in strength and seriousness, but often result in localized pain, reddening, and swelling, and sometimes in nausea, fainting, and breathing problems.

- Aromatherapy
- Conventional medicine
- Herbal remedies
- Homeopathic remedies
- Kitchen medicine

STOMACH ACHE
page **140**

DIGESTIVE SYSTEM

See ❖ Abdominal pain

STRESS
page **60**

NERVOUS SYSTEM

Stress is an ingredient of everyday life; what is important is learning how to cope with it, to avoid the other problems that can accompany unresolved stress.
- ◼ Aromatherapy
- ◼ Conventional medicine
- ◼ Herbal remedies
- ◼ Homeopathic remedies
- ◼ Kitchen medicine
- ◼ Nutrition
- ◼ Preventative measures

See also ❖ Headache ❖ Insomnia ❖ Migraine

STYES
page **87**

THE SENSES

A stye is an abscess in the tiny gland at the bottom of each eyelash and tends to be most common in those in poor general health.
- ◼ Aromatherapy
- ◼ Conventional medicine
- ◼ Herbal remedies
- ◼ Homeopathic remedies
- ◼ Kitchen medicine
- ◼ Nutrition

See also ❖ Conjunctivitis

SUNBURN
page **185**

FIRST AID

Sunburn is caused by ultraviolet rays, and susceptibility to it depends on the amount of pigment in your skin, but any excessive exposure carries a risk of skin cancer.
- ◼ Aromatherapy
- ◼ Conventional medicine
- ◼ Herbal remedies
- ◼ Homeopathic remedies
- ◼ Kitchen medicine

THRUSH
page **166**

REPRODUCTIVE SYSTEM

Thrush is a common infection caused by the yeast organism *Candida albicans* and generally refers to vaginal infection.
- ◼ Aromatherapy
- ◼ Conventional medicine
- ◼ Herbal remedies
- ◼ Homeopathic remedies
- ◼ Kitchen medicine
- ◼ Nutrition
- ◼ Preventative measures

TINEA
page **80**

THE SENSES

See ❖ Ringworm

TONSILLITIS
page **46**

IMMUNE SYSTEM

Tonsillitis is an acute infection of the tonsils, usually caused by a virus, although it may also be bacterial.
- ◼ Aromatherapy
- ◼ Conventional medicine
- ◼ Herbal remedies
- ◼ Homeopathic remedies
- ◼ Kitchen medicine
- ◼ Nutrition
- ◼ Preventative measures

See also ❖ Sore throat

TOOTHACHE
page **94**

THE SENSES

Toothache is usually the result of poor dental hygiene, but tooth decay, an abscess, or gingivitis may all be the cause of the pain.
- ◼ Aromatherapy
- ◼ Conventional medicine
- ◼ Herbal remedies
- ◼ Homeopathic remedies
- ◼ Kitchen medicine
- ◼ Nutrition
- ◼ Preventative measures

See also ❖ Gingivitis ❖ Mouth ulcers

URTICARIA
page **76**

THE SENSES

See ❖ Hives

VAGINAL YEAST INFECTION
page **116**

REPRODUCTIVE SYSTEM

See ❖ Thrush

VARICOSE VEINS
page **114**

CIRCULATORY SYSTEM

Varicose veins are visible, often raised, unsightly, and painful distended veins that commonly appear in the legs.
- ◼ Aromatherapy
- ◼ Conventional medicine
- ◼ Herbal remedies
- ◼ Homeopathic remedies
- ◼ Kitchen medicine
- ◼ Nutrition
- ◼ Preventative measures

See also ❖ Constipation ❖ Hemorrhoids

VIRAL INFECTIONS
page **20**

IMMUNE SYSTEM

See ❖ Infection (bacterial/viral)

WARTS
page **67**

THE SENSES

Warts are caused by a virus and are generally spread from other warts, either on another part of the body or caught from someone else.
- ◼ Aromatherapy
- ◼ Conventional medicine
- ◼ Herbal remedies
- ◼ Homeopathic remedies
- ◼ Kitchen medicine

See also ❖ Corns and calluses

WEIGHT PROBLEMS
page **160**

DIGESTIVE SYSTEM

Severe overweight and painful thinness both increase the risk of suffering from a range of ailments, as well as emotional problems.
- ◼ Aromatherapy
- ◼ Conventional medicine
- ◼ Herbal remedies
- ◼ Homeopathic remedies
- ◼ Nutrition

See also ❖ Cellulite

WHOOPING COUGH
page **38**

IMMUNE SYSTEM

This is an acute, highly infectious bacterial illness, characterized by the typical "whooping sound" caused by uncontrollable bouts of coughing.
- ◼ Aromatherapy
- ◼ Conventional medicine
- ◼ Herbal remedies
- ◼ Homeopathic remedies
- ◼ Kitchen medicine
- ◼ Nutrition
- ◼ Preventative measures

See also ❖ Coughs and bronchitis

WORMS
page **150**

DIGESTIVE SYSTEM

See ❖ Infestation

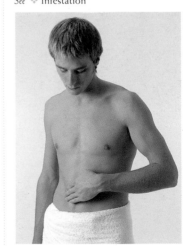

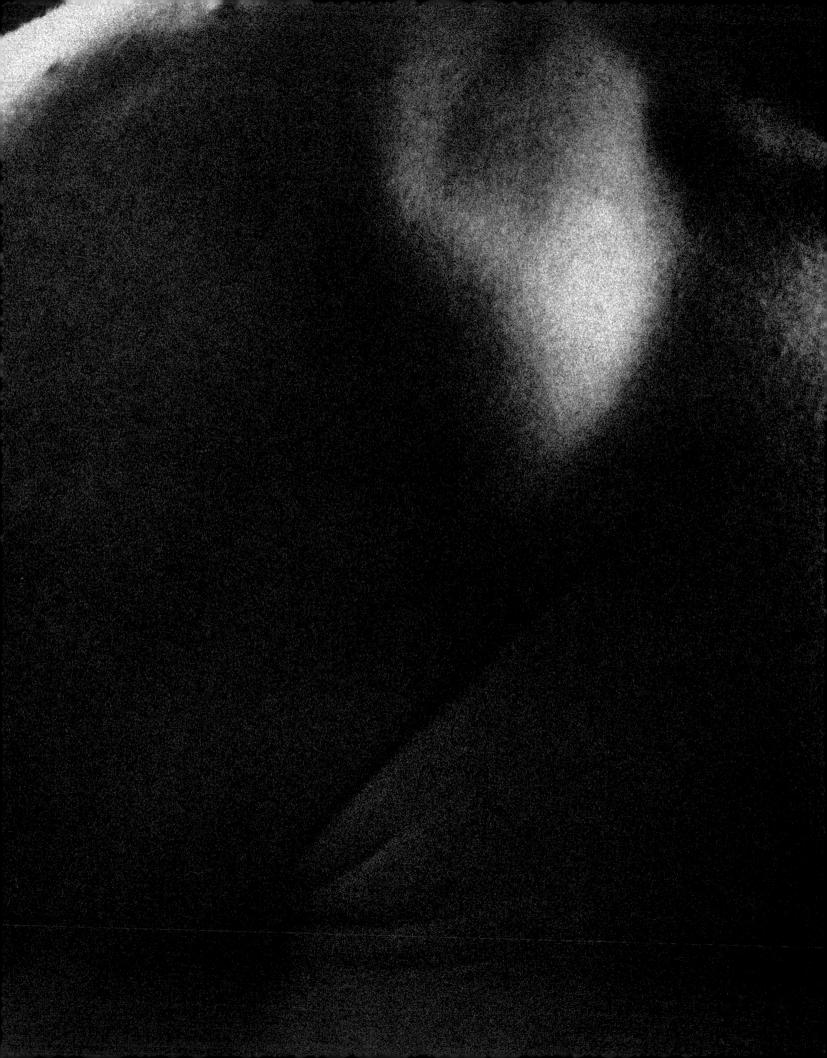

Part Two

THE
AILMENTS

RIGHT Many infections are acquired through the air: we breathe them in. Other routes are through broken skin, skin contact, sexual contact, and contaminated food.

DIAGNOSING
INFECTIONS
● Fever
● Other symptoms depend on the underlying cause

IMMUNE SYSTEM

infections *bacterial/viral*

CAUTION

Always read pain-reliever packages carefully, and do not exceed the stated dose.

KITCHEN MEDICINE

■ In essence, the immune system depends on specific nutrients, and an adequate supply of these depends in turn on a balanced and varied diet. There are, however, two vitally important minerals that are little understood by the general public and not always easily obtainable from everyday food.

■ These are zinc and selenium. Guarantee a surplus intake of both by eating a handful of pumpkin seeds every day for their zinc and five Brazil nuts daily for their selenium.

We share the world we live in with teeming billions of bacteria and viruses. Many have no impact on the human species, some cause minor discomfort, while others cause life-threatening disease. There are even a few that are essential to our healthy survival. The reason that Homo sapiens has survived as a species is because of the body's extraordinary ability to defend itself from attack by all these dangerous organisms. Our natural defense system is a delicate mechanism that needs careful nurturing and when we ignore its needs we can expect to reap a bitter harvest of ill health, disability, and even death. Nurturing this system starts and finishes in the home.

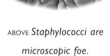

ABOVE Staphylococci are microscopic foe.

CONVENTIONAL MEDICINE

When you feel shivery due to a fever, curling up in bed wearing extra clothes can increase the body's temperature and simply make the problem worse. Instead, try a warm bath, which will help restore normal body temperature (this is particularly useful for children).

Alternatively, try sponging the body with tepid water. Dress in cool clothing and take a pain-reliever. Sometimes antibiotics will be prescribed to treat the infection, although viruses will not respond to them.

Dosage information ~
Adults
■ Take one to two tablets of pain relievers at onset of fever, repeated every 4 hours; see package for details.
Children
■ Give regular doses of liquid pain-reliever; see package or follow medical advice.

HERBAL REMEDIES

 Modern research has shown that many herbs can combat viruses or bacteria.

■ **Use and Dosage:**
Echinacea is one of the most effective herbs—take up to 600mg in tablets three times daily at the first sign of infection.

Garlic is both antiviral and antibacterial, so take up to 2g daily in capsules or add 1–2 cloves to cooked dishes.

Chinese tonic herbs, like astragalus, reishi, and shiitake mushrooms will boost the immune system. Try the mushrooms in soups, or buy them in capsules.

NUTRITION

Building a sound immune system starts three months before conception. Healthy eating by both prospective parents and avoidance of alcohol, large amounts of caffeine, nicotine, and drugs are a vital part of pre-conceptual planning. The nine months of pregnancy must be a period of optimum nutrition. That means: a minimum of five portions a day of a wide selection of fruit and vegetables; lots of complex carbohydrates such as whole wheat bread, brown rice, pasta, oats, all the other cereals, and beans; a sensible intake of low-fat dairy products; half a dozen eggs a week; at least four portions of oily fish each week; plenty of other fish, and poultry, and modest amounts of red meat. The same injunctions are just as relevant when breastfeeding.

In every adult's life there are periods of greater risk: the teens; the student years; the pressures and stresses of building a career; the retirement years, when one partner may be left alone and may lose interest in food. Good nutrition is important throughout life, but at these vulnerable times it is absolutely vital.

AROMATHERAPY

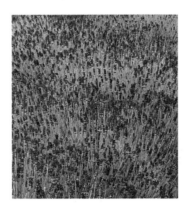

❧ TEA TREE
Melaleuca alternifolia
❧ LAVENDER
Lavandula angustifolia
❧ EUCALYPTUS
Eucalyptus radiata
❧ THYME
Thymus vulgaris
❧ NIAOULI
Melaleuca viridiflora
❧ BERGAMOT
Citrus bergamia

These oils work in three ways: by initially attacking the organisms themselves; by killing airborne germs (thereby preventing further infection); and by strengthening the body's immune system. Most of, if not all, the oils are active against infectious organisms of one kind or another, although the most

ABOVE *Lavender oil is extracted from the flower heads. It is good for flu and throat infections.*

effective and widely used is probably tea tree.

Application:
Depends on what is most convenient or pleasant to use for the user.

EXERCISE

KEEPING ACTIVE plays a key role in the maintenance of natural immunity. The activity hormones produced during physical exercise boost the immune system to an extraordinary extent—athletes and regular exercisers always have a higher count of the T-helper cells—essential components of the body's natural defense mechanisms.

School children seem to take little exercise these days, partly because they rarely walk or bike to school. Organized sports at school are in great decline, but worse still is the fact that so many children spend so much time sitting in front of a television or computer screen. This might explain the ever-increasing amount of infectious illness, allergies, and asthma experienced by the young.

VITAMINS: *the triumvirate of vitamins A, C, and the all-important E provides an enormously powerful and protective antioxidant force that defends the body's cells against attacks by bacteria, viruses, and free radicals.*

LIVE YOGURT: *one of the great immune-boosters is the high natural bacteria content of live yogurt, which plays a dual role in promoting good health. Not only do these beneficial bacteria colonize the gut and control the growth of harmful bacteria, but the enzymes they produce are absorbed directly through the gut wall and strengthen the immune system.*

STRESS: *learning some method of stress control is yet one more piece in the jigsaw of building a strong immune system. Yoga, meditation, or any other relaxation technique is a must, if we are to survive in the modern stressful world.*

ABOVE *Encourage your child to exercise: invite friends round for group games such as soccer. Make the journey to school a walk rather than a car ride.*

HOMEOPATHIC REMEDIES

In homeopathy the patient is treated according to symptoms that the body produces, not necessarily according to the type of infection that leads to those symptoms (so see *Fever on p.24,* *Influenza on p.26, Sore throat on p.44,* etc). It is possible to treat a person to reduce their susceptibility to infection, but this requires a remedy selected for the individual, so consult a homeopath.

RIGHT *Allergies may manifest anywhere in the body and in many ways, such as skin reactions, breathing problems, or stomach upsets.*

DIAGNOSING ALLERGIES

Mild symptoms include:
- Itching skin and/or eyes
- Sneezing fits
- Blocked or runny nose

More severe symptoms include:
- Wheezy breathing
- Difficulty in swallowing
- Swollen lips and tongue

IMMUNE SYSTEM

allergies

Allergies seem to be an ever-growing problem in our polluted, chemical-ridden, and junk-food lives. An allergy is an abnormal response by the body's natural defense mechanisms, very often to something that would not normally be a hazard. The body wrongly identifies a food, a pollen, or an atmospheric pollutant as a dangerous invader; the white cells overreact, causing more harm than the foreign substance; and this "allergic response" then becomes an illness in itself. Sometimes avoidance of the allergen is the only cure, and there are many practical solutions to this problem. In other situations, home remedies can make an enormous difference. (See also Asthma on p.132, Dermatitis on p.72, Eczema on p.74, Hay Fever on p.128, Hives on p.76.)

CAUTION

Violent allergic reactions—anaphylaxis—can be fatal. Sufferers should always carry an emergency injection of adrenalin. Breathing difficulties or swelling of the face should be treated as dire emergencies.

HOMEOPATHIC REMEDIES

Severe allergic reactions require medical help. *(See also Hives on p.76, Asthma on p.132 and Hay Fever on p.128.)*

APIS **30C** For swelling around eyes, sometimes too great to open lids. Swollen face, lips, and tongue.

Dosage: one tablet every 15 minutes. Maximum six doses.

It is also possible to treat allergies using "isopathy," in which a homeopathic dose of the substance causing the allergy (for example, house-dustmite, cat or dog fur, or pollen) is taken.

Dosage: one tablet of 30c potency twice weekly. Maximum six weeks.

CONVENTIONAL MEDICINE

Mild symptoms can be treated with antihistamines or steroid nose drops. For more severe and potentially fatal allergic reactions, such as some cases of peanut allergy, seek urgent medical attention. If you know you have a severe allergic reaction, it is useful to wear a MedicAlert bracelet or necklace, which describes your allergy, in case you fall ill.

Dosage information ~

Adults
- Antihistamines are available as tablets, syrup, or eyedrops; some preparations can cause drowsiness. Most tablets are taken once a day, although eyedrops are applied more frequently; see package for details or follow medical advice. Apply 2 puffs of steroid nose spray per nostril twice a day.

Children
- Doses of antihistamine syrup depend on the age of the child; see package for details or follow medical advice. With steroid nose sprays, apply 2 puffs per nostril twice a day to children over six.

NUTRITION

 Foods are among the commonest causes of allergic reactions, and not just as a result of eating them. Some foods trigger a reaction just through contact (*see Dermatitis on p.72*). It is also possible to become allergic to a food that you have been able to eat for years without problems. Allergies often run in families, but there is evidence that exposure to some foods too early in life can also cause problems. Cow's milk introduced too soon can cause allergic reactions in babies. Children exposed too early to peanuts or peanut products (and peanut oil has even been used in nipple creams) may develop life-threatening allergies.

The most common food allergens are milk, eggs, dairy products, shellfish, nuts, and berries. But allergies—which are very rapid reactions—should not be confused with food intolerance, which produces symptoms hours after consumption. Milk intolerance is a very common problem, whereas true milk allergy is quite rare. Coffee, cocoa, chocolate, tea, cheese, beer, sausages, canned food, red wine, and wheat are common causes of intolerance. Another major difference is that an allergy is triggered by the most minute amount of the culprit, whereas intolerance requires more substantial quantities.

All foods that are rich in B vitamins—as long as you are not allergic to them—can help reduce the severity of allergic symptoms, and oily fish can be a great help in the treatment of eczema, due to its high content of omega-3 fatty acids.

AROMATHERAPY

 MELISSA
Melissa officinalis
ROMAN CHAMOMILE
Chamaemelum nobile
LAVENDER
Lavandula angustifolia

These oils soothe and relax the body after its overreaction to whatever the external stimulus. They are also calming to the emotions.

Application:
This will depend on the form that the allergy takes (*for Hay Fever, see p.128*). If there is irritation on the skin, use a compress, soothing baths or some lotion containing a few drops of the oils, which can be rubbed in regularly. Or use a spray, if the skin is too irritated to be touched.

CAUTION

Most melissa that you can buy will be something called a chemo-type, which is manufactured, but contains all natural ingredients. If you are using true melissa, which is very rare and expensive, be extremely careful about how you use it, for it can cause nasty burns to the skin—so do check what you have bought from your supplier.

OUTSIDE HELP

ALEXANDER TECHNIQUE: this will not cure allergies, but as practicing the technique makes you more aware of your body's needs and responses, it can be a helpful tool in managing yourself and your condition.

REFLEXOLOGY: regular sessions should include the reflex for the area affected (e.g., the skin or the lungs), as well as the endocrine system, liver and kidneys, colon, and diaphragm.

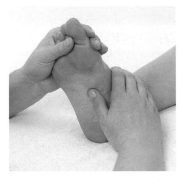

ABOVE *A reflexology treatment may help treat allergies.*

HERBAL REMEDIES

Garlic is traditionally used by many herbalists to combat food allergies—either add cloves to cooking or take daily garlic capsules. Regular cups of agrimony tea can improve the digestive system's ability to cope with allergens, while marigold will help combat the fungal infections often associated with food allergy. Teas made from chamomile, elder, or yarrow flowers can also reduce allergic reactions. While herbalists often recommend ephedra for allergic conditions, its use is limited in many countries to professional practitioners.

CAUTION

Several herbs can trigger allergic reactions; sensitive individuals should be especially careful when handling fresh rue.

PREVENTATIVE *measures*

Food is only part of the allergy story, and identifying the culprits can be a long and tedious business. Many other substances are also potential allergens, and making the effort to identify the source of your personal problems can be well rewarded.

FOOD: *keep a detailed diary of everything you eat and drink for two or three weeks, noting when you suffer allergic reactions. This should reveal distinct patterns, enabling you to track down the offending items and eliminate them from your diet. You will need professional help to make sure that you replace any missing nutrients with the appropriate supplements.*

FOOD ADDITIVES: *artificial colorings, flavorings, and preservatives are a very common cause of allergic reaction, especially in hyperactive children and asthmatics. Read food labels carefully and don't be fooled by "free from all artificial colorings" on the front of the package and other additives in tiny print on the back.*

HOUSEHOLD CHEMICALS: *these are another common trigger. Air fresheners, polishes, cleaning agents, detergents, dishwashing liquids, and fabric softeners can all cause severe reactions in the unsuspecting. Eco-friendly alternatives are now readily available.*

COSMETICS: *another common cause of allergic reactions, mostly in the skin (see Dermatitis on p.72), so try to use hypo-allergenic cosmetics if you are susceptible.*

METALS: *nickel is widely used in costume jewelry, buckles, and the studs on jeans. In contact with the skin, it often causes allergic reactions (see Dermatitis on p.72).*

RIGHT *A fever will cause body temperature to rise: you may feel very hot and poorly, and perspire a great deal.*

DIAGNOSING FEVER
- Shivering
- Hot, dry skin

IMMUNE SYSTEM

fever

A fever or high temperature is the body's way of reacting to an attack by invading bacteria or viruses. The body's temperature is strictly regulated and is normally between 98.4° and 99.5°F (36.9° and 37.5°C). As little as half-a-degree change in temperature may make you feel unwell and suggests there is an infection somewhere in the body. In most cases this is a self-limiting process, and the normal sort of high temperature—as a result of flu, for example—may be left to run its course. However, any prolonged bout of fever for which there is no obvious cause, or very high temperature, must be thoroughly investigated.

CALL THE PHYSICIAN
■ If very high temperatures, above 102.2°F (39°C), do not respond to conventional medication; are accompanied by cystitis, headache, or abdominal pain; or persist for more than 24 hours.

CAUTION
Be particularly alert for fevers starting after trips abroad, after accidents involving cuts and scrapes, contact with animals, or recent surgery.

CONVENTIONAL MEDICINE

Curling up under blankets wearing four layers, if you feel shivery and unwell, can raise the body temperature and simply make the problem worse. Try a warm bath instead, which will help to restore normal body temperature. This is particularly useful for children. Alternatively, try sponging with tepid water. Dress in cool clothing and take a pain-reliever. Sometimes antibiotics will be prescribed to treat the cause of the fever.

Dosage information ~

Adults
■ 1–2 tablets of pain-relievers at onset of fever, repeated every 4 hours; consult package for details.

Children
■ Give regular doses of liquid pain-reliever; consult pack for details, or follow medical advice.

KITCHEN MEDICINE
■ Encourage sweating with this favorite kitchen cordial: add the juice of a lemon, 2tsp/10ml of honey, 1tsp/5ml of grated ginger root, ½tsp/2.5ml each of cinnamon and nutmeg, and 1tbsp/15ml of brandy or whisky to a large mug of boiling water. Sip slowly.

OUTSIDE HELP

YOGA: lying or sitting, inhaling through the mouth helps to cool you. Use Crow Mudra, Shitali, or Sitkari (without head movements), exhaling through the nose. Rest as much as possible.

To inhale in Shitali, the tongue protrudes, with the sides curled up. Close the mouth to exhale.

Sitkari is an alternative for those who cannot shape their tongue for Shitali. Inhale with the tip of the tongue behind the teeth. Close the mouth to exhale.

For the Crow Mudra, purse the lips as though you are going to whistle. Close mouth to exhale.

NUTRITION

 "Feed a cold and starve a fever"—the old adage is absolutely correct. You will not feel like eating anyway, but the body will lose huge amounts of fluid through sweating, so copious drinks are essential.

Drink plenty of diluted fresh citrus juices for their immune-boosting vitamin C; pineapple juice for its soothing enzymes (cartons of juice are fine); and herbal teas—camomile, lime blossom, and elderflower.

ABOVE *Make this easy cordial to relieve a fever. To a large mug of boiling water, add the juice of a lemon, 2tsp/10ml honey, 1tsp/5ml grated ginger, ½tsp/2.5ml cinnamon, ½tsp/2.5ml nutmeg, and 1tbsp/15ml brandy or whisky.*

HOMEOPATHIC REMEDIES

❧ **ACONITE 30**C For first stage of illness. Hot, thirsty, anxious, and restless. If no improvement move on to:

❧ **BELLADONNA 30**C For rapid onset, high fever, red burning face, dry skin, cold feet. Dilated pupils. Hallucinations.

❧ **FERRUM PHOSPHORICUM 30**C For slower onset. Fever fairly high. Sweats and shivering.

❧ **GELSEMIUM 30**C For heavy, aching limbs, reluctance to lift head off pillow. Drowsy, chills up and down spine. No thirst. **Dosage**: one tablet every 30 minutes, for six doses, then every 4 hours. Maximum 3 days.

HERBAL REMEDIES

Herbs have long been used in fever management—cooling the body during the "hot" stages by encouraging sweating (e.g. with yarrow, lime flowers, boneset) and stimulating the digestion (using bitters such as gentian or wormwood), then alternately heating the system during the "chill" stage of the fever (with stimulants like angelica, cinnamon, ginger, or horseradish).

■ **Use and Dosage:**
High fevers require skilled treatment, so confine home remedies to milder cases of fever, using infusions of these herbs as appropriate.

PREVENTATIVE *measures*

Keep your immune system working efficiently by ensuring a regular intake of vitamin C, zinc, selenium, and all the carotenoids. You will get all these nutrients by eating a wide variety of fruit and vegetables, nuts and seeds.

AROMATHERAPY

 ❧ ROMAN CHAMOMILE
Chamaemelum nobile
❧ LAVENDER
Lavandula angustifolia
❧ TEA TREE
Melaleuca alternifolia
❧ JUNIPER
Juniperus communis
❧ PEPPERMINT
Mentha x piperita

Tea tree and juniper encourage the body to sweat, if it needs to eliminate excess fluid. The cooling oils, such as lavender and peppermint, are especially useful for infants, when there is a high temperature that may induce convulsions. Chamomile is soothing and calming.

Application:
Use either in a bath or in low doses in cool water, to sponge the body down at regular intervals.

RIGHT *Flu can make you feel very unwell. Besides a sore throat, coughing, and sneezing, and a high temperature, it's liable to cause muscle pain, lack of energy, and dull your appetite.*

DIAGNOSING INFLUENZA

- High fever
- Backache and muscular pains
- Tiredness and loss of appetite
- Sneezing
- Sore throat and dry cough
- Swollen glands in the neck

IMMUNE SYSTEM

influenza

This is an acute viral infection that recurs throughout the population every year. Approximately every 3 years flu reaches epidemic proportions, as new strains of virus appear, to which the general population has no acquired immunity. So make sure that your kitchen cupboard is always equipped with the necessary home remedies.

CALL THE PHYSICIAN

■ If a cough is getting worse and you are finding it difficult to breathe.

CAUTION

Flu is a serious illness and can be complicated by secondary chest infections and possibly pneumonia. The very young, the elderly, and anyone with asthma, chronic bronchitis, or other obstructive-airways disease, heart disease, kidney problems, diabetes, or undergoing immuno-suppressant therapy is at great, possibly even fatal, risk from flu. They should get medical help at once and avoid contact with any obvious sufferers. Returning to your normal lifestyle too quickly can lead to fatigue.

CONVENTIONAL MEDICINE

There is no specific treatment for influenza, which is caused by a virus infection and so will not respond to antibiotics. Feeling shivery due to a high fever can be eased by taking pain-relievers, which will also ease the muscular aches. Lozenges and hot drinks can soothe a sore throat. Rest in bed and drink plenty of water. Some strains of influenza can be prevented by an annual vaccination.

Dosage information ~

Adults

■ Take one to two tablets of pain-reliever at onset of fever, repeated every 4 hours; see package for details.

Children

■ Give regular doses of liquid pain-reliever; see package for details, or follow medical advice.

RIGHT *Hot lemon and honey is a traditional soother of sore throats.*

HOMEOPATHIC REMEDIES

❧ GELSEMIUM 30c For drowsiness and heavy lids. Head heavy. Chills up and down spine. No thirst. Weakness and trembling legs. Muscular soreness.

❧ EUPATORIUM PERFOLIATUM 30c For pain in bones and aching muscles in back and limbs. Thirsty. Throbbing headache. Aches and pains better for sweating.

❧ BRYONIA 30c For aches, pains, and headaches that are worse for slightest movement. Thirsty for long drinks. Sweats easily. Chill with hot head. Cough that makes headache worse.

Dosage: one tablet every 4 hours until improved. Maximum 12 doses.

HERBAL REMEDIES

Herbs can help to relieve some of flu's more unpleasant symptoms, as well as combat the debilitation that often follows an attack.

Use and Dosage:
Mix equal amounts of boneset, yarrow, elderflower, and peppermint and make an infusion with 2tsp/10ml per cup—add a pinch of cinnamon to this as well.

A compress soaked in lavender tea can be used to ease feverish headaches.

As a post-flu tonic, combine a decoction of elecampane root with an equal amount of an infusion of vervain and St. John's wort.

NUTRITION

The time to worry about nutrition and flu is before you get it. So boost your immune system by following the advice given under Infections (*see p.20*).

If you are unfortunate enough to catch flu— and most of us do from time to time—go to bed, go directly to bed, do not pass Go, do not collect $200. And stay in bed for at least 48 hours. Do not go back to work, school, or college for a week. For the first 24 hours, take plenty of fluids and eat grapes, berries, citrus fruit, and ripe pears only. In the second 24 hours, add cooked vegetables and salad. On the third day, start eating bread, potatoes, rice, and

ABOVE *Citrus fruits fuel-inject the immune system with vitamin C.*

pasta. By the fourth day you should be able to go back to your normal (and, I hope, healthy) diet. The restricted food intake at the start of this plan will push up your white-cell count and, together with the vitamin C in the fruit, will give your immune system a much-needed boost.

During a bout of flu, take 1g of vitamin C three times a day, 5,000 IU of vitamin A and a high-strength B-complex tablet. After a week, reduce the dose to 1g of vitamin C a day, 1,000 IU of vitamin A and continue with the B-complex. Keep taking these supplements for at least 3 weeks.

AROMATHERAPY

🌿 TEA TREE
Melaleuca alternifolia
Tea tree will make you sweat, which should help prevent any worse onset.

Application:
Immediately you feel the onset of a cold or flu, put four to six drops (depending on the size of

person) of tea tree into a warm bath and soak. After your bath, drink a large glass of water, then go to bed. Repeat as necessary. Use steam inhalations and burners to stop cross-infection and for symptomatic treatment. (*See also Common cold on p.124.*)

KITCHEN MEDICINE

■ To help with the miserable symptoms of headache, temperature, aches and pains, and the dry cough that nearly always accompanies flu, drink lots of lemon juice, hot water, and honey as a general soother for the body.

■ Copious amounts of lime-blossom tea will help lower your temperature and relieve the aches and pains of influenza. Adding a generous pinch of cinnamon to all your hot drinks increases their benefit.

■ Drink lots of pineapple juice for the healing enzymes it contains.

■ Cold, wet compresses around the neck and on the front of the chest will help make you much more comfortable while you have a high temperature.

PREVENTATIVE *measures*

Avoiding flu depends on the effectiveness of your body's natural defenses. To keep them firing on all cylinders, see Infections (*p.20*).

OUTSIDE HELP

REFLEXOLOGY: a complete foot reflexology treatment can act as an energy-booster when recovering from flu. Treat the whole foot lightly and briskly every 4 days.

YOGA: lying or sitting, inhaling through the mouth helps to cool you. Use Crow Mudra, Shitali, or Sitkari (without head movements), exhaling through the nose. Rest as much as possible.

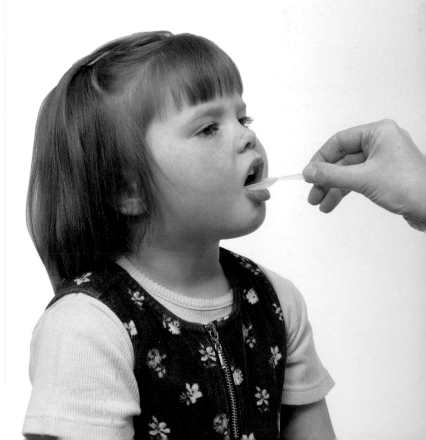

BELOW *Give a pain-reliever to reduce shivers and aches and pains.*

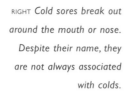

RIGHT *Cold sores break out around the mouth or nose. Despite their name, they are not always associated with colds.*

DIAGNOSING HERPES

- Itchy or sore area, usually around the mouth or nose
- Symptoms may be preceded by a numb or tingling feeling in the same area
- Cluster of small blisters, which may ooze clear fluid before crusting over

IMMUNE SYSTEM

herpes simplex *cold sores*

CALL THE PHYSICIAN
- If you get recurrent herpes.

KITCHEN MEDICINE
- At the very first sign of the tingling lip that heralds the arrival of a cold sore, rub the affected area with a slice of lemon. This may abort the development of a full-blown sore.

These unsightly and uncomfortable skin eruptions are sometimes the result of a cold, but they are always triggered by stress of some sort—either physical or emotional. The Herpes simplex virus may hibernate in the nerves after the initial infection, then spring to life if you get run down, become emotionally stressed or, just as easily, as a result of physical stress to the skin or extremes of temperature. Women often get cold sores at the time of their periods; vacationers get them when exposed to too much sun—and they are most likely to occur on skiing, boating, or beach vacations. Although there are now antiviral drugs, these are best kept for the much more serious problem of shingles (see p.42) and should not be used indiscriminately.

CONVENTIONAL MEDICINE

Treatment with creams containing antiviral drugs may help limit minor outbreaks, particularly if used early. Antiviral tablets are used to prevent frequent recurrences and to limit severe attacks.

Dosage information ~

Adults
- Take antiviral tablets up to five times a day for 5 days;

follow medical advice. Treatment with cream may need rather more frequent application

Children
- Dose depends on the weight and age of the child; follow medical advice. Apply creams every few hours.

OUTSIDE HELP

REFLEXOLOGY: if the cause is stress, then weekly, relaxing complete foot reflexology treatment may well reduce the frequency and intensity of the problem.

HERBAL REMEDIES

Numerous antiviral herbal extracts and oils have been used as a topical treatment for cold sores, including tea-tree oil, oil of cade (a juniper extract), lavender oil, clove oil, *Aloe vera* sap, sliced garlic, and house-leek juice.

■ **Use and Dosage:**
Internally, lemon-balm tea can be effective, as the herb shows significant antiviral activity against *Herpes simplex*.

Capsules containing echinacea (up to 600mg daily) or goldenseal (up to 100mg daily) can also help combat the infection and boost the immune system.

ABOVE *A forest of evergreen eucalyptus in Australia. Essential oil is extracted from the leaves and twigs. It is antiviral, bactericidal, and fungicidal.*

AROMATHERAPY

✿ EUCALYPTUS
Eucalyptus radiata
✿ TEA TREE
Melaleuca alternifolia
These oils are antiviral, so they will kill off the virus causing the problem, especially if you use the tea tree and strengthen the body's immune system, so that the cold sores become less frequent.

Application:
Apply these oils at the onset of cold sores and continue until they have cleared and even beyond, just to make sure that they are completely cured. Put the oils into an alcoholic base (5 drops of either eucalyptus or tea tree in 1tsp/5ml of vodka), then dab the cold sore frequently.

HOMEOPATHIC REMEDIES

✿ NATRUM MURIATICUM 6C For pearly white cold sores. May have mouth ulcers too. Swelling and burning of lower lip. Dry mouth and lips. Cracks in middle lower lip. Person may be introverted and easily hurt.
✿ RHUS TOXICODENDRON 6C For cracks in corners of mouth, cold sores around lips and chin, with scabs. Watery spots. Tongue red and coated, except tip. Thirsty.
Dosage: one tablet taken every 4 hours until improved. Maximum 1 week.

NUTRITION

As cold sores may be a sign of being generally run down, make sure that you really boost your nutritional status if you are suffering from an attack. Because these sores sometimes make eating difficult, rely on puréed vegetable or chicken soups, which are full of the vitamins and minerals you need. Try to boost your resistance by chewing a few pumpkin seeds each day for their zinc, a handful of Brazil nuts for their selenium and puréed avocado with garlic for its vitamin E and the antiviral benefits of garlic itself.

ABOVE *Live yogurt mixed with fruit helps to boost the immune system.*

PREVENTATIVE
measures

Once you have had a cold sore, the Herpes virus will live for ever, dormant in the nerve endings just under your skin, and will rear its ugly head when you least want it to. Preventing recurrent attacks necessitates keeping your immune system functioning at its best and avoiding the physical triggers, which is equally important.

NUTRITION: *the immune-boosting foods already listed should be part of your regular diet. In addition, you should be eating large quantities of whole grain cereals for their vitamin B content and a daily container of live yogurt to maintain your gut flora—essential for some vitamin B production and also an aid to natural immunity. Vitamin C and the bioflavonoids must also be part of your regular daily consumption, so eat lots of citrus fruit, including some of the pith and skin around the segments, and all the berries.*

LIP PROTECTION: *when you are exposed to cold winds or bright sunshine, use a total sunblock on your lips and remember to replenish it regularly if you are swimming or being active and likely to sweat.*

HYGIENE: *cold sores are highly infectious, so do not kiss anyone who has one and never let anyone with a cold sore pick up, hold, or kiss your baby. Do not share towels, facecloths, toothbrushes, flatware, or dishes with anyone who has an active cold sore. However, people prone to cold sores can only transmit the infection through contact with the fluid in the little blisters when they have a cold sore—not at any other time.*

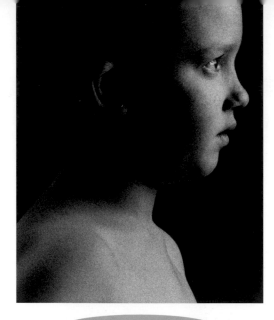

RIGHT *Small red spots with white centers appear in the mouth, before the brownish-red measles rash erupts, starting on the face and spreading down the body.*

DIAGNOSING MEASLES

- Fever
- Runny nose
- Red, watery eyes
- Cough
- Swollen glands
- After 3 or 4 days, an itchy rash develops, starting at the head and neck and spreading downwards, fading after 3 days

IMMUNE SYSTEM

measles

CAUTION

There is nearly always complete recovery from this illness, but watch out for fits caused by very high temperatures and the possibility of meningitis, eye problems, and secondary infections.

Always read pain-reliever packages carefully, and do not exceed the stated dose.

*T*his highly contagious viral infection causes a rash and attacks the respiratory system. The concerted effort to vaccinate all school children against measles now makes it a much rarer complaint than it used to be, but it is still a very serious illness and should not be taken lightly. Home remedies are not a substitute for your physician's advice, but they can make a child much more comfortable. Children with measles must be isolated; the infectious period lasts from the first symptoms—catarrh, conjunctivitis, high fever, and complete misery—until 5 days after the first appearance of the rash. It can take up to three weeks to develop symptoms after you have been in contact with someone with measles.

CONVENTIONAL MEDICINE

Treat the fever with pain-relievers, and use calamine lotion to help soothe itchy skin.
Dosage information ~
Adults
- One to two tablets of pain-relievers at onset of fever, repeated every 4 hours; see package for details. Apply calamine lotion/cream directly to the skin as required.

Children
- Give regular doses of liquid pain-reliever; see package for details, or follow medical advice. Apply calamine lotion/cream directly to the skin as required.

RIGHT *Calamine lotion is an excellent preparation to soothe itchy skin.*

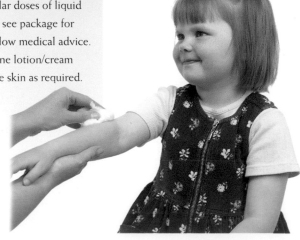

HERBAL REMEDIES

 Herbs can ease symptoms and combat the infection, to support orthodox treatments.

■ **Use and Dosage:**
Make an infusion containing equal amounts of hyssop, marshmallow, catmint, and ribwort plantain (½–1tsp/2.5–5ml of the mix per cup, depending on age of the child) and sweeten with a little honey, to soothe coughs and lubricate dry throats and airways.

Well-strained, cooled infusions of eyebright or self-heal can be used to bathe sore eyes, or to soak a cloth for use as a compress.

Use lemon-balm tea to help reduce fevers and bring down temperatures.

ABOVE *Lemon-balm tea is both cooling and sedating for fevers.*

KITCHEN MEDICINE

■ Fruit juices—especially pineapple, with its soothing enzymes, and orange, for its vitamin C—should be given in large amounts, diluted 50:50 with water.

■ Leeks, garlic, and onions are all protective against the secondary chest infection that often accompanies measles, so use them in abundance.

PREVENTATIVE
measures

VACCINATION: *other than avoiding children with the disease and making sure that your child's general immunity is at its best (see Infections on p.20), vaccination is the only sure prevention. Measles vaccination is safe and effective. Mild side-effects (a faint rash, slight temperature) are comparatively common, but serious side-effects are extremely rare. On the other hand, measles can cause serious complications, such as brain damage and deafness. Any small risk from vaccination is greatly outweighed by the much larger risk of getting the disease itself.*

HOMEOPATHIC REMEDIES

 If the condition worsens, consult a physician.

❧ MORBILLINUM **30C** After contact with measles, this remedy may help to prevent the disease. Take every 8 hours.

❧ BRYONIA **6C** For dryness and hotness. Cough with headache. Worse for any motion. May be used before rash appears.

❧ PULSATILLA **6C** For miserable, clingy child, who wants to be cuddled. Bland, creamy discharge from eyes. Not thirsty. Temperature not very high.

❧ EUPHRASIA **6C** For watering eyes, burning tears, nose discharging bland fluid. Throbbing head and dry cough.
Dosage: one tablet every 4 hours until improved. Maximum 5 days.

CAUTION

Take Morbillinum for three doses only.

NUTRITION

 Few children with measles will feel like eating in the early stages, but as soon as they do, foods rich in vitamin A and C should be given as light meals. Puréed carrot with a poached egg, sweet potatoes cut into small batons and oven-roasted, dried apricots puréed with yogurt and stirred into a package of jelly before setting, kiwi fruit with their tops sliced off and eaten like a soft-cooked egg…these foods are easy to eat, are appealing to children, and will boost the immune system, as well as protect the eyes.

ABOVE *Kiwi fruit is a rich source of vitamins C and E, potassium, and fiber.*

AROMATHERAPY

❧ TEA TREE
Melaleuca alternifolia
❧ EUCALYPTUS
Eucalyptus radiata
❧ ROMAN CHAMOMILE
Chamaemelum nobile
❧ LAVENDER
Lavandula angustifolia
These oils help to fight infection and are calming and soothing.
Application:
Vaporize the sickroom, which should stop the virus being spread by airborne germs. Use the oils with a little warm water to sponge down the patient, or spray them into the air or onto the patient (making sure that the water is warm). You can also use them as inhalations, especially if measles is accompanied by a sore throat.

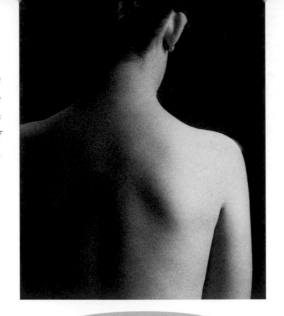

RIGHT *Besides a rash, which may creep over the whole body, German measles is likely to make you feel as if you've got a cold.*

DIAGNOSING GERMAN MEASLES

- Mild fever
- Sore throat
- Rash lasting 2–3 days, starting usually on the face, then spreading to the chest, abdomen, arms, and legs; individual spots may join together to produce a more generally flushed skin
- Swollen glands, particularly behind the ears
- Rarely, rubella causes painful joints

IMMUNE SYSTEM

german measles *rubella*

CALL THE PHYSICIAN

■ If you are pregnant, have been in contact with rubella, and are not sure of your immune status.

CAUTION

If German measles is contracted during the first 3 months of pregnancy, then the effects on the developing fetus can be catastrophic.

*T*he only significant thing about this mild, infectious disease is the risk it carries in pregnancy. It is not so long ago that young girls were deliberately exposed to other children suffering from German measles so that they would catch it and consequently become immune. Today, the majority of children are vaccinated against rubella (the medical term), but any child who does catch German measles must be kept away from all pregnant women, because of the risk to the unborn fetus—including deafness, blindness, heart and lung defects, and even death. Do not forget that many women in the earliest stages of pregnancy may be unaware that they are pregnant. Children with the illness must be kept at home during the infectious period of the disease, which lasts from the start of symptoms until at least 1 week after the appearance of the rash. If you have been in contact with someone with rubella, it can take 2 or 3 weeks before you develop a rash.

CONVENTIONAL MEDICINE

✚ If you have this common viral infection, you should rest if you feel unwell and avoid contact with other people, particularly school-age children and pregnant women. Although most women have had rubella or been immunized, if you are pregnant and worried that you have the illness, or have been in contact with someone with rubella, you should contact your physician.

KITCHEN MEDICINE

■ Camomile tea sweetened with honey helps reduce the fever and, when it is used unsweetened but refrigerated, makes a useful solution with which to bathe the affected area to reduce itching.

HERBAL REMEDIES

 Plenty of fluids are needed and herbal teas are ideal: they can be sweetened or flavored with honey (use pasteurized for very young children), lemon, licorice, or a little peppermint essence. Many soothing, cooling herbs are suitable, including lemon balm, chamomile, catmint, marigold, sage, and hyssop.

■ **Use and Dosage:**
Elderflowers, marigold, and chamomile make a good combination; use ½–2tsp/2.5–10ml per cup of water (depending on age).

Echinacea capsules (100–600mg daily) will help combat the infection of German measles.

Sage, agrimony, cleavers, or cinnamon tea helps to ease sore throats and swollen glands.

ABOVE *Cleavers is an especially good tonic for the lymphatic system and skin conditions. Use a food blender to produce fresh juice.*

AROMATHERAPY

 ✿ LAVENDER
Lavandula angustifolia
✿ ROMAN CHAMOMILE
Chamaemelum nobile
✿ TEA TREE
Melaleuca alternifolia
✿ EUCALYPTUS
Eucalyptus radiata
Chamomile and lavender help to ease any irritation from the rash. Tea tree and eucalyptus, when burned or vaporized, help prevent the virus spreading.

Application:
Use chamomile and lavender in the bath. They can also be used (as can tea tree) in warm water to sponge children down, if they are getting hot, clammy, and distressed. Burn or vaporize the eucalyptus and the tea tree; alternatively, use them in a water spray.

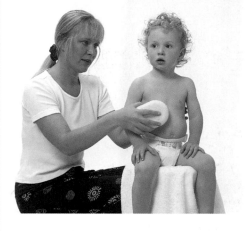

LEFT *Put a few drops of chamomile in some warm water and use this to sponge the child down. It is soothing and will reduce a high temperature.*

HOMEOPATHIC REMEDIES

 This is usually a mild disease and does not require treatment. Because of the danger to the fetus, most women are immunized against it, but if a woman is not immune to German measles and may have been exposed to it, then RUBELLA **30C**, taken every 12 hours for three doses only, may help.

NUTRITION

 Fluids are absolutely vital. **Drink plenty of** diluted fresh citrus juices for their immune-boosting vitamin C; pineapple juice for its soothing enzymes (cartons of pineapple juice are fine); and herbal teas— camomile, lime blossom and elderflower are all ideal.

PREVENTATIVE
measures

There is no way to prevent German measles, apart from vaccination. But it is important, as always, to maintain your child's general immunity in as strong a state as possible (*see Infections on p.20*).

BELOW *The battle to build a strong immune system gets a little help from the citrus army.*

RIGHT *Mumps affects the salivary and parotid glands, causing the neck to swell. Together with flu-like symptoms, mumps can make a child feel very miserable.*

DIAGNOSING MUMPS

- Tiredness
- Mild fever
- Sore throat
- Painful swelling in front of and below the ear, usually on both sides, after a couple of days; temperature will rise sharply
- Swollen glands under the jaw
- Chewing, and sometimes swallowing, is painful
- Men may have tender testicles, sometimes 2 or 3 weeks later

IMMUNE SYSTEM

mumps

CAUTION

Orchitis generally affects just one testicle, with little or few complications, but if both testicles are severely affected, there is considerable risk of sterility, which is seriously increased if the disease occurs in adults.

Always read pain-reliever packages carefully, and do not exceed the stated dose.

*T*his highly contagious viral infection mostly affects children between the ages of 4 and 14. It starts with general malaise and fever, followed by a painful swelling of the salivary gland on one side of the face. In 70 percent of sufferers it goes on to affect the gland on the other side of the face, too. The incubation period lasts 14 to 21 days and sufferers are infectious (via coughs and sneezes or saliva) for 7 days before, and until 9 days after, the first swelling appears. The main complication of mumps is a condition called orchitis—swelling of the testicles—which occurs in one-quarter of boys who catch the disease. There is no specific treatment for mumps, but the symptoms can be dealt with as they arise using the home remedies described below.

CONVENTIONAL MEDICINE

✚ Take a simple pain-reliever to reduce the fever and ease the symptoms. Eat soft food and drink plenty of liquids.
Dosage information ~
Adults
■ One to two tablets of pain-relievers at onset of fever, repeated every 4 hours; see package for details.

Children
■ Give regular doses of liquid pain-reliever; consult package for details, or follow medical advice.

RIGHT *Mumps must be especially carefully monitored in boys for signs of orchitis.*

HERBAL REMEDIES

Swollen glands may be eased by a mixture of cleavers, thyme, and marigold.

■ **Use and Dosage:**
Mix equal amounts of the herbs and make an infusion (½–2tsp/ 2.5–10ml per cup, depending on the child's age); sweeten with honey and a tiny pinch of chili powder or cayenne. Repeat every 2 hours. Take echinacea, which is antiviral, to combat the infection, and if the testicles are affected, use agnus-castus (10 drops of tincture in water three times daily).

Lemon balm or St. John's wort infusion can be used externally in compresses applied to the face and throat; it can also be used to bathe swollen glands.

NUTRITION

Getting sufficient calories into the child is the main difficulty, and soft or blended foods and drinks are best.

Give plenty of vegetable juices diluted with warm water, apple or pear juice, purées of carrot and potato, blended yogurt with honey, fresh non-citrus fruit like dried apricots, mangoes, and papaws which are both nutritious and healing. Pineapple juice will help, too. It is rich in the enzyme bromelain, which is anti- inflammatory and has a high content of natural sugars, to give the child energy. As soon as the patient is able to eat soft foods, give scrambled eggs, rice or tapioca puddings, pasta, mashed potato or avocado, real ice cream, minced chicken, and lots of bananas. A soluble vitamin C tablet (500mg) should be given every day.

Avoid acidic fruit juices, as these increase the flow of saliva, which is very painful.

Sweet potato

Cabbage

Parsnip

Watercress

Carrot

Celery

Parsley

ABOVE *Blend a selection of lightly cooked vegetables for a nutritious, easy-to-swallow soup.*

HOMEOPATHIC REMEDIES

ABOVE *Pulsatilla comes from the pasque flower, Pulsatilla vulgaris. This remedy is often used for treating childhood complaints.*

❧ PULSATILLA **6C** For use if the illness lingers; if there are complications of breasts swelling in girls or testicles swelling in boys (in which case, consult a physician).

❧ LACHESIS **6C** For swollen left side of face, which is sensitive to touch. Person tries to move away if someone tries to touch it. Sore throat, cannot swallow.

❧ MERCURIUS **6C** For right-sided pain, with production of lots of saliva. Smelly breath.

Dosage: one tablet every 2 hours for six doses, then four times daily. Maximum 3 days.

AROMATHERAPY

❧ LAVENDER
Lavandula angustifolia

❧ ROMAN CHAMOMILE
Chamaemelum nobile

❧ TEA TREE
Melaleuca alternifolia

❧ NIAOULI
Melaleuca viridiflora

❧ LEMON
Citrus limon

Lavender and chamomile are calming and soothing, and help to kill the pain. The other oils help to combat infection.

Application:
Put into an oil or a lotion to smooth gently over the affected area, or use as a compress to apply to swollen areas. Air sprays or vaporization will help stop the spread of airborne germs.

PREVENTATIVE *measures*

There is no way to prevent mumps, apart from vaccination. But it is important, as always, to maintain your child's general immunity in as strong a state as possible (*see Infections on p.20*).

KITCHEN MEDICINE

■ Cold compresses applied to the side of the face relieve the pain; they are equally effective if the testicles are involved. Tepid (not cold) sponging of the whole body will help to control the fever and minimize fluid loss. Repeat as often as necessary.

■ Keeping the patient well hydrated and nourished is a problem, as eating and drinking will be painful. Try an alkaline vegetable broth made with celery, cabbage, watercress, carrots, parsnip, sweet potato, and parsley, strained through a fine sieve. Let the child drink it warm, through a large plastic straw.

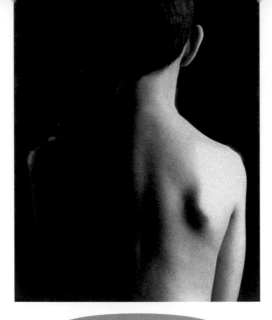

RIGHT *Preceded by a feverish sore throat, the characteristic scarlet fever rash may appear on the neck, chest, stomach, arms, or legs.*

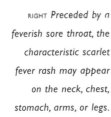

DIAGNOSING SCARLET FEVER

- Fever
- Headache
- Vomiting
- Red rash, which is not itchy; often with flushed red cheeks
- Tongue has a thick white coat with red spots

IMMUNE SYSTEM

scarlet fever

Scarlet fever is nearly always the sequel to a bout of tonsillitis in children. They will often have a sore throat, pain on swallowing, a high temperature, and inflamed tonsils, and if a rash appears 48 hours later on the neck, chest, stomach, arms, and legs, then it is almost certainly scarlet fever. A hundred years ago this was the commonest cause of death in children over the age of one year—now it is rare. It is caused by a bacterial infection and usually lasts about a week. Scarlet fever is infectious, so keep children away from others who have it.

CALL THE PHYSICIAN

■ If you think you have scarlet fever.

CAUTION

Scarlet fever can have serious complications, including rheumatic fever and inflammation of the kidneys, so consult a physician if in doubt or if the condition persists.

Always read pain-reliever packages carefully, and do not exceed the stated dose.

CONVENTIONAL MEDICINE

If you or your child show any symptoms of scarlet fever, you should contact your physician. You can treat the fever with a simple pain-reliever, but if your physician confirms that you have scarlet fever, then you will probably need treatment with antibiotics.

Dosage information ~

Adults

■ One to two tablets of pain-relievers at onset of fever, repeated every 4 hours; see package for details.

Children

■ Give regular doses of liquid pain-reliever; consult package for details, or follow medical advice.

HOMEOPATHIC REMEDIES

Because of the serious complications of this disease, orthodox treatment is recommended. Belladonna may, however, be used, together with orthodox medicine, to help relieve the symptoms.

BELLADONNA 6C For sudden red face and high temperature; could "fry an egg" on the skin. Paleness around mouth, pupils dilated. Hallucinations.

Dosage: one tablet every 2 hours for up to six doses, then every 4 hours as needed. Maximum 3 days.

NUTRITION

A sore throat and tonsillitis will make eating painful and difficult, while a high temperature means that there will be a greatly increased need for fluid replacement (*see Fever on p.24*). Pineapple and papaw juices are of great value, as the natural enzymes that they contain are both soothing and extremely healing to the damaged and inflamed delicate membranes of the mouth and throat.

Drink plenty of vegetable soup made with masses of broccoli, leeks, onions, garlic, and carrots, blended and given warm in a cup. This will help boost the body's levels of the powerful antioxidant nutrients, which increase natural resistance. The onions, garlic, and leeks all have antibacterial properties, which will help speed recovery.

If antibiotics are administered, it is important to replace the natural bacteria in the gut, as these will be killed off by the medication. A twice-daily drink made of a container of live yogurt, 2tsp/10ml of honey, a banana and ½ cup/120ml of milk, blended into a smooth milkshake, should be given morning and evening.

ABOVE *Keep up your fluid intake, and help to replace beneficial intestinal bacteria killed off by antibiotics, by whipping up a live yogurt milkshake.*

HERBAL REMEDIES

Certain herbs can alleviate the discomfort experienced during scarlet fever.

■ **Use and Dosage:**
As an alternative to sage (*see under Kitchen Medicine*), try gargles containing 10–20 drops of either golden seal or myrrh tincture.

To help reduce fevers and ease discomfort, drink a tea containing a mix of catmint, chamomile, elderflowers, and boneset (½–2tsp/2.5–10ml of the mix per cup, depending on the child's age).

Echinacea tablets will help combat the infection: 100–600mg daily in tablets, depending on age.

ABOVE *Resin of the myrrh tree is mixed with alcohol to make myrrh tincture, which is antimicrobial. It boosts production of the white blood cells that fight infection.*

KITCHEN MEDICINE

■ A sore throat can be relieved by gargling with sage tea. Put 1tsp/5ml of fresh chopped sage leaves (or 2tsp/10ml of dried) into a glass, add boiling water, cover and leave to stand for 10 minutes. Strain and use as a mouthwash when cool.

■ Cold compresses applied to the body relieve the pain. Tepid (not cold) sponging of the whole body will help to control the fever and minimize fluid loss. Repeat as necessary.

PREVENTATIVE
measures

It is difficult to prevent any of the infectious childhood diseases, other than by providing good nutrition and a sound immune system, but recurrent bouts of tonsillitis increase the risk of scarlet fever (*see Tonsillitis on p.46*).

BELOW *Young children will benefit greatly from a comforting cuddle to soothe their distress and help recovery.*

RIGHT *The severe, spasmodic coughing of whooping cough will exhaust the sufferer, particularly if accompanied by vomiting.*

DIAGNOSING WHOOPING COUGH

- Sneezing
- Watery red eyes
- Sore throat
- Mild fever
- Cough; irregular bouts of severe coughing fits start nearly 2 weeks later and can last for a month
- Gasping for breath at the end of a coughing fit causes the characteristic whoop while breathing in

IMMUNE SYSTEM

whooping cough

CAUTION

Whooping cough is a serious illness, and although most children recover fully, complications can occur and medical care is essential, especially for children under the age of three.

This highly infectious childhood disease is spread by coughs and sneezes and is most infectious in the early stages. It starts with the symptoms of a normal cold—runny eyes and nose, cough, slight temperature—followed 2 weeks later by violent, uncontrollable bouts of coughing, which frequently end in vomiting. Because the child cannot breathe in during these spasms, they may feel as though they are suffocating, and the typical "whooping sound" as the child fights to breathe in again is extremely distressing. In small babies, oxygen deprivation can become a real hazard. The coughing can also do permanent damage to the lungs. Home remedies can, however, speed recovery and help relieve some of the most distressing symptoms, to make your child more comfortable.

CONVENTIONAL MEDICINE

If your child has been in contact with whooping cough and has not been immunized, then you should be on the lookout for symptoms, as it can only be treated during the first stage, before the coughing fits start. Treatment is with antibiotics prescribed by your physician.

KITCHEN MEDICINE

■ The old wives' favorite of honey and garlic is extremely soothing. Add 2 cloves of finely sliced garlic to a 8oz/225g jar of runny honey, cover and leave overnight. Next day add 1tsp/5ml of the mixture to a cup of warm water and get the child to sip it. Repeat four times a day.

■ Rubbing the soles of the child's feet with the cut end of a clove of garlic is another old wives' tale that really does help. The garlic enters the bloodstream through the skin and its powerful antibiotic chemicals are soon circulating through the lung tissue.

AROMATHERAPY

 ❧ FRANKINCENSE
Boswellia sacra
❧ LAVENDER
Lavandula angustifolia
❧ SANDALWOOD
Santalum album

Frankincense is calming; it slows and deepens the breathing. Lavender is also very calming—not only for the patient but for the carer, too. Sandalwood is antispasmodic, as well as being calming and soothing.

Application:
Burn these oils in the sickroom, or use them to massage the chest and the back.

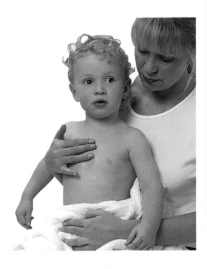

ABOVE *A lavender-oil massage is especially suitable for young children. It must be diluted in a carrier oil before use.*

HOMEOPATHIC REMEDIES

 This is a serious condition and requires medical assessment.
❧ DROSERA **6C** For deep spasms of coughing that start in larynx, retching and vomiting. Worse at night, for lying down. Better for cold drinks.

❧ IPECACUANHA **6C** For spasmodic cough, suffocating, wheezing. Chest feels full of phlegm, but cannot cough it up. Constant feeling of nausea. Nosebleeds with cough.
❧ ANTIMONIUM TARTARICUM **6C** For very sticky phlegm, rattling in chest. Cough worse after eating.
❧ CUPRUM METALLICUM **6C** For violent, spasmodic cough with vomiting. Better for drinking water. Tight feeling in chest.
Dosage: one tablet every 4 hours. Maximum 2 weeks.

LEFT *Drosera comes from Drosera rotundifolia, the sundew. It is recommended for tackling problems of the respiratory system.*

HERBAL REMEDIES

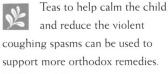 Teas to help calm the child and reduce the violent coughing spasms can be used to support more orthodox remedies.
■ **Use and Dosage:**
Combine a decoction of licorice and elecampane (1tsp/5ml of each per cup) with an infusion of wild lettuce, thyme, and chamomile (1tsp/5ml of each per cup), then give the child between 1tbsp/15ml and ½ cup/125ml of the mix (further diluted with water to make a whole cup), depending on age.

Use a chest rub containing basil, hyssop, and cypress oils (2 drops of each to 1tsp/5ml of almond oil). Give echinacea tablets to support the immune system (100–600mg daily in tablets, depending on age).

PREVENTATIVE *measures*

Avoid contact with other infected children, their siblings, or parents.

The risk of contracting this serious disease is greatly reduced by immunization, which is safe and effective.

OUTSIDE HELP

 REFLEXOLOGY: some symptomatic relief may be found if the reflexes of the respiratory tract are worked. Find the reflexes of the lungs on the balls of the feet, and include the throat and trachea reflexes, as well as the diaphragm. Work firmly and methodically over this area for a few minutes daily.

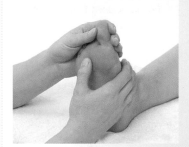

ABOVE *Working the lung, trachea, and bronchi reflexes on the ball of the foot will improve the function of the respiratory system.*

NUTRITION

 It is impossible to feed normal meals to a child with severe whooping cough. **Give plenty of** fluids—especially important when the child is vomiting. Mixtures of warm apple juice, honey, and water; pineapple and blackcurrant juice with warm water; warmed, mixed vegetable juices; warm ginger tea with honey; blended or clear soups, like vegetable or chicken broth; yeast extract drinks—all these will provide nutrients and are soothing. Unless it is the only thing your child will drink, try to avoid large amounts of milk during the first few days. As the child begins to feel better, small light meals between coughing bouts are ideal: a little scrambled egg; ground chicken with rice; fruit purées made with cloves, cinnamon, and honey; thin porridge with lots of honey; very well-puréed potato and carrot, creamed with a tablespoon or two of very low-fat yogurt and a sprinkle of nutmeg.

Do not force food on your child, but you must be insistent about giving regular intakes of liquids, even if they are given just a couple of teaspoons at a time.

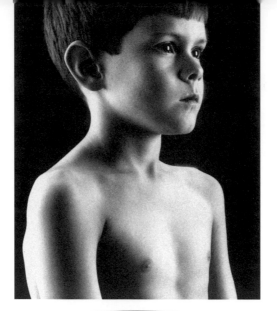

RIGHT *Chicken pox will appear as small raised spots, breaking out first on the trunk, and later on the face and limbs.*

DIAGNOSING CHICKEN POX

- Low fever
- Vomiting and general aches in some cases
- Patches of itchy blisters, affecting the skin, eyes and mouth; blisters will gradually crust and form scabs

IMMUNE SYSTEM

chicken pox

CAUTION

Always read pain-reliever packages carefully, and do not exceed the stated dose.

This highly infectious illness is caused by the Herpes zoster *virus and is most common in children. If you have been in contact with someone who is infected, it may be 2 or 3 weeks before you develop symptoms. Although uncomfortable and irritating—the most serious side-effect is usually the scars left after picking the spots— some children may feel quite poorly if they have a severe infection. In adults, however, chicken pox can be an extremely serious and debilitating illness and can lead to acute pneumonia. After contracting chicken pox, avoid scratching, to prevent the spread of infection and the risk of scars. Keep children's fingernails very short—the hands of youngest children should be kept in cotton gloves whenever possible. Residual scars can be treated with a few drops of vitamin E oil applied every night.*

CONVENTIONAL MEDICINE

✚ Treat the fever with pain-relievers, and use calamine lotion to soothe itchy skin. More severe infections can be treated with antiviral drugs, which may also be used in the early stages for adults.

Dosage information ~

Adults

■ One to two tablets of pain-relievers at onset of fever, repeated every 4 hours. Apply calamine lotion/cream directly to the skin.

Children

■ Give regular doses of liquid pain-reliever; see package for details, or follow medical advice. Apply calamine lotion/cream directly to the skin as required.

ABOVE *Make your child wear cotton gloves to stop him scratching his spots.*

HOMEOPATHIC REMEDIES

 RHUS TOXICODENDRON 6C For intense itching, better for warm applications. Small watery blisters. This is the first remedy to try.

ANTIMONIUM TARTARICUM 6C For spots that are slow to come out. Person is drowsy, sweaty. May have a cough with a rattly chest, but does not bring up any actual mucus.

ANTIMONIUM CRUD. 6C For chicken pox and upset stomach. Person is irritable, sulky. Cries when touched, looked at, or washed. Tongue has a white coat. **Dosage:** one tablet every 2–4 hours until condition improves. Maximum 5 days.

HERBAL REMEDIES

Herbs can ease the fever associated with chicken pox and soothe its rash.

■ **Use and Dosage:**
To ease fevers and irritability, use a tea made from equal parts of boneset, elderflower, and chamomile (½–2tsp/2.5–10ml per cup, depending on patient's age, three times a day).

Rashes can be soothed with a wash made by mixing borage juice (2tbsp/30ml) with standard chickweed infusion (½ cup/100ml) and distilled witch hazel (2tbsp/30ml). Apply gently with a cotton swab as required.

Taking up to 6 x 200mg echinacea capsules daily will help combat the infection.

ABOVE *Borage is in flower in late spring or early summer. Pulp the aerial parts to extract the juice, which can ease irritation.*

NUTRITION

Take plenty of fluids, especially pineapple juice diluted with water (50:50), camomile tea, and water. A short fast (24–48 hours) will boost the body's white-cell count and help to fight the infection.

ABOVE *Pineapples are high in vitamin C, which helps fight infection. The juice makes a soothing drink, rich in the enzyme bromelain.*

AROMATHERAPY

LAVENDER
Lavandula angustifolia
ROMAN CHAMOMILE
Chamaemelum nobile
EUCALYPTUS
Eucalyptus radiata
BERGAMOT
Citrus bergamia
Bathing in these oils or rubbing in a lotion containing them will relieve itching. Vaporization will help stop the spread of the virus, so that hopefully other people will not catch it.

Application:
Use in lukewarm baths, vaporizers, and sprays. Immerse the child in a lukewarm bath containing 1 drop of any of the above oils (but not all of them) every 2 hours. Regular bathing is also soothing for adults with chicken pox, who may be quite ill.

RIGHT *Eucalyptus oil is antiviral and a good local pain-killer. It is also used to treat insect bites and skin infections. Do not use on very young children.*

PREVENTATIVE *measures*

Children almost invariably recover from chicken pox without problems. All you can do is make sure that your child's natural defenses are well nourished by a good, healthy diet.

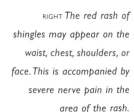
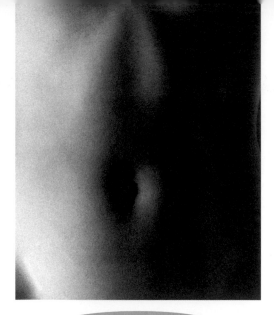

RIGHT *The red rash of shingles may appear on the waist, chest, shoulders, or face. This is accompanied by severe nerve pain in the area of the rash.*

DIAGNOSING SHINGLES

- Burning sensation on an area of sensitive skin, which then develops blisters
- Most commonly affects an area around the shoulder or waist, or one side of the face and one eye

IMMUNE SYSTEM

shingles

Shingles (Herpes zoster is its medical name) is caused by the same virus that causes chicken pox (see p.40). After chicken pox, some of the virus makes its home in the nerve ganglions, where it stays dormant for many years. Exposure to chicken pox in later life if you have never had the illness—or to stressful events—physical or emotional—can then catalyse the virus. Up to 20 percent of adults will be affected at some time, but the elderly and those with a suppressed immune system are at greatest risk. Home remedies can be extremely helpful in reducing both the severity and the duration of an attack of shingles.

For some, shingles is a mild infection that comes and goes in a couple of weeks; for others, an attack can leave them with a wretched condition called "post-herpetic neuralgia." This causes excruciating pain over the area originally affected, and even the lightest touch may be unbearable. Washing, shaving, eating, or even the weight of a bedsheet can be so painful that it can ruin all semblance of normal life, and the condition can persist for months or even years. Powerful drugs, and even neurosurgery, may be of no avail.

CALL THE PHYSICIAN

■ If you think you have shingles.

CAUTION

Shingles that affects the eye may cause serious complications and should be monitored carefully by your physician.

KITCHEN MEDICINE

■ A traditional Dutch folk-remedy for post-herpetic neuralgia is often very successful: coarsely chop 2in/5cm of fresh leek and then, with a mortar and pestle (or the back of a wooden spoon), crush it to extract its juice. Strain the juice and use a cotton ball to paint it over the affected area. Repeat morning and evening for at least a week.

CONVENTIONAL MEDICINE

If you develop symptoms of shingles, you may need treatment from your physician.

If the shingles affects your eye, it could cause permanent damage and you should consult your physician

urgently. Antiviral drugs are only effective if given early. Strong pain-relievers will also help.

HERBAL REMEDIES

 Shingles responds to a variety of herbal remedies.

■ **Use and Dosage:**

During an attack, echinacea (up to 2g in tablets daily) will help combat the viral infection.

Drinking plenty of St John's wort infusion can help to limit the risk of lingering nerve pain, which is so commonly associated with attacks of shingles.

A tea containing equal amounts of passion flower, lemon balm and wild lettuce will also ease the pain and discomfort.

Apply fresh *Aloe vera* sap to any blistering. Afterwards, use cayenne, vervain or St John's wort in either creams or infused oils to combat nerve pain: cayenne is specially effective.

NUTRITION

 The B vitamins, bioflavonoids, and vitamin C are the key nutrients, so **eat plenty of** citrus fruit, with some of the pith and skin between the segments; dark cherries, tomatoes, and mangoes; eggs, poultry, and liver; nuts, seeds, and whole wheat cereals; olive, sunflower, and safflower oils. Do not forget that the probiotic bacteria that are present in live yogurt are an essential factor in the body's production of some B vitamins.

ABOVE *Both mangoes and tomatoes contain valuable nutrients.*

AROMATHERAPY

 ❧ **EUCALYPTUS**
Eucalyptus radiata
❧ **TEA TREE**
Melaleuca alternifolia
❧ **LAVENDER**
Lavandula angustifolia
❧ **ROMAN CHAMOMILE**
Chamaemelum nobile
❧ **BERGAMOT**
Citrus bergamia

These oils are painkilling, antiviral, and help to dry out the blisters. Bergamot is also an antidepressant, and people who develop shingles have often been low or depressed prior to an attack. It is active against the *Herpes zoster* virus that causes shingles. Tea-tree oil will also help to build up the body's immune system, so that afterward the body is much stronger and more able to fight off infection.

Application:

Smooth the oils very gently over the affected area and down either side of the spine, which is where all the nerve endings are, as this area may also be affected and it helps the essential oils get into the system. If the body is too painful to touch, add the oils to a water spray; use a very soft brush to paint the oils on; or use the oils in the bath.

OUTSIDE HELP

ACUPRESSURE: this depends entirely on the site affected by the virus. Traditional acupuncture is one of the few therapies likely to help post-herpetic neuralgia, and a qualified practitioner will be able to advise on appropriate acupressure points in individual cases.

HOMEOPATHIC REMEDIES

❧ **RHUS TOXICODENDRON 6C** For painful, small, watery blisters with a lot of itching. Better for warm applications. Person is restless, which helps to relieve itching. Probably the most often-used remedy for shingles.

❧ **MEZEREUM 6C** For pain-like fire in the muscles, smarting of the skin. Intense itching. Crusts over spots, with pus underneath. Worse for heat and scratching. Neuralgia after shingles, especially in face. Brownish scabs.

❧ **RANUNCULUS BULBOSIS. 6C** For burning pain, itching worse for touch. Bluish appearance of spots, which appear in clusters. Neuralgia of the chest wall.

Dosage: one tablet every 4 hours until blisters have settled. Maximum 5 days.

PREVENTATIVE
measures

It is very difficult to prevent viral infections like shingles. However, people in the at-risk groups—the elderly, those with very low immunity or receiving immuno-suppressant drugs—should be extremely careful to avoid contact with children who have, or may have been exposed to, chicken pox.

SUPPLEMENTS: *the earliest signs of shingles are slight irritation, burning, or pain in the skin segment supplied by the affected nerve. This is commonly on the trunk and round the waist—this is what gives shingles its medical name,* Herpes zoster, *meaning "a belt of fire." But it can also occur on the side of the face, around the eyes, and at the bottom of the spine over the sacrum. The earlier treatment is started, the better, and this is equally true of improved nutrition and supplements. It may be useful to take a small dose (0.5g) of the essential amino acid L-lysine, plus a vitamin B-complex.*

BELOW *Ranunculus flowers. The bulb of the plant is used.*

RIGHT *Sore throats are a recurrent problem in the winter season of coughs and colds. Smoky atmospheres may also cause them.*

DIAGNOSING A SORE THROAT

- Hoarse, sore voice, which may disappear altogether
- Sore cough
- May follow a cold, overusing the voice, or breathing in smoke

IMMUNE SYSTEM

sore throat

A sore throat (*pharyngitis*) may be caused by a viral infection, by dehydration, overuse of the voice or shouting (*laryngitis*), or it may be an early symptom of other infectious diseases. It can also be caused by infection, inflammation, and/or enlargement of the tonsils (see Tonsillitis on p.46). Sore throats are common, uncomfortable, but usually of little clinical significance. A simple sore throat that accompanies a cold or flu is best treated with home remedies, which are infinitely more successful than most proprietary medicines and gargles.

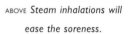

ABOVE *Steam inhalations will ease the soreness.*

CALL THE PHYSICIAN

◼ If there is any change in the quality of your voice that does not return to normal within a week or two.
◼ If you have been hoarse for more than 6 weeks.

CAUTION

Recurrent and chronic sore throats may be caused by smoking, excessive alcohol use, repeated vomiting (as in bulimia), or even by a hiatus hernia.

CONVENTIONAL MEDICINE

Sore vocal cords need rest, which means no talking. Steam inhalations are also useful, as they tend to reduce the swelling around the cords, speeding up recovery, and can be used as often as necessary. Antibiotics are rarely required for a sore throat.

Dosage information ~

Adults

◼ 1–2tsp/5–10ml of linctus or 1 lozenge every 4–5 hours; see package for details or follow medical advice.

Children

◼ 1tsp/5ml of linctus or half a lozenge three times daily; see package for details or follow medical advice.

Adults and children

◼ For steam inhalations, lean over a bowl of boiling water with a towel over your head. You can make this more pleasant by adding eucalyptus or other oils (*see under Aromatherapy*), but the steam itself has most effect on the cough. Or you can invest in a humidifier; put wet towels on the radiators; or fill the tub with hot water and sit in the steamy bathroom with your child.

HERBAL REMEDIES

Soothing, astringent, and antiseptic herbs for use in gargles include sage, lady's mantle, rosemary, thyme, silverweed, agrimony, and echinacea.

■ **Use and Dosage:**
Make a strong infusion (2–3tsp/10–15ml per cup), strain well and gargle every 30 to 60 minutes. (Use the aerial parts of *Echinacea purpurea*, or use a root decoction of any of the three available echinacea species.) Fresh *Aloe vera* sap added to the gargle will also help. Drink additional cups of standard infusion (1tsp/5ml per cup) of any of the above herbs.

KITCHEN MEDICINE

■ The throat's best friend is the kitchen faucet. Four to six glasses of water each day are essential, together with your normal consumption of other drinks.

■ Hot water with 2tsp/10ml of honey and the juice of half a lemon is one of the most soothing of all remedies. Always keep a jar of honey to which you have added half a dozen peeled cloves of garlic, as a teaspoon or two of this mixture several times a day will help both pharyngitis and laryngitis.

■ A thin cotton dish towel soaked in cold water and squeezed, to remove excess moisture, should be wrapped round the neck and throat for 20 minutes, three times a day.

NUTRITION

For an acute sore throat, especially when this is accompanied by a fever, a 24-hour raw fruit and fruit-juice fast (as much of both as you like) will give a boost to the immune system and also provide essential nutrients, which are healing to the mucous membranes located in the throat.

Drink plenty of pineapple juice and citrus juices diluted 50:50 with water; **eat plenty of** avocados, together with all the exotic fruits, like pineapple, papaw, and mango. If you are prescribed antibiotics, make sure you have plenty of live yogurt to recondition the natural bacteria that live in your intestines.

OUTSIDE HELP

REFLEXOLOGY: work the reflexes of the throat around the "neck" of the big toes and thumbs. Work the upper lymphatics with a forefinger, moving up a finger's length toward the ankle or wrist from each web and sliding back down with a gentle pinch.

YOGA: if your throat feels hot, scratchy, or dry, use Shitali or Sitkari for at least 12 breaths, with Nabho Mudra: after breathing in, curl the tip of the tongue upward and exhale. This helps to moisten the throat. Suck soothing candies like butterscotch.

HOMEOPATHIC REMEDIES

 ✿ BELLADONNA **30C** For sudden onset. Throat red, dry, painful, initially on right side. Swallowing very painful.

✿ PHYTOLACCA **30C** For pain in ears on swallowing. Swallowing hot drinks impossible. Dark red

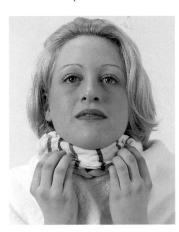

ABOVE *Soak a thin cotton cloth in chilled water to make a soothing cold compress. Use three times a day. Apply, and relax for about 20 minutes.*

tonsils, right side especially swollen. Neck stiff.

✿ LACHESIS **30C** For left-sided pain initially, spreading to right. Sensation of tightness in throat, sensitive to touch. Wakes with sore throat. Difficult to swallow saliva, worse for hot drinks.

Dosage: one tablet every 2 hours for six doses, followed by every 4 hours until improved. Maximum 12 doses.

✿ PHOSPHORUS **6C** For hoarseness worse in evening. Larynx painful and cannot talk. Person is restless and fearful.

✿ CAUSTICUM **6C** For laryngitis after exposure to cold. Hoarseness worse in morning. Burning in windpipe and coughs, but cannot bring up mucus.

Dosage: one tablet every 2 hours for six doses, then every 4 hours. Maximum 3 days.

PREVENTATIVE *measures*

If you use your voice professionally and you keep getting attacks of laryngitis, consult an experienced voice expert or speech therapist, who will be able to teach you the most efficient way of using your voice without causing strain on the vocal cords. If your problem is recurrent episodes of tonsillitis, *see p.46*. Sometimes ongoing chronic sore throats are linked to the postnasal drip of perennial rhinitis (*see Sinusitis on p.130 and Hay Fever on p.128*).

DIET: *to protect your throat, keep your salt consumption to a minimum, drink only modest amounts of alcohol (not spirits), stop smoking, and avoid very hot drinks and cola drinks, which irritate the throat's delicate membranes.*

AROMATHERAPY

 ✿ SANDALWOOD
Santalum album

✿ MYRRH
Commiphora molmol

✿ TEA TREE
Melaleuca alternifolia

These oils are antibacterial, fungicidal, and help to kill the pain and stop it spreading.

Application:
It is possible to gargle with these oils but they do not taste particularly nice, so it is preferable to put them into a massage oil or cream and actually massage them into the throat area. Then wrap something warm around the throat. If the glands in the neck are also swollen, put a drop of lemon into the massage blend, which will take down the swelling in the lymphatic glands.

RIGHT *The tonsils are lymph tissues either side of the back of the mouth. If they are infected, they swell up with fluids, white blood cells, and dead germs. This may make it difficult to swallow.*

DIAGNOSING TONSILLITIS

- Sore throat
- Difficulty swallowing
- Swollen glands in the neck
- Fever

IMMUNE SYSTEM

tonsillitis

Tonsillitis is an acute infection of the tonsils, usually caused by a virus, although it may be bacterial. When the tonsils enlarge and become infected they look red, inflamed, and may be covered in yellow spots of pus. There may also be a fever (see p.24), swollen glands, and a coated tongue. The tonsils are the guardians of the lungs, and when they swell they are simply doing their job—trapping invading organisms before you inhale them. Tonsillitis mostly occurs in children, especially when they are first exposed to a range of illnesses on starting school. Sometimes the problem can become chronic, and it may also affect adults. While severe infections may need treatment with antibiotics (which are only effective for tonsillitis caused by bacterial infection), home remedies are a powerful aid to reducing pain and speedier healing.

CALL THE PHYSICIAN

■ If you are unable to swallow saliva.

NUTRITION

During a bout of tonsillitis eating will be difficult, as swallowing can be excruciatingly painful. Give blended vegetable soups made with carrots, sweet potatoes, and broccoli for their beta-carotene; shredded cabbage and tomatoes for their vitamin C; and leeks, onions, and garlic for their natural antiseptic qualities. **Drink plenty of** hot water, honey, and lemon, together with unsweetened fruit juices.

CONVENTIONAL MEDICINE

Most infections will get better without any treatment, but physicians often prescribe antibiotics if symptoms have been present for several days, although only infections caused by bacteria will respond. Painkilling tablets can relieve the sore throat and fever, and can be dissolved to produce an anesthetic gargle. Lozenges and hot drinks can be soothing. Recurrent infections may be prevented by surgery to remove the tonsils.

Dosage information ~

Adults

■ Take antibiotic tablets up to four times a day; follow medical advice; complete the course.

Children

■ Give antibiotic syrup up to four times a day. Dose depends on age and weight of the child; follow medical advice and remember to complete the course. Bottles often contain more than is required to allow for spillages.

KITCHEN MEDICINE

■ Two of the most ancient culinary ingredients come to the rescue in tonsillitis—garlic and honey. Peel and crush 2 cloves of garlic and stir them into a jar of runny honey. The antibacterial contents of the garlic mix with the soothing properties of the honey. A teaspoonful of this can be given every couple of hours.

■ Homemade ice "lollies" of pure frozen pineapple juice are very easy for the sufferer to suck, and the bromelain enzyme in the pineapple juice helps reduce both the swollen glands and the inflammation of the tonsils.

1 Make some garlic-infused honey to benefit from dual antiseptic qualities. Honey is also very soothing.

2 Buy a container of organic honey. Peel eight cloves of garlic, and crush into the honey. Leave to infuse for several days.

3 Tip the honey out and strain off the pieces of garlic. Return the honey to the jar. Take the honey by the teaspoonful: one for children, and four for adults. It will help to boost the immune system.

HERBAL REMEDIES

 Mild cases will generally respond well to gargling with sage and echinacea tinctures (5ml/1tsp of each) diluted in a glass of warmed pineapple juice. Other suitable gargles are raspberry-leaf tea, marsh cudweed infusion, or 10 drops of thuja or goldenseal tinctures in a glass of water.

■ Use and Dosage:
Support the immune system with echinacea capsules (up to 600mg four times a day).

Drink a mixture of chamomile, cleavers, and sage tea (equal amounts, 2tsp/10ml of the mixture per cup) to help the lymphatic system.

HOMEOPATHIC REMEDIES

 There are many remedies for this condition, and recurrent problems are best treated by a qualified homeopath.

✿ PHYTOLACCA **30C** For dark red or purple tonsils with gray or white pus. Pain goes to ear on swallowing. Worse on right side, worse for warm drinks. Better for cold drinks.

✿ MERCURIUS **30C** For red throat, swollen uvula. Burning pain in throat. Swallowing makes person nauseous. Worse for cold drinks, swallowing liquid.

✿ LACHESIS **30C** For purple tonsils. Wakes with sore throat or worse after sleep. Worse on left side, for swallowing liquids (rather than solids) and saliva. May start on left side and move to right.

Dosage: one tablet every 2 hours for three doses, then every 4 hours. Maximum 2 days.

AROMATHERAPY

✿ THYME
Thymus vulgaris
✿ LAVENDER
Lavandula angustifolia
✿ TEA TREE
Melaleuca alternifolia

Tea tree and thyme both fight the infection, and lavender and thyme are local anaesthetics or have a slightly anesthetic effect.

Application:
Use in steam inhalations or in a warm compress on the throat area. If other symptoms accompany the throat problem, such as earache, headache or abdominal pain, then look under the appropriate ailment for other remedies.

OUTSIDE HELP

REFLEXOLOGY: do not give reflexology while the throat is infected, but to prevent recurrence, regular treatments may help to boost the immune system. The reflexes of the throat and tonsils are found around the "neck" of the big toes and thumbs, and on the nearest webs.

PREVENTATIVE
measures

For children with recurrent tonsillitis, boost the immune system with the appropriate nutrients (*see Infections on p.20*). If the child frequently gets secondary earache, *see p.84*; if sinusitis, *see p.130*. It may be worth cutting down on their intake of dairy products.

BELOW *Working on the throat reflex may help to relieve the discomfort of a sore throat.*

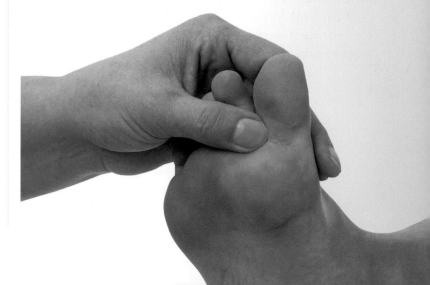

RIGHT *The classic site for neuralgic pain is down one side of the face, where the trigeminal nerve is affected (trigeminal neuralgia). Other parts of the body are also vulnerable.*

DIAGNOSING NEURALGIA

- Pain like a knife or electric shock, often on one side of the face

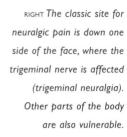

NERVOUS SYSTEM

neuralgia

KITCHEN MEDICINE

■ All nerve tissues need abundant supplies of the B vitamins. Old-fashioned, homemade chicken soup that is enriched with yeast extract, barley, and brown rice offers a simple, nutritious and delicious way of providing them.

BELOW *Simmer a chicken carcass to obtain stock for the basis of a tasty chicken soup.*

Neuralgia is pain in the nervous tissue, usually felt at the ends of the system—that is, near the surface of the skin. It is nearly always a severe, piercing pain to start with, but may then settle down into an extremely painful and continual ache. The most common forms are postherpetic neuralgia (the extreme pain that often follows a bout of shingles and can last from a few days to several years; see p.42) and trigeminal neuralgia (which affects the trigeminal nerve on the side of the face). These can both be so excruciating that washing, shaving, and even the weight of bedclothes may be unbearable. In the treatment of neuralgia, home remedies are not hugely successful, but neither are the very powerful drugs that are normally prescribed. The best chance of success is a combination of orthodox treatment, acupuncture, and self-help.

CONVENTIONAL MEDICINE

Warmth or massage may help during an attack. Pain-relievers may not be sufficient to control the pain, and your physician may prescribe drugs used in other patients to treat depression or epilepsy. In intractable cases your physician can refer you to a pain clinic, where a specialist may recommend a combination of different treatments, including behavioral therapy and acupuncture.

Dosage information ~

Adults

■ Take one to two tablets of pain-relievers at onset of pain, repeated every 4 hours; see package for details.

Children

■ Give regular doses of liquid pain-reliever; see package for details, or follow medical advice.

HERBAL REMEDIES

One simple remedy which many find brings rapid relief is to smooth a little warmed lemon juice or diluted lemon oil on the painful area. Cayenne creams and infused oil are also useful externally, especially if the pain follows shingles, while internally herbs to help restore and repair nerves can be useful.

■ **Use and Dosage:**
Drink a combination of St. John's wort, vervain, and chamomile (equal amounts, 2tsp/10ml of the mix per cup), or try valerian, which is most easily used in tincture or tablets.

ABOVE *Warm some lemon juice and dab it on to the tender area with a cotton ball. It will assist with pain relief.*

NUTRITION

Eat plenty of potatoes, liver (but not if you are pregnant), nuts and seeds, brown rice, Brazil nuts, milk, eggs, poultry, whole wheat bread, dried fruit, green and root vegetables, legumes and fish for their B vitamins, which are essential in the diet of neuralgia sufferers. If chewing is painful, make some soup from a wide variety of the foods containing the B vitamins, so that it can be drunk from a cup or, if this is easier, through a thick straw.

BELOW *Nuts, seeds, dried fruit, and brown rice are rich in B vitamins. Neuralgia sufferers should aim to include these foods in their diet.*

HOMEOPATHIC REMEDIES

🌿 SPIGELIA **6C** For left-sided pain, like hot needles, sharp. Pain above left eye—person can point to the spot.

LEFT *Spigelia anthelmia, or pink root, is a perennial herb from the West Indies and South America.*

Pain worse for stooping or opening mouth.
🌿 CAUSTICUM **6C** For right-sided facial neuralgia. Worse for wind and change of weather. Pain in jaws, worse for opening mouth.
🌿 ACONITE **6C** For use in first stages. Intense pain after going out in cold, dry wind. Often left-sided. May have tingling and numbness. **Dosage:** one tablet hourly for six doses, then every 4–6 hours. Maximum 3 days.

AROMATHERAPY

🌿 LAVENDER
Lavandula angustifolia
🌿 ROMAN CHAMOMILE
Chamaemelum nobile
🌿 MARJORAM
Origanum majorana
🌿 ROSEMARY
Rosmarinus officinalis
These oils are calming and soothing and help to ease the pain and tension of neuralgia.
Application:
They are best used in a cold compress held over the affected area. Do be aware that the condition is aggravated by stress, so look at the oils for stress (*see p.60*) and find something there that you like and can bath in, as well as using the oils for neuralgia on the particular area affected.

CAUTION

Do not use rosemary oil if you have high blood pressure.

PREVENTATIVE *measures*

Unfortunately, you cannot normally prevent this painful condition. Although it is a common aftermath of shingles, it often occurs for no known reason. There is, however, one commonly overlooked cause that can be prevented: problems with the joint between the upper and lower jaws, or with the way in which your teeth come together when you bite, can be a cause of facial neuralgia and trigeminal neuralgia. Regular visits to your dentist can generally prevent this from happening.

OUTSIDE HELP

ACUPRESSURE: this is not usually an option, simply because these conditions are very complex, but treatment by a professional acupuncturist is one of the best therapies I know.
REFLEXOLOGY: work the reflex of the spine along the medial longitudinal arch (the bony ridge on the inside of the feet) and, using the reflexology charts on pp.214–15, work the reflex area corresponding to the problem. For facial neuralgia, work the painful or tender areas on the big toes.

RIGHT *Headaches vary from a mild, inconvenient ache, to a skull-crushing, incapacitating pain. Causes range from stress, eye strain, overindulgence in sun or alcohol, to food allergies and bad posture.*

DIAGNOSING A HEADACHE

- Headache all over scalp, with pain in the neck and shoulder muscles. Likely causes: *stress, tension, poor posture*
- Frontal headache. Likely causes: *eyestrain, sinusitis*
- Throbbing headache on one side, with nausea or vomiting, often preceded by blurred vision. Likely cause: *migraine*

NERVOUS SYSTEM

headaches

Headaches are one of the most common reasons for consulting a physician, yet they are rarely a symptom of any underlying disease. Though they frequently accompany acute infections—more so in the presence of a high temperature—many routine headaches are mechanical in origin. Stress, anxiety, poor posture, badly designed work stations, and the ever-growing use of computers, both at home and at work, can all result in tension developing in the neck and shoulders. And this is by far the most common cause of everyday headaches.

CALL THE PHYSICIAN

■ If the headache is the result of a blow to the head.

■ If there is numbness, confusion, or sudden drowsiness.

■ If you have a headache with a fever, associated with pain on bending your head forward, stiff neck, nausea, or vomiting, dislike of bright light, and drowsiness or confusion.

■ If you have a very severe headache that starts suddenly, often feeling like being hit on the head.

■ If ordinary pain-killers do not help and the pain is severe.

■ If your balance, speech, memory, or vision is affected.

■ If you wake up with headaches that are worse when you cough or sneeze.

■ If you are having recurrent mild headaches.

CAUTION

Always read pain-reliever packages carefully, and do not exceed the stated dose.

CONVENTIONAL MEDICINE

Drink plenty of water. Have a warm bath to relieve the tension. Once a headache has started, rest in a quiet, darkened room and take a pain-reliever.

Dosage information ~

Adults

■ Take 1–2 tablets of pain-reliever at onset of pain, then every 4 hours; see package.

Children

■ Give regular doses of liquid pain-reliever; see package for details or follow medical advice.

NUTRITION

Headaches can be triggered by low blood-sugar levels. Eat at least some whole wheat toast and a banana for breakfast, or a bowl of cereal. Always have a banana and a bag of nuts and dried fruit to nibble on throughout the day. Beware of sudden drastic changes in your eating patterns; very low-calorie diets will also cause headaches. Catarrh (*see p.122*) and sinusitis (*see p.130*) are other common causes. And it is important to differentiate between ordinary headaches and migraine (*see p.52*).

KITCHEN MEDICINE

■ Herbal teas are a good aid—use lime blossom or rosemary for tension headaches, mint for those caused by overindulgence, and chamomile for headaches that are due to exhaustion.

EXERCISE

ANY FORM of general exercise—particularly if it gets you out into the fresh air—will help. Specific exercises to help relax the neck and shoulder muscles are important, too. These should be slow, gentle, stretching exercises, avoiding sudden, jerky movements, which you do a few times each day at regular intervals. This is particularly important if there is any arthritis in the joints of the neck—a common cause of headaches.

(1) Roll the shoulders backward and forward, then turn the neck slowly from side to side. (2)—(3) Push the chin down to the chest and up as far as you can. (4)—(5) Tip the head from side to side toward each shoulder.

HERBAL REMEDIES

 There are various relaxing herbs for headaches.

■ **Use and Dosage:**
Tension headaches often respond to betony and skullcap tea (1tsp/5ml of each per cup).

Use rosemary or a low dose of Korean ginseng (200mg daily) for headaches associated with overexertion and tiredness.

Headaches associated with depression can be helped by a combination of oats and vervain (1tsp/5ml of each per cup).

Lavender is good for burning headaches (eased by an ice package)—use a few drops of tincture neat on the tongue or drink an infusion.

OUTSIDE HELP

ACUPRESSURE: this can be extremely helpful for instant relief. For general headaches, use point 41; for pain in the forehead or around the eyes, points 45 and 46 as well; if the pain is in the temples, use point 47; for the back of the head, use point 42; for most headaches adding points 4 and 18 will help.

ALEXANDER TECHNIQUE: as this improves awareness of your posture during activities, you should be able to avoid the build-up of tension in your neck and shoulders that so often contributes to headaches. Take a moment to realign yourself frequently.

REFLEXOLOGY: the head and neck reflexes are found on the thumbs and big toes, so work these areas deeply with the side of your thumb for symptomatic relief. Rotate the big toes both ways several times, and explore the pituitary gland and cervical reflexes for tender spots.

YOGA: to reduce future risk of headaches, keep the shoulders, neck and face as relaxed as possible. When practicing, be very aware of this area and keep your movements fluid and unstrained. If you feel a headache starting, try slow alternate nostril breathing, then palm your eyes.

AROMATHERAPY

 🍃 LAVENDER
Lavandula angustifolia
🍃 PEPPERMINT
Mentha x piperita
🍃 EUCALYPTUS
Eucalyptus radiata
🍃 BASIL
Ocimum basilicum

Lavender is calming, soothing and a natural painkiller. Peppermint clears the head, as does basil. Eucalyptus clears the sinuses.

Application:
Put onto a facecloth with some cool water and use as a compress. For headaches due to a cold, put one drop of neat lavender on the tips of your fingers and massage into the temples, or a steam inhalation with eucalyptus will help. If the headache is due to an overactive brain, try just a couple of drops of basil on a tissue or handkerchief; a few drops on the pillow at night will calm you.

PREVENTATIVE *measures*

ENVIRONMENT: *make sure that you do not spend hours on end working in a stuffy atmosphere. You can create your own micro-climate by putting green plants near your desk and using a small combined ionizer and humidifier—in the home or workplace.*

MASSAGE: *this is a real boon and it is virtually impossible to do yourself any harm. You cannot massage your own neck and shoulders very well, but you can buy long-handled rollers, which make the task somewhat easier.*

NUTRITION: *avoid excessive alcohol and caffeine, which cause headaches. A low fluid intake is one of the most common causes of headaches. Drink at least 2pt/1l of water every day, as well as other drinks.*

HOMEOPATHIC REMEDIES

🍃 BRYONIA **30c** For pressing, bursting, or splitting headache over left eye. Pain worse for least movement (even of the eye), for light, cough, or stooping. Better for pressure.
🍃 NUX VOMICA **30c** For splitting headache, sore scalp, dizziness, "hang-over" headache. Better for warmth, lying down. Worse for movement, drafts. Person is irritable and oversensitive.
🍃 GELSEMIUM **30c** For head that is heavy and aching, and hard to lift from pillow. Feels like a band around head. Person is chilly. Better for passing urine.
Dosage: one tablet every 4 hours, as needed. Maximum six doses.

LEFT *To disperse a tension headache, blend a few drops of peppermint essential oil in a carrier oil, and use for a firm neck and shoulder massage.*

RIGHT *Migraine headaches are severe, recurrent, and may be accompanied by other unpleasant side effects such as vomiting. Certain foods may trigger an attack.*

DIAGNOSING A MIGRAINE

- Severe headaches, which often start with distorted vision
- Pain is often throbbing and on one side of the head, often near an eye, and associated with nausea or vomiting
- Rarely may experience pins and needles or weakness in parts of the body, during an attack

NERVOUS SYSTEM

migraine

KITCHEN MEDICINE

■ Grow a feverfew plant on your windowsill, but make sure it is the correct variety: *Tanacetum parthenium*. A couple of leaves in a sandwich each day on a regular basis helps prevent migraine attacks for many sufferers. Do not chew the feverfew leaves on their own, though—they are horribly bitter and can cause mouth ulcers.

■ Ginger tea (*see Motion Sickness on p.190*) can help prevent vomiting, but it must be taken at the first sign of an attack, before you start being sick.

■ Two or three glasses of cold water straight from the tap at the very earliest signs of a migraine may be enough to abort an attack.

It is common for people who suffer from regular headaches—particularly when caused by stress and tension—to describe them as migraines, which may seem more acceptable to bosses and friends. Sadly, there is no mistaking a real migraine, with its visual disturbances, nausea, violent vomiting and literally blinding pain. There is now a wide variety of drug treatments, but self-help may be the best long-term key to success. The saddest thing about migraine is that it becomes as much a social as a medical problem, as sufferers tend to become increasingly reclusive, due to the embarrassment of becoming ill when out with friends or repeatedly cancelling engagements at the last minute because of an attack—possibly brought on by the stress of worrying about going out.

Migraines are far more common in women than in men, especially around the time of their periods, so there is certainly some hormonal link. They tend to start after puberty and many women sufferers improve dramatically after menopause. Unfortunately, migraine may occur out of the blue at any time of life, though it is quite common for it to run in families. Children who suffer badly from motion sickness (see p.190) have a greater chance of developing migraine in later life.

ABOVE *Women are more prone to migraine than men.*

CONVENTIONAL MEDICINE

 Avoid anything that may precipitate a migraine. As soon as the migraine begins, take soluble pain-relief combined with an antiemetic prescribed by your physician. Modern prescription medicines may be able to avert an attack. Lie down in a darkened room, if possible, and drink plenty of water.

Dosage information ~

Adults

■ Take one to two tablets of pain-reliever at onset of pain, repeated every 4 hours; see package for details.

Children

■ Give regular doses of liquid pain-reliever; see package for details, or follow medical advice.

NUTRITION

 Naturopaths have known for decades that there is a link between migraine and food. The most common triggers are chocolate, citrus fruit, cheese, and caffeine, though red wine, yeast extracts, pickled herrings, sauerkraut, and other fermented foods are also thought to be causes. Many of these contain the chemical tyramine, which irritates blood vessels in the brain.

PREVENTATIVE *measures*

FOOD DIARY: *keep a detailed diet diary of every single thing you eat and drink for a minimum of 3 weeks (longer if necessary—it should cover at least three attacks). Then go back and identify foods eaten up to 3 hours before an attack started. This will guide you towards the foods that you should eliminate from your diet. If this process is successful, you can then start to add foods back. Do not go for long periods without food or keep yourself going with sweet foods.*

STRESS: *the weekend migraine is very common, especially in men; as soon as they relax, the symptoms start. Yoga, relaxation exercises, or meditation can help overcome this problem.*

ALCOHOL: *avoid red wines and fortified wines, like port, sherry, and Madeira, as these have a very high concentration of tyramines.*

HERBAL REMEDIES

 Lavender and betony are useful migraine herbs.

■ **Use and Dosage:**
Combine equal amounts of both herbs in an infusion and sip while the pain continues.

Drops of feverfew tincture in water are more palatable than the fresh leaves: add 10 drops to a little water and take at 15-minute intervals during an attack.

An equal amount of valerian tincture (a strong sedative) can also help.

CAUTION

Avoid feverfew if taking prescribed blood-thinning drugs such as warfarin or heparin, as it can reduce the blood's clotting ability still further.

EXERCISE

MIGRAINES MAY very occasionally be brought on by exercise, but unless this is the case for you, physical activity can be highly beneficial; it improves the efficiency of the cardiovascular system and there is definitely a link between blood flow to the brain and migraine.

OUTSIDE HELP

ACUPRESSURE: points 1 and 4 encourage the body to eliminate waste products more efficiently and should be used daily, even when you do not have a migraine. During an attack, use the same points, but add points 41, 47, and 51 to relieve the pain.

ALEXANDER TECHNIQUE: this is no cure for migraine, but if practiced regularly it will remedy some of its contributory factors, such as stress, muscular tension, poor respiration, and circulation.

REFLEXOLOGY: if linked with digestive disturbances, work the digestive tract. Work all sides of the big toe deeply with the side of the thumb. Rotate it several times each way, and ease tension in the neck by massaging its base.

YOGA: if you feel a migraine coming on, lie down in a darkened room in the Relaxation Posture: imagine that each time you exhale, your tension gradually dissolves.

RIGHT *Meditation helps to dissipate stress after a hard week at work.*

AROMATHERAPY

🌿 LAVENDER
Lavandula angustifolia
🌿 MELISSA
Melissa officinalis
🌿 PEPPERMINT
Mentha x piperita (if the migraine is accompanied by nausea and sickness)
Lavender is calming, soothing, and a natural painkiller. Peppermint clears the head and stimulates the brain. Melissa is antidepressive and gently sedative.

Application:
These oils may be put onto a facecloth with some cool water and used as a compress, held on the forehead, at the back of the neck, or at the base of the skull. You can either add peppermint or melissa to the lavender or use them separately. Alternatively, put one drop of neat lavender on the tips of your fingers and massage well into the temples.

HOMEOPATHIC REMEDIES

🌿 It is often best to consult a qualified homeopath for the treatment of migraine.

🌿 IRIS **30C** For blurred vision, then right-sided headache with nausea. Better for gentle motion. Often occurs at weekends.

🌿 SANGUINARIA **30C** For pulsating headache, beginning at back of head and extending to right eye. Better for vomiting, lying asleep. Worse for light, noise, fasting. Starts in morning, improving during the day.

🌿 GLONOINE **30C** For waves of congestive, pulsating headache. Dizziness on being upright. Better for vomiting. Flashes of light. Worse for straining or motion.

Dosage: one tablet every 30 minutes until improved. Maximum six doses.

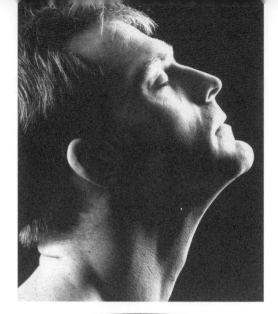

RIGHT *Physical fatigue causes mental fatigue, making it difficult to summon up the effort to try and rectify the problem.*

DIAGNOSING FATIGUE

- Exhaustion
- Sleeping for longer than usual and waking feeling tired
- Inability to concentrate

NERVOUS SYSTEM

fatigue

Extreme fatigue, or TAT (Tired All the Time syndrome), has become a problem of almost epidemic proportions in both US and in Britain, but it should not be confused with Chronic Fatigue Syndrome or ME (myalgic encephalomyelitis, see p.56), in which fatigue is just one symptom of a complex illness. It is important to rule out the presence of any underlying illness—anemia, continual blood loss, thyroid problems, diabetes, glandular fever, and many other conditions could be the cause. In the absence of a more specific diagnosis, extreme fatigue is most likely to be caused by poor nutrition, insomnia (see p.62), snoring, sleep apnea, or anxiety and depression.

CALL THE PHYSICIAN
■ If your symptoms have been present for more than 2 weeks.

KITCHEN MEDICINE
■ The time-honored kitchen remedy for exhausted invalids, immortalized by Charles Dickens in *Oliver Twist*, is gruel. Add 2 heaped tbsp/40ml of oatmeal to 2½ cups/600ml of boiling water and stir continuously until it comes back to a boil. Simmer for 20 minutes, stirring occasionally, then strain through a fine sieve, add 1tsp/5ml of honey and 1tbsp/15ml of light cream. Drink a bowl full every day.

CONVENTIONAL MEDICINE

✚ Try to sleep regularly for 8–9 hours a night. Take regular exercise and eat a balanced diet, avoiding excessive alcohol. If symptoms persist for more than 2 weeks, make a routine appointment to see your physician, who may arrange for some blood tests to rule out a physical cause for your symptoms.

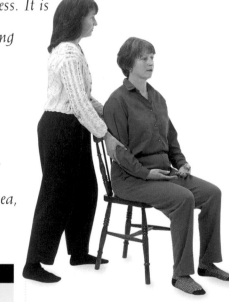

ABOVE *An Alexander Technique teacher will ensure that your posture is not contributing to feelings of fatigue by incorrect use of muscles.*

EXERCISE

SURPRISINGLY, this is one time when exercise is really important, as it stimulates the body's production of adrenalin—the activity hormones. Start gently with two or three easy 10-minute walks each day, and gradually work up to three brisk walks. Then carefully increase your effort, making sure that you always stop before you get too exhausted. Aim for three or four periods of strenuous exercise each week as your final goal. You may feel physically tired, but you will stop feeling permanently exhausted.

HERBAL REMEDIES

 ■ Use and Dosage: Herbal tonics can be extremely effective in boosting energy levels to combat fatigue.

Korean ginseng (600mg daily) is extremely popular but can prove too aggressively stimulating for many—traditionally it should be used only by older age groups (40-plus); American ginseng or codonopsis is gentler, or women may prefer Dang Gui.

Take Siberian ginseng (600mg daily) during busy times to help cope with additional stresses.

ABOVE *Korean ginseng may be conveniently purchased as tablets. The root of the ginseng plant is used. Do not take for more than 4 weeks at a time.*

NUTRITION

 A full complement of the many essential nutrients is the first requirement and this can only be achieved by a well-balanced diet chosen from a wide variety of foods.

Rich sources of iron, like liver (but not if you are pregnant), other organ meat, dates, raisins, watercress, eggs, dark green leafy vegetables, and sardines, must be top of your shopping list. **Eat plenty of** foods rich in vitamin C alongside the iron-rich foods to improve absorption—for instance, tomatoes with the sardines, orange juice with your boiled eggs, green vegetables with the liver.

Avoid absolutely all the commercial energy drinks, which provide little else but sugar, and do not go overboard on the protein. What you need are the starchy foods—but not biscuits, cakes and confectionery. So go for a small steak, plenty of potatoes (not always French fries), and lots of vegetables or salad; a large portion of pasta with a little Bolognese sauce; a bowl of risotto with plenty of rice; or a selection of vegetables and a little chicken.

AROMATHERAPY

 ✺ ROSEMARY
Rosmarinus officinalis
✺ LEMON GRASS
Cymbopogon citratus
✺ BASIL
Ocimum basilicum
✺ PEPPERMINT
Mentha x piperita
For mental fatigue, rosemary, basil, and peppermint are useful and stimulate the brain. Lemon grass and rosemary are probably best for physical fatigue. Lemon grass builds up the body's resistance to fatigue, and gives an extra boost of energy.

Application:
Use these oils in the bath, in massage oils or lotions, in vaporizers, or on a handkerchief.

CAUTION

Do not use peppermint or rosemary oil at night—they are both too stimulating; and peppermint can disturb the sleep pattern. Rosemary should not be used by anyone who has high blood pressure or epilepsy.

OUTSIDE HELP

 ALEXANDER TECHNIQUE: by unconsciously overcontracting some muscles and not using others enough you use fatigable muscles at the expense of nonfatigable muscles. Applying the Technique helps to redress the balance.

REFLEXOLOGY: a complete foot reflexology treatment is a wonderful way of boosting energy levels. If a period of deep sleep is required, the pace should be slow and regular; for an instant pick-me-up, make it brisk.

YOGA: start with relaxation and gentle movements on your back, all coordinated with a long, smooth breath. If you gradually feel more energetic, progress to kneeling, standing and/or seated postures. Use Shitali or Sitkari. Breathe in energy and breathe out tiredness.

HOMEOPATHIC REMEDIES

A consultation with a qualified homeopath is recommended.
✺ NUX VOMICA **30C**
For competitive, ambitious workaholic, who becomes exhausted from overwork or overindulgence.
✺ SEPIA **30C** Often used for the worn out, weepy woman. Feels distant from family. Depressed and dislikes company. Feels the cold easily. May be better for exercise.
✺ KALI PHOSPHORICUM **30C** For mental and physical exhaustion associated with nervousness. After working for exams. Everything seems a big effort. Worse for physical or mental effort.
Dosage: one tablet twice daily. Maximum 5 days.

RIGHT *Chronic fatigue syndrome appears to be a disease of modern times; as yet the cause is unknown. Sufferers may experience such a loss of energy that normal living becomes an impossibility.*

DIAGNOSING CHRONIC FATIGUE SYNDROME

- Fatigue from a particular date onward
- Unexplained generalized muscle weakness
- Often associated with painful joints or muscles, forgetfulness and difficulty in concentrating, mood swings, and depression

NERVOUS SYSTEM

chronic fatigue syndrome *ME*

HERBAL REMEDIES

Herbal immune stimulants, such as echinacea and astragalus, can help in the long term, while traditional tonic herbs (such as ginseng, damiana, or gotu kola) will provide an energy boost during the recovery stage: but taking them too soon can simply exhaust the system further.

■ **Use and Dosage:**
Use drop doses of bitters, like wormwood or gentian tinctures, before meals to improve the digestion, while an infusion using equal amounts of vervain, betony, and oatstraw can help with depression.

A daily bowl of shiitake mushroom soup acts as an immune tonic and restorative.

Take 1g of evening primrose oil daily as a nutritional supplement.

W*hole volumes have been written about this controversial condition and there are still some medical experts who believe that it is entirely a psychological illness. Typified by grinding fatigue and exhaustion, an inability to stay awake, muscle pains, mood swings, and loss of concentration, enthusiasm, and appetite—all of which can lead to severe depression—it is generally a poorly treated illness. No matter what treatment is prescribed, the only route to long-term success is to combine treatment with self-help and the essential support of family and friends. Healthy eating is the foundation of recovery, and extreme dietary regimes of any sort should be avoided at all costs.*

CONVENTIONAL MEDICINE

Because the cause of chronic fatigue syndrome is not known, there is no specific conventional remedy that has been shown to be more effective than any other. Most physicians recommend taking gentle, graded exercise, with rest periods when the symptoms are particularly severe. Eat a healthy diet. Take measures to limit stress, and consider undergoing counseling.

ABOVE *It is vital to ensure nutrition is monitored to give the body the best chance of recovery.*

OUTSIDE HELP

ALEXANDER TECHNIQUE: applying the Alexander principle in daily activities will give you exercise without the risk of exhaustion. It may also help with muscle pains, breathing, and mood swings.

REFLEXOLOGY: to boost energy levels, work every 3–4 days for 10 minutes over the complete left foot, then over the right foot; 5 minutes on the right hand, followed by the left hand—in that order.

ABOVE *The tops of the feet are where most of the reflexes of the lymphatic system are located. A reflexologist will work this area to boost the immune system.*

YOGA: lie in the Relaxation Posture. For 12 slow breaths, every time you breathe out, give yourself up completely to relaxation. Just lie there and enjoy it. Then, for 12 slow breaths, imagine yourself becoming stronger with each inhalation, and that energy is flowing more freely. Do this up to three times daily.

NUTRITION

It is essential to keep blood-sugar levels on an even keel, so do not leave more than 3 hours between eating, and use healthy, natural-sugar foods like dried fruits when you need a bit of a boost. Take a daily high-dose multivitamin and mineral supplement and, to help cope with the inevitable bouts of depression (effect, not cause), use herbal supplements of hypericum.

Eat plenty of brown rice, whole wheat bread and pasta, and potatoes for their energy; liver, all the legumes and dark green vegetables for their B vitamins; citrus fruit, salads, and vegetables for their vitamin C.

Avoid alcohol, all caffeine, sugar, candies, cakes, and foods with poor nutritional value.

AROMATHERAPY

The oils you choose depend on your symptoms:

For muscular fatigue:
- THYME
 Thymus vulgaris
- LEMON GRASS
 Cymbopogon citratus
- MARJORAM
 Origanum majorana

For insomnia:
- CLARY SAGE
 Salvia sclaria
- VALERIAN
 Valeriana fauriei
- MARJORAM
 Origanum majorana
- ROMAN CHAMOMILE
 Chamaemelum nobile
- LAVENDER
 Lavandula angustifolia

For depression:
- NEROLI
 Citrus aurantium
- ROSE
 Rosa centifolia/Rosa damascena

The oils for muscular fatigue are warming, soothing, and stimulating; those for insomnia are relaxing, soothing, and warming; those for depression are again both warming to the mind and uplifting.

Application: Use these essential oils in baths, foot spas, for massage and in inhalations. Do get professional help from an aromatherapist who can see you through this problem, and who will be able to get some of the oils that you may find it difficult to obtain.

EXERCISE

DURING recovery you need to make gradual improvements in the amount of physical and mental activity that you undertake. Get plenty of rest and learn a technique such as meditation, relaxation, or yoga that you can practice at home. When you feel up to it, take as much exercise as you think you can tolerate, but ignore all the well-meaning friends and family who try to encourage you to "go for a brisk walk" or "take up jogging." Too much exercise before you are really on the mend will set your progress back by weeks. Help to keep your mind active by reading and playing card games, chess, or checkers. Jigsaw puzzles are therapeutic.

PREVENTATIVE *measures*

The general consensus is that this problem is caused by a viral infection, frequently attacking an individual during, or immediately after, some other acute infection—influenza, gastroenteritis, or even a severe cold. The only preventative measure may be maintenance of an adequate and efficient immune system, which can only be achieved through a healthy lifestyle and high-quality, nutritious diet.

HOMEOPATHIC REMEDIES

This is a complicated problem to treat, so a consultation with a qualified homeopath is recommended. The following remedies are suggestions only; they may also be used to treat fatigue.

- CARBOLIC ACID **6C** For mental and physical fatigue. Very sensitive sense of smell. Band-like headaches. Belching and nausea. Craves stimulants.
- PICRIC ACID **6C** For heavy, tired feeling. Breakdown after mental exertion. Headache better for bandaging head tightly. Dread of failure at exams.
- CALCAREA CARBONICA **6C** For chilly, sweaty head, especially at night. Hard working, conscientious, takes on too much, practical. Lots of sore throats.
Dosage: one tablet daily. Maximum 2 weeks.

RIGHT *An onset of depression and lethargy, concurrent with the shortening days as fall slips into the bleak chills of winter, are the main symptoms of SAD.*

DIAGNOSING SEASONAL AFFECTIVE DISORDER
- Mood changes related to the seasons—commonly depressed in winter and picking up again in the spring
- Often associated with a craving for carbohydrates, lethargy, and insomnia

NERVOUS SYSTEM

seasonal affective disorder *SAD*

ABOVE *Cold, stark days make most of us feel a little down. But for SAD sufferers, the depression is magnified and cannot be shrugged off.*

S*AD is much more than just the winter blues. When the retina at the back of the eye is stimulated by light, the pineal gland is affected, so that the amount of the hormone melatonin circulating in the body is reduced. During the winter months—certainly in northern parts of the United States, the UK, and northern Europe—there is not much sunlight, so more melatonin is released. This prepares us for hibernation and we tend to slow down, eat more, and gain weight. Some people are much more severely affected by this lack of daylight than others and become extremely depressed, displaying severe symptoms of Seasonal Affective Disorder.*

CONVENTIONAL MEDICINE

Exposure to a bright light source for several hours a day can help in some cases.

HERBAL REMEDIES

Both St. John's wort and lemon balm are effective antidepressants, which can provide a little symptomatic relief. Basil is also very uplifting.

■ **Use and Dosage:**
Fresh basil is available throughout the winter from supermarkets, so eat plenty, and regularly inhale the scent of the crushed leaves, or a few drops of the oil on a handkerchief.

Siberian ginseng helps the body cope with additional stresses: try taking 600mg daily for 4 to 6 weeks in early winter, before symptoms become too severe.

HOMEOPATHIC REMEDIES

 Like chronic fatigue syndrome, this problem is complex to treat, so consult a qualified homeopath. The following remedies offer only a brief guide.

SEPIA 30c For person who cannot be bothered, even with family. Feels separated from family and depressed. Guilty feelings and tearful. Slow mentally and sharp-tongued. Better after exercise.

AURUM 30c For depressed, sulky, weepy person. All emotions are felt in the extreme. Critical of both self and others.

HELLEBORUS 30c For person whose mind is a blank, memory poor, feels separate from the world. Answers questions slowly, sometimes feels guilty.
Dosage: one tablet daily. Maximum 5 days.

ABOVE *Sepia is made from the ink of the cuttlefish.*

NUTRITION

Do not go for more than 3 hours without eating. **Eat plenty of** almonds, apricots, bananas, broccoli, spinach, brown rice, sesame and sunflower seeds; whole wheat bread, potatoes, pasta, and porridge; and sensible amounts of eggs, fish, poultry, lean meat, and low-fat dairy products. Eat masses of fruit, vegetables, and salads.

EXERCISE

EXERCISE is an important factor in overcoming SAD. Get as much fresh air and daylight as you can: a brisk 10-minute walk once or twice a day can make all the difference. Exercise also produces the body's own "feel-good" chemicals in the brain.

OUTSIDE HELP

REFLEXOLOGY: while symptoms of SAD persist, it may provide some relief to work the reflexes of the endocrine system. Press firmly with the side of the thumb and hold sensitive points for 15 seconds. Do this three times.

YOGA: meditate on the golden, life-giving sun; feel its heat and its energy. Then imagine it glowing and radiating from your solar plexus throughout your body. Practice Salute to the Sun daily, with visualization, and vigorous expansive postures, such as Warrior and Triangle, Upward-Raised Dog and Bow.

AROMATHERAPY

However SAD affects you, look up the oils given under stress (*see p.60*) and use them in the way that you find most soothing for your condition.

DIET: *first, avoid the energy-robbers. It is bad enough feeling miserable all the time, without eating or drinking things that deprive your body of what little energy you have. So refined carbohydrates (like sugar, white flour, cakes, cookies, candies and puddings) should be reserved for very occasional treats. Avoid excessive amounts of animal fat and do not have more than one alcoholic drink a day—a glass of good red wine or 1¼ cups/300ml of real beer are best (too much alcohol destroys the B and C vitamins). The caffeine in tea, coffee, chocolate, and cola drinks interferes with iron absorption, and nicotine not only reduces the oxygen levels in your blood, but also interferes with vitamin B absorption.*

SUPPLEMENTS: *give your body and mind a boost with vitamins A, C, and E, a B-complex supplement, and the minerals iron, zinc, and selenium. And take a regular dose of co-enzyme Q10, which helps release energy from food, throughout the winter months.*

LIGHT: *SAD responds well to treatment with high-intensity light. Light is measured in a unit called a lux: the average office has an intensity of 500 lux; a normal home 300 lux; while if you look out of the window at a sun-drenched garden, you are getting 2,500 lux, and this is the level that you need to beat depression and keep down your levels of melatonin. You can create this with a special light box, which is best kept in the kitchen of your home or at your workplace and provides the level of illumination needed to control melatonin.*

KITCHEN MEDICINE

■ If you are suffering from SAD, or just feeling tired and worn out after months of winter weather, there are lots of kitchen herbs and spices that can help. Parsley, thyme, rosemary, mint, sage, horseradish, ginger, and cinnamon are all good stimulants, so use them generously in cooking and to make your own teas.

① Put 2tsp/10ml of your chosen fresh chopped herb (or 1tsp/5ml of dried herb) into a cup of boiling water.

② Cover, leave for 10 minutes, then strain.

③ Add a little honey and sip slowly while sitting down to relax for 20 minutes; ½in/1cm of peeled grated ginger root can be used in exactly the same way.

RIGHT *Raised blood pressure, heart disease, headaches, skin problems, ulcers, and even a stroke can be the end result of long-term and unresolved stress.*

DIAGNOSING STRESS

- Lots of minor medical ailments, often all at the same time
- Fast heartbeat
- Diarrhea
- Edgy or depressed feeling
- Difficulty sleeping
- Poor or increased appetite
- Irritability

NERVOUS SYSTEM

stress

It is most important to realize that some stress—the kind that excites us and gives an edge to our performance or our relationships—is an essential ingredient of everyday life. What varies is the way in which people cope with, and adapt to, different levels of stress. Once you have learned the stress levels you can comfortably withstand, it is not difficult to learn the skills necessary to cope with higher stress levels. Whatever causes your stress, your body's response is the same. Large amounts of adrenalin are poured into your system, preparing you for "flight or fight." Difficulties arise when, as in most situations in modern life, you cannot do either. In most instances stress counseling, psychotherapy, and relaxation techniques can help, but home remedies have a major part to play, too.

CALL THE PHYSICIAN

■ If you have been feeling consistently stressed for more than 2 weeks

KITCHEN MEDICINE

■ Many of the common culinary herbs have powerful calming effects. Among the best are rosemary, thyme, lemon balm, basil, lemon verbena, marjoram, and nutmeg, so use them lavishly in appropriate recipes.

■ A tomato, lettuce, and basil sandwich makes a wonderful destressing snack, especially at bedtime, if stress is causing sleep problems.

CONVENTIONAL MEDICINE

Following a stressful episode, try to reorganize events to avoid further upset. Eat regular meals and take regular exercise—consider yoga or meditation relaxation therapy. Try to avoid resorting to alcohol or cigarettes. If the symptoms become unmanageable, then your physician may be able to make a referral to a counselor. Drugs to control the symptoms or to lift your mood are not a panacea, but are useful as they may improve the symptoms to a point at which you are more able to help yourself.

ABOVE *Exercise lifts the mood and dissipates physical symptoms of stress.*

HERBAL REMEDIES

 Relaxing herbs like betony, lemon balm, lavender, chamomile, vervain, or skullcap make ideal teas to soothe tensions and nervous stress. Valerian is sometimes referred to as "nature's tranquillizer," but without the usual sleep-inducing side-effects, so it is ideal for easing tensions: the taste is distinctive, so tablets may be preferable.

■ **Use and Dosage:**
Use 1–2tsp/5–10ml of the relaxing herbs per cup of tea.

Siberian ginseng will help the body cope with stress: take 600mg daily in the week before expected stresses occur.

HOMEOPATHIC REMEDIES

 A consultation with a qualified homeopath is recommended.

❧ DYS. CO. (BACH) 30C For anxiety before an event like an exam. Reacts to any criticism, cannot keep still.
Dosage: one tablet every 12 hours. Maximum three doses.

❧ NUX VOMICA 30C For a competitive, impatient, ambitious go-getter. Symptoms of abdominal pain, which is cramping. Likes coffee, spices, alcohol, and fats. Stress from overwork at the office.
Dosage: one tablet twice daily. Maximum 5 days.

NUTRITION

It is hard to overemphasize the role of nutrition in helping to calm a stressful life. Serotonin and tryptophan both have a calming effect on mind and body. For serotonin, **eat plenty of** nuts (especially walnuts), dates, figs, pineapples, papaws, passion fruit, tomatoes, avocados, and eggplant.

For tryptophan, **eat plenty of** potatoes, beans, pasta, rice, and whole wheat bread. Porridge and muesli make a good start to the day. Get your protein from modest amounts of fish, poultry, and low-fat dairy products, as well as beans and cereals. The B vitamins and iron are also key requirements in a stressful life.

EXERCISE

EXERCISE IS without question one of the most effective ways of reducing your body's stress levels. Stress-related headaches, digestive problems, menstrual problems, insomnia, hyperactivity (mental and physical), and the muscular aches and pains that result from a stressful existence can all melt away thanks to exercise.

Do not create more stress by trying to stick to a punishing regime or an over-burdensome schedule. Any activity that you enjoy can be beneficial, as long as you are burning up the surplus adrenalin and releasing all those feel-good hormones.

AROMATHERAPY

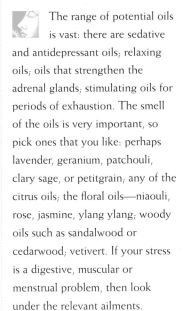 The range of potential oils is vast: there are sedative and antidepressant oils; relaxing oils; oils that strengthen the adrenal glands; stimulating oils for periods of exhaustion. The smell of the oils is very important, so pick ones that you like: perhaps lavender, geranium, patchouli, clary sage, or petitgrain; any of the citrus oils; the floral oils—niaouli, rose, jasmine, ylang ylang; woody oils such as sandalwood or cedarwood; vetivert. If your stress is a digestive, muscular or menstrual problem, then look under the relevant ailments.

Application:
Whatever oil you choose, try not to make a regime for yourself that is difficult or creates even more stress. Put the oil in the bath, in a burner, into a massage oil or body lotion, and just enjoy the pleasure of it. Try and make the time.

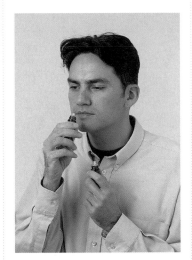

ABOVE *Certain oils will be more appealing to you than others: use these, rather than something you don't like! There are plenty to choose from for various therapeutic effects.*

PREVENTATIVE
measures

Planning your life to minimize over-commitment and learning how to say "no" are the first steps toward avoiding stress-related problems. Yoga, meditation, relaxation exercises, massage, aromatherapy, and calming baths are all protective against stress.

DIET: *avoiding excessive consumption of mental irritants, like alcohol and the caffeine in cola drinks, coffee, tea, and chocolate, is important. Beware of taking unnecessary behavior-modifying drugs. Although these are sometimes essential, in many cases self-help, home remedies, and natural therapies are even more effective and have no side-effects.*

OUTSIDE HELP

ALEXANDER TECHNIQUE: stress is often accompanied by a build-up of muscle tension, bad posture, and poor breathing. The Alexander Technique cannot take these stress factors away, but practicing it makes you more aware of your body's reaction and enables you to manage yourself better in stressful situations.
REFLEXOLOGY: a complete reflexology foot treatment is a wonderful way of relieving stress-related symptoms. Slow, light, and rhythmic treatment relaxes; but if a boost of energy is needed, the treatment can be brisk and stimulating. Treat twice-weekly.
YOGA: don't be competitive in your yoga practice. Focus on slow movements coordinated with the breath, and long exhalations. Practice Aruloma Ujjayi: in through both nostrils, out through alternate. Humming as you exhale, sitting or lying, is very peaceful.

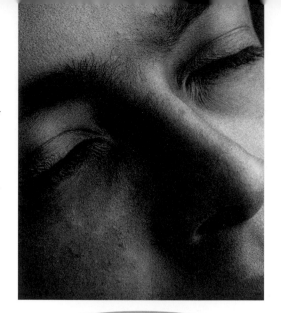

DIAGNOSING INSOMNIA

- Difficulty getting to sleep, which may occur at any time during normal sleeping hours

NERVOUS SYSTEM

insomnia

CAUTION

Avoid sleeping pills, which are addictive. They may, however, be suitable for short-term treatment under medical supervision.

KITCHEN MEDICINE

■ A bottle of milk, a jar of honey, a loaf of bread, and a lettuce are all you need. A glass of warm milk and honey is a time-honored aid to sleep; with a lettuce sandwich you will be off to the land of nod before you can count ten sheep. The starch in bread stimulates the brain to release the relaxing natural substance known as tryptophan, while lettuce has been used as a soporific since the time of the ancient Romans.

■ Chamomile and lime-blossom tea are also gently soothing for insomniacs.

*N*one of us can escape the occasional bad night's sleep. Indigestion, toothache, backache, anxiety about something happening the next day, being too hot or too cold…these and many other factors can conspire to rob us of our usual beauty sleep. Real insomnia, however, is a state of habitual sleeplessness, repeated night after night, often for months or even years on end. Worrying about insomnia, to the point of obsession, does more damage than the lack of sleep itself. But in most instances there is no need to take sleeping pills, tranquilizers, or alcohol. Better sleep hygiene and a wealth of home remedies can help you get the sleep of the just.

CONVENTIONAL MEDICINE

Stop working at least an hour before bedtime. Have a hot milky drink and a bath (but not too hot). Avoid alcohol. Go to bed, but if you are still awake after 30 minutes, get up and settle into a relaxing activity, such as reading a newspaper or magazine. After 30 minutes go back to bed.

Repeat as many times as necessary. During the day (never just before bedtime), take regular aerobic exercise, at least three times a week. Seek medical advice if the symptoms of insomnia persist.

LEFT *A glass of warm milk and a lettuce sandwich.*

EXERCISE

MOST CHRONIC insomniacs say they are too tired to exercise, but in fact regular exercise releases endorphins (the body's own "feel-good" chemicals) from the brain. No matter how tired you feel, exercise will help you to a better night's sleep—as long as there is no underlying medical condition causing your insomnia for which exercise would not be advised.

HERBAL REMEDIES

 A simple remedy suitable for all ages is Californian poppy, which can be grown in the garden as an annual and is an effective sleep-inducing remedy, with none of the side-effects associated with more potent types of poppies.

■ **Use and Dosage:**
Use Californian poppy fresh or dried in an infusion.

Also worth trying are passion flower, lavender, and betony—use in equal amounts in an infusion as a nighttime drink.

Cowslip flowers are a traditional and effective remedy for insomnia associated with overexcitement. Use a tincture and take 20–40 drops in hot milk before bed.

ABOVE *A dreamy field of Californian poppies. Grow them in a sunny spot in your garden, dry, and store.*

NUTRITION

 What you eat plays a key role in the pattern of insomnia. Going to bed too full or too hungry interferes with your normal sleep habits, and it is the disturbance of these regular patterns that leads to insomnia. Eating too late—especially a meal based on animal protein—is a great mistake, as such foods are stimulating and trigger greater production of the activity hormones. Starchy foods, on the other hand, encourage the body to manufacture more of the nonactive, growth and repair hormones, which function best during sleep. Ideally, evening meals should therefore be based on foods like rice, pasta, potatoes, root vegetables, and beans, saving meat meals for eating during the middle of the day.

Eat plenty of organ meats (but not liver if you are pregnant), fish, poultry, eggs, potatoes, brown rice, whole wheat cereals, whole wheat bread, and soy products, which are the best sources of vitamin B_6, lack of which can be a factor in insomnia. Culinary herbs can also be a tremendous help and the ones you should use most in your cooking are sage, fennel, rosemary, and basil.

AROMATHERAPY

 LAVENDER
Lavandula angustifolia
CLARY SAGE
Salvia sclarea
ORANGE
Citrus aurantium/Citrus sinensis
MARJORAM
Origanum majorana
BASIL
Ocimum basilicum

These oils are calming and soothing. Basil helps to clear the mind, while oils like marjoram are warming muscle-relaxants.

Application:
Use in warm baths, or put a couple of drops on the pillow, in a burner or a light ring in the bedroom. Use the oils in combinations and find the ones you like best—smell is an extremely important factor, as a smell that you do not like is not very conducive to sleep.

CAUTION

Never drink alcohol if you are going to use clary sage, or drive after using it. It is very sedative and can have quite a nasty effect in combination with alcohol.

PREVENTATIVE *measures*

This is one condition for which prevention really is better than cure. The first step is to recognize that insomnia is not a disease—nobody dies of it and nobody should let their lives be dominated by it.

SLEEPING HABITS: *a regular sleep routine is vital and depends on going to bed and getting up at roughly the same time every day—insomnia is quite rare in those who have to be up at 6.00 a.m.. If your sleep pattern has been disrupted—by illness or a stay in hospital, or by traveling across time zones—it is crucial to get back into your normal pattern as quickly as possible. Do not allow yourself to sleep during the day, as this will make getting back to normal even more difficult.*

CAFFEINE: *most people are aware that too much coffee can keep you awake, but they forget there are considerable amounts of caffeine in tea, cola drinks, chocolate, and cocoa. Insomniacs should avoid it in all forms, from lunchtime on.*

HOMEOPATHIC REMEDIES

PASSIFLORA 30C
For restless, wakeful sleep. Try this remedy first.

NUX VOMICA 30C For overworked person, who wakes in early hours thinking of work. Falls asleep just before time to wake up. Wakes with hungover feeling.

ARSENICUM ALBUM 30C For anxious, restless sleep. Sleeps with the head raised. Particularly if a chilly person.

COFFEA 30C For waking in early hours, mind full of ideas, dozing afterward. Wakes suddenly, dreams disturb sleep.
Dosage: one tablet before bed for 10 days or until improved.

OUTSIDE HELP

ACUPRESSURE: points 34 and 38 will help.
ALEXANDER TECHNIQUE: reducing unnecessary tension, as well as inhibiting its build-up, is part of what the technique teaches. Practicing, especially in semi-supine, before you go to bed—as well as while you are lying awake—may greatly improve the quality of rest you are getting. It may even send you to sleep!

REFLEXOLOGY: a full foot reflexology treatment often produces sufficient relaxation to induce a good night's sleep. The treatment should be slow and rhythmic and the pressure light.
YOGA: before going to bed, do a very peaceful, meditative practice. Incorporate Cat and one or two lying postures, all with slow breathing. Finish lying or sitting: ask God, or your Higher Self, for help with any problems and give thanks for the day.

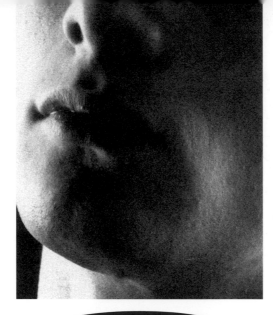

RIGHT *Acne is most distressing when it occurs on the face, as it can't be hidden, but it may also erupt on the shoulders, back, and chest.*

DIAGNOSING ACNE
- Blackheads
- Spots
- Greasy skin

THE SENSES

acne

Acne is a distressing skin problem that affects around 80 percent of young people between the ages of 12 and 24. It occurs as a result of a build-up of oil or sebum secreted through the pores. The pores become blocked, then infected, causing spots. It is more common in boys than girls and is triggered by the fluctuating levels of hormones during adolescence. Though not directly caused by diet, food can play a vital part in the improvement, or worsening, of the angry red pustular spots which most commonly appear on the face, neck, top of the shoulders, and back.

HERBAL REMEDIES

Combine cleansing herbs taken internally with external antiseptic washes, steam baths or lotions.

■ **Use and Dosage:**
Drink three cups daily of a tea made by infusing ⅓ cup/10g each of agrimony, burdock leaves and marigold petals to 1pt/500ml of water.

Apply a lotion of 4tbsp/60ml each of distilled witch hazel and rosewater with 1tsp/5ml each of tea-tree and thyme oils.

A traditional remedy is simply to rub acne pustules with a garlic clove each night.

EXERCISE

THERE is no specific exercise that will help with acne, but any general physical activity that improves the circulation and breathing is always beneficial for the skin.

CONVENTIONAL MEDICINE

Treatment varies according to how severe the condition is and which parts of the skin are affected. The aim of conventional treatment is to unplug the blocked pores, kill any germs, and reduce the inflammation. Mild acne may only require a lotion that dries the skin. In moderately severe cases, an antibiotic preparation applied to the skin may be used in combination with a drying lotion. If acne is persistent, antibiotic tablets may be more effective.

In severe cases, oral treatment with a derivative of vitamin A may help, but this has to be prescribed by a dermatologist. Most treatments take up to 3–6 months to work and may need to be continued beyond this to prevent acne recurring.

Dosage information ~
Adults and children

■ Apply lotions and creams to the whole area, not just the spots, twice a day. Tablets may be taken once a day or more frequently; follow medical advice.

OUTSIDE HELP

REFLEXOLOGY: regular sessions that might help could include the endocrine system, the liver and kidney reflexes, the colon, and the diaphragm.

YOGA: in yoga terms, this is a problem of overheating. Cool the system through closing postures, such as Forward Bends; emphasize long exhalations, and practice Shitali or Sitkari. You also need to reduce stress on the liver, so be careful with fried foods and sugars.

AROMATHERAPY

✿ LAVENDER
Lavandula angustifolia

✿ BERGAMOT
Citrus bergamia

✿ TEA TREE
Melaleuca alternifolia

These oils are bactericidal and relaxing, which will help anybody who is stressed due to severe acne. Lavender is also calming for the skin, as well as the emotions. Tea tree builds up the body's immune system, which should prevent infection from getting into the open spots.

Application:
Apply lavender neat, using a cotton bud, directly to the spot. Tea tree, bergamot, and lavender can all be used in a compress or facial steamer. Using the three oils together, or separately, in a bath can be especially useful with teenagers, who do not want a fussy routine. They can simply put their facecloth in the bath, then over their face, to get a compress effect. Do ensure you are drinking plenty of water—the body needs water to flush the system out.

CAUTION

Do not apply any oil other than lavender directly to the skin.

NUTRITION

Your diet should be low in animal fats and high in the immune-boosting nutrients. Sugar consumption should be minimal to reduce the production of sebum (the skin's natural protective grease) and deprive bacteria of their favorite food.

Eat plenty of all the dark green and orange vegetables and fruit for their beta-carotene; citrus fruits for their vitamin C; nuts, seeds and vegetable oils for their vitamin E. Eat some cabbage every day—it helps regulate hormone levels, as well as containing lots of beta-carotene and vitamin C.

Avoid high-fat, high-sugar convenience foods. Eliminate chocolate, ice cream, salt, burgers, hot dogs, and all manufactured meat products. A detox program of just raw fruit, vegetables, and salads with unlimited water, unsalted vegetable juices, and herbal teas should be followed for 3 days each month. After the third day add whole grains and cooked vegetables, returning to your normal diet on the fourth day.

Your standard diet should be rich in all the whole grains and fresh produce, with limited amounts of dairy produce. Complex carbohydrates, like potatoes, brown rice, whole wheat bread, and beans, can be eaten in abundance. Use vegetarian protein sources or fish and lean poultry. Tropical fruits are especially good, due to their high enzyme content, so include mangoes, papaws, pineapple, and kiwis.

Cabbage
Carrot
Pineapple
Papaw
Broccoli
Curly kale
Kiwi fruit
Mango

ABOVE *Fruit and vegetables are vital for their vitamins and cleansing effect on the body.*

HOMEOPATHIC REMEDIES

A consultation with a qualified homeopath is recommended.

✿ KALI BROMATUM 6C For acne of face, cheek, and forehead. Spots look bluish-red, discharge pus, and produce scars.

✿ CALCAREA SULPHURICUM 6C For lots of pimples, spots that discharge pus on face and around ears. Heal slowly. Pus can form a crust on the skin. Scalp has pimples.

✿ SULPHUR 6C For spots on forehead and nose. Skin worse for washing, sensitive to cold air. Spots that are scratched discharge pus. Patient intolerant of heat, lazy, and produces smelly sweat.

Dosage: one tablet daily. Maximum 2 weeks.

PREVENTATIVE
measures

Acne is not just a physical condition but, when severe, can lead to depression and social isolation. Bad cases should be seen by a dermatologist for specialist treatment. But even they can be helped by taking preventative measures.

SUPPLEMENTS: *daily doses of vitamin A (500μg), zinc (5mg) and evening primrose oil (1,500mg). For premenstrual flare-ups take 50mg of vitamin B_6 each day for the 10 days preceding onset.*

HYGIENE: *use tea-tree oil skin-wash and cleanse daily with a container of natural live yogurt containing a heaped teaspoon of coarse sea salt. Although cosmetics can be useful to cover inflamed skin, try to avoid heavy, oil-based cosmetics. Picking at the skin may make things worse by spreading the infection or causing scars.*

ABOVE *Stimulating blood flow to the skin by brushing with a loofah.*

HYDROTHERAPY: *after your bath or shower, stimulate the blood flow to the skin by brushing vigorously with a loofah or back brush and cold water.*

SUNLIGHT: *acne usually improves during the summer months due to the antibacterial effect of ultraviolet light. Get as much natural daylight on your skin as possible—in the early morning and late afternoon during the summer and any time during the winter. But never sunbathe when there is a risk of burning.*

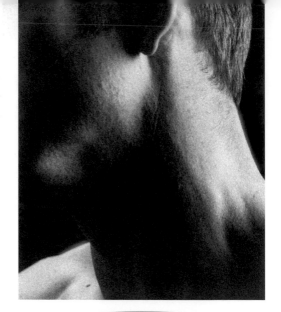

RIGHT *Boils are infections which start around a hair follicle, forming pus. The back of the neck, nostrils, armpits, between the legs, and buttocks are likely sites.*

DIAGNOSING A BOIL
- Localized swelling
- Hot, red skin over the affected area
- Pain, often throbbing
- Possibly a yellow discharge of pus

THE SENSES

boils

Anyone can get a boil at any time, and the occasional episode is painful and unpleasant, but not of great significance, as long as it is treated correctly. Repeated boils may, however, be a sign of underlying illness (for example, diabetes) or an indication that your natural resistance has declined for some reason.

HERBAL REMEDIES

Apply slippery elm or chickweed ointments, or make a slippery elm poultice by mixing 1tsp/5ml of the powdered herb with enough hot water, or hot marigold infusion, to make a thick paste, then apply to the boil. Internally, garlic or echinacea (2 x 200mg capsules, twice a day) will help improve resistance.

OUTSIDE HELP

REFLEXOLOGY: it is possible that complete and regular reflexology treatment may help to stimulate all the systems of elimination and may therefore be beneficial for acne.

CONVENTIONAL MEDICINE

A boil may burst spontaneously or it may need lancing to release the pus. Treatment at an early stage with antibiotics can sometimes prevent a boil from developing, as can cleaning all cuts well with soap and water.

Dosage information ~
Adults
- Take antibiotics three or four times a day for 3–7 days; follow medical advice.

Children
- Antibiotic syrup up to four times a day; take medical advice.

AROMATHERAPY

- TEA TREE
Melaleuca alternifolia
- LAVENDER
Lavandula angustifolia
- BERGAMOT
Citrus bergamia
- JUNIPER
Juniperus communis

Application:
Use tea tree, lavender, and bergamot in a hot compress; juniper and lavender in the bath.

KITCHEN MEDICINE
- **The traditional bread poultice is the best way to treat a boil** (*see Kitchen medicine on p.189*).

HOMEOPATHIC REMEDIES

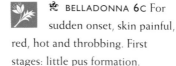

- BELLADONNA 6C For sudden onset, skin painful, red, hot and throbbing. First stages: little pus formation.
- HEPAR SULPHURIS CALCAREUM 6C For splinter-like pains at slightest touch. Bad-tempered. Brings boil to a head.
- SULPHUR 6C For crops of boils. One boil finishes as another starts.
Dosage: one tablet every 4 hours for 2–3 days.

NUTRITION

Eat plenty of vitamin C-rich food—currants, citrus fruit, kiwis, and fresh fruit juices; liver, carrots, broccoli, and spinach for their vitamin A; pumpkin seeds and shellfish for their zinc; garlic for its antibacterial properties. Avoiding high-sugar and high-fat foods substantially reduces the risk of getting boils.

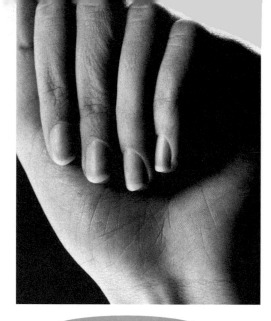

RIGHT *The common wart is most often found in children, especially on the hands. These are more of a nuisance than anything. Plantar warts, or verrucae, however, can be painful.*

DIAGNOSING WARTS

- Most warts cause no symptoms, but may cause pain if found on the sole of the foot
- Can be unsightly, depending on their position

THE SENSES

warts

Warts are caused by the human papilloma virus and are generally spread from another part of the body or caught from someone else. Most people with warts will lose them as the wart virus dies off. For the remainder, they can vary from a mildly irritating single wart to painful verrucae and large, conjoined groups of distressing genital warts, which may also put these women's babies at risk. Genital warts can be sexually transmitted and both partners should receive medical attention.

HERBAL REMEDIES

Thuja is extremely antiviral and antifungal.

Use and Dosage:
A couple of drops of tincture on the wart night and morning will usually clear it reasonably quickly. Also take 5 drops of tincture in a little water twice a day.

Other useful herbs include tea-tree oil, marigold, *Aloe vera*, house leeks, and the sap of freshly picked greater celandine.

AROMATHERAPY

❧ LEMON
Citrus limon
❧ TEA TREE
Melaleuca alternifolia
Tea tree is antiviral, while both oils are antiseptic.

Application:
Apply neat oil using a toothpick, so that you get one drop directly onto the wart or verruca. Cover with a dry plaster or dressing and repeat at least twice a day. Alternate the oils after 2 or 3 weeks.

CONVENTIONAL MEDICINE

Most warts will disappear eventually with no treatment, but because they can spread or be painful, many people prefer to treat them. The principle of all treatment for warts is to try and destroy the wart tissue without harming the surrounding normal skin. Keep the wart covered to avoid spreading the infection. Before applying a treatment, file the surface of the wart to remove any hard skin. Seek medical advice for persistent or spreading warts.

Dosage information ~
Adults and children
- Apply the treatment daily after filing the surface with an emery board or pumice stone; see package for details.

HOMEOPATHIC REMEDIES

❧ THUJA **6C** For large, jagged, cauliflower warts. Large, flat warts located on hands and fingers. Nails deformed. Painful verrucae.
❧ CAUSTICUM **6C** For warts on hands, face, lips. Bleed easily. Warts inflamed and hard; near or under fingernails.
❧ NITRIC ACID **6C** For large, soft, yellow warts. Especially on eyelids and nose. Bleed on washing.
❧ DULCAMARA **6C** For smooth, large warts on face or palm.
Dosage: one tablet taken twice daily until improved. Maximum 3 weeks.

KITCHEN MEDICINE
- Simple, non-genital warts may respond to rubbing them with the cut end of a clove of garlic, a cut dandelion stalk, or even undiluted lemon juice. Repeat twice daily for a week or two.

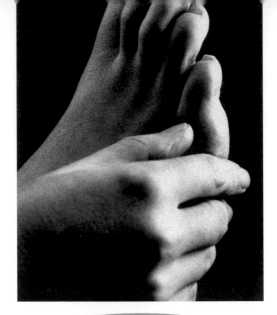

RIGHT *Corns and calluses usually occur on the feet, but may also appear on the hands after rough, repetitive manual work.*

RIGHT *Corns and calluses usually occur on the feet, but may also appear on the hands after rough, repetitive manual work.*

DIAGNOSING CORNS & CALLUSES

- An area of thick, hard skin, often on the toes
- Corns can be painful

THE SENSES

corns & calluses

Corns and calluses of the feet are the inevitable result of wearing ill-fitting shoes. If there are deformities of the foot, these can also lead to areas of excessive pressure or a change of weight distribution when standing or walking. Either way, corns or calluses—areas of hard, thick skin—may result. Corns should be dealt with by a qualified podiatrist or chiropodist and not hacked at with any of the patent corn-removing gadgets. Calluses may also occur on the palms of the hand and the fingers—for example, as the result of gardening or manual work.

CONVENTIONAL MEDICINE

You can gently file a callus and then moisturize the skin. It may be easier to file the skin after a bath, when the skin is soft. Covering a corn with a cushioned bandaid, which is designed to avoid pressure on the corn itself, can relieve the pain. Otherwise seek advice from a podiatrist.

HOMEOPATHIC REMEDIES

ANTIMONIUM CRUDUM **6C** For thick and distorted nails. Horny lumps on hands and soles. Callosities from slight pressure. Inflamed corns. Feet very tender.

GRAPHITES **6C** For thick, ingrown, and crumbling nails. Callosities on hands, with skin that cracks and discharges sticky substance.

FERRUM PICRICUM **6C** For corns with yellowish discoloration. May also be many warts on the hands.

Dosage: one tablet twice daily. Maximum 2 weeks.

ABOVE *Gardening is a particular risk factor for calluses on the hands. Gardeners should protect their hands with thick gloves, and use a barrier cream.*

EXERCISE

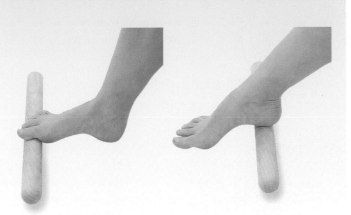

IF CALLUSES form as a result of a fallen arch or some injury to the foot or ankle that alters the gait, the joints and muscles of the foot can be exercised using an old-fashioned wooden rolling pin. Place the rolling pin on the floor at right-angles to the foot, then start with your toes on the rolling pin and your heel on the floor. Exerting

some pressure on the rolling pin, move the foot forward until the heel is on the rolling pin and the toes are on the floor in front. Repeat 20 times with each foot. Then turn the rolling pin round and place the foot along its length. While gripping with the toes, roll the pin from left to right. Repeat 20 times, then change feet.

Rounded shape

Plenty of space

ABOVE *It pays to ensure that you buy sensible, correctly fitting shoes from childhood, to avoid problems in later years.*

PREVENTATIVE *measures*

FOOTWEAR: *shoes should have a round rather than pointed shape, and there should be at least 1in/2.5cm between the end of the longest toe and the tip of the inside of the shoe. For reasons of vanity, women always buy shoes at least half to one size smaller than they should—and their feet pay the price. Avoid high-heeled shoes and pumps, both of which cram the foot down into the toe end, squeezing the toes together, deforming the shape of the foot and applying greatly increased pressure in all the wrong places. Lace-up shoes hold the foot back into the heel end and ensure proper weight distribution.*

FOOTCARE: *at least twice a week soak the feet for 10 minutes in hot soapy water, rub any callused areas carefully with a pumice stone, dry thoroughly, then apply liberal amounts of moisturizing cream.*

HERBAL REMEDIES

 There are numerous traditional herbal remedies for corns, such as mashed house leeks, onions, garlic cloves, or lemon rind and juice applied directly to the affected area. Inflammation can be soothed with St. John's wort cream or comfrey oil while easing pressure on the area with thick felt rings. Rubbing the feet with fresh plantain leaves was traditionally believed to prevent corns.

KITCHEN MEDICINE
■ For corns, apply crushed garlic to a piece of gauze, put over the corn, and secure in place with a bandaid.

AROMATHERAPY

🕊 ROMAN CHAMOMILE
Chamaemelum nobile
🕊 LAVENDER
Lavandula angustifolia
🕊 GOOD-QUALITY VEGETABLE OIL
(or calendula oil: available from reputable suppliers)

These oils are anti-inflammatory, so they will bring the swelling down and thus lessen the pain. Using a good-quality vegetable oil will reduce the areas of hard skin.

Application:
Use in daily massage, especially with the essential oil mixed with the good-quality vegetable oil. If there is inflammation and the affected area is too tender to touch, then foot baths (or hand baths, if the calluses are on the hand) will be more relevant.

1 Treat yourself to a pedicure twice a week. First, soak the feet in hot, soapy water for 10 minutes.

2 Use a pumice stone to rub gently at hard skin. This obviates the need for proprietary hard-skin removers.

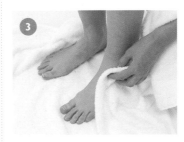

3 Dry your feet thoroughly. This is good practice and helps stop fungal infections such as athlete's foot.

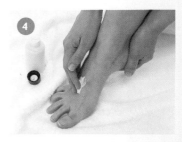

4 Massage plenty of moisturizer into your feet. While you are at home, go barefoot as often as possible.

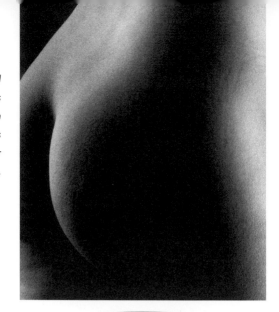

RIGHT *The thighs and buttocks are the areas where women most often complain of cellulite: areas where women have a higher proportion of fat than men.*

DIAGNOSING CELLULITE

● Pitted orange-peel appearance on the skin, often on the upper thighs, buttocks, and arms

THE SENSES

cellulite

ABOVE *Swimming is great exercise because it ensures both arms and legs get a workout. Gradually build up the length of the session.*

EXERCISE

REGULAR physical activity is a major factor in the prevention and treatment of cellulite, which most commonly occurs on the buttocks, thighs, and back of the upper arms. So cycling, swimming, skipping with a rope, and a regular, brisk, arm-swinging walk will all help: 20 minutes three times a day is the minimum in order to see any real benefit.

*T*his much-discussed and written about "ailment" is not an illness at all. The orange-peel-like skin that characterizes cellulite is not the result of a build-up of toxins but rather something that happens to the skin of most women—and it's almost only women who complain of this problem (98 percent of sufferers being female). This is because women have a thinner outer skin than men, a thinner underlying level of the dermis and a different composition of fat cells in the subcutaneous layer. Cellulite is caused by a combination of hormone changes, skin structure, and fat deposits, and though it occurs in women of all shapes and sizes, it is undeniably more common in those who are overweight. Despite being a cosmetic problem, cellulite is the cause of considerable distress to those suffering from it. And, since a woman's total number of fat cells is partially determined by her mother's nutrition during pregnancy, there are certain women who are more prone than others to experience this particular condition.

CONVENTIONAL MEDICINE

✚ Cellulite may improve by taking regular exercise and shedding excess weight, although it tends to worsen in pregnancy. There is no evidence to suggest that rubbing in expensive moisturizers and oils has any positive effect.

NUTRITION

 Weight loss is the first step toward the reduction of cellulite, but do take care: lose weight too quickly and the condition gets worse. So no crash diets, no ridiculous regimes of meal replacements and pills, just sensible eating (*see Weight Problems on p.160*), together with a reduction of refined carbohydrates—from sugars, biscuits, cakes, candies and soft drinks.

Eat plenty of brown rice, oats, beans, whole wheat bread, and pasta for their soluble fiber content; plenty of bell peppers, broccoli, spinach, and sweet potatoes for their beta-carotene.

Reduce your intake of salt and cut down on alcohol.

AROMATHERAPY

☙ JUNIPER
Juniperus communis
☙ FENNEL
Foeniculum vulgare
☙ ROSEMARY
Rosmarinus officinalis

Fennel is a diuretic. Juniper will help the body to detoxify and rosemary will help to stimulate the lymphatic system, which enables the body to remove waste products. If a hormone imbalance is suspected, then geranium (which is another diuretic) could also be used.

Application:
Use these oils as a massage and in baths (including foot baths). You are looking for long-term benefits, as there is no short-term relief. The skin will feel better before it looks better. Remember that stress can be a factor (*see p.60*).

ABOVE *Fennel is a feathery-leaved herb, the seeds of which are used in medicine.*

CAUTION

Rosemary and fennel oils must not be used by those with high blood pressure or epilepsy.

RIGHT *Juniper essential oil is stimulating and rubefacient, and is an ingredient in proprietary skin rubs.*

HERBAL REMEDIES

Popular demand has created a variety of "over-the-counter" herbal products purporting to reduce cellulite. Most are based on metabolic stimulants, such as kelp, to encourage weight loss and should not be used for more than 2 to 3 weeks. Avoid over-the-counter cellulite remedies based on powerful laxatives (for example, senna, cascara sagrada, rhubarb root), which are designed to cause sudden weight loss. Patent skin rubs are often based on rubefacient oils, such as juniper or pepper, which increase surface blood flow in an attempt to revive tired tissues.

PREVENTATIVE *measures*

Keep your weight down, keep active, and avoid high-fat, high-sugar, high-salt foods.

SKIN CARE: *stimulate circulation to the skin by vigorous brushing with a loofah or soft brush in the bath or shower. Massaging the areas of cellulite briskly—always in the direction of the heart—stimulates the lymph flow, although it will not rub away the cellulite. Using gels containing extracts of horse chestnut has been shown to increase the effectiveness of skin-brushing.*

OUTSIDE HELP

REFLEXOLOGY: a brisk reflexology treatment every 3–4 days over the entire feet can help to boost circulation.
YOGA: circulation in the thighs will generally be helped by postures like the Dancer, Cobbler, Locust, and Bow, as well as by all the standing postures.

ABOVE *The Half Locust (left) and the Full Locust (right) can be done in various ways. They tone the buttocks and strengthen the lower back.*

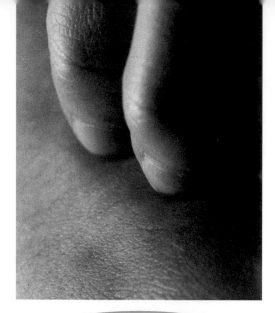

RIGHT *Dermatitis may occur anywhere on the body. It can be triggered by frequent contact with a substance: hairdressers are prone to it through immersing their hands in shampoo many times a day.*

DIAGNOSING DERMATITIS

- Starts as a patch of itchy skin covered with small blisters
- Area may become raw if it is scratched
- Often starts after prolonged contact with a mild irritant such as some soaps and detergents

THE SENSES

dermatitis

CALL THE PHYSICIAN

■ If the dermatitis is weeping and crusting, since it may be infected.

Dermatitis is often an allergic reaction of the skin, producing an acute local inflammation. This may be caused by contact with irritant substances, such as metals, perfumes, cosmetics, or even plants, or it may be part of a general allergic or "atopic" condition, often linked with asthma and hay fever (see pp.132 and 128). Even a local patch of dermatitis caused by direct contact can spread to distant parts of the body. Self-help and simple home remedies are a real must in the treatment and long-term control of all forms of dermatitis.

KITCHEN MEDICINE

■ Oats make a wonderful emollient, or soothing application, for all inflamed skin problems. Make up a bag of cheesecloth containing 4tbsp/60g of uncooked oats. Hang it under the taps as you run the bath, then use the bag as a sponge for cleaning the skin. The natural oils and vitamins will soothe inflamed areas and stimulate the growth of new skin. Use for three or four baths before replacing the oats.

CONVENTIONAL MEDICINE

Moisturize your skin regularly. If the dermatitis is severe, consult a physician, as treatment with steroid creams may be necessary.

Dosage information ~
Adults and children

■ Choose a non-perfumed moisturizer and apply it as often as possible.

OUTSIDE HELP

ACUPRESSURE: point 38 may help reduce the itching, but it is not a treatment for the condition.

REFLEXOLOGY: it is possible that regular complete reflexology treatment might increase resistance to contact or food allergy and reduce stress reaction. Wipe affected areas of the hands and feet with witch hazel before reflexology.

ABOVE *The substances causing dermatitis are as diverse as the people who suffer from it. Common culprits are metal, cosmetics, plants, and rubber gloves.*

NUTRITION

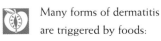

 Many forms of dermatitis are triggered by foods: both by their natural constituents and by a variety of artificial food additives. Handling foods can also set off episodes of dermatitis on the hands and fingers, and garlic, raw fish, and mangoes are common triggers. This type of allergic reaction usually occurs in professional cooks who are handling large amounts of such foods.

Avoiding the consumption of all artificial additives is the first step towards healing. But after that it is a question of detective work. Keep a careful diary of everything you eat and drink, with a note of when your skin looks better or worse. This will provide some pointers to the culprit, but the most common

ABOVE *Tomatoes, bell peppers, oats, wheatgerm, and brown rice help boost the essential nutrient content in the diet. Include them in meals as often as possible, together with other fruit and vegetables, oily fish, and nuts.*

irritant foods (in descending order) are milk and all dairy products, shellfish, eggs, citrus fruit, strawberries, red meat, and wheat products.

A high intake of vitamins A and E, beta-carotene, and essential fatty acids is very important, so drink a large glass of carrot juice every day. Eat plenty of broccoli, spinach, parsley, tomatoes, apricots, sunflower seeds and oil, oily fish, nuts, soy products, red and green bell peppers, oats, wheatgerm, and brown rice. Drink copious amounts of water and eat parsley and celery to stimulate the kidneys, so that more waste products are eliminated in the urine rather than through the skin.

HOMEOPATHIC REMEDIES

 RHUS TOXICODENDRON 6C For small watery blisters. Itchy and better for placing in hot water. "Poison ivy" rash.

KALI ARSENICOSUM 6C For itching that is intolerable. Worse for warmth, at night and for undressing. Skin dry and scaly.

KREOSOTUM 6C For dermatitis on hands and backs of fingers, face

and eyelids. Very itchy. Worse in evening. Better for warmth.

PETROLEUM 6C For dry, leathery, rough skin with cracks. Burning and itching. Skin may be red, raw, and bleed. Worse in winter.

Dosage: one tablet daily. Maximum 2 weeks.

See also Eczema on p.74.

HERBAL REMEDIES

Borage, and other herbs, are useful in soothing the irritant rash of contact dermatitis.

■ **Use and Dosage:**
Use a lotion made from equal amounts of borage juice and distilled witch hazel. Fresh borage juice can be made by pulping the leaves in a food processor, or it is available commercially.

Evening primrose or comfrey creams can also help; or you can apply the sap squeezed from a fresh *Aloe vera* leaf.

Internally, garlic has an antihistamine effect to combat the allergic response (use cloves in cooking or take up to 1g daily in capsules), while burdock and cleavers tea can be soothing.

AROMATHERAPY

TEA TREE
Melaleuca alternifolia

LAVENDER
Lavandula angustifolia

ROMAN CHAMOMILE
Chamaemelum nobile

Tea tree is antiviral, antifungal, and antibacterial, so it helps to stop the infection spreading and becoming even more infected. Lavender and chamomile are both calming, soothing, anti-inflammatory, and painkilling.

Application:
Use in a bath and as a topical cream to put on the skin. Tea tree can also be used in the laundry of towels and facecloths, which will stop the spread of the infection (and make sure that you have a separate towel and facecloth from the rest of the family). (*See also Eczema on p.74 and Stress on p.60.*)

See also Eczema on p.74.

PREVENTATIVE *measures*

METALS: *for contact dermatitis, avoid skin contact with nickel (used in most costume jewelry) and metal alloys—found in foreign silver, gold plate, rolled gold, zippers, clips, studs (jeans are a common offender), hooks and eyes, watchstraps, and buckles.*

COSMETICS: *perfumes, soaps, detergents such as bubble baths, and cosmetics, including nail polish, are common causes of contact dermatitis, so buy hypoallergenic varieties. And avoid hair dyes. Problems commonly arise after years of use, when an attack of dermatitis erupts without warning.*

Regular moisturizing is the most vital part of your daily routine. Do not be put off by the idea of lanolin causing allergies (you are more likely to be allergic to strawberries), for it is the best of all moisturizers and 95 percent of the population tolerate it with no allergic problems whatsoever.

OTHER IRRITANTS: *rubber gloves, many medicated creams and ointments, and some plants—particularly poison ivy, primulas, chrysanthemums, euphorbias, and rue—can trigger instant reactions, so try to avoid these irritants if you are susceptible.*

SUPPLEMENTS: *regular doses of 3g a day of evening primrose oil have been shown to be highly effective. When the problem subsides, stick with a maintenance dose of 1g a day. This should be taken together with a B-complex vitamin and 5,000 IU of vitamin A daily.*

RIGHT *Eczema often first occurs in infancy, though it may start at any time in life. There are five types of eczema: contact, atopic, seborrheic, discoid, and varicose, commonly affecting different parts of the body.*

DIAGNOSING ECZEMA

- Starts with a patch of itchy skin covered with small blisters
- Area may become red and raw if it is scratched
- In long-standing eczema, the skin may become thick, with accentuated skin markings
- In some cases eczema can cause flaky skin

THE SENSES

eczema

Those unfortunate people who suffer from asthma, hay fever, and eczema are described as atopic. They may have to endure all these problems, and frequently pass them on to their children, for these conditions are often familial complaints and—though some individuals, or even generations, may escape—atopic illness spreads throughout the family tree. There are many similarities between eczema and dermatitis (see p.72) and some conditions labeled dermatitis are in fact eczema.

CALL THE PHYSICIAN

■ If the eczema is weeping and crusting, as it may be infected.

KITCHEN MEDICINE

■ Oats or wheatgerm make a soothing application for the relief of the discomfort caused by eczema. Using a 12in/30cm square double thickness of cheesecloth or thin cotton, place 8 heaped teaspoons of either cereal in the middle, bring the four corners together and tie in a knot to form a bag. Hang under the running bath faucet so that the emollient substances dissolve in the water, then use the pad as a sponge instead of soap. Rich in vitamin E and healing demulcents, this makes an effective remedy.

CONVENTIONAL MEDICINE

Moisturize the skin regularly using bath oil, soap substitute, or lotion. If eczema is severe, consult a physician, as treatment with steroid creams may be necessary.
Dosage information ~
Adults and children

■ Choose a nonperfumed moisturizer and apply it as often as possible.

HOMEOPATHIC REMEDIES

There are many remedies for this condition and consultation with a qualified homeopath may be helpful to find the best one.

❧ CLEMATIS 6C For eczema that starts with small, watery spots. Then burning, stinging, itching. Worse for heat and cold water.

❧ ARSENICUM ALBUM 6C For dry, rough, scaly skin. Itching and burning. Scratching until skin is raw briefly alleviates this.

❧ GRAPHITES 6C For rawness in bends of elbows and knees, and behind ears. Oozes pale fluid. Corners of mouth crack. Skin dry and hard.

❧ SULPHUR 6C For dry, burning, scaly skin. Scalp dry. Itching worse for scratching and water. **Dosage:** one tablet twice daily. Stop after 2 weeks or on improvement. Repeat if necessary.

ABOVE **Clematis erecta,** *the remedy source, is a climbing plant with beautiful, star-shaped flowers.*

OUTSIDE HELP

ACUPRESSURE: point 38 may help relieve intense itching of the skin.

REFLEXOLOGY: it is possible that regular complete reflexology treatment might increase resistance to contact or food allergy and reduce stress reaction. Wipe affected areas of the hands and feet with witch hazel beforehand.

ABOVE *Acupressure on point 38 helps to relieve one of the most annoying symptoms: the itching which drives the sufferer to scratch and so worsens the problem.*

HERBAL REMEDIES

Herbalists generally treat atopic eczema with cleansing herbal teas and limited use of creams to reduce the discomfort.

■ **Use and Dosage:**
Mix equal amounts of red clover, heartsease, burdock leaves, fumitory, and stinging nettles, which will help to reduce inflammation, stimulate the digestion and circulation, and clear any toxins that are contributing to the problem. Use 2tsp/10ml of the mixture to a cup of boiling water, three times a day.

Evening primrose used as an external cream or taken internally (2g per day) can also help.

Chickweed, marshmallow, and chamomile creams can all be beneficial.

NUTRITION

Food is frequently a major factor in controlling the flare-up of symptoms, but is not a cure for the condition. Food culprits vary from individual to individual, but in asthmatic children, one of the most common food groups implicated is chemical additives—colorings, flavorings, preservatives, and flavor enhancers—which should all be avoided. Early exposure to cows' milk is often the original cause of infantile eczema and may result from a high maternal consumption during pregnancy or breastfeeding, or when given in bottles. It is best to avoid giving cows' milk to babies for as long as possible.

All dairy products and citrus fruit can make eczema flare up, but the offending food is often very personal to the individual, and allergic reactions may be precipitated by any food—from shellfish to strawberries, chocolate to cashew nuts.

The careful compiling of a diet diary, and noting when the condition becomes either better or worse, often supplies pointers to foods that should be excluded. Unless the trigger foods are few and not essential nutritionally, then long-term exclusion diets (especially for children) should be undertaken only under professional guidance.

AROMATHERAPY

🌿 LAVENDER
Lavandula angustifolia
🌿 ROMAN CHAMOMILE
Chamaemelum nobile
🌿 GERANIUM
Pelargonium graveolens
🌿 JUNIPER
Juniperus communis
🌿 ROSE
Rosa damascena/Rosa centifolia
🌿 CEDARWOOD
Cedrus atlantica

Eczema is very varied in its manifestations, but all these oils are calming, soothing, and anti-inflammatory. Juniper also has a detoxifying effect, which is useful if the body needs to eliminate toxins (it may, however, make your condition worse before it gets better, but do persevere).

Application:
Mix calendula base oil or aqueous cream (available from any pharmacy) with the oils, then rub them gently into the affected area. You may need to alter the formula until you find one that suits you and helps your condition. Check for allergies (*see p.22*) and stress levels (*see p.60*) and make sure that your clothes are made of natural fibers, if possible.

ABOVE *Rose oil is distilled from fresh rose petals, and has a very high odor intensity. It is recommended for the treatment of eczema sufferers.*

CAUTION

Do not apply essential oils to broken, weeping skin without first getting professional advice.

PREVENTATIVE *measures*

BEDROOM HYGIENE: *a very common cause of eczema is an allergic reaction resulting from contact with the droppings of the house-dustmite—of which there are five million in your bed. All the necessary measures should be taken to minimize the dustmite population surrounding anyone with eczema (see Asthma on p.132).*

SUPPLEMENTS: *these can play a key role in reducing the inflammatory process that causes eczema and in boosting the nutrient intake that builds healthy skin: 1–3g of evening primrose oil, together with a B-complex supplement and 7,500 µg of beta-carotene, should be taken every day.*

CLOTHING: *avoid wearing wool next to the skin, as it can make the itch worse. and try to avoid getting overheated. Wear cotton (which is cooler than wool) and manmade fabrics. Keep fingernails short—this applies particularly to babies, who may cause further damage to the skin by scratching their eczema.*

EXERCISE

EXERCISE with caution, because sweating is a common irritant to the sensitive skin of the eczema sufferer. Chlorinated water in swimming pools may also have to be avoided.

RIGHT *An urticaria rash can flare up anywhere on the body. An allergic reaction causes fluid to seep from the skin's blood vessels and swell the surrounding tissues.*

DIAGNOSING HIVES

- Itchy rash that looks like nettle- or poison-ivy rash, affecting anything from a small area of skin to the whole body; tends to come and go, leaving no marks
- May get better after a few days, but can continue for months

THE SENSES

hives *urticaria*

H ives—or urticaria, to give it its medical name—is also known as nettle-rash, as its appearance is similar to the lumpy skin eruptions caused by stinging nettles. It is an allergic reaction and can be caused by foods, contact with plants (and not necessarily nettles), cosmetics, the whole range of domestic cleaning chemicals, alcohol, sudden exposure to cold or hot air, and, very often, by sunlight. Food additives and colorings are frequent culprits, but eruptions of these irritating lumps and bumps can also be triggered by stress and anxiety.

CALL THE PHYSICIAN

■ If the rash persists, or becomes widespread.

KITCHEN MEDICINE

■ Unless your hives are caused by exposure to cold temperatures, placing a few ice cubes in a plastic bag on the offending area may help relieve the itching.

CONVENTIONAL MEDICINE

If you know what triggers the rash, you can avoid it, but in most cases this is difficult and all you can do is try and reduce your symptoms. The rash will be more comfortable if you keep cool. Antihistamines may prevent the rash from developing, although some preparations will make you drowsy. Try calamine lotion to soothe hot, itchy skin.

Dosage information ~
Adults
■ Most antihistamine tablets are taken once a day; consult package details or follow medical advice. Apply calamine lotion/cream directly to the skin as required.
Children
■ Doses of antihistamine syrup depend on the age of the child: see package for details, or follow medical advice. Apply calamine lotion/cream directly to the skin as required.

NUTRITION

The only long-term treatment is to identify and then avoid the foods that cause attacks by following the Exclusion Diet (*see p.211*). The most common irritating foods are shellfish, chocolate, strawberries, eggs, nuts, dairy products, wheat (rarely), and, very commonly, food additives (particularly tartrazine).

OUTSIDE HELP

REFLEXOLOGY: working the reflex of the area that is affected may be of benefit to those suffering from hives. If stress is a trigger, then include the diaphragm and solar plexus in a relaxing treatment.

YOGA: this ailment is often stress-related. Explore different ways of relaxation to see what technique works best for you. Finish your practice with 12 breaths of alternate nostril breathing, using long, slow exhalations.

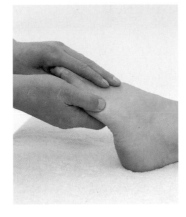

ABOVE *Treating the reflex of the arm, for an outbreak of urticaria brought on by a day in the sun.*

HOMEOPATHIC REMEDIES

Severe allergic reactions require medical help.

✿ URTICA URENS **30C** For nettle-rash, very itchy red blobs with white center. Allergic reactions, particularly to shellfish. Worse for cold bathing. Urticaria with joint pains. This is probably the most common remedy.

✿ APIS **30C** For swelling and puffiness of skin, which feels it will tear. Stinging, burning pains, worse at night. Urticaria from insect bites and bee stings.

Dosage: one tablet every 15 minutes until improved. Maximum ten doses.

HERBAL REMEDIES

Minor or occasional outbreaks of hives can be soothed with chamomile cream or borage juice, as well as with such traditional standbys as dock leaves, freshly sliced onion, or crushed cabbage leaves.

LEFT *The juice of crushed borage is an excellent tonic for the adrenal glands.*

■ **Use and Dosage:**
For persistent problems, generally associated with food allergy, make a tea containing agrimony and chamomile (2 parts each) with heartsease and stinging nettles (1 part each), to combat the action of histamine and improve resistance to allergens in the gut. Use 2tsp/10ml of the mixture per cup, three times daily.

ABOVE *Broccoli is rich in beta-carotene, and may also protect against cancer.*

RIGHT *Zucchini are beneficial for skin problems.*

AROMATHERAPY

 ✿ ROMAN CHAMOMILE
Chamaemelum nobile

✿ LAVENDER
Lavandula angustifolia

✿ MELISSA
Melissa officinalis

Chamomile and lavender soothe the irritation; melissa and chamomile calm the allergic reaction.

Application:
Use in a light cream base to rub onto the irritated area; in a spray, if the area is too tender to be touched; or in water—either sponge the affected area down or use in the bath.

PREVENTATIVE *measures*

Anyone with hives should wear loose-fitting cotton clothes, especially underwear, and avoid synthetic materials and "scratchy" fabrics. Some sufferers find that taking 1,500mg of vitamin C a day prevents, or at least lessens the severity of, their attacks.

ASPIRIN AVOIDANCE: *aspirin and its derivatives, like nonsteroidal anti-inflammatory drugs (NSAIDs, commonly prescribed for arthritis and now available "over the counter" for everything from toothache to period pains), are a very common factor in this condition. For those who have identified aspirin as a culprit, it may be worth eliminating all foods that contain natural aspirin as well (most berries, dried and fresh fruit, some nuts and seeds). Dairy products, vegetables, poultry, fish, meat, cereals, and legumes contain very little or no aspirin.*

SUNLIGHT SUFFERERS: *if your nettle-rash is triggered by sunlight, eat lots of foods rich in beta-carotene. The richest sources are the bright orange, red and dark green fruit and vegetables— carrots, apricots, spinach, broccoli, bell peppers, and tomatoes. You should avoid Earl Grey tea (it is flavored with bergamot) and buckwheat (or anything made from it). Both may make the skin more sensitive to sunlight and aggravate the condition.*

RIGHT *Psoriasis most often erupts on the trunk of the body and the limbs. It sometimes occurs after a bout of illness, and may be hereditary.*

DIAGNOSING PSORIASIS
- Thick red patches of skin covered by silvery-white scales

THE SENSES

psoriasis

KITCHEN MEDICINE
- Soothing and moisturizing the skin are vital steps in the relief of this condition. Fill a cheesecloth bag with wheatgerm and hang it under the faucets when running a bath, then use the bag as a sponge when washing. The vitamin E in the wheatgerm dissolves in the water and is both soothing and healing.
- Do not have the bath too hot.

Psoriasis is a chronic skin condition, which tends to run in families and affects approximately one person in 50 in both United States and the Britain, although it is much rarer in the black population. It occurs because the skin cells are reproducing far more quickly than normal—the normal cycle for cell reproduction takes 311 hours, but in psoriasis it takes just 36. It is more common in smokers and heavy alcohol drinkers, although it can start at any age (from diaper rash onward), most frequently in the late twenties to thirties. Attacks may start with a bacterial throat infection, particularly in children, or following a stressful event; psoriasis can also be a reaction to some drugs. The unique silvery, scaly eruption of the skin often starts on the knees and backs of the elbows, but can spread to be a life-ruining illness covering most of the body surface. Unlike eczema (see p.74), psoriasis is not an allergic reaction, although dietary changes may help mitigate the symptoms.

CONVENTIONAL MEDICINE

It is important to keep the skin well moisturized using bath oil, soap substitute, or lotion. Rehumidify the air using a bowl of water near radiators. If the symptoms persist, seek medical advice—conventional treatment includes prescribed lotions, shampoos, and creams to put on the skin. In cases that do not improve with creams, treatment with ultraviolet light may help.

Dosage information ~
Adults and children
- Choose a nonperfumed moisturizer and apply it as often as possible.

HERBAL REMEDIES

 Small areas of psoriasis often respond well to cleavers cream.

■ **Use and Dosage:**
Add a cup of strained cleavers infusion to 1 cup/250g of melted emulsifying ointment (available from pharmacies) and stir constantly as it cools and thickens.

Cleansing teas will also help: mix equal amounts of the roots of blue flag, burdock, and yellow dock for a decoction (1tsp/5ml per cup) or use an infusion of cleavers, red clover flowers, and burdock leaf (2tsp/10ml per cup). Where stress is a factor, add skullcap or passionflower to the mix.

HOMEOPATHIC REMEDIES

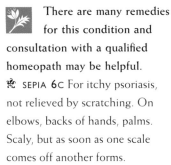 There are many remedies for this condition and consultation with a qualified homeopath may be helpful.

❀ SEPIA **6C** For itchy psoriasis, not relieved by scratching. On elbows, backs of hands, palms. Scaly, but as soon as one scale comes off another forms.

❀ ARSENICUM IODATUM **6C** For dry scales, itching. Scales come off, leaving raw, moist surface. Thickened skin. Psoriasis on wrists and palms.

❀ PETROLEUM **6C** For dry, cracked, rough, leathery skin. Cracked ends of fingers. Worse in winter. Itching at night. Psoriasis on hands.

Dosage: one tablet twice daily. Stop after 2 weeks or on improvement. Repeat if necessary.

NUTRITION

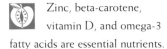 Zinc, beta-carotene, vitamin D, and omega-3 fatty acids are essential nutrients.

Eat plenty of oily fish for their vitamin D and fatty acids; orange, red and dark green fruit and vegetables for their beta-carotene; and shellfish, oysters, and pumpkin seeds for their zinc.

Although psoriasis is not an allergic condition, specific foods may aggravate it in some individuals. Fish, shellfish, citrus fruit, red meat, dairy products, caffeine, and alcohol are the most common triggers, but only apply to a very small percentage of sufferers. If you notice that any of them make your skin worse, it is obviously sensible to avoid them.

Avoid liver and other organ meat, because they can increase the body's production of prostaglandins—complex chemicals, which, though normally beneficial, can aggravate psoriasis.

ABOVE *Oily fish, shellfish, and oysters are especially rich in beneficial nutrients.*

AROMATHERAPY

 ❀ LAVENDER
Lavandula angustifolia
❀ BASIL
Ocimum basilicum
❀ BERGAMOT
Citrus bergamia
❀ VETIVERT
Vetiveria zizanoides

The body/mind connection is very important here, as it can be a nasty link in a vicious circle: you have psoriasis, so you become stressed because it looks unsightly and feels awful, and the stress only makes the psoriasis worse and creates further tension. So you need to break the cycle with these de-stressing oils.

Application:
Good base oils are essential—unrefined avocado (if you can get it), or just ordinary avocado; or carrot oil. You can add just a few drops to these if you do not want your aqueous cream base to be particularly greasy. Regular massage from a professional, as well as localized massage done by yourself, will also be really useful.

OUTSIDE HELP

ACUPRESSURE: self-help by means of acupressure is not appropriate to this condition, although professional acupuncture may be a great help.

REFLEXOLOGY: regular reflexology treatment could be given and may help to alleviate some of the symptoms of psoriasis.

YOGA: stress usually worsens this condition, so incorporate into your daily practice enough relaxation time, and at least 12 slow breaths, with the exhalation twice as long as the inhalation.

ABOVE *Getting out into the sunshine is often a help, but protect yourself with sunscreen and suitable clothes.*

PREVENTATIVE
measures

There is no specific way to prevent psoriasis, but it is often possible to keep it in check by following the nutritional advice already given. Supplements of vitamin D, beta-carotene, and zinc can also play a certain part in controlling this most unpleasant illness.

SUNSHINE: *this is known to be beneficial and, in severe cases of psoriasis, ultraviolet lamps are used in conjunction with drugs that increase the skin's sensitivity to sunlight. There is, of course, a balance between the severity of the condition and the increased risk of skin cancer, and the usual precautions must be taken in hot countries (and even in the UK in midsummer).*

RELAXATION: *stress is known to be a major factor in increasing the severity of psoriasis. Relaxation techniques like yoga, meditation, and stress control have a great deal to offer.*

CENTRAL HEATING: *avoid central heating wherever possible, as it tends to make dry skin conditions worse.*

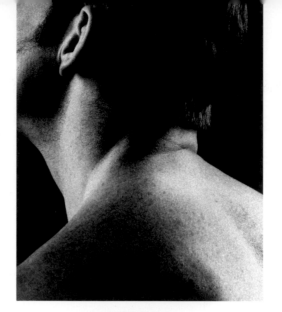

RIGHT *The ringworm fungus lives on skin in any part of the body, but is particularly happy in areas which are both moist and warm, such as the armpits, groin, and feet.*

- One or more round areas of scaly, slightly itchy, abnormal-looking skin
- The center of the abnormal area may look more normal, leading to the appearance of a ring

THE SENSES

ringworm *tinea*

ABOVE *When your friendly feline rubs up against you, she may be giving you more than affection: cats can transmit ringworm.*

Ringworm is an inflammatory infection of the skin caused by mold or fungi (and 90 percent of all fungal infections are caused by the molds Microsporum epidermophyton *and* M. trichophyton). *Ringworm infections (so called because of the red circular patches with the raised outside edge, and actually nothing to do with worms) or—to give it its medical name—tinea may appear on the skin, hair or nails, in the groin, on the feet, and sometimes on the head. Home remedies work well in the treatment of these conditions. Ringworm is a common complaint and highly contagious, as it is spread by direct physical contact. It can often be acquired from horses, farmyard animals, and particularly from cats* (Microsporum canis).

CONVENTIONAL MEDICINE

✚ Ringworm on the body can usually be treated effectively with antifungal creams. If the rash has not cleared up after two weeks, then consult your physician. Ringworm affecting the scalp or nails can be more difficult to treat and you should discuss it with your physician.

Dosage information ~
Adults and children
■ Most creams are applied twice a day; see package for details.

HOMEOPATHIC REMEDIES

✿ TELLURIUM 6C For ringworm over whole body, lower limbs. May be more on left side. Itching worse after going to bed, for cool air and rest. Intersecting rings over whole body.
✿ SEPIA 6C For ringworm in isolated spots, mainly on upper body. Itching not better for scratching. May occur every springtime. **Dosage:** one tablet daily. Maximum 2 weeks.

AROMATHERAPY

 🌿 TEA TREE
Melaleuca alternifolia

🌿 MYRRH

Commiphora molmol

🌿 LAVENDER

Lavandula angustifolia

Since ringworm is a fungal infection, oils that have a fungicidal action, such as tea tree and myrrh, are obviously going to be the most relevant. If lavender is the only oil you have, you can use this, as it has a slight fungicidal effect.

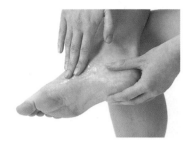

ABOVE *Tea tree oil is antibacterial and fungicidal.*

Application:
Apply as a compress, as a water spray (but do not spray too near the eyes), or in a massage medium. Do be aware, however, that ringworm is infectious, and make sure that your hygiene is good, especially if you are applying oils to somebody else. Make sure that you wash your hands well afterward and use the oils in the hand wash.

HERBAL REMEDIES

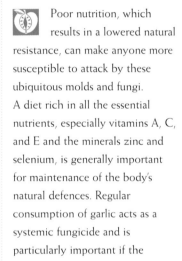 Tea tree, thyme, and marigold all show antifungal activity and can be very effective for infections such as ringworm.

■ **Use and Dosage:**
Apply tea-tree, thyme, or marigold creams to affected areas three or four times a day.

If the scalp is affected, use a strained marigold infusion as a rinse, or add 5 drops of tea-tree or thyme oil to the rinsing water after shampooing (ideally, with a strong soapwort infusion, which is very cleansing).

Internally, cleavers and chickweed tea will also help (1tsp/5ml of each per cup).

NUTRITION

Poor nutrition, which results in a lowered natural resistance, can make anyone more susceptible to attack by these ubiquitous molds and fungi. A diet rich in all the essential nutrients, especially vitamins A, C, and E and the minerals zinc and selenium, is generally important for maintenance of the body's natural defences. Regular consumption of garlic acts as a systemic fungicide and is particularly important if the ringworm has affected finger- or toenails.

PREVENTATIVE
measures

HYGIENE: *keep the towels, facecloths and bed linen of those with ringworm separate from the rest of the family and make sure that you use high temperatures in your washing machine to kill off the fungus.*

CLOTHING: *if ringworm affects feet or toenails, wear cotton socks, leather or canvas shoes, and change your socks and wash your feet twice a day, drying them by patting, not rubbing. If the infection is in the groin, wear only cotton underwear; shower, bath, or wash the area at least once a day (more in hot humid weather); and again dry by patting, not rubbing.*

KITCHEN MEDICINE

■ Garlic and cider vinegar, which no kitchen should ever be without, are sovereign remedies for these fungi. When combined together and left to infuse, they can be used to soak feet or hands, or as a lotion applied to any other infected area.

1 To make a lotion for treating ringworm, peel two cloves of garlic, and crush into a bowl.

2 Pour on 2½ cups/600ml of boiled water, which has been allowed to cool slightly.

3 Add 1tbsp/15ml cider vinegar. Leave to infuse for 10 minutes, then dab on the affected area.

THE SENSES

RIGHT *If you have one too many bad hair days, look at your lifestyle. Stress, poor nutrition and unkind chemical treatments all take a toll.*

DIAGNOSING HAIR PROBLEMS

- Flaking scalp. Likely cause: *dandruff*
- Men's hair receding at the temples. Likely cause: *male-pattern baldness*
- Generalized thinning of women's hair, often starting 3–4 months after the birth of a baby. Likely cause: *hormonal changes*
- Patches of complete hair loss, in men or women, often with very short hairs visible. Likely cause: *Alopecia areata*
- Generalized thinning and dry hair. Likely cause: *underactive thyroid gland*

hair problems

EXERCISE

ANY FORM of exercise that stimulates the circulation on a regular basis will help maintain healthy hair. There is a suggestion that the head and shoulderstand yoga postures encourage blood flow to the scalp and carry extra nutrients to the hair follicles—but no scientific evidence for this.

Hair problems are frequently a sign of underlying illness, as hair is a true barometer of health. Many of the difficulties that arise are, however, simply the result of not caring for your hair properly. Naturally hair health depends on nutrition, but constant blow-drying, coloring, perming, and heavy overuse of sticky cosmetic products all combine to make your crowning glory look drab, brittle, and lackluster. Save money and revitalize your hair with easy, do-it-yourself home remedies. Most women lose hair after childbirth, but don't panic; it does grow back again. The same is true—for men and women—after any serious illness.

CONVENTIONAL MEDICINE

✚ Excessive hair growth can be treated with bleaching, but beware that it can make dark hair look orange. Other treatments include electrolysis, which is painful and can be expensive, but is permanent. Waxing needs repeating every few months and can cause ingrowing hairs. Hair loss after pregnancy or due to *Alopecia areata* tends to regrow,

and may not need treatment, though your physician may arrange for some blood tests, to ensure that your thyroid gland is working normally. Male-pattern baldness can be treated, but the new hair is thin and downy. Treatment is expensive and if it is stopped, the hair will fall out again. Dandruff can be controlled with shampoo or lotion. In severe cases consult your physician.

Dosage information ~
Adults and children

■ For male-pattern baldness, apply solution containing minoxidil twice a day. For dandruff, use a mild detergent shampoo once or twice a week. Products containing Ketoconazole are probably the most effective. If using bleaching cream, apply to hairy skin and leave, usually for 10–15 minutes; see package for details.

KITCHEN MEDICINE

■ Rinsing fair hair with diluted lemon juice and dark hair with a vinegar solution, gives them extra shine.

■ For a dry, flaky scalp, massage half a cup of warm olive oil (stand it in a bowl of hot water; do not heat it on the stove) well into the scalp after washing your hair. Wrap your head in a towel, leave for a half hour, then shampoo again, and rinse.

HOMEOPATHIC REMEDIES

KALI SULPHURICUM 6C
For yellow, flaking dandruff, which may be moist or sticky. Hair may fall out, leaving bald spots.

GRAPHITES 6C
For crusts on scalp. Also eczema behind ears, which may be moist. Oozes sticky fluid.

OLEANDER 6C
For large white flakes falling from hair. Scalp dry or itchy. Psoriasis or cradle cap (in babies). Generally worse for eating oranges. **Dosage:** one tablet twice daily. Maximum 2 weeks.

ABOVE *Nerium oleander is the source for the homeopathic remedy of oleander.*

HERBAL REMEDIES

Herbs have a beneficial effect on a wide range of hair problems.

■ **Use and Dosage:**
For dandruff, try adding 1–2 cups of rosemary or stinging-nettle infusion to the final rinse when shampooing.

Hair loss will sometimes respond to arnica, rosemary, or southernwood (massage an infused oil into the scalp).

Dry hair can best be treated by cleansing and demulcent herbs taken internally, such as marshmallow and burdock as a tea (1tsp/5ml of each per cup).

Itchiness can be soothed by a final rinse of catmint or camomile infusions.

OUTSIDE HELP

REFLEXOLOGY: nails are the reflexes for the hair and scalp, and 5 minutes daily buffing of the fingernails of one hand against the other may help hair and scalp problems. For hair loss caused by stress, work the diaphragm and adrenal reflexes.

YOGA: many people say that inverted postures like Downward-Facing Dog, Standing Forward Bend, Shoulderstand, and Headstand help keep hair healthy.

The Downward-Facing Dog. Start on your hands and knees. Rock back and up on to your feet, straighten your arms, chin on chest. Hold, then return to the starting position.

The Headstand increases blood flow to the scalp. Use a wall for support. Avoid if you have heart problems or high blood pressure.

NUTRITION

This is a vital factor in maintaining healthy hair, and anemia is one of the most frequent causes of hair loss.

Eat plenty of iron-rich foods, like liver (but not if you are pregnant), all other organ meat, whole grain cereals, dark green leafy vegetables, eggs, dates, and raisins. Do not forget that vitamin C improves the absorption of iron, so eat fruit or vegetables at the same time. Vitamin E is also important for healthy hair growth, so eat avocados, nuts, seeds, and olive oil on a regular basis.

Reduce your intake of animal fat and sugar, as these can aggravate the production of sebum and make the scalp more greasy, so they are best eaten in moderation.

AROMATHERAPY

ROSEMARY
Rosmarinus officinalis

ROMAN CHAMOMILE
Chamaemelum nobile

LEMON
Citrus limon

GRAPEFRUIT
Citrus x paradisi

CEDARWOOD
Cedrus atlantica

Aromatherapy can improve the condition of the scalp and of the person in general, so improving the growing conditions for hair. Rosemary is usually used for dark hair and chamomile for fair hair. Rosemary, lemon, grapefruit, and cedarwood also stimulate the circulation and balance the body's secretions, so reducing dandruff.

Application:
Add 2 drops of your chosen essential oil either to the rinse water or to a good vegetable oil, then massage into the scalp. Wrap all the hair on your upper head in plastic wrap, then place a warm towel around it and leave the essential oils in the hair for 2 to 3 hours, or overnight if you can bear it. Then shampoo the hair as usual, using a mild shampoo (not a medicated one), so that you do not damage the sebum balance (sebum being the body's natural oil, which coats the hair, making it look shiny and healthy).

PREVENTATIVE *measures*

REGROWTH PREPARATIONS:
male-pattern baldness is strongly familial, so men whose father or grandfather went bald early probably will too. There are now some licensed medicines that stimulate the regrowth of hair, but they are not without side-effects and the results are on the whole disappointing. Although pills are not a substitute for a balanced diet, there are some vitamin and mineral supplements specifically formulated for hair care— they will maintain the condition of your hair and may slow down the genetic march of time.

HAIR CARE: *do make sure that you use good-quality hair brushes and combs, because harsh nylon bristles and sharp teeth may damage the hair and scalp, particularly if used when the hair is wet and vulnerable.*

CAUTION

Avoid rosemary oil if you have high blood pressure. If you have sensitive skin, keep lemon and grapefruit doses low as they may be slightly irritating.

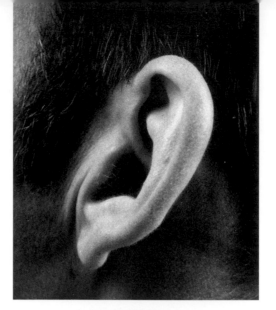

RIGHT *Earache is often the result of the spread of a throat infection to the middle ear.*

DIAGNOSING EARACHE

- Throbbing pain and a fever, often during or after a cold; may be worse if taking off or landing in an airplane; child may scream and possibly pull at one ear. Likely causes: *middle-ear infection or fluid in the middle ear*
- Pain after syringing or after swimming. Likely cause: *external ear infection*

THE SENSES

earache

T his is a very common problem, especially in young children, and is generally caused by an infection. The Eustachian tube, which links the back of the nose and throat to the middle ear, can allow bacteria access to this sensitive region. The lining of the ear canal is very thin and can easily be damaged if you scratch or clean it overenthusiastically; an infected ear canal will be sore and often produces a discharge. In some cases, pain is referred to the ear from other places—a classic example is when children complain of earache after having their tonsils removed. Earache in children should always be regarded as serious and seen by your physician, although it is not necessary to resort to antibiotics on every occasion. Home remedies can help and often avoid the need for stronger medication.

CALL THE PHYSICIAN

- If earache persists in young children.
- If you have severe earache.

CAUTION

Always read pain-reliever packages carefully, and do not exceed the stated dose.

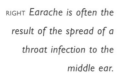

CONVENTIONAL MEDICINE

To prevent damage to the ear canal, avoid cleaning the ears with cottonwool swabs or scratching them too vigorously. A pain-reliever will usually ease earache, but if the pain persists, there is a discharge, or a high fever consult your physician. In the meantime, keep the ear dry by putting cotton in it while showering.

Dosage information ~
Adults
- One to two tablets of pain-reliever at onset of pain, repeated every 4 hours; see package for details.

Children
- Give regular doses of liquid pain-reliever; consult package for details, or follow advice from your physician.

KITCHEN MEDICINE

- Fill a sock with bran and heat in the microwave, or gently in a very low oven inside a heatproof dish. Wrap the sock in a towel and use it as a hot compress on the affected ear. The warmth is very soothing, relieving the pain, and the bran will retain the heat for quite a time.

HERBAL REMEDIES

 It is very important to avoid putting anything in the ear if there is the slightest risk that the eardrum has perforated.

■ **Use and Dosage:**
Warmed herbal oils (infused mullein or St.-John's-wort, for instance) can be helpful as ear drops, or you can infuse a chamomile teabag for a few minutes, then place this over the ear while it is still warm.

AROMATHERAPY

❧ LAVENDER
Lavandula angustifolia
❧ ROMAN CHAMOMILE
Chamaemelum nobile

ABOVE *Roman chamomile flowers produce an analgesic, antiseptic oil.*

Chamomile is beneficial for a dull ache and lavender for sharp pain.
Application:
Put a drop of lavender on some cotton and make a plug of it to place in the ear. Use chamomile in a warm compress on the side of the face.

CAUTION

Do not pour essential oil directly into the ear. If there is no improvement within 24 hours, or if pus appears from the ear or you develop a fever, seek medical help.

NUTRITION

Children with recurrent earache may respond to a diet free of dairy products for a short period of time, as this does seem to reduce the amount of mucus that the body produces. Though there is no scientific proof, naturopaths have used this dietary plan with great success since the start of the twentieth century. Plenty of pineapple juice should be drunk for its healing enzymes, and citrus juices for their vitamin C, to fight off infection. Otherwise, most children with earache will want little food apart from light snacks, as chewing and swallowing often make the pain even worse.

For adults, the decongestant spices, such as cinnamon, ginger, chili, horseradish, and mustard, are a great help.

CAUTION

If your child is on a reduced dairy-product diet, seek professional advice to make sure that there are no nutritional deficiencies.

HOMEOPATHIC REMEDIES

❧ Earache can respond well to homeopathic treatment. For recurrent earache, consult a qualified homeopath; if worsening, consult a physician.

❧ PULSATILLA **6C** For heavy, pressing pain outward from eardrum. Worse for applied heat. Thick, bland, smelly discharge. Child is miserable, clingy, and wants to be cuddled.

❧ CHAMOMILLA **6C** For severe, sharp pains in the ear driving person frantic. Child is irritable, angry, better for moving.

❧ BELLADONNA **6C** For sudden onset. Throbbing earache worse for heat. Hypersensitive hearing. Face very hot and red. Skin dry, may be delirious.

❧ ACONITE **6C** For initial stages of earache. Pains may be worse in left ear.

Dosage: one tablet every 4 hours for 2–3 days or until better.

OUTSIDE HELP

ACUPRESSURE: point 42, just behind the tip of the mastoid bone at the bottom of the back of the ear, can relieve the pain of earache.

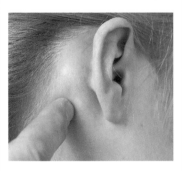

ABOVE *The acupressure point 42 helps pain relief.*

REFLEXOLOGY: work the ear, nose, throat, and Eustachian-tube reflexes in the webs between the fingers and toes—particularly between the third, fourth, and fifth—as well as the entire fingers or toes.

RIGHT *Kitchen spices can help to decongest catarrh-filled passages, which often cause earache. Add them to your cooking.*

PREVENTATIVE *measures*

BEDROOMS: *it is important that sinuses be kept as clear as possible in susceptible children. A mixture of lavender and eucalyptus oils in a fragrancer (electric, not candle) in a child's bedroom, with a few drops of decongestant oil on the pillow, will help. Keeping the bed and bedroom dustmite-free (see Asthma on p.132), well ventilated, and not too hot is also important.*

NUTRITION: *susceptible children should be on a diet rich in all fresh produce and low in refined sugars, animal fats, and dairy produce.*

Ginger is anti-catarrhal and helps the circulation

Cinnamon is warming and aromatic

Mustard is a pain-reliever and expectorant

Chili powder is stimulating and rich in vitamin A

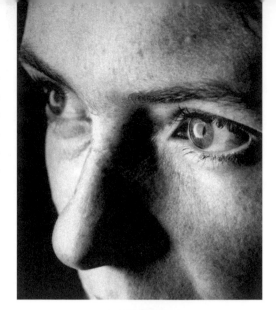

RIGHT *The white of the eye and the inner surface of the eyelids are covered by a membrane called the conjunctiva. When this becomes inflamed, it is called conjunctivitis.*

DIAGNOSING CONJUNCTIVITIS

- Symptoms may affect one or both eyes
- Eyes appear red
- A gritty feeling
- Eyes are often itchy
- Watery or sticky discharge

THE SENSES

conjunctivitis

T*his acute inflammatory condition of the mucous membrane covering the surface of the eye and lining the eyelids is caused by an infection or allergy. A foreign body in the eye can also result in similar symptoms. Conjunctivitis can be serious and is highly infectious.*

KITCHEN MEDICINE

■ Thin slices of cucumber or used, cold, teabags placed over the closed eyes for 6 minutes help to relieve the inflammation.

HERBAL REMEDIES

 Herbal eyebaths are soothing and easy to make.

■ **Use and Dosage:**
Add 1tsp/5ml of herb to a cup of boiling water, then simmer gently for 5 minutes before straining well. Let cool and then use in an eyebath. Try marigold flowers, eyebright, chamomile flowers, rose petals, raspberry leaves, elderflowers, or fumitory.

Take echinacea (6 x 200mg capsules daily) to combat any infection and strengthen the immune system.

AROMATHERAPY

 No essential oils can be used near the eyes.

CONVENTIONAL MEDICINE

 For minor infections, bathe the eyes with water that has been boiled and then cooled. If this does not help, then antibiotic drops or ointment may be helpful. For allergic conjunctivitis, antihistamine eyedrops can ease the symptoms.

Dosage information ~
Adults and children
■ Pull down the lower lid and insert antibiotics or ointment; consult package, or seek medical advice. Continue for 48 hours after the symptoms have resolved themselves.

NUTRITION

Foods rich in beta-carotene and vitamin A are important for all eye conditions—so eat orange and red fruit and vegetables, all dark green leafy vegetables and liver.

OUTSIDE HELP

REFLEXOLOGY: eye reflexes are on and between the second and third fingers and toes. Pinch the webs until tenderness is located, then massage for 5 minutes each side, four times daily.

HOMEOPATHIC REMEDIES

✿ APIS 6c For swollen, red, puffy eyelids. White of eye red, intolerance of light.
✿ ARGENTUM NITRICUM 6c For yellow or white discharge, white of eye red. Babies with sticky eye.
✿ PULSATILLA 6c For white or yellow discharge. Lids inflamed. Itching and burning.
✿ EUPHRASIA 6c For white of eye that is red, constantly watering. Tears burn, lids swollen.
Dosage: one tablet every 4 hours. Maximum 2 days. Euphrasia tincture can be diluted (two drops in an eggcup of cooled boiled water) to bathe the eye.

ABOVE *The remedy Euphrasia comes from a plant known as eyebright.*

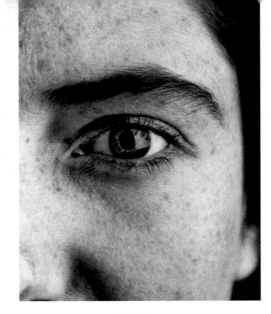

RIGHT *A stye is a small boil at the root of an eyelash, caused by bacterial infection. It is infectious: wash your hands after touching it, and do not share a towel.*

DIAGNOSING STYES

- Starts with a painful lump near an eyelash
- Pain may become severe and throbbing and the stye may discharge pus

THE SENSES

styes

A stye is an abscess in the tiny gland at the bottom of each eyelash. It comes to a head or "point" on the outside of the lid and can cause extreme inflammation of the eyelids. Infection may spread to the eye itself, so styes are not to be treated lightly. They tend to be more common in those with low resistance and in poor general health.

KITCHEN MEDICINE

■ Compresses are very soothing: make one from a used teabag dipped in cold water and rest it on the closed eye for 10 minutes.
■ Alternatively, add 1tsp/5ml of sodium bicarbonate to 2½ cups/ 600ml of hot water and use this to bathe the affected eyelid with cotton balls. Use a clean ball each time.

HERBAL REMEDIES

Marigold or eyebright decoctions can be used to bathe the affected area, or a little marigold cream will also help.
■ **Use and Dosage:** Simmer the decoction for 5 minutes to help ensure a sterile mixture for bathing the eye.

If styes are recurrent and linked to overwork, taking Siberian ginseng in the build-up to any especially stressful period will help the body to cope.

CONVENTIONAL MEDICINE

A stye will often get better with no treatment except pain-relievers, as required. If it does not improve, then a course of antibiotics may be necessary.

Dosage information ~
Adults
■ One to two tablets of pain-relievers at onset, repeated every 4 hours.
Children
■ Regular doses of liquid pain-reliever; see package for details.

NUTRITION

Foods that are rich in zinc, beta-carotene, and vitamin C are important to raise natural immunity. A high-dose supplement of these vitamins would also be useful once a stye appears.

AROMATHERAPY

A little bit of lavender in a base oil, rubbed onto the cheek underneath the stye, will be fine, but do *not* put any essential oils actually on the stye or anywhere near the eye.

OUTSIDE HELP

REFLEXOLOGY: the eye reflexes are found on and between the second and third fingers and toes. Press firmly with the thumb and work on the tender areas located. Work the lymphatics/immune system.

HOMEOPATHIC REMEDIES

❧ PULSATILLA **6C** For stye on upper lid. May also have a creamy, bland discharge from eye.
❧ STAPHYSAGRIA **6C** For recurrent styes, and styes that leave a hard, inflamed area in the skin.
Dosage: one tablet every 4 hours until stye is improved. Maximum four days.

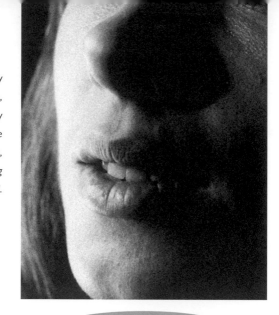

DIAGNOSING BAD BREATH
- Unpleasant smell on the breath

THE SENSES

bad breath *halitosis*

KITCHEN MEDICINE
■ Chew a few caraway seeds, mint leaves, or a coffee bean.
■ Use a mouthwash of thyme tea (see p.92).

Aromatic caraway seeds help digestion and relieve flatulence

Mint leaves are refreshing and stimulate digestive juices

Medically, bad breath is not usually very significant. Sometimes, however, it can be a pointer toward the diagnosis of more serious illness—the fish-like smell caused by liver failure, the ammoniac odor of kidney disease, or most obviously, the smell of nail-polish remover (or very ripe pears) found in diabetic coma.

Nearly always halitosis is the result of bad dental hygiene—a build-up of plaque, infected gums, a tooth abscess, a rotting filling, or lazy brushing techniques. People often become obsessive about their breath, but dentists in the US, Israel, and the UK are now using electronic machines that measure the odors in exhaled breath, enabling them to tell exactly how bad the problem is and to demonstrate to patients with halitophobia (fear of having bad breath) that they are not actually suffering— nor are their friends. It is worth noting that more people lose their teeth through gum disease than tooth decay (see Gingivitis on p.92), so heed the following advice.

CONVENTIONAL MEDICINE

✚ Looking after teeth and gums by regular brushing, flossing, and dental check-ups will help ensure that teeth and gums are not responsible for unpleasant smells in the mouth. Sensible eating habits will often avoid the problem, but it is important to seek medical advice if there is no obvious cause.

HERBAL REMEDIES

 Identifying the cause of bad breath is important.

■ **Use and Dosage:**

If hyperacidity is to blame, then meadowsweet tea can help; if sluggish digestion is at fault, then agrimony or fenugreek seeds (1tsp/5ml of herb to a cup of boiling water) can be useful.

Where bad breath is associated with catarrh, use peppermint or tea-tree oil inhalants.

A traditional remedy is to chew a few lovage or fennel seeds.

An effective herbal mouth spray can be made by adding 1tsp/5ml each of tea-tree and rosemary oils to scant 1/2 cup/100ml oz of water and pouring into a spray bottle.

ABOVE *Meadowsweet (Filipendula ulmaria) reduces stomach acidity. Make a tea by infusing 2tsp/10ml of dried herb in boiling water for 10 minutes.*

HOMEOPATHIC REMEDIES

 Ensure that there is no serious cause for this particular complaint.

❧ MERCURIUS **6C** For offensive breath, metallic taste in mouth. Dribbles on the pillow at night. Bleeding gums.

❧ PULSATILLA **6C** For halitosis in the morning. Dry mouth with greasy taste. Not thirsty. Food may taste bitter.

❧ KALI BICHROMICUM **6C** For offensive breath, sensation of a hair on the tongue. Thick, saliva, ropy, yellow catarrh.

Dosage: one tablet twice daily. Maximum 2 weeks.

OUTSIDE HELP

REFLEXOLOGY: if bad breath is a digestive problem, work the digestive reflexes on the entire palms of the hands or the soles of the feet.

YOGA: look at your diet and lifestyle; something about them probably needs changing. Keep your mouth cleaner like this: first thing every morning gargle with salted water, then scrape your tongue gently with the back of a spoon. Massage your gums, then gargle once again.

AROMATHERAPY

 ❧ TEA TREE

Melaleuca alternifolia

❧ PEPPERMINT

Mentha x piperita

❧ THYME

Thymus vulgaris

❧ LEMON

Citrus limon

❧ NIAOULI

Melaleuca viridiflora

These oils kill off any unnecessary bacteria or viral infection that was in the mouth or throat, and which might be causing bad breath, and also freshen that area.

Application:

Use in a mouthwash or gargle.

CAUTION

Do not give these mouthwashes to children.

NUTRITION

 Constipation is thought to be a common cause of bad breath and is easily remedied by following the appropriate advice (*see Constipation on p.156*). Sinus infections, catarrh, and chronic chest diseases can also be responsible (*see Catarrh on p.122, Sinusitis on p.130*). Some people find the smell of garlic, onions, curries, and other highly spiced food unpleasant, although all these foods are extremely healthy—so avoid them if you feel you must.

Regular daily helpings of natural live yogurt, plenty of water and adequate amounts of fiber-containing foods—apples, pears, carrots, whole grain cereals, and beans—all improve the digestive function and will help bad breath.

PREVENTATIVE
measures

TOOTH CARE: *see your dentist regularly. Brush your teeth after eating and before going to bed. If this is not always possible, chew sugar-free gum after meals to stimulate the production of saliva, neutralize acids, and prevent the formation of plaque, which leads to decay. Use dental floss and change your toothbrush at least every 3 months. Avoid excessive amounts of high-sugar foods and drinks, especially the acidic carbonated ones (even sugar-free).*

LEFT *The smell of onions, and another member of its family, garlic, tends to linger on the breath.*

RIGHT *Mouth ulcers may appear on the tongue, the roof of the mouth, the groove between the gums and cheek, or elsewhere on the cheek.*

DIAGNOSING MOUTH ULCERS

- Painful white craters, often with bright red borders
- May occur singly or in clusters and often recur

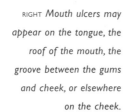

THE SENSES

mouth ulcers

These are painful, irritating sore patches inside the mouth, generally occurring on the inside of the lips (especially the lower one) and cheeks, although they can appear on the gums and roof of the mouth. Their medical name is apthous ulcers and, though frequently caused by injury—biting the cheek or lip, badly fitting dentures or the jagged edge of a damaged tooth—there may equally be no clear cause. In rare cases they are associated with an underlying disorder affecting the whole digestive tract.

CALL THE DENTIST

■ If you have an ulcer that recurs regularly in the same place, because it is quite likely to be traumatic in origin and caused by a dental problem.

■ If an ulcer fails to heal after 3 weeks.

ABOVE *Infuse 2tsp/10ml of raspberry leaves in a cup of boiling water, allow to cool, strain and use as a mouthwash.*

CONVENTIONAL MEDICINE

Most ulcers improve with no treatment after a few days, but they can last for two weeks. Pastilles or ointment containing local anesthetic can relieve the pain. These can be used with a paste containing steroid, which may speed up the healing process. Try rinsing the mouth with warm, salty water. Avoid hot, spicy, or acidic foods.

Dosage information ~
Adults and children

■ Apply a paste containing steroid combined with a local anesthetic pastille or ointment to the ulcer at regular intervals; see package for details. Salt-water mouthwashes used three or four times a day may be helpful to you.

HERBAL REMEDIES

As well as sage (*see under Kitchen Medicine*), suitable herbs for mouthwashes include rosemary, marigold, raspberry leaves, cloves, or chamomile.

■ **Use and Dosage:**
Myrrh and golden seal both taste extremely bitter but can be very effective: buy the tinctures from a pharmacy or health-food store and add 10–20 drops of either to a glass of warm water.

Strengthening the immune system with regular garlic capsules can be helpful for recurrent ulcer problems.

KITCHEN MEDICINE

■ An old wives' tale from southern Europe is the most effective remedy I know, albeit not the most pleasant. Cut a clove of garlic in half, squeeze it until the oils appear on the cut surface, then dab on the ulcer two or three times a day. Although this treatment stings and smells, the ulcer will normally disappear within 24 hours.

■ A mouthwash with sage tea is very soothing and antiseptic and helps prevent ulcers becoming infected.

1 Put 1tsp/5ml of fresh chopped sage leaves (or 2tsp/10ml of the dried herb) into a glass.

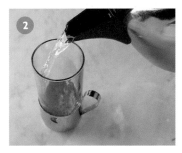

2 Add boiling water, cover and leave to stand for 10 minutes.

3 Strain off the leaves and use as a mouthwash when cool enough.

ABOVE *Garlic is a natural antiseptic and antibiotic. It has been used for healing since ancient times.*

OUTSIDE HELP

 REFLEXOLOGY: the reflexes of the mouth, teeth, and gums are found on the joints of the fingers and toes.

In addition, give some attention to the digestive tract on the soles or palms, and to the lymphatic/immune system.

NUTRITION

As this condition is so often related to stress, it is really important to have a diet that is extra-rich in all the B vitamins, so make sure that you **eat plenty of** meat, poultry, wheatgerm, brewer's yeast, leafy green vegetables, whole grain cereals, and whole wheat bread.

Avoid foods that may be damaging to the delicate mucous membranes of the mouth, including very salty food, such as chips, cocktail snacks, salted nuts, vinegar, pickles, chilies, and very hot curries. If you have ulcers, all these foods will make them much more painful.

AROMATHERAPY

🌿 MYRRH
Commiphora molmol
Myrrh helps to kill the pain and the infection, and stop it spreading. If you cannot get hold of myrrh essential oil, then myrrh tincture (available from herbal suppliers) can be used in place of the myrrh and vodka solution.

Application:
Put 2 drops of myrrh in 1tsp/5ml of vodka, then dab directly onto the mouth ulcer. This mixture can also be added to a cup of warm water and used as a mouthwash.

PREVENTATIVE *measures*

SUPPLEMENTS: *regular sufferers of mouth ulcers should take a daily dose of 5,000IU of vitamin A, 200mg of vitamin E, and 10mg of vitamin B_2. It is also extremely helpful to suck a combined vitamin C and zinc lozenge every day— and take three or four a day when you actually have the ulcers. When attacks are specifically associated with periods, then taking 50mg of vitamin B_6 and 2,000mg of evening primrose oil every day during the week before your period is due may help to ward off the ulcers.*

HOMEOPATHIC REMEDIES

Check with your physician that there is no anemia. Consult a homeopath to treat the tendency toward ulcers.

🌿 BORAX 6C For painful, white ulcers that bleed easily on contact, or when eating. Mouth hot and tender. Bitter taste in mouth.

🌿 MERCURIUS 6C For ulcers on tongue and soft palate. Tongue yellow, thick, coated, and shows the imprint of teeth. Metallic taste in mouth. Lots of saliva.

🌿 NITRIC ACID 6C For blisters and ulcers in mouth that bleed easily. Ulcers on tongue and soft palate. Tongue clean, red.

🌿 NATRUM MURIATICUM 6C For recurrent mouth ulcers, cold sores, and colds. Person may be introverted and easily hurt.
Dosage: one tablet twice daily until improved, then stop. Maximum 5 days.

LEFT *Make your own treatment lotion from myrrh, vodka, and water. Myrrh is soothing, antiseptic, and healing.*

RIGHT *If your gums bleed easily when you clean your teeth, it may be a sign of gingivitis, especially if the gums are tender. The condition needs treating to prevent eventual loss of teeth.*

DIAGNOSING GINGIVITIS

- Sore gums, which may be red and may bleed easily

THE SENSES

gingivitis

*F*ar more teeth are lost through gum disease than through tooth decay, and gingivitis— when the gums bleed very easily and dental plaque and tartar accumulate around the gum line—is by far the most common cause of gum disease. If gingivitis is left untreated, then pockets of infected pus can develop at the base of teeth, followed by abscesses and loose teeth, which may eventually fall out. Good oral hygiene is essential to the prevention of this painful condition, but home remedies can be an extremely effective cure once infection occurs.

KITCHEN MEDICINE

■ The antiseptic Thymol— the pink wash you are given by the dentist in order to rinse your mouth—was originally extracted from the culinary herb thyme. And you can use thyme to make an effective mouthwash at home—add 1 heaped tsp/5ml of dried thyme leaves (1 tsp/5ml level teaspoon if they are fresh) to a glass of hot water, cover and leave to stand for 10 minutes. Strain and, when cool enough, use the whole glass, a mouthful at a time.

■ One item you will find in every kitchen is salt: 1 level tsp/15ml added to a glass of hot water produces another extremely cheap and effective mouthwash, which will help keep the mouth germ-free.

CONVENTIONAL MEDICINE

✚ Antiseptic mouthwashes and pain-relievers may help in the first instance. Seek the advice of a dentist or hygienist if the symptoms persist.

Adults

■ Use a recommended mouthwash twice a day. Take one to two tablets of pain-relievers at onset of pain, repeated every 4 hours; see package for details.

Children

■ Use a recommended mouthwash twice a day. Give regular doses of liquid pain-reliever; see package for details, or follow advice from your physician.

CAUTION

Some mouthwashes may cause brown stains on the teeth, which improve when the mouthwash is discontinued.

AROMATHERAPY

 ❦ MYRRH
Commiphora molmol
❦ TEA TREE
Melaleuca alternifolia
❦ THYME
Thymus vulgaris
❦ FENNEL
Foeniculum vulgare
These oils are all healing and help to stop infection; thyme is antiseptic and myrrh is antimicrobial; tea tree helps build up the body's immune system.

Application:
Use in a mouthwash, putting a few drops of oil into a cup of warm water. Alternatively, massage myrrh tincture (available from herbal suppliers) into the gums to improve the circulation (obviously making sure that your hands are very clean before you do this).

ABOVE *Fennel essential oil is extracted from its seeds. These are harvested in the fall, when ripe.*

HERBAL REMEDIES

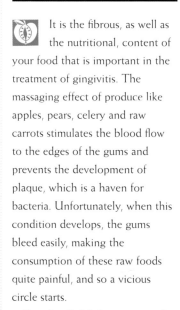 Herbal mouthwashes can help to tonify and improve gum tissues, as well as combating infection and soothing ulceration.

■ **Use and Dosage:**
Use a cooled, well-strained infusion or decoction containing such herbs as echinacea, lady's mantle, marigold, marjoram, rosemary, sage, or tormentil (2tsp/10ml per cup), or dilute 2 drops of tea-tree oil in a cup of water and use this instead.

Myrrh is very effective, if available: use 10 drops of tincture in a cup of water as a mouthwash.

Take echinacea or golden seal capsules in order to boost the immune system.

OUTSIDE HELP

REFLEXOLOGY: the reflexes of the gums can be found on the fingers. Working over the fingers and thumbs two or three times a day for about 5 minutes, paying particular attention to the tender areas on the joints, might be of benefit.

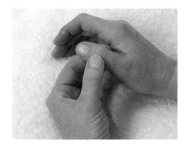

ABOVE *This reflexology treatment is easy to do yourself.*

HOMEOPATHIC REMEDIES

 ❦ MERCURIUS SOLUBILIS 6C For inflamed, bleeding gums. Produces lots of saliva. Breath is offensive and teeth may be loose. Metallic taste in mouth. Mouth moist but person is thirsty.
❦ KREOSOTUM 6C For spongy, bleeding gums. Teeth painful, decay easily, and are crumbly. Bitter taste.
❦ PHOSPHORUS 6C For gums that bleed easily and ulcerate. Bleeding after tooth extraction.
❦ NITRIC ACID 6C For teeth that become loose; spongy, bleeding gums. Tongue clean, red. May have ulcers on soft palate.
Dosage: one tablet three times daily. Maximum 1 week.

NUTRITION

It is the fibrous, as well as the nutritional, content of your food that is important in the treatment of gingivitis. The massaging effect of produce like apples, pears, celery and raw carrots stimulates the blood flow to the edges of the gums and prevents the development of plaque, which is a haven for bacteria. Unfortunately, when this condition develops, the gums bleed easily, making the consumption of these raw foods quite painful, and so a vicious circle starts.

Eat plentiful daily amounts of citrus fruit and all other fresh produce, as vitamin C is the most important single nutrient.

Reduce your intake of sugar, which (apart from poor nutrition) is your gums' worst enemy—eat as little as possible and try to clean your teeth immediately after you have had any high-sugar foods.

ABOVE *Phosphorus is recommended for hemorrhage.*

TOOTH CARE: *learning the correct way to brush your teeth is essential, so if you don't know, ask a dental hygienist to explain. And make sure that you change your toothbrush at least every 3 months. Sadly, gum disease and dental decay are on the increase, as cost keeps more and more people away from regular visits to the dentist. But gum disease can have generally debilitating effects on your health, as well, so whatever economies you make, avoiding your dentist will be a false one.*

NUTRITION: *do not forget that natural fruit juices may be full of nutrients, but they also have a high sugar content, although they are infinitely healthier than all the soft drinks (including those of the diet, lite, and low-calorie variety). No matter how much you may hate the idea, sugar-free chewing gum is a great protector of teeth and gums. If you cannot brush your teeth after a meal, chewing gum for 15 minutes will do part of the job.*

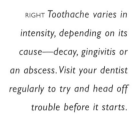

RIGHT *Toothache varies in intensity, depending on its cause—decay, gingivitis or an abscess. Visit your dentist regularly to try and head off trouble before it starts.*

DIAGNOSING TOOTHACHE

● Pain, often severe and throbbing, around a tooth

THE SENSES

toothache

KITCHEN MEDICINE

■ Cloves are one of the best pain-relievers for all types of toothache. If you have some clove oil, dip a tiny piece of cotton into the oil, roll it into a ball, and stick it into the painful part of the tooth.

■ Alternatively, holding a clove between the teeth, or between the side of the mouth and the painful tooth, will release enough essential oil to dull the pain.

CLOVES

Toothache is usually the result of poor dental hygiene. Scrupulous attention to oral hygiene—proper flossing, careful brushing, and a reduced consumption of soft drinks and sugar in general—is the first step. Next come regular visits to your dentist. But many of the problems can be avoided by healthy eating.

Dental caries (tooth decay), an abscess, or gingivitis (see p.92) may be the cause of the pain. Pain may come in short bursts, triggered by sweet foods or hot/cold drinks, which suggests caries, with slight inflammation of the tooth pulp; or in long periods, triggered by heat or cold. Severe sudden pain that is worse at night-time means that the pulp is badly inflamed. Intense and throbbing pain with a sensitive area on the gum is likely to be an abscess, which may cause fever, with inflammation and swelling of the tissues around the tooth. Go to your dentist! Weeks of painkillers will keep you going until the tooth pulp dies off and the pain stops, but then you will almost certainly lose the tooth.

CONVENTIONAL MEDICINE

✚ Take a pain-reliever as necessary to ease the toothache, and contact your dentist.

Dosage information ~

Adults

■ One to two tablets of pain-relievers at onset, repeated every 4 hours; see package for details.

Children

■ Give regular doses of liquid pain-reliever; see package for details, or follow medical advice.

NUTRITION

 Dental problems can be avoided by healthy eating although this must be combined with good oral hygiene.

Eat plentiful daily amounts of citrus fruit and all other fresh produce, as vitamin C is the most important single nutrient.

Reduce your intake of sugar, which (apart from poor nutrition) is your gums' worst enemy—eat as little as possible and try to clean your teeth immediately after you have had any high-sugar foods.

ABOVE *Swill your mouth after eating citrus fruit to reduce acid levels.*

HOMEOPATHIC REMEDIES

 This condition requires dental assessment.

✿ CHAMOMILLA **30C** Teething remedy for children. Person is intensely irritable, has intolerable pains, and cries angrily. Child has to be carried constantly. Better for warm food.

✿ COFFEA **30C** For toothache eased with ice-cold water.

✿ PLANTAGO **30C** For teeth that are sore to touch, swelling in cheeks. Produces a lot of saliva. Worse for cold air and contact. Better for eating.

✿ MAGNESIUM CARBONICUM **30C** For toothache in pregnancy. Teeth very sensitive to touch, painful to bite. Worse at night. Pain from cutting wisdom teeth.

Dosage: one tablet hourly for six doses, as needed.

HERBAL REMEDIES

For abscesses and similar infections, strong antibiotic herbs—especially Chinese figwort (Xuan Shen), forsythia berries, and echinacea—can sometimes solve the problem completely.

■ **Use and Dosage:**
These antibiotic herbs are best taken in tinctures (1tsp/5ml three times daily).

AROMATHERAPY

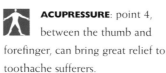 ✿ CLOVE
Syzygium aromaticum
✿ ROMAN CHAMOMILE
Chamaemelum nobile
These oils only represent first-aid help until dental treatment can be organized. Clove has an anaesthetic effect and is also a strong antiseptic, so it should help prevent any infection setting in until you can get dental treatment.

Chamomile is soothing and helps to kill the pain.
Application:
To use the clove oil, *see under Kitchen Medicine.* You can also rub clove oil all around the gum as well. If you just have toothache, rather than full-blown pain, then a warm chamomile compress on the facial area is very soothing.

OUTSIDE HELP

ACUPRESSURE: point 4, between the thumb and forefinger, can bring great relief to toothache sufferers.

REFLEXOLOGY: the reflexes of the teeth are found on the joints of the fingers and toes. Press across the big toe joints to locate the reflex for the painful tooth. Hold this point firmly for 2 minutes.

YOGA: to cope with pain, use Ujjayi: lengthen your exhalations by 1 second each time, until you reach your maximum. Continue for a while longer, breathing out as slowly as possible.

RIGHT *Acupressure on point 4 will help to numb the throbbing pain.*

Good oral hygiene, low consumption of sugars and high-sugar foods, and healthy eating are all you need to prevent tooth problems leading to toothache.

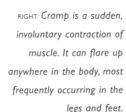

RIGHT *Cramp is a sudden, involuntary contraction of muscle. It can flare up anywhere in the body, most frequently occurring in the legs and feet.*

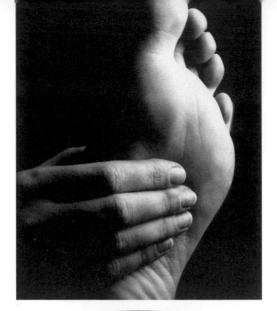

BONES AND MUSCLES

DIAGNOSING CRAMP

- Sudden and continuous pain in a muscle, often the calf or foot
- Pain may develop during exercise or at night

cramp

This sudden and severely painful condition always seems to strike at the most inappropriate moments. It is most common in the calf muscles, but it can happen anywhere in the body and is excruciatingly uncomfortable, often leaving you feeling as though you have been kicked by a mule. The common wisdom is that it is due to a deficiency of salt, but unless you are standing in front of a roaring fire all night in the tropics, or playing a five-set Grand Slam tennis final in 104°F/40°C this is never the case. Potassium deficiency is a far more likely cause of cramp than salt loss. Cramp can also occur if the muscles are not receiving enough oxygen because the blood supply is damaged. Cramps at night are common in pregnant women and the elderly, although they may be a sign of a more serious underlying condition, such as diabetes.

CALL THE PHYSICIAN

- If you have had pain in the chest or calves during exercise.

EXERCISE

EXCESSIVE EXERCISE can lead to a build-up of lactic acid in the muscles, which can itself cause cramp. Gentle, regular exercise on the other hand helps to tone the muscles and improve the blood flow, so it is a good weapon in the fight against night cramps.

CONVENTIONAL MEDICINE

➕ Cramp-like pain will usually go away when the muscle is relaxed. This generally means resting for a few minutes. Cramps at night are often relieved by stretching and rubbing the affected muscle. Pain in the chest or calves during exercise, which stops after resting, can be more serious and requires medical attention.

KITCHEN MEDICINE

- A glass of tonic water at bedtime—without the gin—often helps, due to its quinine content.

OUTSIDE HELP

REFLEXOLOGY: work the corresponding area on the hands or feet.

YOGA: use gentle lying twists and Knees-over-Chest posture, and Shitali or Sitkari, regularly.

To do the Knees-over-Chest posture, lie on your back and bring your knees up to your chest.

For a gentle but effective lying twist, bend the legs, with feet on the floor. Exhaling, take knees to right; inhale, return to center, then go to left.

You can also do a lying twist with the feet and knees apart: experiment and see which version you prefer.

HERBAL REMEDIES

Decoctions of cramp bark or black haw can help persistent night cramp, while teas of wild yam, chamomile, or fennel can ease stomach cramps.

■ **Use and Dosage:**
Add 1tsp/5ml of cramp bark or

black haw to 1½ cups/350ml of water and simmer for 10 minutes to make a decoction.

Make an external rub using 5 drops each of cypress, marjoram, and basil oils in 1½tsp/7.5ml of almond oil.

AROMATHERAPY

℞ GERANIUM *Pelargonium graveolens*
℞ GINGER *Zingiber officinale*
℞ CYPRESS *Cupressus sempervirens*
These oils are stimulating and increase the circulation, warming up the muscles so that cramp does not set in.

Application:
Use in a compress, in the bath, or in a foot spa. You really need to be looking at prevention, rather than cure, so make sure that you massage the feet and legs in the evenings, before you go to bed, if you are susceptible to cramp.

NUTRITION

This is often the key to relieving attacks of cramp, but it must be seen as a long-term benefit, not an instant cure. If you suffer regularly from cramp, eat at least one banana each day. Vitamin E is a great aid to the circulation, so eat avocados, nuts, seeds, and lots of good olive oil. Sardines contain beneficial omega-3 fatty acids and also are a rich source of calcium, as are all dairy products. Eat natural yogurt for its riboflavin and eggs for their vitamin B_{12}.

HOMEOPATHIC REMEDIES

℞ CUPRUM METALLICUM **6C** For violent, sudden cramps in the calves at night. Useful for cramps during pregnancy. Try this remedy first.
℞ MAGNESIUM PHOSPHORICUM **6C** For writer's cramp, cramps from prolonged exertion. Cramps in the calves better for rubbing.

℞ NUX VOMICA **6C** For cramps in the calves and soles, with lots of muscle spasms. Sleeplessness, particularly toward morning, with dreams of arguments. Person may be irritable.
Dosage: one tablet before retiring. Maximum 2 weeks.

PREVENTATIVE
measures

If cramp is due to poor circulation, rub the legs from the knees down with alternate hot and cold sponges for 5 minutes before bedtime.

RELAXATION: *occupational cramps, often suffered by writers, musicians, typists, and the like, are caused by relentless but controlled repetitive movements. These problems are greatly* aggravated by stress or tension, so *practicing some relaxation techniques and taking regular breaks from the activity will alter the pattern. If the problem persists, seek specialist referral.*

NUTRITION: *take 400 IU of vitamin E each day and a good mineral supplement containing calcium, potassium, and magnesium.*

ABOVE *As part of your bedtime routine, rub the cramp-prone area with sponges soaked alternately in hot and cold water.*

DIAGNOSING REPETITIVE STRAIN INJURY

- Pain in the hand, arm, or neck
- Often related to using a keyboard for long periods

BONES AND MUSCLES

repetitive strain injury *RSI*

R*epetitive strain injury is a result of overuse of the upper body at work. While the term RSI has become popular in the media, the condition should properly be called work-related upper-limb injury, as it nearly always involves pain in the wrist, forearm, shoulder and neck. The pain can occur in any one or more (even all) of these areas. Many treatments have been tried, often with little success, but the best results may come from a combination of rest and home remedies.*

KITCHEN MEDICINE

■ Keep a large bag of frozen peas (loosely packaged, or empty them into a larger plastic bag) in the freezer, for use as an ice pack. Use a permanent-ink marker to mark the package, so that you do not eat the peas by mistake.

First cover the skin with a thin cotton dish towel (do not forget to do this, unless you want freezer burns). Apply the ice package and leave in place for 10 minutes. Then give the area a brisk rub with a warm facecloth, followed by a rough towel. Repeat up to three times a day.

CONVENTIONAL MEDICINE

✚ Prevent pain by taking a break from the keyboard at regular intervals. Ensure that your keyboard, monitor, and desk are comfortable and ergonomically safe. If pain develops, rest until the pain has completely disappeared. If it persists, try a nonsteroidal anti-inflammatory pain-reliever. Your physician may suggest that you seek the advice of a specialist.

Dosage information ~

Adults

■ Take one to two tablets of pain-reliever at onset of pain, repeated every 4 hours; see package for details.

AROMATHERAPY

 ❦ LAVENDER
Lavandula angustifolia

❦ ROMAN CHAMOMILE
Chamaemelum nobile

❦ ROSEMARY
Rosmarinus officinalis

❦ GINGER
Zingiber officinale

❦ MARJORAM
Origanum majorana

❦ JUNIPER
Juniperus communis

Essential oils should not be used to mask the pain so that you can carry on—they should be used as treatment once you have stopped doing the movement that created the problem. These oils will help the circulation, warming the muscles and killing some of the pain. Juniper also helps to remove the toxins that are creating the pain.

Application:
Use to massage around the affected area; or use in hand or foot baths, or soak the affected area in the bath. But do identify what it is you are doing that is creating the problem and try either to stop it totally or to do less of it.

HERBAL REMEDIES

 Anti-inflammatory herbs such as meadowsweet, white willow, or St.-John's-wort may be helpful in teas.

■ **Use and Dosage:**
Use 2tsp/10ml of these herbs per cup. Herbal rubs suggested for rheumatism and arthritis (*see pp.110*

and *104*) may give some relief.

Some sufferers find that tonic herbs used to help the body cope with physical stresses—notably Siberian ginseng, astragalus, or shiitake mushrooms—can bring about improvements in chronic RSI conditions.

HOMEOPATHIC REMEDIES

 ❦ ARNICA **6C** For bruised sensation in muscles and tendons. Aching muscles after overexertion. Worse for damp weather and continuing movement. Person says they are fine, even when obviously not.
❦ CAUSTICUM **6C** For burning pain, inflamed tendons. Pain worse for drafts, cold, or overuse. Carpal

tunnel syndrome. Person is very idealistic and intense.
❦ STAPHYSAGRIA **6C** For tearing pains in arms, which may feel beaten. Worse for motion and touch. Person is very sensitive, deeply hurt. May appear very sweet but be angry underneath.
Dosage: one tablet twice daily. Maximum 2 weeks.

OUTSIDE HELP

 ACUPRESSURE: this is not really appropriate for RSI, although traditional acupuncture can be effective.
ALEXANDER TECHNIQUE: RSI, like many other conditions, involves overexercising some muscles at the expense of others. Practicing the Alexander Technique, with its emphasis on overall good use of your body, will

certainly alleviate the symptoms, if not help actually prevent recurrence of RSI.
REFLEXOLOGY: it is possible that reflexology treatment may be of benefit in treating RSI: try applying techniques to the hand or foot on the affected side.

NUTRITION

RSI is an inflammatory condition, so you should **eat plenty of** the natural anti-inflammatory foods—oily fish, orange, red, and dark green fruit and vegetables, citrus fruit, nuts, seeds, and olive oil for their antioxidant vitamins A, C, and E; eggs, brewer's yeast, and Brazil nuts for the antioxidant mineral selenium. Regular consumption of all these foods will help the body's own self-healing mechanisms.

Avoid too much red meat; stick to poultry, white fish, legumes and whole grains for your protein.

EXERCISE

APPROPRIATE EXERCISES will help, but the wrong sort of activity can make matters much worse. This is not the time for "Do-it-yourself"—you need to see a specialist osteopath or physiotherapist, who will assess your individual needs and prescribe specific exercises accordingly.

PREVENTATIVE
measures

RSI is caused by continual repetitive activities—on an assembly line, in a kitchen, at a supermarket checkout, and, most often, at the computer keyboard—so the workplace is where you must start taking preventative measures.

OFFICE FURNITURE: *to minimize the risks you must have a properly designed chair, with a height adjustment, tilt mechanism, variable rake, and adjustable height for the back support (and for the arms, if any). There should also be a foot-rest, and the height of the desk must be appropriate to the work being done on it. The center of your PC screen should be as near as possible to your eyeline; there must be a paper holder if you are copy-typing or constantly referring to documents; and ideally room at the edge of the desk for a padded wrist-bar. If your work involves using the telephone and keyboard at the same time, and for long periods, you need a hands-free, headset telephone.*

REST: *it is crucial that you take regular breaks from the keyboard. I consider 10 minutes out of every hour an absolute minimum for proper protection; and in a perfect world, no one would spend more than 3 hours at a keyboard (with a total of 30 minutes off) before taking a complete hour away from it.*

EARLY WARNING SIGNS: *if you experience the slightest sign of pain in the wrists, forearms, elbows, or shoulders after an hour or two at work, speak to your immediate boss or human-resources manager and get immediate medical advice. If you allow RSI to become well established, it can mean weeks or months off work– and, at worst, being forced to change the type of job you do.*

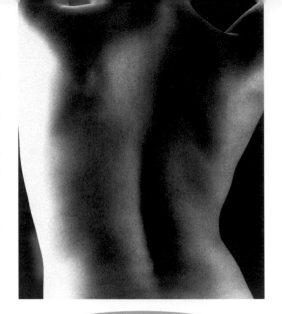

RIGHT *Back pain may occur along any part of the spine, but low back pain is probably the most common. The back carries the weight of the head and body, and most movement involves it, so it is subject to many stresses.*

DIAGNOSING BACK PAIN

- Pain may come on suddenly or may be more long-standing
- Often worse after sitting or standing for long periods
- Low back pain may be associated with pain down the leg

BONES AND MUSCLES

back pain

Y ou have an almost 90 percent chance of suffering from back pain at some time in your life, and once you have had it, you are twice as likely to suffer again. More than 10 percent of the population suffers all the time. Most causes of back pain can be relieved by manipulative therapy within the first 6 weeks, though in some cases surgery may be the only answer. Prevention is the best treatment, but if you are already a sufferer, you should take steps to minimize the risk of repeated attacks and to maintain your back in a strong, healthy and mobile state. Do not stay in bed for more than 48 hours, even with a severe attack of back pain—seek professional help as soon as possible.

CALL THE PHYSICIAN

- If you cannot control when you pass urine or open your bowels.
- If you have numbness in a limb or difficulty moving it.
- If you have pain passing down your leg.
- If you cannot control the pain.
- If there is no improvement after 4–6 weeks.

CAUTION

Whatever the cause of your back pain, make sure that it is properly diagnosed.

Always read pain-reliever packages carefully, and do not exceed the stated dose.

CONVENTIONAL MEDICINE

Take a pain-reliever regularly. This may need to be combined with a prescribed muscle-relaxant, which may help to relieve muscle spasm and avoid the need for strong pain-relievers. Try to avoid prolonged bed rest. There is evidence to suggest that continuing normal activities may help to hasten recovery and will reduce the chance of developing a long-term back problem. Most back pain is short-lived and self-limiting, but if problems persist for more than a few days, then early referral to a physiotherapist is recommended.

Dosage information ~
Adults
- One to two tablets of pain-relievers at onset of pain, repeated every 4 hours; see package for details.

Children
- Give regular doses of liquid pain-reliever; see package for details, or follow medical advice.

KITCHEN MEDICINE

■ Apply a hot package made from bruised, warmed cabbage leaves, or try one of my favorite recipes—a bran and mustard poultice. Mix 4 cups of bran with 4tsp of dry mustard powder. Put into the top of a double boiler, cover and heat over boiling water until hot. Fill two small bags made of two or three layers of cheesecloth. Apply one bag to the painful area, keeping the other hot between two plates in the oven. Change the bags over when the first one is cool. Continue applications for 15 minutes, two or three times a day.

NUTRITION

ABOVE *Celery seed combats water retention; turnips relieve inflamed muscles.*

Eat plenty of celery and parsley to encourage fluid elimination; turnips for their anti-inflammatory action; pineapple for its pain-relieving enzymes; and oily fish to maintain mobility.

Reduce your intake of caffeine. **Avoid** carrying excessive weight, which puts even more strain on the spine.

HERBAL REMEDIES

Herbal remedies can ease symptoms, but where back pain is related to a mechanical fault, such as a slipped disc, then manipulative treatment is generally preferable.

■ **Use and Dosage:**
Low back pain can be associated with kidney problems, so remedies like buchu, corn silk, and couchgrass (2tsp/10ml of each per cup of tea) can be helpful.

To ease local discomfort, soak a compress in scant ½ cup/100ml of hot water containing cramp bark (1tbsp/15ml) and cinnamon (1tsp/5 ml) tinctures, then apply.

CINNAMON

ABOVE *Cinnamon is a warming kidney tonic, useful in a compress for low back pain.*

Reheat the mix and reapply as required. Anti-inflammatories such as devil's claw (6 x 200mg capsules daily) can also help.

OUTSIDE HELP

ACUPRESSURE: use points 17, 24, and 25; points 31, 35, and 39 are also useful.

ALEXANDER TECHNIQUE: muscular imbalance and excessive shortening of some muscles, which leads to ineffectiveness of others, are often contributory factors to back pain. Practicing the Alexander Technique may sometimes be beneficial in curing the problem. It will certainly help avoid recurrence of it, by teaching you a more balanced use of your own body.

REFLEXOLOGY: the spinal reflexes are found on the medial longitudinal arches of the feet (the bony ridges on the inside). Work these areas, particularly sore or tender parts. Check the neck and pelvic reflexes. First-aid treatment for symptomatic pain relief requires firm pressure.

YOGA: if you can, lie down with the legs bent, feet flat on the floor. Rest in this position as much as possible, exhaling fully and slowly for at least 12 breaths. If it feels right, try some simple arm movements, coordinating them with the breath, but do nothing that seems to feel painful or wrong.

ABOVE *An Alexander teacher will show you a good resting posture to adopt, lying down. The head is first brought into line with the body.*

BELOW *The legs are bent, with feet flat on the floor, positioned about shoulder-width apart. Hands rest on the stomach, and elbows on the floor. Do this for 20 minutes every day.*

PREVENTATIVE *measures*

POSTURE: *maintain good posture at work, in your hobbies and at home. Proper chairs, work stations, work benches, beds, and armchairs—of the right height, with good upright support and firm seating—are essential.*

DAILY ACTIVITIES: *don't wear high heels or use shoulder bags. Avoid combinations of twisting and bending, and keep your weight down, learning to lift with your back straight and avoiding excessive loads. When working in the house or garden, keep a variety of different tasks on the go at the same time, in order to avoid long periods of a single repetitive movement.*

HOMEOPATHIC REMEDIES

Numbness in the bottom, or difficulty knowing when you want to pass urine or open the bowels, requires urgent medical assessment.

❦ BRYONIA 6C For stiffness in small of back at change of weather. Slow onset, worse for slightest movement. Better for pressure, rest, and cold applications.

❦ GNAPHALIUM 6C For pain extending down the leg, "sciatica" with numbness. Worse on right side, for lying down and motion. Better for sitting in chair and drawing legs up.

❦ TELLURIUM 6C For pain extending down the leg, sciatica, right-sided. Pain worse for cough, sneezing, opening the bowels, or touch. Also lumbago.

Dosage: one tablet every 2–4 hours, as needed, for 3–4 days.

AROMATHERAPY

It is important to have a good diagnosis before deciding which oils to use.

For muscular problems:

❦ LAVENDER

Lavandula angustifolia

❦ GINGER

Zingiber officinale

❦ MARJORAM

Origanum majorana

For kidney pain:

❦ LAVENDER

Lavandula angustifolia

❦ ROMAN CHAMOMILE

Chamaemelum nobile

For disc problems:

❦ LAVENDER

Lavandula angustifolia

❦ ROMAN CHAMOMILE

Chamaemelum nobile

❦ MARJORAM

Origanum majorana

The oils for muscular problems are warming and soothing, while those for kidney pain and disk problems are soothing and calming and will also help to kill the pain.

Application:

The oils for muscular pain can be used in a massage, in the bath, or in a compress; those for kidney pain and disk problems also in a compress or in the bath (if you can manage to get into a bath), to help relieve inflammation. If back pain is due to period pains, then the best oil would be clary sage, used in a compress or in a lotion, which you can rub in periodically. For back pain due to stress, have a good massage, using the destressing oils (*see p.60*) and the warming muscular oils.

FOR MOST BACK PROBLEMS these 12 exercises will build strength and mobility. Do daily for 10 minutes. If any of them make your pain worse, skip for a few days, then try them again. Take it gently—you're not training to be an Olympic weight lifter. Many of my patients get distressed and angry with their problems. Don't get mad—get even. The way to get even is to get fit.

1. THE TAIL TUCK
POSITION: Lying on your back, knees bent, feet flat on the floor.
EXERCISE: Flatten hollow of back on the floor, using abdominal muscles to pull the abdomen down. Raise pelvis just off the floor. Do not lift lower back. Hold for 5 seconds. Relax pelvis for 5 seconds, keeping back flat on the floor. Repeat five times, breathing regularly.

1.   THE TAIL TUCK

2. THE STRAIGHT-LEG TAIL TUCK
POSITION: As in 1.
EXERCISE: As in 1, but gradually straighten the legs. This prepares you for exercise 3.

3. THE STANDING TAIL TUCK
POSITION: Stand with back against a suitable wall, feet 6–9in/15–24cm away from bare board.
EXERCISE: Flatten small of back against wall, using the abdominal muscles. Do not bend the knees. Hold for 5 seconds. Relax and repeat five times. Keep breathing regularly. You can practice this exercise against an imaginary wall at any time when you are standing.

3.   THE STANDING TAIL TUCK

EXERCISE

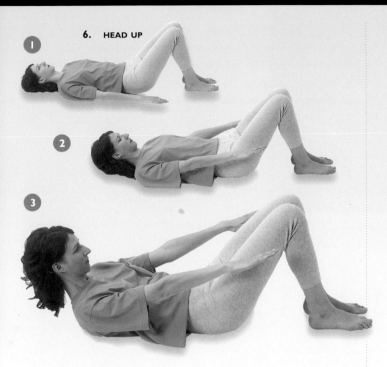

6. HEAD UP

4. THE SKIER'S TAIL TUCK

POSITION: As in 3.

EXERCISE: As in 3, but slowly bend the knees, keeping back flat against the wall. Hold for 15 seconds. Repeat three times with 5-second rests. Do not let your flattened back come away from the wall. As you get better at this exercise, you can increase the amount you bend your knees, until they are at 90°—as if sitting on an imaginary chair. Carry on until you can hold this position for a full 60 seconds.

5. THE QUARTER BUM

POSITION: Erect, with a quarter gripped between the cheeks of your buttocks.

EXERCISE: Flatten lower part of back and, keeping the coin held firmly in place, walk around the room for 1 minute.

6. HEAD UP

POSITION: Lying on your back, knees bent, feet flat on the floor.

EXERCISE: Flatten back to floor. Lift arms up, put chin on chest. Roll forward until shoulder blades are off the floor. Hold for 5 seconds. Roll back to floor. Keep tail tucked in. Build up to 10 repeats.

7. THE SIT-DOWN

You must be proficient at this one before you can even consider the Sit-Up.

POSITION: Sitting on floor, knees bent, arms around knees.

EXERCISE: Lean slowly backwards, using arms to support the weight of the trunk. Then use arms to pull back to a sitting position. Rest for 5 seconds. Repeat 10 times. As your abdominal muscles gain in strength, you can reduce the support of your hands and arms, until you can perform the sit-down exercise 10 times without holding your knees. You can then move on to:

8. THE SIT-UP WITH TOE TOUCH

POSITION: Lying on your back, knees bent, feet flat on the floor.

EXERCISE: Tuck in tail, put chin on chest, with hands along sides. Roll upright from the neck, keeping tail tucked in. When upright, straighten legs, stretch fingers to toes, then roll slowly back to floor, bending the knees. Work up to 10 repeats.

9. THE ONE-HAMSTRING PROTECTED STRETCH

Hamstrings are located at the back of the thigh. Stretching both at once can do more harm than good.

POSITION: Sitting on floor, one knee fully bent, with foot flat on the floor.

EXERCISE: Allow bent knee to fall outward, then stretch both hands towards foot of straight leg as far as is comfortable. Now start a gentle, rhythmic, bouncing movement, reaching for the foot. Continue for 20 seconds. Rest, change legs and repeat.

10. THE LEG-UP

Lifting both legs strains the back. Until you are several weeks into your exercise plan, stick to lifting one at a time, then switch to both legs, but starting with your feet resting on a low stool.

POSITION: Lying on your back, one leg bent with foot flat on the floor, other leg straight. Tuck in tail and maintain this position throughout the exercise.

EXERCISE: Without bending the knee of the straight leg, raise it upward until level with knee of the bent leg. Hold for 5 seconds, lower slowly, rest for 5 seconds. Repeat five times, change legs, then do five more lifts with the other leg.

11. THE CROSS-OVER LEG PRESS

This is an isometric exercise (one that tones the body by opposing one muscle to another) to strengthen the abdominal muscles.

POSITION: Lying on your back, knees bent, feet flat on the floor.

EXERCISE: Tuck in tail and maintain this position throughout exercise. Raise right knee until calf is parallel with the floor. Now place left hand on right knee, keeping your arm straight. Raise head and tuck chin into chest. Now push hand against knee, and knee against hand, using the muscle strength of shoulder and arm against knee and hip. Hold pressure for 5 seconds, then relax. Repeat five times, then change over hand and leg, and repeat another five times.

Remember: isometric exercise = no movement.

12. THE CROSS-OVER SIT-UP

POSITION: Lying on your back, legs straight.

EXERCISE: Tuck in tail and maintain this position, spreading legs apart to 45°. Tuck chin into chest and place right arm across body. Now, pushing your right shoulder toward your left leg, raise your trunk until both shoulder blades are off the floor. Relax and repeat five times. Change arms and stretch left shoulder to right leg. Repeat another five times.

9. THE ONE-HAMSTRING PROTECTED STRETCH

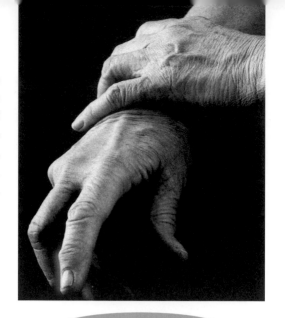

RIGHT *Arthritis affects the joints, causing them to swell. In rheumatoid arthritis, these are commonly the fingers, wrists, elbows, shoulders, knees, ankles, and feet.*

DIAGNOSING ARTHRITIS

- Joints are often sore and swollen and may be an abnormal shape
- Aching, stiff joints

BONES AND MUSCLES

arthritis

There are more than 200 different forms of arthritis that cause problems with the joints. Pain, stiffness, swelling, and inflammation are usually present, but conditions may range from the inconvenience of arthritis in a finger, caused by an injury 20 years before, to the severe disablement that can result from rheumatoid arthritis. Some of the severe conditions do not lend themselves to treatment with home remedies, but whatever form of arthritis you have, diet can play a key role in reducing the severity of your symptoms. Osteoarthritis and rheumatoid arthritis also respond to self-help, though this is not a substitute for surgery or drug therapy.

KITCHEN MEDICINE

■ Cabbage leaves make a great poultice for inflamed joints (gout, osteo- or rheumatoid arthritis). Bruise one or two large, outer, dark green leaves with a rolling pin or knife handle, and warm in a microwave, steamer, oven, or on a hot radiator, then wrap around the affected joint. Cover with a towel and leave in place for 15 minutes, repeating two or three times a day. You will be amazed at the relief this simple country woman's recipe provides.

■ Ginger is also worth a try—there is no scientific proof of its efficacy, but lots of anecdotal stories. Drink ginger tea (*see p. 190*) and make sure that you add plenty of fresh ginger root and dried ginger to recipes when you are cooking.

CONVENTIONAL MEDICINE

✚ Relieve arthritis with simple pain-relievers such as aspirin. Sore joints may feel better when they are supported with a firm bandage. You may find that keeping your joints warm helps, too. Gentle exercise is important in order to keep your joints supple.

Dosage information ~
Adults
■ One to two tablets of pain-relievers at onset of fever, repeated every 4 hours; see package for details.
Children
■ Give regular doses of liquid pain-reliever; consult package for details, or follow advice from your physician.

EXERCISE

EXERCISE is vital, as keeping supportive muscles in good shape greatly relieves the pain of arthritic joints and movement keeps them supple. The exercise must be appropriate to your condition and, where there is severe joint damage, should be non-weight-bearing. Swimming is ideal, specially with water aerobics (exercises in water).

HERBAL REMEDIES

 Anti-inflammatory herbs such as birch, black cohosh, meadowsweet, poplar, and willow are widely used—usually as teas, although birch sap (collected in the fall and taken in teaspoonful doses) was once a popular folk remedy. Devil's claw-root, from the Kalahari, is now popular.

■ **Use and Dosage:**
Take up to 3g of devil's claw root powder daily in capsules, for at least 4 weeks.

Ease painful symptoms by combining 10 drops of rosemary or wintergreen oil with 1tsp/5ml of infused comfrey oil, then using the mixture as a gentle massage.

HOMEOPATHIC REMEDIES

 It is helpful to consult a qualified homeopath about this ailment (*see also Rheumatism on p.110*).

❧ BRYONIA **6C** For joints that are red, hot, with tearing pains. Worse for slightest movement. Better for holding joint tightly and applying heat. Dry mouth and thirst.

❧ GUAIACUM **6C** For knobby joints, feeling that is necessary to stretch tendons. Worse for applied heat and movement. Better for applied cold.

❧ RHODODENDRUM **6C** For arthritis that affects smaller joints, which feel weak. Worse for changes of weather, and before storms and cold winters. Better for warmth.

Dosage: one tablet taken three times daily. Maximum period 1 month.

OUTSIDE HELP

ACUPRESSURE: an excellent way to help control your own pain levels using points 6, 7, 8, and 9 for arm, shoulder, and finger pain, and points 13, 14, 15, and 16 for pain in the hips and lower limbs. It is also worth using points 17, 18, and 19 for generalized discomfort.

ALEXANDER TECHNIQUE: this can be of great benefit to arthritis sufferers. It helps to reduce deep-held muscular tensions, which results in relieving excessive pressure on the joints, thus alleviating pain and improving the circulation.

REFLEXOLOGY: all joints of the hands and feet should be worked for pain relief and mobility of the corresponding body joints. Hip joints can be eased by pressure

ABOVE *Rotating the ankles eases pain in the hip joints.*

and rotation of the ankles; the neck by rotation of the big toe.

YOGA: don't give up in despair when you can no longer achieve things that you used to do easily. Your yoga is more important now than ever before. Practice very slowly and meditatively, seeing how far you can move affected joints without causing yourself pain. Do not exercise joints when they are inflamed.

AROMATHERAPY

 ❧ LAVENDER
Lavandula angustifolia
❧ ROMAN CHAMOMILE
Chamaemelum nobile
❧ EUCALYPTUS
Eucalyptus radiata
❧ JUNIPER
Juniperus communis
❧ GINGER
Zingiber officinale

These oils have a painkilling effect, especially for localized pain. They are also warming and soothing. But there are many oils that can be used for this condition and it is up to you to find out which ones suit you best.

Application:
Use in baths—foot or hand baths, depending on where the affected joints are—or massage an oil or a lotion into the body. If your joint problem is a very recent one, do check that your stress levels are as low as they can be.

CAUTION

If you are using a compress, or a warm hand or foot bath (or just a warm bath), make sure that you mobilize the joints as much as possible after heat treatment, because the heat can cause congestion, making matters worse.

NUTRITION

 For all arthritic conditions, except gout:

Eat plenty of oily fish and shellfish, for their omega-3 fatty acids; sweet potatoes, broccoli, apricots, carrots, and liver for their vitamin A and beta-carotene; citrus fruit, strawberries, kiwis, and dark green vegetables for their vitamin C and bioflavonoids; olive oil, sunflower seeds, unsalted nuts, and avocados for their vitamin E.

Reduce your intake of red meat, coffee, and game.

Gout sufferers must **avoid** all alcohol, game, organ meat, yeast and meat extracts, all oily fish, fish roe, mussels, and scallops.

PREVENTATIVE *measures*

WEIGHT CONTROL: *being seriously overweight adds greatly to the stresses on all weight-bearing joints and will predispose you to arthritis in the lower spine, hips, knees, ankles, and feet.*

FOOT CARE: *inappropriate shoes—those with stiletto heels, very pointed toes or, worst of all, both—are an almost certain guarantee of bunions (arthritis in the big toe joint).*

JOGGING AND MARATHON RUNNING: *as man is designed to run, it is fine to do so on soft sand, grassy meadows, or the carpet of leaves in a forest. It is not quite the same when you pound around on city sidewalks—your foot hits the ground a thousand times each mile. This high impact, even in modern, high-quality trainers, dramatically increases the risk of arthritis in all weight-bearing joints.*

DIET: *a high intake of oily fish and shellfish (see under Nutrition) increases your consumption of the protective omega-3 fatty acids. It also ensures a constant supply of vitamin D, which, combined with a good calcium intake, means strong bones that are less likely to be damaged. Include parsley, celery, and watercress in your diet to eliminate uric acid.*

RIGHT *Osteoarthritis mainly affects the hip, knee, spine, and fingers, as the cartilage between the bones, which acts as a cushion, wears away.*

DIAGNOSING OSTEOARTHRITIS
- Stiff, painful joints
- May affect any joint, but common in the hips, knees, and fingers
- Affected joints are often hard and swollen

BONES AND MUSCLES

osteoarthritis

Osteoarthritis is commonly seen as the result of long-term wear and tear on weight-bearing joints, often as the result of occupation or sporting activities. However, this is not the only cause, and previous injury or fracture, damage to the cartilage (especially in the knee), previous infection, or congenital deformity such as spinal curvature or bunions may also lead to osteoarthritis.

NUTRITION

 Oily fish are an important group of foods for anyone suffering from osteoarthritis. The omega-3 fatty acids in the fish are naturally anti-inflammatory and help to maintain the mobility of affected joints.

Eat plenty of liver, carrots, sweet potatoes, spinach, broccoli, apricots, mangoes, and bright orange cantaloupe melons for their vitamin A and beta-carotene, which are equally important nutrients; all the green leafy vegetables, citrus fruit, kiwis, red, yellow and green bell peppers for their vitamin C, which helps to protect the joints from further damage. This is one condition for which it is best to avoid red meat and meat products as far as possible—instead fish, poultry, nuts, seeds, and beans, together with eggs and modest amounts of low-fat dairy products, should be used as protein sources.

CONVENTIONAL MEDICINE

Try to keep as active as possible, which helps to keep the affected joints supple and increases muscle tone and strength. It also helps to control weight gain, which can aggravate osteoarthritis. Staying active may mean taking pain-relievers and using mechanical aids, such as a walking frame or stick. Your physician can arrange for physiotherapy, if required. In severe cases, a joint replacement can provide a new lease of life.

Dosage information ~
Adults
- Take one to two tablets of pain-reliever at onset of pain, repeated every 4 hours; see package for details.

EXERCISE

EXERCISE IS vital for all people suffering from osteoarthritis. Obviously the amount and type of exercise will depend on the individual's condition, but maintaining strong supportive muscles is a sure way to reduce pain. Lack of mobility leads in turn to increasing stiffness and decreasing muscle strength—the worst possible combination for arthritic joints.

KITCHEN MEDICINE

■ Ginger tea can be very soothing to painful joints. Peel and grate ½in/1cm of fresh ginger root, and add to a mug of boiling water. Cover and leave to stand for 10 minutes. Strain and add 1 tsp of honey, then drink two or three mugs a day.

■ For individual painful joints, use a cabbage poultice. Take a large leaf of dark green cabbage, cut out the thick center stalk, and bruise the leaf all over with a rolling pin or knife handle. Heat the leaf in a microwave, steamer, or low oven, or round a hot-water pipe, then wrap it round the affected joint (checking the temperature first!). Cover with a towel and leave for 15 minutes.

■ Take warm baths with 3tbsp/45ml Epsom salt and soak for 20 minutes; and use regular alternate hot-and-cold contrast bathing of painful areas.

HERBAL REMEDIES

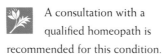

A number of herbs may help this condition.

■ **Use and Dosage:**
The "wear and tear" contributing to osteoarthritis can often be helped by regular use of comfrey cream or infused oil: massage a little into the aching joint every night for at least 2 months.

Internally, herbs to stimulate circulation and clear toxins can be helpful—try a decoction of angelica, yellow dock, prickly ash and willow bark (1–2tsp/5–10ml per cup).

Devil's claw root is very effective (*see Arthritis on p.104*).

HOMEOPATHIC REMEDIES

A consultation with a qualified homeopath is recommended for this condition.

❧ RHUS TOXICODENDRON **6C** For tearing pains, worse at night, restless with them. Pain worse for initial movement, then improves as gets moving. Joints feel sore and stiff. Worse for wet or cold weather.

❧ PULSATILLA **6C** For pains that are wandering from joint to joint. Weepy with the pains and emotional. Pains better for gentle motion. Worse for warmth.

❧ CALCAREA CARBONICA **6C** For joints that swell, particularly knees. Pain worse in morning. Cold feet in bed at night. Weakness of legs, tires easily. Sweaty, cold feet. **Dosage:** one tablet three times daily. Maximum 2 weeks.

PREVENTATIVE *measures*

Maintaining a sensible weight and avoiding activities that are most likely to lead to stress-related arthritis are the key factors. Marathon running, relentless jogging on hard surfaces, and high-impact aerobics can all damage joint surfaces and predispose you to osteoarthritis later on.

DIET: *maintaining a diet that is rich in oily fish will protect your joints—and your heart and circulation, too. Including plenty of nuts and seeds, olive oil, and avocados for their vitamin E also offers a degree of joint protection.*

LEFT *Rhus toxicodendron comes from the leaves of poison ivy. It particularly targets problems of the joints, ligaments, tendons, and skin.*

OUTSIDE HELP

ACUPRESSURE: use points 6, 7, 8, and 9 for the arms, shoulders and fingers; points 13, 14, 15, and 16 for the hips and legs; and points 17, 18, and 19 as general pain-relieving points for arthritic conditions.

ALEXANDER TECHNIQUE: in osteoarthritis, as in arthritis, too much pressure on afflicted joints, due to deep-held muscular tension and uneven weight-bearing, almost certainly aggravates the condition. Practicing the Technique will ease these symptoms.

REFLEXOLOGY: work the reflex of the area affected, together with the eliminatory channels. Check the cross-reflex—if a knee or shoulder joint is affected, for example, massage the corresponding area in the other knee or shoulder.

YOGA: don't give up in despair when you can no longer achieve things that you used to do easily. Your yoga is more important now than ever before. Practice very slowly and meditatively, seeing how far you can move affected joints without causing yourself pain. Do not exercise joints when they are inflamed.

AROMATHERAPY

❧ LAVENDER
Lavandula angustifolia
❧ ROMAN CHAMOMILE
Chamaemelum nobile
❧ MARJORAM
Origanum majorana
❧ GINGER
Zingiber officinale
❧ BLACK PEPPER
Piper nigrum
❧ ROSEMARY
Rosmarinus officinalis
❧ JUNIPER
Juniperus communis

These oils are warming and soothing. Juniper also helps detoxify the system.

Application:
Use in warm baths, in hand or foot baths. You can also add them to massage oils or lotions, but do not massage over any area where there is inflammation.

ABOVE *A few drops of marjoram oil in a bowl of warm water makes a pain-relieving foot bath.*

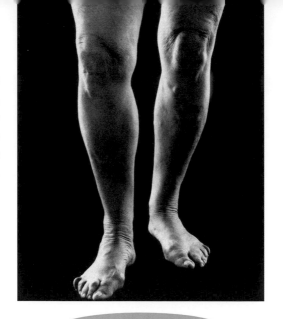

RIGHT *Osteoporosis is a weakening of the bones, making them vulnerable to fracture anywhere in the body. Keeping active helps to prevent its onset.*

DIAGNOSING OSTEOPOROSIS

- Does not cause any symptoms but is the commonest cause of fractured bones in people over the age of 75 years

BONES AND MUSCLES

osteoporosis

O steoporosis—the condition in which the bones become weak, brittle and easily broken—normally occurs in women after menopause, though men can get it, too. It is growing at an alarming rate in the US, Europe and Britain and must be seen as an extremely serious problem. Any medical condition that causes a premature menopause (see p.172) increases the risk of osteoporosis; this is also true of long-term treatment with some drugs (particularly cortisone and its relatives) and of eating disorders like anorexia and bulimia. Diseases that affect the body's absorption of nutrients (including calcium)—particularly Crohn's disease, colitis, and diverticulitis—also predispose you to a greater risk. Osteoporosis carries a strong familial link and, although you cannot choose your parents, forewarned is forearmed. The best home remedy is prevention.

OUTSIDE HELP

ALEXANDER TECHNIQUE: the body alignment achieved by practicing the Technique will help toward the desired quality of weight-bearing and ease in all activities.

REFLEXOLOGY: great care should be taken when handling the feet or hands. It is, however, possible that reflexology treatment may benefit this condition.

YOGA: most yoga postures are weight-bearing, so practice daily to strengthen your bones. Be sensible and avoid postures such as Headstand, which might cause you to fall and hurt yourself.

CONVENTIONAL MEDICINE

To avoid the risk of osteoporosis, encourage children to take regular weight-bearing exercise and drink plenty of milk. Calcium and vitamin D supplements are also recommended in older women, either through the diet or prescribed tablets. Avoid smoking and excessive alcohol consumption. HRT prevents osteoporosis and can be taken at any stage after menopause, usually for at least five years. If osteoporosis is already present, it can be treated with prescribed drugs. Try to continue taking regular exercise to improve muscle tone and bulk.

HOMEOPATHIC REMEDIES

In homeopathy the patient is treated according to the symptoms that the body produces. As a disease, osteoporosis does not have symptoms until a fracture occurs, so there are no specific remedies for this ailment.

EXERCISE

WEIGHT-BEARING exercise throughout life is essential as part of the mechanism that builds strong bones. Lack of exercise by today's school children and the virtual absence of it in the lives of most young women predicts an appalling picture of pain, suffering and disability by the time they reach their sixties. Walking, golf, tennis, badminton, bowling, ballroom or disco dancing—in fact, any activity (even gardening or strenuous housework) that keeps you on your feet and moving for an hour or so, three or four times a week—is a great insurance policy.

Apart from the benefit to your bones, regular physical activity builds strong muscles, which help to keep you fit, active, and mobile well into old age. The more you do, the more you will be able to do and the less likely you will be to develop osteoporosis.

CAUTION

Though exercise is vital, it is important to be aware of the risks of excessive exercise. Many women, while not being anorexic, strive to maintain ridiculously low weights through intensive exercise. This often leads to the cessation of periods and an artificial menopause—the greatest of all risks for osteoporosis.

HERBAL REMEDIES

 Herbs rich in minerals, vitamins, and steroidal compounds are generally recommended to combat bone loss in old age and can make an important contribution to dietary needs.

■ **Use and Dosage:**
Drink a daily tea containing stinging nettles, alfalfa, and sage (2tsp/10ml per cup) and take 2tsp/10ml of horsetail juice in water three times daily.

Chinese angelica (Dang Gui) also provides nourishment and is becoming more widely available in tablets from health-food stores.

AROMATHERAPY

❧ FENNEL
Foeniculum vulgare
❧ ROSEMARY
Rosmarinus officinalis
❧ BLACK PEPPER
Piper nigrum
❧ LAVENDER
Lavandula angustifolia
❧ ROMAN CHAMOMILE
Chamaemelum nobile
❧ MARJORAM
Origanum majorana

❧ BENZOIN
Styrax benzoin
These oils are warming, soothing, and anti-inflammatory. Fennel contains plant estrogens.

Application:
Use in baths, in foot baths or in bowls of warm water. They can also be massaged in. Do not use rosemary or fennel oil if you have high blood pressure or epilepsy.

NUTRITION

 The key to avoiding osteoporosis is building strong bones from the teens onward, but unfortunately this is also the time when many girls get on the treadmill of dieting and weight loss—a treadmill they often stay on until their forties and fifties. Having a low calcium intake in the early years is almost a guarantee of having problem bones later on. The average woman who is modestly active needs around 2,000 calories per day; it is impossible to get all the nutrients you need to build strong bones on very low-calorie diets (under 1,250 calories per day).

The diet of all women should be rich in foods that contain calcium, vitamin D, bioflavonoids, vitamin K, and magnesium. For calcium, **eat plenty of** low-fat dairy products, nuts, beans, and canned sardines (with their bones); for vitamin D, eat eggs and oily fish; you will get substantial amounts of vitamin C and bioflavonoids from citrus fruit (eating some of the pith and skin between the segments), blackcurrants, bilberries, blueberries, and blackberries; for vitamin K, eat spinach, broccoli, and cabbage; eat tofu, almonds, and cashews for magnesium.

ABOVE *Blackberries have a very high vitamin C content, and are a good source of calcium and magnesium.*

PREVENTATIVE
measures

Of course it is best to start preventative measures as early as possible, but don't believe the physicians who say it is too late for dietary changes to make any difference to you. You may have to take drugs prescribed by your physician, but even these will work better if you improve your diet and do weight-bearing exercise.

CALCIUM: *avoid anything that increases the risk of excessive elimination, or poor absorption, of calcium. Too much protein, too much sugar, excessive amounts of refined carbohydrates, too much salt, overindulgence in alcohol, and vast amounts of soft drinks all increase the body's loss of calcium. Large amounts of bran interfere with its absorption. Smoking and the oxalic acid in rhubarb have the same effect. Caffeine also increases calcium loss, so tea and coffee should be drunk in modest amounts.*

VITAMIN D: *without sufficient vitamin D, the body cannot absorb enough calcium. During the summer, vitamin D is manufactured in the body by the effect of ultraviolet light from the sun on the skin. Today we are rightly concerned about the risks of sunbathing and skin cancer, but there is a happy medium: early-morning, late-afternoon, and evening exposure to the sun is quite safe, particularly in the spring and fall (and even in the summer in most parts of the world). It is the gray months of winter that are a problem. This is when you need to eat more oily fish and take a good vitamin D and calcium supplement.*

HRT: *Hormone Replacement Therapy is now big news, but there are many women who either cannot, or do not want to, take it (see Menopause on p.172).*

RIGHT *Rheumatism is the lay person's term for general aches and pains in muscles and joints, which may be accompanied by stiffness. Most people will suffer from rheumatism by the time they are in their seventies.*

DIAGNOSING RHEUMATISM
● Aching joints or muscles

BONES AND MUSCLES

rheumatism

R heumatism is a vague and general term that describes painful problems affecting muscles, tendons, and connective tissue—often, but not always, surrounding joints—but it is not a specific disease. RSI (see p.98), tennis elbow, frozen shoulder, and tendonitis are just some of the disorders that can be grouped together under the broad heading of rheumatism. Even fibrositis is part of this collection. None of them is linked to osteoarthritis or rheumatoid arthritis. Your physician may offer you anti-inflammatory drugs or even steroid injections, but there are home remedies that may be just as effective. Unless you are in severe pain, try these first, as none of them has any side-effects.

CALL THE PHYSICIAN
■ If your symptoms persist for longer than 3–4 weeks.

KITCHEN MEDICINE
■ Cold compresses and ice packages can be particularly effective and should be applied to the painful area following the directions given under RSI (*see p.98*).

■ Celery seeds increase the body's elimination of uric acid, which can aggravate the inflamed tissues, so use them liberally in cooking. Beware celery salt, however; it does contain celery, but also has a high salt content, which encourages fluid retention and will make painful joints even worse.

CELERY SEEDS

CONVENTIONAL MEDICINE

✚ Often resting for a few days, followed by gentle stretching exercises, is all that is required. A warm hot-water bottle or an ice package can help. Some people find that a firm supportive bandage provides enormous relief. Take pain-relievers as required. Your physician may want to arrange for further investigations if the symptoms persist.

Dosage information ~
Adults
■ Take one to two tablets of pain-reliever at onset of pain, repeated every 4 hours; see package for details.
Children
■ Give regular doses of liquid pain-reliever; see package for details, or follow medical advice.

EXERCISE

EXERCISES ARE a vital part of restoring your affected tissues to normal. Any general activity that does not increase pain levels is fine, but you really need to get specific guidance from an osteopath or physiotherapist before trying to exercise affected muscles, tendons, or joints.

HERBAL REMEDIES

 Anti-inflammatory rubs (such as 5 drops of chamomile essence in 1tsp/5ml of infused St.-John's-wort oil) can be helpful for conditions like tennis elbow or frozen shoulder. Rheumatism may respond to cleansing teas, which remove accumulated toxins in the tissues.

■ **Use and Dosage:**
Try an infusion of bogbean, meadowsweet, and yarrow leaves (2tsp/10ml), which you have flavored with a little lemon juice.

Warm compresses can also help: soak a cloth in cramp-bark and angelica decoction, reheating the mix and resoaking as necessary.

HOMEOPATHIC REMEDIES

 If the following remedies do not help, then consult a qualified homeopath. *(See also Arthritis on p.104 and Osteoarthritis on p.106.)*

🜍 COLCHICUM **6C** For severe inflammation of joints, with severe pain. Person is irritable. Worse for any motion. May affect several joints at once, or move from left to right side of the body. Worse at night. Also used for gout.

🜍 RANUNCULUS BULBOSUS **6C** For neck stiffness, especially of left scapula. Fibrositis. Worse for cold and damp.

🜍 DULCAMARA **6C** For stiff and painful joints. Worse in the fall, for cold and damp, getting wet. Better for moving, dry weather. May also have diarrhea.

Dosage: one tablet three times daily. Maximum 2 weeks.

AROMATHERAPY

 🜍 LAVENDER
Lavandula angustifolia

🜍 ROMAN CHAMOMILE
Chamaemelum nobile

🜍 JUNIPER
Juniperus communis

🜍 MARJORAM
Origanum majorana

🜍 GINGER
Zingiber officinale

🜍 BENZOIN
Styrax benzoin

🜍 ROSEMARY
Rosmarinus officinalis

You may find that some of these oils are more beneficial to you than others—so experiment until you find the oils that work best.

Application:
Use in the bath, or in a compress over the affected area. Benzoin is not particularly effective in the bath, as it sits on the bottom in little globules. You can also use

ABOVE *Roman chamomile.*

these oils in a massage medium, but never massage over swollen and inflamed joints—instead, massage over the affected area between flare-ups.

CAUTION

Do not use rosemary oil if you have high blood pressure or epilepsy.

NUTRITION

 Follow exactly the same nutritional guidelines as are given for arthritis *(see p.104)*.

Eat plenty of oily fish and all the powerful antioxidant foods, which are rich in vitamins A, C, and E and in the minerals zinc and selenium.

Avoid foods that will aggravate your inflammation, like red meat, and those likely to increase your levels of uric acid, such as offal, yeast, yeast extracts, meat extracts, roe, taramasalata and even caviar; avoid all red and fortified wines, and be modest in your consumption of other forms of alcohol. Don't drink more than one or two cups of coffee a day.

OUTSIDE HELP

ACUPRESSURE: this depends largely on where your problem is and it is important that you get detailed instructions from a qualified acupuncturist.
REFLEXOLOGY: work the reflex of the area affected. Work all eliminatory channels, and the lymphatic system.
Work the cross-reflexes *(see Osteoarthritis on p.106)*. Very gentle work over the small joints may reduce pain and swelling.
YOGA: practice with great awareness of all affected joints: see how far you can move them without pain. Emphasize opening, stretching movements, such as Arm Raising, Warrior, Two-Foot Support, and Cobra.

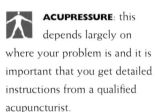

LEFT Arm Raising and (RIGHT) Warrior. One position leads naturally to the other. Benefits shoulders, elbows, and knees.

BELOW The Two-Foot Support aids hip and knee flexibility, and strengthens the back.

BELOW The Cobra helps preserve mobility and strength in the spine, improving posture and freeing the chest.

PREVENTATIVE *measures*

NUTRITION: *if your normal diet is deficient in the vitamins A, C, and E and the minerals zinc and selenium, there is a greater chance that you may develop some form of rheumatism. Following the nutritional guidelines for arthritis (see p.104) and taking a daily supplement of these essential nutrients will give you added protection against rheumatism and many other diseases besides.*

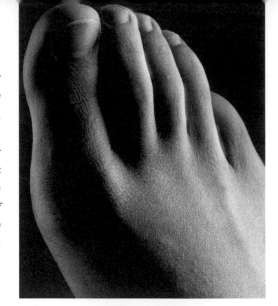

RIGHT *Cold weather or pressure on the skin, or a combination of the two, causes chilblains. The inflammation lasts for 2 or 3 weeks. Prevent chilblains by wearing warm gloves, a couple of pairs of socks, thick trousers, and a woolly hat.*

DIAGNOSING CHILBLAINS

- Painful, itchy, dark red swellings
- Often affect the fingers and toes, but can also affect the ears, cheeks, and nose

CIRCULATORY SYSTEM

chilblains

CALL THE PHYSICIAN

■ If a chilblain begins to ulcerate.

These sore, itching, inflamed, and frequently swollen patches of skin occur most commonly on the backs of the fingers or tops of the toes. Sometimes they crop up on the ears, outer thighs, and other parts of the body that are subject to cold and/or pressure. The cause is restriction of the circulating blood supply in the capillaries—the tiniest blood vessels at the very end of the system—leading to lack of oxygen and nutrients, and consequent cell damage. Prevention is the only cure.

EXERCISE

REGULAR physical exercise is essential to improve the efficiency of the whole circulatory system.

KITCHEN MEDICINE

■ Cut a thick slice of lemon, dip it in coarse sea salt, and rub over the surface of the chilblain— but only if the skin is not broken or cracked.

CONVENTIONAL MEDICINE

Avoid chilblains, or frostbite, by wrapping up warmly in cold weather. Several thinner layers can be more effective than one thick one. Once developed, a chilblain may take several weeks to recover. Take pain-relievers if required.
Dosage information ~
Adults
■ Take one to two tablets of pain-reliever at onset of pain, repeated every 4 hours.

Children
■ Give regular doses of liquid pain-reliever; consult package for details or follow medical advice.

RIGHT *Winter can be fun, but make sure your children are well protected.*

OUTSIDE HELP

REFLEXOLOGY: working the fingers and toes will stimulate the blood supply to these areas and help to prevent chilblains. Avoid the chilblains themselves—work the cross-reflex instead (the corresponding finger or toe on the same side).
YOGA: do all you can to improve circulation to the feet. Be particularly aware of them when you practice, especially in inverted postures. Massage them gently last thing at night and in the morning.

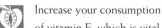

HERBAL REMEDIES

 For habitual sufferers, circulation can be improved by teas containing prickly ash bark, ginger, cinnamon twigs or angelica root.

■ **Use and Dosage:**
Simmer 1tsp/5ml of dried herb—singly or in combination—with 2 cups of water for 10 minutes; add a dash of cayenne powder before drinking.

Cayenne cream can ease discomfort, or try compresses or foot baths using oak-bark decoction.

Topical itching can be eased with arnica (do not use if the skin is broken), *Aloe vera* or marigold creams.

ABOVE *Angelica root is a warming herb for the blood circulation.*

AROMATHERAPY

🌿 GERANIUM
Pelargonium graveolens
🌿 BLACK PEPPER
Piper nigrum
🌿 LAVENDER
Lavandula angustifolia
These oils are warming, soothing, increase the circulation, and have a slight painkilling effect.

Application:
Rub the oils, blended with either a carrier oil or a lotion, vigorously into the chilblains. Do this only to unbroken chilblains. In the long term you should be looking

at improving your circulation, either by massaging your feet or by using oils in the bath or in a foot bath. As well as geranium and black pepper, you could use rosemary, lemon grass, ginger, or marjoram for this purpose. All these oils are warming and stimulating to the circulation.

CAUTION

Anybody who has high blood pressure or epilepsy should avoid using rosemary oil.

HOMEOPATHIC REMEDIES

 The application of Tamus ointment is often soothing for chilblains.
🌿 AGARICUS **6C** For burning, itching and redness that is worse for cold.
🌿 PULSATILLA **6C** For bluish discoloration of skin, sharp pains worse for warmth. Person may be weepy.
🌿 PETROLEUM **6C** For burning chilblains that itch, skin cracks.

🌿 PLANTAGO **6C**
For skin that itches and burns and is sensitive.
Dosage: one tablet three times daily. Maximum 2 weeks.

PLANTAIN
(*PLANTAGO MAJOR*)

ABOVE *The homeopathic remedy made from the greater plantain is recommended for healing sore, inflamed skin.*

NUTRITION

Increase your consumption of vitamin E, which is vital for healthy blood vessels, by **eating plenty of** avocados, all nuts and seeds, and olive oil; buckwheat (added to bread, cake, or cookie recipes, or as pancakes) for its rutin content; citrus fruit, blackcurrants, cherries, and blueberries for their vitamin C and bioflavonoids, which are essential

nutrients for effective peripheral circulation.

One unit of alcohol per day for women (two for men) will help open up the tiniest blood vessels But be warned: larger amounts of alcohol have the opposite effect and make chilblains worse. Caffeine in any form is a vasoconstrictor and reduces blood supply, as does nicotine.

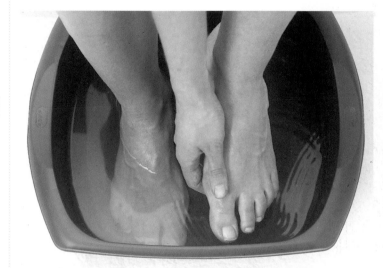

ABOVE *For chilblains on the toes, bathe the feet in hot water followed by cold water (for 5 minutes each) to boost circulation.*

PREVENTATIVE *measures*

CLOTHING: *keep hands and feet warm with thin cotton gloves and socks, covered by thicker woollen or fur-lined gloves and boots. Make sure that gloves, socks and shoes/boots are large enough—there should be at least 1in/2.5cm of clear space between the end of the toe and the shoe/boot, and ¹/₂in/1.2cm for gloves.*

NUTRITION: *take a daily dose of 400 IU of vitamin E and 1g of vitamin C with bioflavonoids. Also take a B-complex that includes nicotinic acid.*

BATHING: *contrast bathing of the affected areas with alternate hot and cold water for 5 minutes, at least once a day, stimulates the blood flow.*

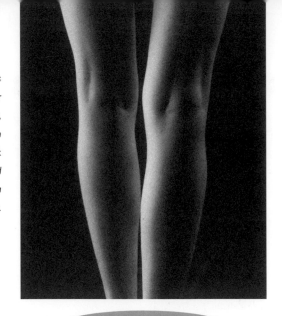

DIAGNOSING VARICOSE VEINS

- Often there are no symptoms, apart from their unsightly appearance
- Veins may ache after standing for long periods of time

CIRCULATORY SYSTEM

varicose veins

CALL THE PHYSICIAN

■ If the skin starts to ulcerate over or near a varicose vein.

KITCHEN MEDICINE

■ The cheapest and most abundant ingredient in any kitchen is water, which makes one of the finest home remedies. Fill a large plastic bucket with comfortably hot water and a second bucket with 4in/10cm of shingle and cold water. Stand in the hot bucket for 30 seconds, then stomp up and down in the cold bucket for 10 seconds. Repeat for 10 minutes every day to stimulate the blood flow and strengthen the muscles of the vein walls.

■ If you have a varicose ulcer, then a dressing of sterile gauze spread with thick organic honey will aid healing.

*V*aricose veins are visible, often raised, unsightly, and painful distended veins that commonly appear in the legs, although they can also occur in the walls of the rectum (see Hemorrhoids on p.176). Though they are generally hereditary, they are frequently made worse by pregnancy, obesity, lack of exercise, jobs that involve prolonged standing, a sedentary lifestyle and by constipation. If they become chronic, the skin condition of varicose eczema may develop, and poor blood supply to the skin may result in severe ulcers from the most minor knocks and bumps.

CONVENTIONAL MEDICINE

✚ For varicose veins in the legs, a well-fitting supportive elastic stocking that includes a heel, worn all day, may improve the symptoms. Surgical treatment may relieve them, although they may recur.

LEFT *Organic honey has healing properties.*

HOMEOPATHIC REMEDIES

❦ VIPERA 6C For swollen, sensitive varicose veins, with bursting pains. Also phlebitis.

❦ HAMAMELIS 6C For varicose veins that feel bruised and sore. Veins large, blue. Varicose veins in pregnancy.

❦ PULSATILLA 6C For legs that feel heavy. Varicose veins itchy in warmth.

❦ FLUORICUM ACIDUM 6C For painful varicose veins. Varicose ulcers with red edges.

❦ FERRUM METALLICUM 6C For varicose veins during pregnancy. **Dosage**: one tablet twice daily until improved, or for 10 days. May be repeated.

HERBAL REMEDIES

 Herbs like buckwheat, which is rich in rutin, can be used to strengthen the veins, while melilot, horse chestnut, motherwort, prickly ash, or yarrow can be used to improve the circulation, combat any tendency to thrombosis, and counter the deposit of fibrin that can cause further damage.

■ **Use and Dosage:**
These herbs can be taken in teas or tinctures (try equal amounts of melilot, motherwort, or yarrow, for example).

Externally, distilled witch hazel or horse chestnut ointment can be used in gentle massage.

EXERCISE

EXERCISE IS vital, and any activity that you enjoy will pay huge dividends by improving the circulation in your legs. Walking, cycling, ball games, swimming, or any other activity will do, as long as you do it at least three times a week.

If you have to stand for long periods, then shifting your weight from heel to toe, walking for a few seconds on your toes and then on your heels, constantly wriggling your toes, flexing your feet, and tightening and relaxing your calf muscles will all help to keep the blood coursing through your veins and arteries.

ABOVE *Cycling exercises the legs, while avoiding the need to bear body weight.*

AROMATHERAPY

❀ CYPRESS
Cupressus sempervirens
❀ GERANIUM
Pelargonium graveolens
These oils are stimulating and increase the circulation.
Application:
Put the essential oils into a carrier oil or lotion that can be massaged above the varicose veins—never over the veins. A warm compress can be placed on the vein if it is very painful and throbbing, but never massage below or over the vein—this just puts more pressure onto an already overloaded area. Putting your legs higher than your head for at least 10 minutes twice a day will also help.

Avoid constipation, as this simply puts even more pressure on the veins (*see p.156*).

NUTRITION

Avocado is packed with vitamin E

Eggs are rich in zinc

Buckwheat contains rutin, which strengthens blood vessels

ABOVE *Prepare meals which include an abundance of foods that are known to improve blood circulation.*

If you already have varicose veins, your nutrition should be improved to provide an abundance of nutrients that are beneficial to the circulation. Eat buckwheat—as pancakes, or added to bread or cookie recipes, for its rutin, a bioflavonoid that specifically strengthens blood vessels.

Eat plenty of avocados, olive oil, and all the nuts and seeds for their vitamin E; liver, sardines, eggs, shellfish, and pumpkin seeds for their zinc; and citrus fruit, black-currants, blackberries, blueberries, bilberries, and dark red cherries for their bioflavonoids and vitamin C.

OUTSIDE HELP

REFLEXOLOGY: circulation in the legs and pelvis can be generally improved by foot reflexology. Pressure to the feet can be brisk and firm, but do not work over-prominent veins. Cover the whole of both feet every 3–4 days.

YOGA: any postures that raise the feet above the hips will help. Modify the Relaxation Posture at the end of your practice by resting your legs over a chair, or up against the wall. Then massage, with slow sweeping movements, from the feet upward.

PREVENTATIVE *measures*

The major preventative step is to avoid constipation (*see p.156*)—plenty of fluid and the right kind of fiber are the key. Make lifestyle changes to control your weight and minimize the other causative physical factors.

DIET: *smoking, excessive amounts of caffeine and alcohol all have an adverse effect on the heart and blood vessels, thus reducing the efficiency of the circulatory system. A high salt intake encourages fluid retention, swelling, and high blood pressure, while refined carbohydrates and too much sugar lead to constipation and weight gain.*

RIGHT *Restless legs are an annoying disturbance just as you are drifting off to sleep, when the legs twitch for no apparent reason.*

RIGHT *Restless legs are an annoying disturbance just as you are drifting off to sleep, when the legs twitch for no apparent reason.*

DIAGNOSING RESTLESS LEGS

- Burning, weakness, or numbness, or jerky movements in the legs
- Commonly occurs in women just before going to sleep or soon after sitting down

CIRCULATORY SYSTEM

restless legs

CALL THE PHYSICIAN

■ If you suddenly start suffering from this problem and the condition is severe and intractable.

*S*ymptoms of this usually minor, but nonetheless unpleasant, problem start as soon as you sit down or go to bed. An uncontrollable need to move the legs, jerky spasms of the leg muscles, and uncomfortable feelings deep within them are part-and-parcel of restless legs syndrome. It may be caused by prescribed drugs or possibly by a problem in the central nervous system, but both these situations are rare. More often it is a symptom of iron-deficiency anemia or caused by circulation problems, although sometimes it occurs for no apparent reason.

CONVENTIONAL MEDICINE

✚ Restless legs are occasionally due to an iron deficiency, which can be treated easily with iron supplements.

LEFT *The remedy Tarantula hispanica is made from tarantula spiders pickled in alcohol. This remedy is often prescribed for hyperactivity.*

HOMEOPATHIC REMEDIES

❧ ZINCUM 6C For twitching, constant movement of feet night and day.

❧ CAUSTICUM 6C For restless legs during sleep, twitching. Excitable people.

❧ TARANTULA 6C For restless feet and legs in bed, with weakness and numbness. Restless sleep. Legs restless in evening and before going to bed.

❧ RHUS TOXICODENDRON 6C For aches in legs. Worse for initial movement. Better for continued movement. Legs often restless in bed at night.

Dosage: one tablet three times daily. Maximum 2 weeks or until improved.

EXERCISE

THOUGH ANY physical activity improves circulation to the lower limbs, there is no specific evidence that it will help relieve restless legs. Anecdotally, however, many patients have told me that taking a brisk walk before bedtime seems to improve the situation.

HERBAL REMEDIES

 Teas to soothe and relax the nerves are worth trying, especially chamomile, lemon balm, skullcap, vervain, and passionflower. If the problem is severe at night, it is worth bathing the legs in cramp-bark decoction or massaging a little cream containing the herb into the legs before going to bed.

■ **Use and Dosage:**
1–2 drops of chamomile, rose, or lavender oil in 1tsp/5ml of almond oil also makes a good massage.

ABOVE *A bedtime massage with fragrant, relaxing oils may inhibit the syndrome.*

AROMATHERAPY

 LEMON GRASS
Cymbopogon citratus
Lemon grass is good for stimulating poor circulation.
Application:
Use lemon grass in a bowl of warm water or a foot spa, or add the essential oil to a lotion or carrier oil, to make a medium that can be massaged into the legs. Treatment can be carried out two or three times a day, if practical. This condition is usually worse at bedtime, so that is probably the best time to apply it. Make sure that your legs are raised regularly, so in the evenings put your feet up; you may also find that putting a book under the end of the bed just to raise it slightly will help.

① Put 4–6 drops of lemon grass essential oil into a carrier oil, such as sweet almond.

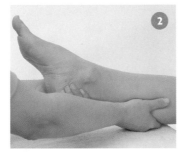
② Give a relaxing massage to the legs and feet, which will stimulate the circulation.

OUTSIDE HELP

REFLEXOLOGY: it is possible to apply reflexology to the feet to relax the muscles.
YOGA: emphasize postures such as Upward Raised Legs, plus Shoulderstand and Headstand if these are appropriate. Rest with your feet higher than your hips— against a wall, or over a chair. Massage the feet and legs with upward, flowing movements.

NUTRITION

Follow the advice given for anemia (*see p.118*); even if this is not the cause of your problem, it is a healthy way to eat.

In order to improve blood flow to the legs, it is also important that you have a high intake of vitamin E, vitamin C, and bioflavonoids.

Eat plenty of avocados, sunflower, safflower or olive oils, nuts, seeds, and dark green leafy vegetables for their vitamin E; dark-colored berries for their vitamin C and bioflavonoids. It is also useful to use buckwheat flour in your cooking—make pancakes from it and add it to bread, pastry and cookie recipes—as this valuable member of the rhubarb family contains rutin, a natural substance that strengthens blood-vessel walls. And do not forget to use loads of garlic in your cooking, which improves blood flow by reducing the stickiness of blood and thus the risk of clotting.

Very small amounts of alcohol do improve the circulation, but anything more than one drink an evening does exactly the opposite. Caffeine and nicotine also act as vasoconstrictors, closing up the smallest blood vessels situated at the end of the system and reducing the blood flow. So do not smoke, and drink tea and coffee only in reasonable quantities.

> **KITCHEN MEDICINE**
> ■ Chili, ginger, and horseradish all help to stimulate the circulation and improve blood flow. Using these herbs liberally in your cooking can help relieve the symptoms of this irritating condition.

ABOVE *Garlic is helpful for the circulation.*

PREVENTATIVE *measures*

It is very difficult to prevent a condition for which there is not always an obvious cause. Making sure that your diet is rich in all the iron-containing foods and vitamin C, and staying physically active, are the best things you can do.

DIAGNOSING ANEMIA

- Tiredness
- Pale skin
- Shortness of breath on mild exertion
- Rapid heart rate and palpitations
- Swollen ankles
- Feeling of faintness

CIRCULATORY SYSTEM

anemia

A nemia is a condition in which the blood has a reduced ability to absorb oxygen and transport it around the body in the form of hemoglobin. This may occur because insufficient haemoglobin is being produced or because it is being destroyed prematurely. Around 90 percent of all cases are the result of iron deficiency, and heavy or prolonged periods, blood loss from ulcers, piles, or gum disease are all likely causes. Many women of childbearing age are iron-deficient, but poor diet, deficiencies of folic acid and vitamin B_{12}, leukemia, sickle cell anemia, and thalassemia are comparatively rare causes. Vegetarians and pregnant women are vulnerable to anemia. Dietary improvement is nearly always the answer, particularly for vegetarians and vegans.

CALL THE PHYSICIAN

■ If you think you are anemic.

KITCHEN MEDICINE

■ Nettle soup and dandelion leaves added to salads are unusual but effective ways of getting lots of extra iron. You can also make both into tea, by adding 1 tsp/5ml of chopped leaves to a cup of boiling water.

■ Add parsley, chives, lovage, fennel, watercress, and elderberries to salads and fruit dishes.

CONVENTIONAL MEDICINE

Because there are several different types of anemia, you should consult your physician before taking any treatment. Often a course of iron tablets is all that is required, but some kinds of anemia do not need any treatment, and iron may even make the condition worse. Your physician may need to arrange for a blood test to be done before advising you. Pregnant women often need iron and folic acid supplements.

Dosage information ~

Adults and children

■ Usually take 1 iron tablet a day; see package for details. Be aware that iron often causes constipation.

ABOVE *Pregnant women often become anemic.*

NUTRITION

Always eat vitamin C-rich foods together with those containing iron, in order to improve absorption. For vegetarians a traditional vegetable curry cooked in a cast-iron container is an excellent source of iron that is well absorbed. In severe cases of anemia, food sources are not sufficient and supplements will form an essential part of your recovery.

Eat plenty of organ meat for its vitamin B$_{12}$; meat, green vegetables, watercress, legumes, whole grain cereals, molasses, dried fruits, cashew nuts, wheatgerm, tomato paste, yeast extracts, and brewer's yeast for their iron and folic acid.

ABOVE *Black pudding, made from pigs' blood, is rich in iron.*

LEFT *The vegetables in a curry will absorb iron from the cooking vessel if cooked in a cast-iron container.*

HERBAL REMEDIES

Many plants are rich in minerals and nutrients and can therefore be helpful for iron-deficient anemia: those plants said to "rob the soil"—such as stinging nettles, and parsley—are especially rich in iron. Bitter herbs (like gentian) will improve the digestion and mineral absorption.

■ **Use and Dosage:**
Make a tonic by steeping 3 cups/100g each of stinging nettle, Chinese angelica (Dang Gui), and dandelion root in 2pt/1*l* of red wine for 2 weeks; strain and drink one sherry glass per day.

Echinacea (2 x 200mg capsules daily) can help stimulate red blood-cell production.

ABOVE *Yellow gentian root stimulates a sluggish digestive system, to aid the absorption of essential nutrients.*

PREVENTATIVE
measures

Most anemia is self-induced by careless or faddy eating. The majority of women with this complaint are iron-deficient. Improve your eating habits and you can wave goodbye to the draining symptoms of exhaustion, lethargy, constipation, restlessness, headaches, irritability, and lack of concentration.

DIET: *eat well and regularly, including all the foods listed below and under Nutrition. Avoid restrictive weight-loss diets or any other nutritional regime that seems extreme. Exclusion diets should only be carried out under professional supervision, and in my experience the so-called "Candida diet" inevitably does more harm than good.*

ANTI-NUTRIENTS: *uncooked bran, tea, coffee, cola drinks, and chocolate can all interfere with your absorption of iron, so keep these to a minimum and eat or drink them separately from iron sources.*

PRO-NUTRIENTS: *iron absorption is greatly improved in the presence of vitamin C, so eat tomatoes with your omelet, half a grapefruit before your boiled egg, and a large mixed salad with your steak or liver.*

SUPER IRON: *some surprising foods are extremely rich in iron and should be eaten in great abundance: fresh dates and unsalted cashew nuts (twice as much iron as steak), as well as watercress, stinging nettles, dandelion leaves, parsley, lovage, chives, and fennel.*

LEFT *Iron-rich foods: dates, watercress, and cashew nuts. Make an iron-clad salad!*

HOMEOPATHIC REMEDIES

The cause of anemia should be established before trying homeopathic treatment and the remedies should be used together with efforts to treat the cause. A consultation with a qualified homeopath, who may work in conjunction with your physician, is suggested.
☙ FERRUM METALLICUM **6C** For person who appears strong, flushed, has cold hands and feet, but feels weak after any effort. Hammering headache. Flushes easily from pain or emotions. Ringing in the ears before periods. Anemia due to heavy periods.

☙ CALCAREA PHOSPHORICA **6C** For children who are growing rapidly. Anemia after illness. Person dissatisfied with life and always looking for something new. Tends to be irritable.

☙ CHINA **6C** For anemia from blood loss. Feels weak, sensitive, and nervous. Easily upset and feels chilly.
Dosage: one tablet twice daily. Maximum 2 weeks.

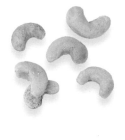

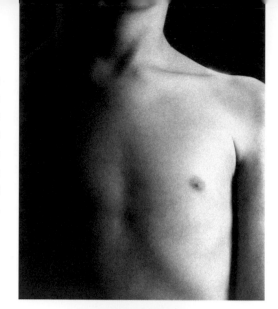

RIGHT *Hiccups can be embarrassing or give you a fit of the giggles. The spasm of the diaphragm that causes them is often brought on by too much food or drink, swallowed too quickly.*

DIAGNOSING HICCUPS

- Sudden intake of breath associated with a characteristic sound and sensation, often repeated several times before stopping

RESPIRATORY SYSTEM

hiccups

*I*t is a sudden spasm of the diaphragm that causes a hiccup, but this spasm is triggered by irritation of the major nerve that supplies this muscle. The diaphragm contracts suddenly, making you breathe in quickly. This breath is interrupted by your throat closing suddenly, which makes the characteristic hiccup sound. Hiccups usually come in clusters and an attack may last anything from a minute or so to an hour or two, or even months. Attacks are nearly always the result of indigestion, overeating, rushing through a meal, or consuming large quantities of soft drinks—when the gas distends the stomach, which presses against the underside of the diaphragm, thereby causing irritation. Surprisingly, even medical textbooks suggest the traditional remedy of the cold key down the back or drinking from the wrong side of a glass as possible cures.

CAUTION

Hiccups may sometimes be a sign of underlying and serious disease—liver abscess, chronic kidney failure, or even a symptom in the later stages of severe cancer.

KITCHEN MEDICINE

■ Eat 2tsp/10ml of granulated sugar or try a dose of babies' gripe water—its main constituent is dill, which helps settle the stomach if the hiccups are caused by indigestion.

CONVENTIONAL MEDICINE

Virtually everyone has the occasional attack of hiccups, and they can even occur in babies in the womb. In most cases there is no obvious cause, but if the diaphragm is irritated by something, such as an abnormally swollen stomach, the hiccups can be persistent. Most hiccups stop within a few minutes; if they persist, you should consult your physician, who may prescribe a drug to relax the diaphragm.

ABOVE *Even an unborn baby may give its mother a start by an attack of hiccups.*

AROMATHERAPY

 ❧ LAVENDER
Lavandula angustifolia
Lavender is calming and soothing.
Application:
Put a drop of lavender in the bottom of a brown paper bag, then place the bag over the mouth and nose, and breathe in and out, slowly and deeply. This slows and deepens the breathing, calms the diaphragm, and will stop the hiccups. Or you could use frankincense instead.

ABOVE *The essential oil extracted from lavender is anti-convulsive and has a mild sedative effect.*

NUTRITION

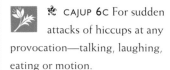 It is not really what you eat, but *how* you eat that is important. Make sure that you chew your food well, that you sit down to eat, take your time, and always have a glass of water with your meals.

Avoid excessive amounts of carbonated drinks (mineral water included). This is particularly important when travelling by air, as the pressure differential between the inside of your body and the atmosphere in the cabin forces gases out of the drinks and causes abdominal distension. This is uncomfortable and a common cause of hiccups.

HOMEOPATHIC REMEDIES

❧ CAJUP **6C** For sudden attacks of hiccups at any provocation—talking, laughing, eating or motion.
❧ RANUNCULUS BULBOSIS. **6C** For hiccups associated with drinking alcohol; hiccups when drunk.
❧ IGNATIA **6C** For hiccups from emotional causes. Hiccups and burping when eating, drinking, or smoking. Empty sensation in the stomach.
❧ CYCLAMEN **6C** For hiccup-like burping. Worse for fatty food. Hiccups during pregnancy or while yawning.
❧ HYOSCYAMUS **6C** For hiccups after eating.
❧ NUX VOMICA **6C** For hiccups from overeating or -drinking.
Dosage: one tablet every 30 minutes until improved. Maximum 12 doses.

OUTSIDE HELP

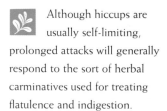 **ACUPRESSURE**: point 43 on the ring finger is a good one to try. If it works, it is instant.

ABOVE *Point 43 lies on the Small Intestine meridian, which runs from the neck, down the arm, to the fingertips.*

HERBAL REMEDIES

Although hiccups are usually self-limiting, prolonged attacks will generally respond to the sort of herbal carminatives used for treating flatulence and indigestion.
■ **Use and Dosage**:
Sip peppermint or fennel infusion, or take 2–3 drops of cinnamon or clove oil on a lump of sugar.

Eating papaw fruit or juice, or chewing candied ginger, can also help.

PREVENTATIVE *measures*

Follow the eating rules given under *Nutrition*.

EXERCISE

HERE IS A simple exercise, which may help stop an attack of hiccups. ① Lie on your back on the floor with your knees bent.

② Bring your knees up, and, with your hands, pull them toward your chest as hard as you can.

③ Hold for a count of three. Relax and repeat several times. This puts pressure on the underside of the diaphragm, and may stop the spasms.

RIGHT *Catarrh is mucus in the nose, throat, and chest caused by infection, allergy, or irritation of the mucous membranes. Consult your physician if the catarrh contains blood, or persists for longer than a month.*

DIAGNOSING CATARRH

- Excessive amounts of thick mucus in the nose and throat
- Blocked or runny nose

RESPIRATORY SYSTEM

catarrh

I rritation of the mucous membranes in the nose and throat, or allergic reactions, can cause an increase in the amount of mucus produced by these tissues. Viral or bacterial infections can also produce the same reaction and, if the sinuses become congested and infected, this can lead to sinusitis (see p.130).

KITCHEN MEDICINE

■ Mix one-third beet juice with two-thirds tepid water and take two or three sniffs of the mixture through each nostril, sniffing hard enough to force the juice into the back of the throat. Then spit it out. This sounds revolting but it's not too bad after the first sniff and the beet juice is gently healing and antiseptic. Do not use your favorite linen or embroidered handkerchief for at least 2 hours after the treatment, unless you want it stained red; stick to paper tissues.

CONVENTIONAL MEDICINE

Catarrh, or nasal congestion, will improve without any treatment, usually within a week or two. However, inhaling steam makes breathing more comfortable, since steam makes mucus thinner and helps to reduce the swelling. Both adults and children can have a steam inhalation as often as is necessary. Decongestants can help too, particularly ones that are sprayed up the nose.

Beware: if continued for more than a week, a nasal decongestant will actually make the nose more stuffy than it was before.

Dosage information ~
Adults and children
■ For steam inhalations, lean over a bowl of boiling water with a towel over your head. You can make this more pleasant by adding eucalyptus or other oils (*see under Aromatherapy*), but the steam itself has most effect on the congestion. Or you can invest in a humidifier; put wet towels on the radiators; or run the hot tap into the bath and sit in the steamy bathroom with your child. Most nasal decongestants are sprayed into the nose at least twice a day.

HERBAL REMEDIES

A combination of astringent and soothing herbs will help clear catarrh and ease inflamed membranes.
Use and Dosage:
Try mixing equal amounts of dried elderflower, eyebright, marshmallow leaves, and ribwort plantain, then use in infusions (2tsp/10ml to a cup of boiling water, four times a day).

Steam inhalants can also help: mix 5 drops each of sandalwood and eucalyptus oils with 1tsp/5ml of friar's balsam (compound tincture of benzoin) in a basin of boiling water and inhale for 10 minutes. If you have a eucalyptus tree in your garden, use a handful of fresh leaves in boiling water instead.

HOMEOPATHIC REMEDIES

 There are many catarrh remedies. If the following do not help, it is advisable to consult a homeopath (*see also Sinusitis on p.130*).

🌿 KALI BICHROMICUM **6C** For thick, ropy, gluey, green, or yellow catarrh. Pressing pain in root of nose. Dry crusts in nose. Worse for hot weather.

🌿 EUCALYPTUS **6C** For stuffed-up nose, chronic catarrh and pus-like discharge.

🌿 PULSATILLA **6C** For stuffed-up nose, white/yellow-green discharge. Better in open air. Loss of smell or foul smell in nose from catarrh. Ears may discharge.

🌿 SAMBUCUS NIGRA **6C** For snuffles in babies, with difficulty suckling.

Dosage: one tablet every 4 hours until condition improves. Maximum 12 doses.

AROMATHERAPY

🌿 EUCALYPTUS
Eucalyptus radiata

🌿 BENZOIN
Styrax benzoin

🌿 BASIL
Ocimum basilicum

🌿 THYME
Thymus vulgaris

These oils relieve congestion and help to fight infection. But if catarrh is due to an allergy, then lavender or chamomile may be more beneficial (*see Allergies on p.22*).

Application:
Steam inhalation and/or facial massage from a therapist for specific pressure points are generally beneficial.

CAUTION

These oils (excluding the lavender and chamomile) are all very strong and should probably not be used for small children.

OUTSIDE HELP

ACUPRESSURE: points 26, 41, 46, and 47 help stimulate the flow of mucus.

REFLEXOLOGY: working the fingers and thumbs, and the spaces between the metacarpal bones located on the backs of the hands, may provide some relief.

YOGA: experiment with both postures and breathing techniques, and do what works best. Sometimes inverted postures like Standing Forward Bend, Dog, and Shoulderstand help; at other times it seems best to avoid them. Likewise, Kapalabhati, Ujjayi, and alternate nostril breathing are

worth trying, but always gently, without strain.

LEFT *The Standing Forward Bend may help to clear passages blocked with catarrh.*

NUTRITION

 Naturopaths believe that a high consumption of dairy products can increase the production of mucus. So cut down on all milk-based foods for a couple of weeks. If you do this for any longer, however, get professional guidance about your diet and about supplements, to prevent calcium and other nutritional deficiencies.

Leeks are rich in sulphur and vitamin C

Chives are a circulatory tonic

Onions strengthen the lungs

Garlic is a decongestant

Scallions are a cleansing antiseptic

Eat plenty of onions, chives, scallions, leeks, and garlic, all traditional foods for the relief of catarrh; sweet potatoes, carrots, broccoli, and red or dark green cabbage for their beta-carotene.

Be sure to add thyme, rosemary, ginger, chilis, and horseradish to all appropriate recipes, as these are decongestants.

ABOVE *Inhaling pungent essential oils will help penetrate stubborn mucus.*

PREVENTATIVE *measures*

Stop smoking and avoid exhaust fumes, chemical smells, and other pollutants that are irritant. Avoid allergens (*see Allergies on p.22*). Blow your nose frequently to reduce the risk of infection, but never block one nostril and blow the other—the increased pressure can force mucus into the Eustachian tube. Regular inhalations over a bowl of boiling water containing 3 drops each of eucalyptus, lavender, and thyme oils will usually help.

RIGHT *Cold symptoms are miserable, affecting head, throat, and chest, and often accompanied by temperature, aches and pains, and a lack of energy. Attack colds positively by boosting the body's immune system.*

DIAGNOSING A COLD

- Fever
- Runny nose
- Sneezing
- Tickly cough
- Sore throat

RESPIRATORY SYSTEM

common cold

CAUTION

Always read pain-reliever packages carefully, and do not exceed the stated dose.

KITCHEN MEDICINE

■ Time and again tests have shown that hot water containing the juice of a lemon and plenty of honey is more soothing and healing than a whole bunch of cold cures added together.

ABOVE *Hot honey and lemon drink.*

There are hundreds of different viruses responsible for the symptoms of a cold, and coughing or sneezing in confined spaces can transmit the virus via infected mucus. The common cold has defied the combined efforts of all the world's physicians, virologists, and other medical experts, and this is one condition for which the old wives' tales often produce the best results. Vast amounts of money are spent worldwide on "over-the-counter" remedies, which at best make little difference and at worst can have serious side-effects. So encourage your body's natural defenses to overcome a cold, by taking plenty of rest, eating nutritiously and enjoying the benefits of steam treatment and other simple home remedies.

CONVENTIONAL MEDICINE

✚ There is no cure for a cold, although there are lots of remedies that alleviate the symptoms (but surprisingly little evidence to support the use of cough medicine). Fever and malaise can be treated with pain-relievers, which often need to be continued on a regular basis for several days until the symptoms subside. Inhalations of steam as often as possible make the mucus thinner, helping to clear the nasal passages and make breathing easier. Babies may need nose drops to enable them to breathe more easily while feeding. Colds usually last between 3 and 10 days.

Dosage information ~
Adults

■ One to two tablets of pain-relievers at onset of fever, then every 4 hours; see package for details.

Children

■ Give regular doses of liquid pain-reliever; consult package for details, or follow advice from your physician.

AROMATHERAPY

🌿 EUCALYPTUS
Eucalyptus radiata
🌿 TEA TREE
Melaleuca alternifolia
🌿 PINE
Pinus sylvestris

Tea tree will make you sweat, which helps to eliminate the virus and make you feel better (make sure that you have a large glass of water before you go to bed, because if you are going to sweat, you need extra fluid). Eucalyptus and pine help to ease stuffiness; at night, you could also add lavender, to help you sleep.

Application:
Use these oils in vaporizers or inhalations (on handkerchiefs, tissues, and bedcovers) to ease that stuffy, congested feeling. In a burner they will help to reduce the risk of secondary infections and alleviate cold symptoms. You can also put these essential oils in the bath, especially at bedtime, using tea-tree oil at the first onset of cold symptoms.

OUTSIDE HELP

ACUPRESSURE: if sinuses become blocked and painful, see Catarrh (p.122).
REFLEXOLOGY: work the fingers and thumbs, the webs between the fingers, the pads beneath the fingers, and the spaces between the metacarpal bones on the back of the hands for the reflexes of the head, lungs, and upper lymphatics.
YOGA: avoid inverted postures. Emphasize backbends such as the Warrior and Cobra. When the nostrils are clear enough, practice Surya Bhedana for 12 breaths followed by Ujjayi.

NUTRITION

Eat plenty of fresh fruit, salads, and raw vegetables; at least two cloves of raw garlic daily—in parts of Eastern Europe they eat a whole bulb of garlic, to kill off the cold virus as well as keeping away the vampires; thick onion soup or oven-baked onions daily (onions and garlic have a very powerful antiseptic and decongestant effect). **Drink plenty of** fluids to replace those lost through sweating and sneezing, but stick mainly to fruit juices, plain water, herbal teas, and the hot water, lemon, and honey mixture (*see Kitchen Medicine*).

Avoid dairy products and all sugary food for 2 or 3 days.

HERBAL REMEDIES

Herbs can ease many symptoms of a cold, and many display antiviral activity to combat the cause.

■ **Use and Dosage:**
A tea that is made from equal parts of elderflower, peppermint (use catmint instead for children), yarrow, and hyssop (1tsp/5ml per cup, taken up to four times daily) will ease chills and coughs.

Gargling with a standard infusion of sage will soothe sore throats; you can improve the flavor with fresh lemon juice.

Use plenty of garlic in cooking and take up to 10 x 200mg echinacea capsules daily, for up to 4 days, in order to boost the immune system.

HOMEOPATHIC REMEDIES

🌿 ACONITE **30c** For first signs of cold. Frequent sneezing, nose stuffed up. Thirsty, worse for stuffy rooms.
🌿 ALLIUM CEPA **30c** For profuse sneezing, streaming eyes and nose. Hot, thirsty, better in fresh air. Nose sore.
🌿 DULCAMARA **30c** For cold from getting chilled when hot. Severe sneezing, eyes red and sore. Sore throat. Neck stiff and pains in limbs.
🌿 NATRUM MURIATICUM **30c** For cold that begins with sneezing. Discharge from nose, like the white of an egg. Nose may also be blocked. Cold sores, mouth ulcers and cracked lips.
Dosage: one tablet up to every 4 hours, as needed. Maximum 3 to 4 days.

ABOVE *The remedy Dulcamara comes from the woody nightshade. It is a powerful enemy of catarrh.*

PREVENTATIVE *measures*

NUTRITION: *eat plenty of pumpkin seeds, oysters and other shellfish to keep your zinc intake up to the mark. When there are lots of colds around, suck three or four zinc and vitamin C lozenges each day to boost your immunity.*

ENVIRONMENT: *try to avoid overheated, overcrowded places like department stores, movie houses, and theaters—especially important if you suffer from asthma, diabetes, heart disease, kidney disease, or any illness that compromises your natural immunity. If possible, travel to work earlier or later than usual, to avoid the rush hour, and make sure that you get plenty of fresh air and exercise to keep your respiratory system functioning well. Feeling stressed, tired, or depressed can increase your chances of catching a cold. Getting wet or sitting in a draft cannot give you a cold.*

LEFT *Get out into the fresh air of open spaces as often as you can. The exercise will do you good, and you'll be well away from sources of cold germs!*

DIAGNOSING COUGHS & BRONCHITIS

- Explosive release of air from the lungs
- Mucus that is clear or colored, often yellow or brown
- Dry, tickly throat

RESPIRATORY SYSTEM

coughs & bronchitis

A straightforward cough may be due to nothing more than inhaled irritants like dust, exhaust fumes, smoke, or a crumb of food. But of all symptoms in the respiratory tract a cough is the commonest and it may be a sign of underlying illness. Acute bronchitis, however, is caused by an infection, often following flu or a severe cold. Chronic bronchitis is most common in cool, damp climates and is caused by repeated irritation from smoking, foggy weather, and damp air, leading to an overproduction of mucus in the lungs. Though not always infected, this mucus clogs up the airways and reduces the amount of oxygen available, making the heart work harder. A chest infection on top of chronic bronchitis causes severe breathing problems.

CALL THE PHYSICIAN

- If you have a deep cough.
- If you are coughing up bloodstained mucus, which may be a sign of more serious illness.

NUTRITION

 Acute or chronic bronchitis and a simple irritant cough will all respond to dietary changes.

Eat plenty of celery, parsley, and fresh dandelion leaves (dandelion teabags are now available if you do not have a garden) to increase your urinary output and get rid of body fluids; onions and leeks (the same family as garlic); fish, legumes, brown rice, and bananas for their B vitamins; liver, carrots, sweet potatoes and spinach for their vitamin A; oily fish for their anti-inflammatory properties.

Cut out all salt in order to prevent fluid retention. **Reduce** your intake of all dairy products to help lessen mucus formation.

CONVENTIONAL MEDICINE

A dry cough will often be relieved by a steam inhalation, which you can have as often as necessary. If a cough does not clear up within 2–3 weeks, see your physician. A deeper cough, such as the type that develops after a cold into bacterial lung infection (most common in children and the elderly), may require antibiotics. There is no evidence that cough medicines have any effect on a cough.

Dosage information ~
Adults and children

- For steam inhalations, lean over a bowl of boiling water with a towel over your head. You can make this more pleasant by adding eucalyptus or other oils (*see under Aromatherapy*), but the steam itself has most effect on the cough. Or you can invest in a humidifier; put wet towels on the radiators; or fill the tub with hot water and sit in the steamy bathroom with your child.

HERBAL REMEDIES

Herbal cough remedies can ease bronchial spasms, expel phlegm, lubricate a dry cough, or suppress an irritant one.

■ **Use and Dosage:**
For chesty coughs or bronchitis, use herbs like thyme, elecampane, mullein, cowslip, white horehound, or Iceland moss in teas (1tsp/5ml per cup) sweetened with honey. A general syrup can be made by layering slices of onion or turnip with sugar; leave overnight, then drink the liquid in 1tsp/5ml doses.

Cough suppressants like wild cherry can ease nervous, irritant coughs but should be avoided when trying to expel phlegm.

HOMEOPATHIC REMEDIES

❧ RUMEX **6c** For throat tickling with cold air, spasmodic dry cough preventing sleep. Hoarseness. Phlegm tough, worse for talking and cold air. Better for covering mouth.

❧ STANNUM **6c** For forceful cough, which brings up green mucus. Worse evening until midnight. Worse for laughing, talking, lying on right side. Chest feels weak.

❧ BRYONIA **6c** For dry, hacking, spasmodic cough. Must sit up. Worse for eating, drinking, at night. Cough on entering warm room. Holds chest on coughing. **Dosage:** one tablet three times daily until improved. Maximum 2 weeks.

OUTSIDE HELP

REFLEXOLOGY: work the lung and diaphragm reflexes on and beneath the balls of the foot, paying particular attention to the webs between the big toes and second toes—the throat and trachea.

YOGA: try Shitali or Sitkari, raising the head slightly as you inhale and lowering it as you exhale. Coughs sometimes signify difficulty with communicating: reflect on whether you have been saying too much, too little, or the wrong things.

EXERCISE

THIS BECOMES more difficult, particularly for those suffering from chronic bronchitis, but it is vital to keep the lungs working, as the less they do, the more they will become inelastic and the less they will be able to do. Walking, deep-breathing exercises, and swimming are all a great starting point, but amazing improvements can also be seen as a result of taking up a wind instrument—a recorder, penny whistle, or mouth organ works fine—or even by learning to sing.

ABOVE *Playing the recorder is a good way to exercise the lungs.*

AROMATHERAPY

❧ SANDALWOOD
Santalum album
❧ BENZOIN
Styrax benzoin
❧ EUCALYPTUS
Eucalyptus radiata
❧ FRANKINCENSE
Boswellia sacra
❧ TEA TREE
Melaleuca alternifolia
Steam inhalations using these oils soothe the throat and airways, and assist in expelling excess mucus. Massage of the throat and chest eases the tension there, especially if you are coughing a lot. Gargling ensures that no infection sets in in the throat.

Application:
Use the sandalwood, benzoin, eucalyptus, or frankincense in steam inhalations. Massage the throat and chest with any of these and use tea tree for gargles.

KITCHEN MEDICINE
■ For all respiratory problems a daily bowl of garlic soup is a must, as it is both decongestant and antibacterial. ① Crush six cloves of garlic and sweat in a little hot olive oil. ② Add a level teaspoon of crushed aniseeds and 2pt/1*l* of water. ③ Boil for 15 minutes, then crumble in two or three thick slices of stale whole wheat bread. ④ Cook for 4 minutes. Serve at once.

PREVENTATIVE
measures

Don't smoke. Don't smoke. Don't smoke. Avoid other smokers. Keep the lungs in good condition through regular exercise. Keep bedrooms cool and well aired and wear a protective mask for all dusty home improvements jobs and when air-pollution levels are bad.

RIGHT *Hay fever, like asthma, is on the increase. At one time it described seasonal allergies to plants, but the term now covers reactions to other pollutants.*

DIAGNOSING HAY FEVER

- Sneezing fits
- Blocked or runny nose
- Sore, itchy eyes
- Tickle in the roof of the mouth

RESPIRATORY SYSTEM

hay fever

Hay fever is an allergic reaction to the pollen produced by grasses that mainly flower in the spring and summer. The sore, puffy eyes, streaming nose, and violent bouts of sneezing are instantly recognizable. But it is not only grass pollens that cause hay fever—and today the term is often used to describe allergic reactions to any type of pollen or, for that matter, other airborne irritants, like exhaust fumes, general atmospheric pollution, and even strong smells, like some perfumes. There are some unfortunate people who suffer constantly from the symptoms—a condition known as perennial rhinitis, which is most often caused by the droppings of the house dustmite (see Asthma on p.132 for preventative measures).

ABOVE *Buy organic honey for the added benefit of its healing properties.*

KITCHEN MEDICINE

■ If you have a pollen allergy, a jar of locally produced honey could be your salvation. Studies have shown that eating 4tsp/20ml daily of honey made by bees feeding on the pollen from flowers in your locality can provide considerable relief from the symptoms.

CONVENTIONAL MEDICINE

✚ Drug treatments work by preventing the allergic reaction and are available as eyedrops, tablets and nose sprays. Antihistamines sometimes cause drowsiness, although this is less of a problem with the more recent formulations.

Dosage information ~
Adults
■ Most tablets are taken once a day, although eyedrops are applied more frequently; follow package details or medical advice. Apply two doses of nose spray per nostril twice a day.

Children
■ Doses of antihistamine syrup depend on the age of the child; consult package for details or follow medical advice. For children over 6 years, apply two doses of nose spray per nostril twice a day.

HOMEOPATHIC REMEDIES

 Hay fever can be treated by using mixed pollens (30c taken once fortnightly during the season). Homeopathic hay-fever tablets can be bought "over the counter," alternatively try one of the following:

❧ ALLIUM CEPA **6C** For constantly running sore nose, watering but not sore eyes. Worse for warm rooms. Better in the open air.

❧ EUPHRASIA **6C** For watery and sore eyes, running but not sore nose. Worse for light and warmth.

❧ SABADILLA **6C** When bouts of violent sneezing are the main problem. Itching and tingling in nose, worse for perfume.

Dosage: one tablet twice daily. Maximum 2 weeks.

AROMATHERAPY

 ❧ ROMAN CHAMOMILE
Chamaemelum nobile
❧ BASIL
Ocimum basilicum
❧ MELISSA
Melissa officinalis
Chamomile and melissa are anti-allergens and basil helps to clear the sinuses and the head of the nasty effects of hay fever.
Application:
Place 1 drop of each oil on a handkerchief, which you can then carry with you everywhere for instant relief. You can also use these oils for massaging the upper back and chest.

HERBAL REMEDIES

Herbalists often treat hay fever by using strengthening and cleansing herbs for the respiratory tract early in the year, before the problem becomes too severe.

■ Use and Dosage:
Make an infusion containing elderflower (3 parts), white horehound (2 parts), fumitory (1 part), and vervain (1 part), then drink 1–2 cups daily from late January until Easter.

To relieve symptoms during the hay-fever season, take eyebright in capsules (up to 8 x 200mg daily) and bathe the eyes with well strained, sterilized marigold or eyebright infusions.

ABOVE *Use marigold* (Calendula officinalis, *not* Tagetes spp.) *flowers to make a soothing eyebath for hay-fever symptoms.*

NUTRITION

Following a regime that reduces the body's production of mucus may be helpful. So **reduce** your intake of dairy produce—naturopaths believe this to be mucus-forming. If this helps and you make permanent changes to your diet, make sure that you replace the missing nutrients (especially the calcium) from other sources.

Vitamin C and its accompanying bioflavonoids are important protectors of the mucous membranes. All berries and fresh currants supply large quantities of both, and citrus fruit, including some of the pith and skin around the segments, should also be eaten in abundance.

OUTSIDE HELP

ACUPRESSURE: points 50 and 51 may help stop a violent attack of sneezing; points 41 and 47 can be useful to increase mucus drainage.
REFLEXOLOGY: work the reflexes of the eyes, nose, and throat, which are located on and between the fingers and toes; plus the reflexes to the lungs and diaphragm.
YOGA: focus on closing postures such as Forward Bends. Practice

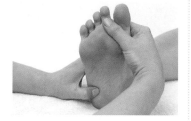

ABOVE *Working the reflex to the bronchi helps to make labored breathing easier.*

Kapalabhati and Pranayama techniques regularly, throughout the year.

PREVENTATIVE *measures*

The only real prevention is to avoid inhaling allergenic material, but this is seldom practical. If you suffer from pollen allergy, staying indoors early in the morning and late in the evening, keeping the windows closed and wearing wrap-around sunglasses will help to some extent. If you have perennial rhinitis, follow the advice on controlling the dustmite population in your bedroom (*see Asthma on p.132*). Take a daily dose of 1000mg of vitamin C, 400IU of vitamin E and vitamin B-complex.

RIGHT *The sinuses are bony cavities located around the nose. When their mucous membranes become infected, these swell, causing a blockage of mucus which may be very painful.*

DIAGNOSING SINUSITIS

- Pain in the face or teeth
- Persistent headache, often over the eyes
- Pain worse on leaning forward
- Foul taste in the mouth
- Blood-stained discharge from the nose
- Completely or partially blocked nose

RESPIRATORY SYSTEM

sinusitis

A heavy cold, allergies, irritant fumes, smoking, upper respiratory infections, nasal polyps, or adverse reactions to some foods may all be the cause of sinusitis. This inflammation of the membranes lining the sinuses, and their consequent overproduction of mucus, is what produces the symptoms of headaches, facial pain, stuffiness, loss of smell, pain in the teeth, repeated episodes of chest and ear infections, and thick, infected mucus. While antibiotics may be essential for severe infections, home remedies are best for milder conditions and also for prevention.

KITCHEN MEDICINE

■ Garlic, which is powerfully antibacterial, and horseradish are powerful weapons in the fight against sinus problems. Eat the equivalent of one good-sized clove of garlic a day—or if you hate the taste and smell, use a garlic tablet.

■ Horseradish is a very strong decongestant, and a couple of teaspoons of peeled, grated horseradish root in a sandwich will soon get the mucus flowing out of your nose.

■ Onions and leeks are both traditional foods for the treatment of chest and sinus infections, so eat lots of them—they are particularly good when cooked together to make a decongestant soup.

■ The natural enzymes in pineapple juice are especially healing to the sinuses. Drink at least three glasses, diluted 50:50 with water, each day.

CONVENTIONAL MEDICINE

✚ Treatment depends on improving drainage from the sinus, together with treating the infection. Steam helps to make the mucus thinner and reduces nasal congestion. Nose sprays containing decongestants may help, but if used for too long can make the congestion worse. Antibiotics may be necessary to clear the infection. Recurrent sinusitis may require surgical treatment.

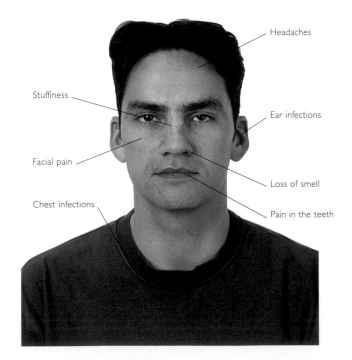

Headaches

Stuffiness

Ear infections

Facial pain

Loss of smell

Chest infections

Pain in the teeth

HERBAL REMEDIES

 Anticatarrhal herbs, such as elderflower, chamomile, ground ivy, coltsfoot, yarrow, eyebright, or plantain, can all help.
■ **Use and Dosage:**
Make teas using 2tsp/10ml of herb per cup: add a pinch of goldenseal or bayberry powder or 5 drops of tincture to the mix, if available.

Gently massaging the sinus areas with a cream or infused oil containing any of these herbs will also help.

Steam inhalants are also beneficial: add 10 drops each of eucalyptus, peppermint, pine, and sandalwood oils to a basin of hot water and inhale for up to 10 minutes.

HOMEOPATHIC REMEDIES

There are many remedies that help sinusitis. If the following do not help, consult a qualified homeopath.
❧ HYDRASTIS **6C** After a cold, for pressing pain in forehead. Scalp and neck also painful. Thick mucus at back of throat.
❧ KALI BICHROMICUM **6C** For thick, yellow, ropy catarrh. Pulsating pain at root of nose and

frontal sinuses worse for stooping. Pressure in ear. Worse for cold, dry weather. Loss of smell.
❧ HEPAR SULPHURIS CALCAREUM **6C** For thick, white or yellow, smelly mucus that makes nose sore. Person irritable. Facial bones sore. Right-sided shooting pains.
Dosage: one tablet three times daily until improved. Maximum 10 days.

NUTRITION

The food that most commonly increases the production of mucus, especially in children, is cow's milk. Even breastfeeding mothers who consume a large amount of milk may make their babies more prone to chest and sinus problems. Try excluding cow's milk and milk products from your diet for a few weeks. If this does help and you are going to exclude them in the long term, make sure you get plenty of calcium and vitamin D from other sources (*see Osteoporosis on p.108*).

To maintain healthy sinuses, vitamins A, C, and E and bioflavonoids are important, so **eat plenty of** carrots, apricots, and dark green leafy vegetables; citrus fruit, with some of the pith

and skin; dark cherries, tomatoes, and mangoes; avocados, olive, sunflower, and safflower oils.

Reduce the amount of salt in your diet, as this encourages fluid retention and swelling of the sinus membranes; go easy on the alcohol, which causes dehydration that will irritate already inflamed sinuses.

BELOW *Fruit and vegetable defenders.*

EXERCISE

EXERCISE of any sort can help to improve breathing and clear the nasal passages. However, if hay fever is involved, take care to avoid exercising outside when pollen counts are likely to be high and take precautions against house-dustmite dung, if you are exercising at home (see *Asthma* on p.132).

OUTSIDE HELP

ACUPRESSURE: the points around the eyes and nose and the back of the head—49, 50, 51, and 52—are useful to relieve the symptoms of sinusitis.

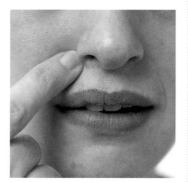

ABOVE *Use strong pressure on point 49 on the Large Intestine meridian. It will help to clear the head.*

REFLEXOLOGY: the sinus reflexes are found on the tips of the fingers and toes. Work up and down every part of these areas, and lift and straighten each toe in turn, pushing up each bulb with your thumb. Working the upper lymphatics and ileo-caecal valve reflexes might help.
YOGA: rapid breathing techniques like Kapalabhati and Bhastrika are excellent at keeping the sinuses clear, but they should not be used during an acute stage.

PREVENTATIVE
measures

If allergies are the root of the problem, take the appropriate preventative measures (*see under Nutrition*). If perennial rhinitis— all-year-round sinus problems— is the problem, then special care must be taken to keep the home allergen-free (*see Asthma on p.132*).

DIET: *a diet that is constantly enriched with the nutrients already recommended will help to ensure strong and healthy mucous membranes in the sinuses. For those susceptible to sinus problems, a monthly 2-day cleansing regime of nothing but raw fruit, vegetables and salads—as much as you like—with plenty of fruit and vegetable juices is a highly protective bonus.*

AROMATHERAPY

❧ BASIL
Ocimum basilicum
❧ EUCALYPTUS
Eucalyptus radiata
❧ TEA TREE
Melaleuca alternifolia
These oils help to fight infection and clear the sinuses.
Application:
Put the essential oils onto a handkerchief, or vaporize them into the air, in a burner, an electric vaporizer, a light ring, or simply in a bowl of warm water, if that is all you have handy. Steam inhalation is an effective way of employing them. Most of these oils are a bit too strong to put directly on the face, but you can do a facial massage combining them with either plain oil lotion or whatever ordinary night-cream you use. It is worth finding a therapist who will show you how to carry out this facial massage treatment.

132

RIGHT When the bronchial passages in the lungs are inflamed, or narrowed by a bronchospasm (surrounding muscles tighten), wheezy, difficult breathing results.

DIAGNOSING ASTHMA
- Recurrent periods of difficulty in breathing
- Tightness in the chest, associated with wheezing
- Cough, particularly at night (this may be the only symptom in children)

RESPIRATORY SYSTEM

asthma

Asthma is an extremely serious illness and can be life-threatening. The following advice must be taken in context with any advice given by your medical practitioner. These simple home remedies should not replace your regular medication, but, used in a complementary way with other therapy, can greatly improve your quality of life and reduce both the frequency and severity of asthma attacks. In recent years, the incidence of asthma has dramatically increased—partly, I believe, due to ever-increasing amounts of atmospheric pollution; partly due to the growing addition of complex chemicals to food and drink; and partly to double glazing, insulation, and draft-proofing of our homes. Twice as many boys as girls suffer from asthma and around 3 percent of the total American population endures this illness. It most commonly affects children, but adults can also suffer from late-onset asthma.

CALL THE PHYSICIAN
- If you are already asthmatic but have noticed that you need more medication recently than usual.
- If there is a rapid deterioration in your condition.

CAUTION
Avoid non-steroidal anti-inflammatory drugs, such as ibuprofen or aspirin, which may make your asthma worse.

ABOVE We are continually contributing to our own health problems.

CONVENTIONAL MEDICINE
Most asthmatics will already be taking prescribed medication, which will need to be increased when an attack starts. If you are experiencing your first asthma attack, seek urgent medical attention.

HERBAL REMEDIES
Herbal antispasmodics and broncho-dilators are very effective in treating asthma—although the most potent herbs, such as ephedra and lobelia, are confined to professional use.
- **Use and Dosage:**
For mild cases, a steam inhalant of chamomile flowers (1tbsp/15ml to a basin of boiling water) can often avert an attack.

Drinking cups of elecampane can also help: macerate 2tsp/10ml of the root overnight in a cup of cold water, then heat to boiling point; strain and sweeten with 1tsp/5ml of honey and sip as required.

HOMEOPATHIC REMEDIES

Asthma is a serious condition and may require medical attention. Do not stop medication from your physician. It would be helpful to consult a qualified homeopath.

ARSENICUM ALBUM 6C For wheezing, anxiety, restlessness, fear of suffocation. Worse 1:00–3:00 A.M., in cold air. Better for bending forward, warm drinks.

IPECACUANHA 6C For rattly chest, unable to cough up phlegm. Wheezy, chest feels tight. Cough with each breath. Nausea. Better for sitting up and in open air.

NATRUM SULPHURICUM 6C For coughing green sputum. Worse for damp weather and 4:00–5:00 A.M.. Occurs with hay fever.

Dosage: one tablet three times daily. Maximum 1 week.

NUTRITION

In children, asthma is nearly always an allergic response and although this is mainly to inhaled allergens, food and food additives can also be triggers. Start by keeping a detailed food diary, noting when the attacks occur. This should give you some clues as to the foods that might be better avoided.

Food additives like colorings, flavorings, and preservatives can be severe triggers, and all these chemicals are best avoided. A diet rich in all the protective antioxidants that are so important for the health of lung tissue is essential. Salad, greens, grapes, melons, tomatoes, bell peppers, kiwis, whole grain cereals, and lots of all the green vegetables should be the basis of the asthmatic's diet.

One of the most common food groups to cause problems are dairy foods, as milk and milk products tend to increase the body's production of mucus.

You may need professional guidance to make sure that the child does not suffer nutritional deficiencies when you start excluding major foods.

EXERCISE

ABOVE *Exercise helps to increase the lungs' efficiency: very important for asthmatics.*

EXERCISE IS absolutely essential, but advice on this is rarely given to asthmatics or their parents. Asthma is rarely a bar to physical exercise, so long as it is well controlled with appropriate medication. Any exercise that improves the efficiency of the lungs and increases the amount of air that can be breathed in and out is of great benefit. Singing, playing a wind instrument, swimming (although the chlorine in pools can sometimes upset asthmatics), or any sport that the child really enjoys should be encouraged.

PREVENTATIVE
measures

BEDROOM HYGIENE: *turn down heating in the bedroom and increase the ventilation. Use a high-powered-suction vacuum cleaner with a medical-grade filter, and vacuum the mattress, bedclothes, all flat surfaces, shades, and drapes regularly. Use a plant mister to spray windowsills, bedheads, closet tops, and bookshelves, then wipe to remove all dustmite droppings daily, and use anti-dustmite shampoo on carpets. Cover bedding with impregnated netting in order to kill all dustmites, and use high-temperature washes for all bed linen. All these practical steps help to remove dustmites and their droppings, which are highly allergenic.*

SMOKING: *don't smoke or allow smoking anywhere in the house where an asthmatic lives.*

PETS: *don't have cats, dogs, cage birds, or other furry pets in the house. Snakes and other reptiles are fine.*

OUTSIDE HELP

ACUPRESSURE: points 4, 18, 20, and 23 are useful during attacks.

ALEXANDER TECHNIQUE: in 1973 consultant physician Dr. Wilfred Barlow stated, "The asthmatic needs to be taught how to stop his wrong way of breathing." Asthmatics often overuse certain respiratory and postural muscles at the expense of others. Practicing the Technique will help toward a more relaxed way of breathing and enable you to manage yourself better during an asthma attack.

REFLEXOLOGY: during an asthma attack, work the diaphragm and lung reflexes located on the balls of the feet, and especially the adrenal glands.

YOGA: focus on expansive postures such as Warrior, Triangle, Two-Foot Support, and Cobra. In both, postures and breathing practices aim to increase the length of your exhalation. Make friends with your breath through this meditation: inhaling freely, gradually slow your exhalations, with a sense of ease.

AROMATHERAPY

FRANKINCENSE
Boswellia sacra
Frankincense slows and deepens the breathing. It is used by monks when they are going into deep meditation. But if asthma is an allergic reaction, try chamomile instead (*see also Stress on p.60*).

Application:
Use in a vaporizer, compress, or bath, or for localized massage around the chest/facial area. Frankincense can also be put on a tissue or on your pillow at night to help you breathe. And a large towel concertinaed (not rolled), then placed on the floor under the length of your spine will open the chest and drop your shoulders backward, which will help your breathing.

CAUTION

Do not use frankincense in a steam inhalation, as the heat will increase the inflammation of the mucous membrane, making the congestion worse.

RIGHT *A hot, burning feeling behind the breastbone is caused by stomach acids flowing back up into the esophagus, either because of lax muscles, eating too much, or tight clothing.*

DIAGNOSING ~~EARTBURN~~

~~ng~~ sensation in upper part of the
which goes up the center
the back of the
~~ated with~~
an ~~th~~

● Pain is ... when lying
flat, or whe~~r~~ ...

● Pain may start a~~r~~ ...ks
or alcohol and is agg~~r~~...
fatty foods, and being ov~~er~~...

DIGESTIVE SYSTEM

heartburn

Heartburn, also known as acid indigestion, may be caused by obesity, the late stages of pregnancy, or a hiatus hernia, but most often it is the result of too much of the wrong kind of food or plain overeating. The acid contents of the stomach escape upward into the esophagus, causing the characteristic burning sensation behind the breastbone. Whatever the cause, home remedies can help resolve the pain and the often severe discomfort of this common symptom.

CALL THE PHYSICIAN

■ If heartburn continues for a long period of time, as it can be indicative of complaints such as ulcers or gallstones.

■ If the symptoms persist or are not relieved by an antacid.

CAUTION

If you are pregnant, do not take any medicines without first consulting your physician.

Antacids usually contain magnesium or aluminum salts: the former (e.g. Milk of Magnesia) tend to cause diarrhea; the latter (e.g. Aluminum hydroxide) may cause constipation.

EXERCISE

PHYSICAL activity stimulates the function of the whole digestive system and any activity that tones and strengthens the abdominal muscles is an added bonus. Hiatus hernia sufferers should avoid exercises that involve lots of bending, as this can allow stomach acids to flow through the hernia into the esophagus.

CONVENTIONAL MEDICINE

Avoid eating fatty foods or drinking hot drinks or alcohol. Try to stop smoking and lose weight if necessary. If the symptoms are worse at night, then try drinking a glass of milk before bedtime and raising the head of the bed. Try taking an antacid if the symptoms continue.

*Dosage information—**Adults and children over 16***

■ Many types of antacid are available in tablet or liquid form. Antacids contain magnesium or aluminum salts, or both; some are combined with alginic acid and are particularly helpful for heartburn; see package for full details.

RIGHT *Milk is alkaline and will help to reduce acid levels in the stomach.*

HERBAL REMEDIES

 Soothing, demulcent herbs, such as marshmallow and slippery elm, are widely used for heartburn.

■ **Use and Dosage:**
Take these herbs in tablets or capsules (200mg) before meals.

Teas of antacid herbs, such as meadowsweet, centaury, bogbean, dandelion, or black horehound, can also be useful.

Carminative teas used for indigestion (see p.136) can also help, or make a thin gruel by mixing 1tsp/5ml of powdered slippery-elm bark with a little water, then adding a hot chamomile infusion. Drink before meals.

HOMEOPATHIC REMEDIES

 Persistent heartburn requires medical assessment, but a consultation with a homeopath may help.

❧ ROBINA 6C For heartburn with acidity. Worse at night and for lying down. Prevents sleep. Abdomen bloated with wind and colic. Headaches.

❧ CAPSICUM 6C For acid dyspepsia, burning in stomach or icy coldness. Water brash. Craves stimulants such as coffee, but this causes nausea. Thirsty for water, but this causes shuddering.

❧ SULPHUR 6C For heartburn from eating either too much, or spicy, food. Big appetite, craves spices, alcohol, fats. Thirsty for cold drinks.

Dosage: one tablet hourly for six doses. May be repeated.

OUTSIDE HELP

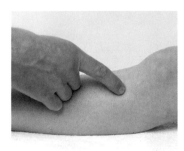

ABOVE *Point 23 is on the Pericardium meridian, which is said to protect the heart. Stimulation helps digestion.*

ACUPRESSURE: points 23, 27 and 28 will all stimulate the digestive system and encourage it to perform more efficiently.

REFLEXOLOGY: the reflexes involved in the relief of heartburn symptoms are the esophagus, diaphragm, and stomach on the hands and feet. Work these reflexes on the feet or the entire palms of both hands.

ABOVE *These starchy foods are easy to digest. Live yogurt replenishes intestinal bacteria.*

NUTRITION

 Avoiding the symptoms of heartburn is simply a matter of applying common sense to your eating habits.

Avoid alcohol, nicotine, and caffeine. Do not overeat or eat very acidic or irritant foods, such as chili, pickles, raw onion, sour fruit, or very hot curries. Deep-fried foods can also set off an uncomfortable bout of heartburn. If your problem is a hiatus hernia or you are in the later stages of pregnancy, make sure that you eat a little and often—not more food in total, but spreading your daily intake over five meals instead of the usual three.

Heartburn for which there is no obvious reason sometimes responds well to a few weeks on the Food Combining (Hay) Diet (see p.210).

PREVENTATIVE *measures*

NUTRITION: *eating small meals at regular intervals is the kindest way to treat a digestive system prone to hyperacidity. Make sure that you use all the good digestive herbs routinely in your cooking and end your meals with a glass of mint tea. Eat a container of live yogurt every day for its gut-friendly bacteria and lots of good starches—potatoes, rice, pasta, sweet potatoes, bananas, and bread—which are all easy to digest.*

LOSING WEIGHT: *obesity must be dealt with, because it is a major cause of heartburn. Simply losing weight and avoiding tight, restrictive clothes will make an enormous difference.*

RAISING THE BEDHEAD: *if you are very pregnant or have a hiatus hernia, raise the head of your bed by 2–3in/5–7cm; do not use extra pillows, which will just give you a stiff neck and will end up on the floor anyway.*

KITCHEN MEDICINE
■ As with most digestive disorders, there are many common and effective kitchen remedies. Mint, dill, fennel, ginger, and slippery elm (see Gastritis on p.146) can all be used to great advantage.

AROMATHERAPY

 ❧ FENNEL
Foeniculum vulgare
❧ PEPPERMINT
Mentha piperita
❧ BLACK PEPPER
Piper nigrum
❧ ROMAN CHAMOMILE
Chamaemelum nobile

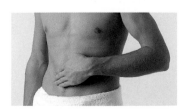

ABOVE *Massage the stomach with a soothing oil.*

❧ GINGER
Zingiber officinale
These oils calm and soothe the digestive tract.
Application:
Use in a massage oil or massage lotion, or in a warm compress over the stomach area.

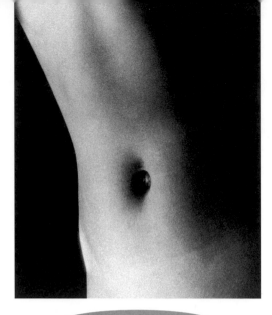

DIAGNOSING INDIGESTION

- Pain or discomfort in the upper part of the abdomen, related to food
- May be associated with nausea and belching

DIGESTIVE SYSTEM

indigestion

There cannot be a single person who has not had the occasional bout of indigestion and, with the exception of underlying diseases being the cause, it is always self-inflicted. Do not waste your money on expensive "over-the-counter" remedies. Indigestion starts in a kitchen—your own, the gourmet restaurant's, or the takeout's—and that is where you will find the answer.

CALL THE PHYSICIAN

- If you have a persistent problem with indigestion.
- If you have the symptoms of indigestion and have lost weight unintentionally.
- If it is the first time you have had these symptoms and you are over 40 years old.

CAUTION

Severe pain after eating or when you are hungry, blood in the stool, and long-standing chronic digestive problems could be symptoms of a more serious underlying condition and must be investigated.

Avoid aspirin and NSAIDS, which may make the symptoms worse.

CONVENTIONAL MEDICINE

Avoid eating immediately before bedtime, plus drinking and smoking. Raising the head of the bed may alleviate nighttime symptoms, while being overweight or wearing tight-fitting clothes may make the symptoms worse. When the pain starts, try drinking milk; if that does not help, take an antacid to relieve the pain. If the symptoms do not respond to an antacid, then a short course of cimetidine or ranitidine may help.

Dosage information ~

Adults and children over 16
Many types of antacid are available in tablet or liquid form; see package for details. Be aware that antacids usually contain magnesium or aluminum salts: the former (e.g. Milk of Magnesia) tends to cause diarrhea; the latter (e.g. Aluminum hydroxide, Alu-Cap) may cause constipation. Other indigestion mixtures contain dimethicone to relieve wind.

Take 200mg cimetidine when the symptoms appear, then repeat after 1 hour if symptoms persist. Maximum daily dose: 800mg, but not more than 400mg in any period of 4 hours. If symptoms continue after 2 weeks, seek medical advice. To prevent nighttime heartburn take 100mg 1 hour before bedtime. *Avoid cimetidine in pregnancy.*

Take 75mg ranitidine with water when the symptoms appear. If symptoms persist for more than 1 hour, or return, another tablet can be taken. Maximum: 300mg in 24 hours. If symptoms continue after 2 weeks, seek medical advice. *Avoid ranitidine in pregnancy.*

KITCHEN MEDICINE

MINT

- Of all the culinary plants, mint is king of indigestion remedies. A glass of mint tea is an almost instant cure—even more so when sweetened with a little honey, one of the great digestive soothers.

- Another traditional remedy is a generous pinch of baking soda dissolved on the tongue. This is not the most pleasant of medicines, but it is extremely effective and does not have the high aluminum content of many of the proprietary antacids.

AROMATHERAPY

🜨 FENNEL
Foeniculum vulgare
🜨 PEPPERMINT
Mentha x piperita
🜨 BLACK PEPPER
Piper nigrum
🜨 ROMAN CHAMOMILE
Chamaemelum nobile
🜨 GINGER
Zingiber officinale
These oils calm and soothe the digestive tract.
Application:
Use in a massage oil or massage lotion, or in a warm compress over the stomach area.

HERBAL REMEDIES

 There is an enormous variety of herbal carminatives to use for indigestion, ranging from familiar culinary herbs and spices (such as caraway, cardamom, and ginger) to more exotic Eastern remedies (like galangal and dried tangerine peel/Chen Pi).

■ **Use and Dosage:**
All can be made into a standard infusion or used in tinctures (1/2tsp/2.5ml diluted with water, or up to 20 drops on the tongue).

Slippery elm or marshmallow-

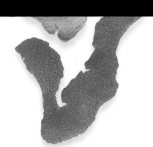

ABOVE *Chinese herbalists use Chen Pi to direct energy downward and ease indigestion.*

root capsules will help protect the stomach lining.

Also worth trying are lemon balm and agrimony teas—both ideal for children.

HOMEOPATHIC REMEDIES

Persistent symptoms require medical attention, but a consultation with a homeopath may be helpful.
🜨 LYCOPODIUM **30**C For burning in throat from indigestion. Pressure in stomach and bitter taste in mouth. Bloating immediately after meals. Craves warm drinks.
🜨 NUX VOMICA **30**C For pain, like a stone, in the stomach some time after meals, together with nausea. Indigestion from drinking strong coffee.
🜨 CARBO VEGETABILIS **30**C For heaviness, fullness, sleepiness after

ABOVE *Lycopodium 30c is made from Lycopodium clavatum, a moss.*

food. Food turns to gas in stomach, with lots of belching and flatus.
Dosage: one tablet hourly for six doses, then three times daily. Maximum 1 week.

OUTSIDE HELP

 ACUPRESSURE: points 23, 27, and 28 will relieve nausea and encourage the wave-like contractions of the colon that speed up the digestive process.
REFLEXOLOGY: starting beneath the knuckles or toe joints, work across the palms and soles to the wrists or heels, covering the reflexes of the stomach, liver, pancreas, intestines, and colon.

YOGA: if you already have indigestion, use Shitali or Sitkari. To avoid indigestion in the future, be very mindful of what and how you eat, so that you find out what does and does not suit you. Some people need to eat several small meals rather than two or three large ones. Be peaceful when you eat: avoid rushing your food.

PREVENTATIVE
measures

Follow the guidelines given under *Nutrition* and you will not go far wrong.

NUTRITION

If you choose to overeat—and who doesn't sometimes?—you must be prepared for the consequences of indigestion. Once in a while it is probably worth it. Chronic indigestion, however, is another matter and can make your life a misery. Long gaps between meals, eating on the run, large, rich meals late at night, and a surfeit of burgers, hot dogs, and other greasy or deep-fried fast-food represent an assault on your digestive system. So eat a sensible, well-balanced diet and make sure you eat regular meals.

Avoid eating too much of the obvious culprits—raw onions, pickles, hot, spicy chili and curry, radishes, cucumber, and bell peppers. Unripe bananas are particularly indigestible—do not eat them until the skin has a few brown speckles, as that shows that the starch is changing into sugar.

EXERCISE

TO COUNTERACT the occasional one-off bout of indigestion, a quick walk round the block might be all you need—and this is a good idea after a large meal anyway. If you are a chronic indigestion sufferer, then abdominal exercises to strengthen the stomach muscles can make all the difference (see *Irritable Bowel Syndrome* on p.154).

RIGHT *Nausea is a very common, though unpleasant, part of life, and may be precipitated by many factors.*

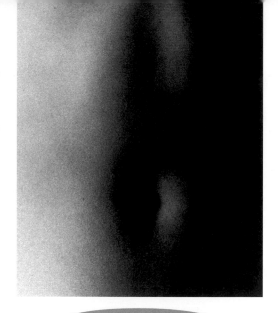

DIAGNOSING NAUSEA

- Sensation of impending vomiting, often accompanied by sweating, excessive salivation, dizziness, and pale skin
- In pregnancy, nausea tends to be worst in the first 3 or 4 months, but can continue throughout the pregnancy in rare cases; although often called morning sickness, it may occur at any time of the day, even at night

DIGESTIVE SYSTEM

nausea

Nausea, that familiar feeling of sickness, may be followed by vomiting. This violent expulsion of stomach contents may bring considerable relief, if the vomiting has been triggered by overindulgence in either food or alcohol, or by the ingestion of some toxic substance (accidental or otherwise). But it may also be the first of a series of repeated bouts in a prolonged episode, if the underlying cause is food poisoning or some other form of viral or bacterial infection (see Gastroenteritis on p.148). High temperatures in children, appendicitis, motion sickness, pregnancy, migraine, liver and gallbladder disease, whooping cough, vertigo, Ménière's disease, and severe anxiety can all cause varying degrees of nausea. But whatever the cause, you can help yourself with simple home remedies.

CALL THE PHYSICIAN

- If nausea is a recurring problem.
- If bouts of nausea and vomiting have no obvious explanation
- If you have been feeling nauseous for more than a week, the nausea is associated with abdominal pain, or you are not pregnant.

CAUTION

If you are pregnant, do not take any medicines without first consulting your physician. Do not take medicines containing hyoscine if you have glaucoma.

KITCHEN MEDICINE
- Exactly the same remedies apply here as in motion sickness (see p.190). If you are suffering from vacation food poisoning, see gastroenteritis (p.148).

CONVENTIONAL MEDICINE

Avoid eating, but take frequent sips of plain water and lie down until the sensation passes. Antinausea treatments can be helpful, particularly for travel sickness, but consult your physician to choose the best remedy, which may depend on the cause of the nausea. Nausea due to pregnancy may be relieved by eating. Try eating frequent light snacks throughout the day, possibly even before getting out of bed in the morning. Get as much sleep and rest as possible, as being tired tends to make the nausea worse.

Dosage information ~
Adults and children
- Treatments for travel sickness are usually taken before traveling and then repeated at regular intervals, if required; see package for details (see also Motion Sickness on p.190).

HERBAL REMEDIES

 Ginger is probably the most widely used herb for nausea (*see Motion Sickness on p.190*), but other useful remedies include chamomile, peppermint, lemon balm, and bitter orange.

■ **Use and Dosage:**
Take these herbs in teas or, more easily during bouts of nausea, as drops of tincture (diluted 50:50 with water) on the tongue.

Black horehound is often recommended and can be extremely effective, but some people find that the distinctive flavor makes them feel worse.

HOMEOPATHIC REMEDIES

Ensure there is no serious medical condition. These remedies can be useful for morning sickness experienced during pregnancy.

IPECACUANHA **6C** For constant nausea, not relieved by vomiting. Clean tongue, needs to keep swallowing an excess of saliva.

SEPIA **6C** For nausea at sight, smell or thought of food. Morning sickness before eating, vomits on rinsing mouth. Craves vinegar.

GLOSSYPIUM 6c For nausea and vomiting worse before breakfast, movement or standing up. No appetite, sensitive stomach with a lot of gas.

Dosage: one tablet every half-hour. Maximum 12 doses.

AROMATHERAPY

GINGER
Zingiber officinale

PEPPERMINT
Mentha x piperita

LAVENDER
Lavandula angustifolia

ROMAN CHAMOMILE
Chamaemelum nobile

Lavender and chamomile are soothing and calming, while peppermint acts as a mild anesthetic to the stomach wall and ginger is the universal remedy for nausea.

Application:
Use as a compress, and accompanied by herbal teas.

ABOVE *Ginger is indicated for nausea resulting from any cause, whether it is an infection, travel sickness, or pregnancy. Ginger oil can be used for a gentle stomach massage.*

NUTRITION

This very much depends on the cause of the nausea, but in general terms a bout of food poisoning should be treated with the BRAT diet, followed by a gradual return to normal eating (*see Gastroenteritis on p.148*). Vomiting caused by ulcers needs a specific pattern of eating (*see Gastritis on p.146*). For nausea caused by vertigo or Ménière's disease follow the advice for motion sickness (*see p.190*).

OUTSIDE HELP

ACUPRESSURE: frequent pressure applied to point 38 on the wrist will bring great relief from nausea.

REFLEXOLOGY: for symptomatic relief, work the stomach reflexes on both hands, starting beneath the knuckles and working down to the wrists. Carry out the thumb- and finger-walking technique across the palms, from side to side, to do this.

YOGA: use Shitali or Sitkari, keeping the head still, breathing out more slowly than you inhale. These exercises often help to settle the stomach.

ABOVE *Yoga breathing exercises calm an irritated stomach.*

RIGHT *For nausea induced by anxiety, it is important to learn to relax as much as possible. Set aside time every day to do this.*

PREVENTATIVE
measures

MÉNIÈRE'S SUFFERERS: *if you suffer from Ménière's disease, then severely reducing your salt intake, avoiding all but very small quantities of alcohol, and trying to keep your life as stress-free as possible will curtail your symptoms.*

GALLSTONE SUFFERERS: *where vomiting is caused by gallstones, a very low-fat diet is necessary to prevent recurrent attacks (see Gallbladder Problems on p.144).*

RELAXATION: *vomiting brought on by anxiety or nervous tension requires relaxation techniques—try meditation, yoga, or relaxation exercises. It is easier to learn from a teacher, but a wide variety of audio and video tapes, as well as books, is available.*

DEHYDRATION: *the young and the elderly can dehydrate rapidly as a result of repeated vomiting—even more so if this is accompanied by diarrhea. It is essential to replace lost fluids with very frequent but small amounts of isotonic solution. You can buy remedies or make your own (see Gastroenteritis on p.148).*

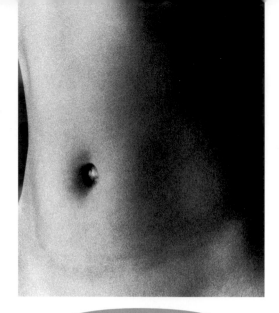

DIAGNOSING ABDOMINAL PAIN

- Waves of cramping pain, often associated with diarrhea and/or nausea and vomiting. Likely cause: *gastroenteritis or food poisoning*
- Severe, constant pain in the lower right side of the abdomen. Likely cause: *appendicitis*
- Lower abdominal pain associated with pain when passing urine. Likely cause: *cystitis*
- Burning, acidic pain in the top of the abdomen. Likely cause: *stomach problems*
- Dull, cramping pain in lower abdomen around menstruation. Likely cause: *period pain*

DIGESTIVE SYSTEM

abdominal pain

stomach ache

Abdominal pain (stomach ache) is the result of abusing your digestive system. Overeating, overindulgence, excessive alcohol, too much fat, or unwise combinations of food may all be the culprit. It is a problem that most people will suffer from occasionally; it can also be triggered off by stress and anxiety. Regular attacks of abdominal pain need investigation to rule out underlying disease. (See also Constipation p.156, Diarrhea p.158, Flatulence p.142, Gallbladder Problems p.144, Gastroenteritis p.148, Irritable Bowel Syndrome p.154, Peptic Ulcers on p.152).

CALL THE PHYSICIAN

- If abdominal pain becomes more severe, or has been unchanged for more than a day or two.
- If you are in severe pain and unable to hold down fluids for more than 12 hours.
- If a child has severe abdominal pain.

CAUTION

Avoid taking aspirins or ibuprofens, as they may irritate an already sore stomach lining.

KITCHEN MEDICINE

- When cooking vegetables, add a few caraway seeds.
- Chew a few dill seeds and drink mint tea after meals.

CONVENTIONAL MEDICINE

Abdominal pain may be a minor problem or it can be life-threatening. Stomach ache can initially be treated with a simple pain-reliever, such as paracetamol (but not aspirin or ibuprofen, which may irritate the stomach lining). Drink plenty of water, and eat only if you are hungry. Avoid spicy or fatty foods until the pain subsides. If the pain becomes worse, or remains unchanged for several days, seek medical advice.

Dosage information ~
Adults
- Take one to two tablets of pain-relievers at onset of pain, repeated every 4 hours; see package for details.

Children
- Give regular doses of liquid pain-reliever; consult package for details, or follow advice from your physician.

HERBAL REMEDIES

Carminative herbs—such as aniseed, clove, coriander, fennel, ginger, parsley, peppermint, and thyme—can help relieve the pain associated with wind, while soothing remedies like bogbean, centaury, Irish moss, or meadowsweet can also ease the inflammation and irritation associated with overindulgence.

If stress and anxiety are to blame, try regular cups of lemon balm or chamomile infusion.

■ **Use and Dosage:**
Use the herbs in standard infusions and decoctions; drink a cup every 3 to 4 hours while symptoms persist. Avoid laxative herbs if the cause of pain is uncertain.

HOMEOPATHIC REMEDIES

These remedies may also be used for infantile colic.

❧ MAGNESIUM PHOSPHORICUM 6C
For cramping abdominal pains. Better for heat, pulling legs up to abdomen, pressure, and rubbing. Belching gives no relief.

❧ DIOSCOREA 6C For colic pains. Better for stretching or for bending backward.

❧ COLOCYNTHIS 6C For cutting colic pains. Better for pressure, heat. Pains after anger. Bends over double; presses on abdomen for relief.

❧ CHAMOMILLA 6C For infant colic. Greenish stool, infant's cry is angry, pains are unbearable.

Better for being carried.
Dosage: one tablet every half-hour. Maximum six doses.

ABOVE *Irritable babies suffering from colic may respond well to homeopathic remedies.*

OUTSIDE HELP

ACUPRESSURE: use at point 27 in the middle of the abdomen and point 23 on the outside of the leg, just below the knee joint.

REFLEXOLOGY: for the relief of discomfort in the digestive system, work the soles of the feet, beginning just below the ball of the foot, or on the entire palms of the hands.

YOGA: lie down with the legs bent, feet on the floor. Place your hands gently over the painful area and feel the warmth from them. Breathe out easily and quietly, but

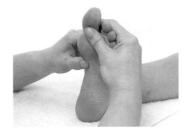

ABOVE *A reflexology treatment to ease abdominal pain.*

more slowly and fully than usual, and imagine that each time you exhale the pain is dissolving. Remain like this for a little while.

AROMATHERAPY

❧ LAVENDER
Lavandula angustifolia
❧ ROMAN CHAMOMILE
Chamaemelum nobile
Both oils are soothing and calming and help to kill the pain.
Application:
Place a warm compress on the stomach area and possibly on the lower back. A hot-water bottle can be used on top of the compress. If the pain continues and the reason is unknown, then good diagnosis is important. If the pain is due to constipation, gentle circular massage of the abdomen with lavender and chamomile will also be of benefit.

CAUTION

If using on small children, make sure that the doses are the relevant sizes.

NUTRITION

Everyone knows the proverb "You are what you eat," and this is never truer than in relation to all digestive problems.
Eat plenty of foods containing soluble fiber (think of it as smoothage, not roughage), such as oats, apples, pears, root vegetables and all the bean family.
Reduce your intake of alcohol, coffee, and all soft drinks. Eat little and often and cut down on all animal fats.
A few weeks on the Food Combining (Hay) Diet (*see p.210*) often work wonders for chronic digestive difficulties.

PREVENTATIVE
measures

Good digestion starts in the mind, so make sure that you always eat in a relaxed situation. Chewing your toast on your way to work or school in the morning, wolfing down a sandwich at your desk, and rushing through your evening meal because you're going out will all guarantee digestive discomfort.

CHEWING: *saliva is a vital digestive enzyme and it is essential to chew your food thoroughly so that by the time it reaches your stomach, starch and cellulose are already being broken down and the rest of the process made easier. Make time to sit and savor even the simplest of meals, and never eat standing in the kitchen while doing something else at the same time.*

FOOD DIARY: *keep a diary of what you eat and when you feel discomfort — it is surprising how often patterns emerge that enable you to avoid your personal trigger-foods.*

EXERCISE: *after eating, don't be tempted to slump in your favorite armchair—the dreaded stomache ache will follow. It's no good scrunching up your whole digestive system when it is full of food and has work to do. Take your stomach for a 10-minute walk after you have eaten.*

LEFT *High-fiber foods such as apples, pears, root vegetables and oats, speed through the digestive system efficiently.*

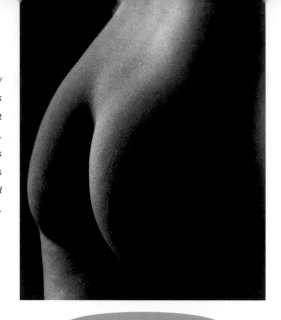

RIGHT *Although potentially embarrassing, flatulence is an absolutely normal result of the digestive process. Certain foods will make its occurrence more likely, as does eating too quickly and swallowing air.*

DIAGNOSING FLATULENCE

- Excessive wind, either through the mouth or the anus
- Often associated with a bloated abdomen

DIGESTIVE SYSTEM

flatulence

*C*omedians joke about it; Shakespeare and Chaucer even wrote about it; everyone has it, but pretends they don't; no one in polite society ever talks about it. Yet nothing is more natural than flatulence—which is the normal by-product of digestion and fermentation that takes place in the gut. Many people feel obsessive anxiety about flatulence, but unless it becomes excessive, there is no need for concern. Any sudden change in the everyday build-up and release of these gases could, however, herald an underlying problem. Possible causes are hiatus hernia, Irritable Bowel Syndrome (see p.154), diverticulitis, or severe constipation (see p.156). But in the absence of other disease, home remedies will usually overcome this problem.

KITCHEN MEDICINE

■ As with most digestive problems, simple kitchen remedies will be found in any well-stocked store cupboard. Dill—both seeds and fronds (the leaves)—caraway and fennel seeds, licorice, parsley, and mint can all be added to cooking and taken as tea, both to prevent and relieve excessive wind.

EXERCISE

AS WITH ALL digestive problems, exercise improves the overall function of the system, while toning up the abdominal muscles has added benefit.

CONVENTIONAL MEDICINE

✚ A change in diet can be helpful, cutting down on legumes such as beans and lentils. Other foods that could be reduced include brussels sprouts, peas, cabbage, and eggs. If the problem persists, try taking an antacid that contains dimethicone.

Dosage information ~
Adults and children
■ Many suitable preparations are available, either as tablets or in liquid form; see package for details.

RIGHT *Eggs and beans cause problems for some.*

HERBAL REMEDIES

...de choice of
...natives to
...estive tract and
...:

...common
... as aniseed,
... (chili),
...ilantro, garlic,
...ge, and thyme,
... to cooking is an
... digestive
...ively, drink
... or try teas of

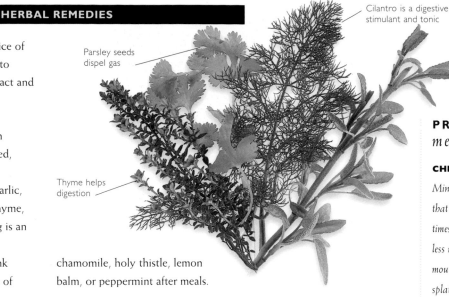

Cilantro is a digestive
stimulant and tonic

Parsley seeds
dispel gas

Thyme helps
digestion

Sage is
carminative

chamomile, holy thistle, lemon
balm, or peppermint after meals.

HOMEOPATHIC REMEDIES

RAPHANUS 6C For
flatulence after abdominal
operations when wind feels
trapped. Distended abdomen,
colicky pains.

LYCOPODIUM 6C When food
seems to ferment in stomach.
Feels full after little food. Bloating
abdomen. Flatus rumbles in
abdomen. Passing flatus eases

abdominal pains. Belching.

CARBO VEGETABILIS 6C For
heaviness after meals, sleepiness
and belching. Flatus smells
offensive. Craves both sweet and
salt foods.

Dosage: one tablet hourly for six
doses, then twice daily. Maximum
1 week.

OUTSIDE HELP

REFLEXOLOGY: work the
soles and palms in order
to stimulate the functioning of
the digestive tract. For chronic
conditions, massage and
squeeze gently down the back
of the lower leg.

YOGA: emphasize twisting
postures and forward bends,
contracting the lower abdomen
each time you exhale, releasing it
as you inhale. Try: standing—
Forward Bend, Twisted Triangle,
Squat; lying—Relax, Twist, Knees-
over-Chest; sitting—Twist,
Forward Bend. Finish with Two-
Foot Support and relaxation.

AROMATHERAPY

ROMAN CHAMOMILE
Chamaemelum nobile

FENNEL
Foeniculum vulgare

GINGER
Zingiber officinale

MARJORAM
Origanum majorana

PEPPERMINT
Mentha x piperita

These oils aid gas dispersal and
calm down the pain associated
with flatulence.

Application:
Use in either an oil-based or
lotion-based massage and rub
onto the abdomen.

NUTRITION

In order to prevent
flatulence you must allow
time for the digestive process to
work—so savor the look and
aroma of your meal and take time
to appreciate its flavor, because
mixing your food with saliva is the
first step toward good digestion.

Avoid all carbonated drinks and
reduce your consumption of sugar
in all forms, as it increases the
amount of fermentation in the
stomach; also **avoid** foods like
beans, brussels sprouts, cauliflower,
and other "windy" foods if you are
suffering from flatulence. But as
your eating habits improve and
you add to your diet more live
yogurt and other fermented milk
products, with all their beneficial
bacteria, you will find that you can
return to eating virtually anything.
It helps, too, if you add caraway
seeds when cooking cabbage, and
summer savory to all bean dishes.

Constipation is an extremely
common cause of excessive and
uncomfortable wind and will be
exacerbated greatly if you start
adding bran to your daily food
intake. Instead, eat foods that
contain soluble fiber, such as oats
(*see Constipation on p.156*).

(*see Constipation on p.156*)

PREVENTATIVE *measures*

CHEWING: *the Victorian Prime
Minister William Gladstone maintained
that all food should be chewed 30
times—and thorough mastication means
less wind. And not speaking with your
mouth full not only prevents you
splattering your neighbor with half-
chewed food, but stops you swallowing
air with your food—a common
aggravating factor.*

FOOD COMBINING: *this way of
eating, frequently known as the Hay
Diet (see p.210), involves separating
protein foods (like meat, fish, cheese, and
eggs) from starchy foods (like bread,
potatoes, rice, pasta, cereals, cookies, and
cakes). It may be a long-term solution for
some people.*

ABOVE *Proteins (top) and starches
(bottom) should be eaten at separate
times on a food-combining diet.*

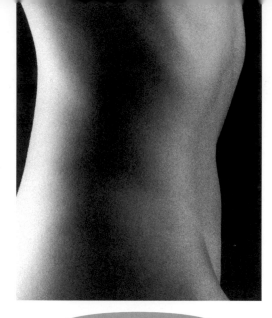

RIGHT *The gallbladder is attached to the liver and connected to the bile duct. It receives and stores bile. Gallstones are small solid masses consisting of cholesterol, bile pigments, and lime salts.*

DIAGNOSING GALLBLADDER PROBLEMS

Most people with gallstones never experience any symptoms, but:

- Gallstones can cause recurrent, painful attacks in the upper right side of the abdomen
- Whites of the eyes and skin may appear yellow, a condition known as jaundice
- Pain may be associated with a fever
- Nausea and vomiting are common

DIGESTIVE SYSTEM

gallbladder problems

CAUTION

Always read pain-reliever packages carefully, and do not exceed the stated dose.

CALL THE PHYSICIAN

■ If pain persists, especially if accompanied by jaundice and a raised temperature.

KITCHEN MEDICINE

■ Every French housewife will serve a fresh globe artichoke as the first course of a meal that has a rich, fatty main course. If you have gallbladder problems, you should eat this wonderful vegetable at least two or three times a week. The chemicals in the artichoke plant have a specific stimulating effect on the gallbladder and liver.

---

*T*he five Fs are one of the aides-mémoires that should stick in any medical student's mind: fair, fat, forty, female, and flatulent are the common denominators for women suffering from gallstones—and women are twice as likely as men to get them. At their worst, gallstones can block the flow of bile from the gallbladder to the stomach and, without bile, the digestion of fats becomes almost impossible. Bile works in the same way as dishwashing liquid on greasy dishes: it emulsifies the fats by breaking them down into millions of tiny globules, vastly increasing the total surface area on which the digestive enzymes can work. Without this process the sometimes horrendous symptoms of projectile vomiting and violent pain ensue. Home remedies are not the answer for acute gallbladder symptoms, but they can prevent them recurring.

CONVENTIONAL MEDICINE

✚ Pain from a gallstone can be excruciating. If the pain continues, despite taking simple pain-relievers, contact a physician immediately. Seek immediate medical help if the pain is associated with fever or jaundice.

Dosage information~

Adults

■ One to two tablets of pain-relievers at onset of pain, repeated every 4 hours; see package for details.

ABOVE *Globe artichokes are known to improve the gallbladder's efficiency.*

HERBAL REMEDIES

 Professional help is essential for severe or persistent problems, but general discomfort can be soothed by anti-inflammatory and bitter herbs, to dilute the bile and ease excretion.

■ **Use and Dosage:**
The "olive oil and lemon" remedy is often successful for gallstones. After breakfast eat nothing more until early evening, then drink 2–4 tbsp/30–60ml of olive oil, followed by the fresh juice of 1–2 lemons diluted with as little warm water as possible. Continue alternating this combination every 20–30 minutes through the evening until you have consumed 1pt/500ml of olive oil and the juice of about 9–10 lemons. The remnants of the gallstones should then be passed with stools over the next 3 days, appearing as small stones and gritty sand.

Try decoctions of milk-thistle seeds, fringe-tree bark, or wild-yam root (1tsp/5ml per cup), or an infusion of fumitory and agrimony (1tsp/5ml each per cup).

For gallstone sufferers, bitters before meals (e.g. 2–5 drops of gentian, wormwood, or centaury tincture) can encourage bile flow; a tea containing parsley piert, milk thistle, and dandelion root (1tsp/5ml of each) may also help.

HOMEOPATHIC REMEDIES

 Consult a physician for gall-bladder problems.

❧ CHELIDONIUM **6c** For pain under right ribs extending to right shoulder blade. Colic, jaundice, gallstones, "bilious vomiting." Stools pasty/yellow.

❧ BERBERIS **6c** For pain under right ribs radiating to stomach and all over body. Worse for pressure. Watery stools that are clay-colored.

❧ HYDRASTIS **6c** For gallstones, tenderness over liver. No appetite or thirst. Jaundice. Stools white.

Dosage: one tablet every 2–3 hours for six doses, then three times daily for 2–3 days.

OUTSIDE HELP

 REFLEXOLOGY: the whole feet or hands should be treated to address all areas of imbalance. The liver reflex is located in the mid-section of the right palm and sole, and the gallbladder reflex beneath the fourth right finger and toe.

AROMATHERAPY

❧ LAVENDER
Lavandula angustifolia
❧ ROMAN CHAMOMILE
Chamaemelum nobile

These oils help to reduce the pain—aromatherapy is not going to cure gallstones or any other gallbladder problems, but it can help to alleviate some of the symptoms.

Application:
The easiest way to use these essential oils would be in a massage oil or massage lotion, which could be applied over the area of the gallbladder.

NUTRITION

A problematic gallbladder necessitates quite a strict food regime. If you have had one acute attack, you certainly will not want another, and you can virtually eliminate the risk by adhering to the following nutritional advice. Apart from controlling the return of your symptoms, this dietary regime has the added bonus of helping you toward a considerable loss of weight—and obesity is a common cause of gallstones.

Eat plenty of vegetables and fruit, and generous portions of whole grain cereals, particularly oats, which help to eliminate cholesterol, the most common constituent of gallstones; plenty of fish, including oily fish (but avoid smoked fish, as it has a high fat content and too much salt); and beans, which also help the body to get rid of cholesterol. And make sure that you have at least one large clove of garlic (or a high-strength garlic pill) every day. **Avoid** alcohol and caffeine, but you must drink a minimum of 3½pt/1.7l of water, in addition to other drinks, every day.

Avoid all animal fats (no beef, pork, lamb, duck, or goose). Chicken without skin is all right, as long as it is roasted (unbasted) on a rack, broiled or boiled. Eat no butter, cream, cheese (except cottage cheese), eggs, or fried food. You can use skim milk, very low-fat yogurt, and a little olive, sunflower or safflower oil. Do not eat sausages, salami, pâté, ham, bacon, meat pies, pasties, or any processed meat whatsoever.

PREVENTATIVE
measures

The best way to prevent gallstones is to be a vegetarian, since they are only half as likely to suffer as meat-eaters. Taking the contraceptive pill increases the risk, and a high-fat diet combined with being overweight increases it even further. But beware: constant alternating between drastic diets and bingeing, with the resultant loss and regain of weight over and over again, will predispose you to an even greater risk of gallbladder problems.

ABOVE *A vegetarian diet avoids many foods that trigger gallbladder problems.*

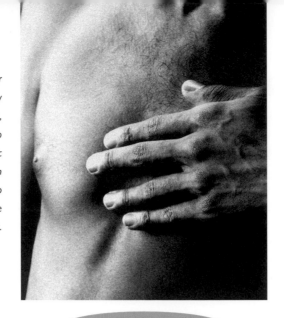

RIGHT *Gastritis is either acute, and brought on by something eaten or drunk, or chronic, when there is no particular cause. Chronic gastritis usually occurs in elderly people, and is due to the breakdown of the stomach lining.*

DIAGNOSING GASTRITIS

- Pain or discomfort in the upper part of the abdomen, related to food
- May be associated with nausea or belching

DIGESTIVE SYSTEM

gastritis

CALL THE PHYSICIAN

■ If the symptoms persist or are not relieved by antacids.

Severe and sudden gastritis—inflammation of the stomach lining—is nearly always self-inflicted. Too much alcohol, too many cigarettes, very hot chili or curry…all these can be the trigger. Some medicines—both prescribed and "over-the-counter"—can also cause damage to these sensitive tissues: aspirin, nonsteroidal anti-inflammatory drugs (NSAIDs), oral steroids, and some antimalarial pills are among the culprits.

CONVENTIONAL MEDICINE

✚ Avoid spicy foods, hot drinks, alcohol, and smoking. Avoid nonsteroidal anti-inflammatory drugs, which are often taken for pain relief. Eating frequent, regular small meals of bland food may relieve the symptoms. Antacids can also be helpful.

Dosage information ~

Adults and children over 16

■ Many types of antacid are available as tablets or in liquid form; see package for details.

CAUTION

Antacids usually contain magnesium or aluminum salts: the former (e.g. Milk of Magnesia) tend to cause diarrhea; the latter (e.g. Aluminum hydroxide) may cause constipation.

AROMATHERAPY

 ℞ ROMAN CHAMOMILE
Chamaemelum nobile
℞ LAVENDER
Lavandula angustifolia
℞ MELISSA
Melissa officinalis

These oils help to relieve the pain and irritation of gastritis.

Application:

Apply as a massage over the abdominal area, or as a compress.

OUTSIDE HELP

REFLEXOLOGY: when the acute phase of diarrhea and vomiting has passed, work the stomach and intestine reflexes on the soles of the feet. Work lightly for a few minutes daily to help restore normal function.

ABOVE *Acidic foods may be a culprit.*

HERBAL REMEDIES

 Herbs will soothe and protect the inflamed stomach lining, as well as reduce acidity and ease associated nausea.

■ **Use and Dosage:** Slippery elm and marshmallow are popular and widely available in tablets or powders (make into a paste with warm water).

Fenugreek seeds (2tsp /10ml per cup) in a decoction with a pinch of powdered cinnamon can bring relief; or use lemon balm, meadowsweet, and fennel in an infusion (½– 1tsp /2.5–5ml of each per cup).

Use licorice root in a decoction or dissolve a 1in/2.5cm licorice stick in a cup of hot water.

HOMEOPATHIC REMEDIES

Severe pains, vomiting blood or dark "coffee-grounds" fluid, or persistent pain require medical attention. A consultation with a qualified homeopath is recommended. (*See also Peptic Ulcers on p.152.*)

✿ BISMUTH **6C** For burning pains in stomach, severe cramps. Person is frightened, wants someone with them all the time. Thirsty for cold water, which they vomit very soon afterward.

✿ NUX VOMICA **6C** For gastritis from alcohol. Cannot stand pressure around waist. Cramping pains, worse for eating, anger. Workaholic and irritable.

✿ CAPSICUM **6C** For burning or icy-cold feeling in stomach. Wants coffee but this makes them nauseous. Lots of flatulence.

Dosage: one tablet taken every 2 hours for six doses, then three times daily. Maximum period 3 days.

NUTRITION

It is not normally difficult to identify foods that trigger bouts of acute gastritis and, once isolated, these can then be avoided. In addition to those already listed, coffee (particularly instant coffee), pickles, vinegar, raw onions, and all the very sour fruits may be implicated.

Long periods without food can result in discomfort, even more so at times of stress, when the secretion of acid from the stomach lining is increased. Chronically, this pattern can lead to stomach ulcers, now known to be caused by the bacteria *Helicobacter pylori* (*H. pylori*)—a bug that is particularly susceptible to the naturally occurring chemicals in manuka honey.

A sensible eating pattern of frequent small meals combined with avoidance of known or suspected irritants is the key to solving gastritis.

PREVENTATIVE
measures

Avoiding food irritants and following the dietary advice given are essential for anyone with a history of recurring gastritis. Modest consumption of alcohol and total avoidance of nicotine are important. Include regular use of all the culinary herbs that are aids to digestion—parsley, sage, rosemary, thyme, mint, ginger, dill, fennel, and caraway in particular.

SLIPPERY ELM: *one of the many great traditional medicines of the Native North Americans is the bark of the slippery, or red, elm. It is sold as a powder in health-food stores and, to make a soothing drink, simply mix 1tsp/5ml with a little cold water, add 2tsp/10ml of honey and a cup of boiling water, stirring thoroughly. The resulting gruel should be taken every morning before breakfast.*

KITCHEN MEDICINE

■ A quarter of a teaspoon of baking soda in a glass of warm water helps neutralize excess acid.

■ A tea made of licorice, fennel, dill, or peppermint can be instantly soothing, particularly when a spoonful of honey is added.

■ Honey itself is a centuries-old traditional remedy for peptic ulcers and gastritis—and manuka honey from New Zealand is a tried-and-tested remedy of the Maoris.

ABOVE *Manuka honey, used by the Maoris of New Zealand, fights the bacteria that cause peptic ulcers.*

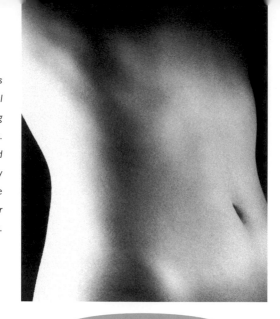

RIGHT Gastroenteritis is caused by bacterial or viral infection, and eating poisonous substances. Although the vomiting and diarrhea are very unpleasant, this is how the body expels the poison or infection.

DIAGNOSING GASTROENTERITIS

- Nausea and vomiting
- Diarrhea
- Crampy abdominal pain
- Mild fever

DIGESTIVE SYSTEM

gastroenteritis
including food poisoning

CALL THE PHYSICIAN

■ If diarrhea or vomiting is prolonged, to rule out any underlying illness.

■ If you have been unable to hold down fluids for longer than 12 hours.

CAUTION

Severe gastroenteritis, especially in children or the elderly, who are at particular risk of dehydration, may be extremely grave or even life-threatening.

Avoid medicines that claim to stop diarrhea, as they tend to prolong the illness; reserve them for occasions when it may be difficult to use a lavatory frequently, such as while traveling or taking an examination.

*A*cute and violent diarrhea and vomiting may be caused by an infection that you catch from someone else—bouts of this type of bug can run through closed communities like the proverbial dose of salts—but, most commonly, acute gastroenteritis is caused by food poisoning and is transmitted by food that has spoiled, been improperly cooked or handled, or prepared by someone with contaminated hands. For an otherwise fit and healthy adult, home remedies can help bring about an effective and rapid recovery.

CONVENTIONAL MEDICINE

Take a sip of fluid every 5 minutes. If the vomiting continues and symptoms persist for more than 12 hours, seek urgent medical attention. If the symptoms are less severe, drinking extra water will help, but this needs to be combined with salt and sugar to be most effective. Special oral rehydration fluid preparations are available, which taste like strong mineral water. They can be flavored or made into ice cubes to make them more palatable. Prolonged diarrhea may require further treatment, so seek medical advice.

Dosage information~
Adults and children

■ Dissolve the contents of an oral rehydration packet in water and drink after each episode of diarrhea; see package for full details.

OUTSIDE HELP

REFLEXOLOGY: when the acute phase of diarrhea and vomiting has passed, work the stomach and intestine reflexes on the soles of the feet. Work lightly for a few minutes daily to help restore normal function.

YOGA: when the pain is really bad, place your hands where it hurts most. Feel their warmth. Inhaling, imagine them healing you. Exhaling, imagine that the pain is gradually dissolving.

HERBAL REMEDIES

 Herbs can ease the symptoms, while nature gets rid of the irritant.

■ **Use and Dosage:**
Combine bistort and fenugreek decoction with an agrimony and gotu kola infusion (1 cup of the mixture, three to five times daily) to soothe the lower bowel.

Take slippery elm or marshmallow capsules to protect the gut lining. Bilberry or cranberry juice will combat fluid loss while easing bowel discomfort.

Aloe vera juice is often recommended and is an ideal remedy, if available.

Take 10 drops of echinacea tincture in a little water every few hours in order to combat any infecting organisms.

LIVE YOGURT

KITCHEN MEDICINE

■ Apart from the culinary herbs, many of which have a soothing effect on the lining of the intestinal tract (*see Gastritis on p.146*), yogurt plays a vital role in recovering from gastroenteritis. The natural bacteria present in yogurt, known as probiotics, attack and destroy unwelcome bacteria, play a key role in the digestive process and have an immune-boosting effect on your natural resistance. This is also true of fermented milk products. Unfortunately, none of these benefits is provided by most commercial yogurts, which contain none of the live bacteria, after being treated a second time. For this reason, you must choose live yogurt, which is a rich source of the beneficial probiotic bacteria.

HOMEOPATHIC REMEDIES

 Starve for 24 hours, maintaining hydration by taking sips of water every 15 minutes. The following remedies may be used for travelers' diarrhea.
❧ **ARSENICUM ALBUM 6C** For gastroenteritis from food poisoning. Diarrhea and vomiting at the same time. Chilly, better for warmth. Patient restless, anxious, and weak. Heat improves burning abdominal pain. Thirsty for sips of liquid.
❧ **VERATRUM ALBUM 6C** Give if Arsenicum album fails, for very profuse watery stool. Thirsty for large quantities of cold drinks.
Dosage: one tablet hourly until improved, then every 4 hours. Maximum 5 days.

AROMATHERAPY

❧ ROMAN CHAMOMILE
Chamaemelum nobile
❧ LAVENDER
Lavandula angustifolia
❧ MELISSA
Melissa officinalis
❧ TEA TREE
Melaleuca alternifolia

ABOVE *Roman chamomile soothes emotional distress.*

Tea tree will stop cross-infection, because it is antiviral and antibacterial. Chamomile and lavender calm and soothe but are also painkillers. Lavender also relieves the stress that accompanies gastroenteritis, while melissa is an antidepressant and relieves spasms in the digestive tract.

Application:
Tea tree is useful in the home, especially to protect other members of the family—so have it burning, and make sure that you use it to wash all surfaces down, and wash out the bath and any soiled linen. Use the other oils in the bath, in a body lotion or for massage.

PREVENTATIVE
measures

PERSONAL HYGIENE: *most food poisoning still occurs at home, where scrupulous cleanliness in the kitchen and careful attention to personal hygiene are the first lines of defense. It should, but sadly does not, go without saying that washing your hands after going to the bathroom is essential. But remember to scrub your nails, too.*

KITCHEN HYGIENE: *frozen meat and poultry must be thawed slowly and thoroughly before cooking; poultry and burgers must be cooked until all the juices run clear; separate chopping boards must be used for raw and cooked meat and poultry (and separate cloths to clean up afterward). In the refrigerator, carefully separate raw meat and poultry from all other foods: put them at the bottom in deep containers so that blood cannot drip onto other food.*

TRAVELERS' TIPS: *protect yourself with a few simple rules and lots of common sense. Remember the old adage when traveling to far-flung places: "Cook it, peel it, or forget it." Do not eat undercooked meat, fish or poultry or raw shellfish. Don't touch salads anywhere in Asia or Africa. And be very wary of the hotel buffet, sweltering in the fly-infested sunshine. Water can be a great hazard—beware ice cubes!*

NUTRITION

The first step is to replace lost fluids and electrolytes. Over-the-counter products are available, but in an emergency make your own by adding 8tsp/40g of sugar or honey and 1tsp/5ml of salt to 2pt/1l of boiled water, then drink a wineglassful every half-hour. Give children 2–4tsp/10–20ml every 10 minutes.

You will not feel like eating until the worst symptoms have abated. When you do, avoid all dairy products for at least 48 hours and, during that time, stick to the BRAT diet—ripe Bananas, boiled Rice, Apples, and dry whole wheat Toast. Do not have any ice-cold drinks and avoid all citrus juices.

ABOVE *Try the BRAT diet as a first step back on the road to normal eating.*

RIGHT *Lice live on the skin and feed by sucking blood, causing intense itching. Intestinal parasites enter the body through contaminated food, and may cause anal itching or more serious symptoms.*

DIAGNOSING INFESTATION

- Parasitic skin infections cause an itchy rash
- Worms in the digestive tract may be passed in the stool and may cause itching around the anus

DIGESTIVE SYSTEM

infestation
worms and parasites

CALL THE PHYSICIAN

■ If you suspect that you are suffering from an intestinal parasite.

CAUTION

Infants and asthmatics should avoid using alcoholic solutions for head lice.

Parasites like head lice and scabies and the wide variety of intestinal worms, such as pinworm, are no respecters of person or position. Any one of us can come into contact with an affected child's head or eat a piece of infected meat or fish. Intestinal parasites require medical attention, while skin infestations can take several treatments to clear, particularly in the case of some head lice, which have become resistant to some currently available medicated shampoos and treatment lotions. In both cases, however, there are home remedies that can help with the infestation.

CONVENTIONAL MEDICINE

✚ Pinworms are easily treated with a single dose of mebendazole, although it may need to be repeated after 2–3 weeks. The whole family should be treated at the same time. Parasitic skin infestations can be treated with insecticides, which are available as lotions and shampoos, and the whole

affected area needs treatment. Do not use insecticides too frequently on children; instead, for head lice, try regularly combing the hair with a fine nit-comb. This is easily done after washing. Put on conditioner and leave for 5 minutes before combing, then wash off.

Dosage information ~
Adults and children

■ For scabies, apply a water-based solution all over the body.

■ For head lice, apply a water-based lotion to the whole scalp. Repeat after 7 days.

■ For pinworms, take one dose of mebendazole, repeated 2 weeks later.

ABOVE *Conventional treatment relies on insecticidal shampoo. Do not use too often.*

KITCHEN MEDICINE

■ Pumpkin seeds are a traditional remedy for worms, and here is an effective, but long and not exactly pleasant treatment. Scald ⅓ cup/50g of pumpkin seeds with boiling water and remove the outer skin. Add a little milk to the husks and grind to a paste—most easily done with a mortar and pestle, though the back of a wooden spoon will do. After 12 hours without food, eat all of the resulting paste and wait another 2 hours without eating. Then take 4tsp/20ml of castor oil mixed with orange juice. You can have a light meal now and should pass the worms after about 3 hours.

CAUTION

Under no circumstances, take castor oil for any other purpose. Do not use it as a laxative. With repeated use it can be extremely damaging to the intestines.

■ Two other traditional foods may not be quite as effective, but are certainly more palatable. Naturopaths have long advocated eating a big portion of carrots or drinking a large glass of carrot juice each day, as well as drinking the juice of a whole lemon vigorously mixed with 1tbsp/15ml of olive oil.

HERBAL REMEDIES

 As well as carrots (*see under Kitchen Medicine*), cabbage is a traditional remedy for pinworms and can be used in the same way. And there are other herbal remedies for infestation.

■ **Use and Dosage:** Take garlic as a preventative when you are traveling.

Wormwood is one of the most effective herbal remedies, but is very bitter and unpleasant to taste: 1tsp/5ml (¼tsp/1ml for children) of the tincture, well diluted in water or carrot juice and taken on an empty stomach, may be sufficient to clear the problem. Repeat the dose after 14 days (to match the threadworm's life cycle).

Head lice can best be treated by putting a few drops of neat tea-tree or thyme oil onto a fine comb and then combing the hair well night and morning; use a strong tansy infusion as a rinse after shampooing.

HOMEOPATHIC REMEDIES

 The following remedies have a reputation for helping to clear worms. However, if the symptoms persist, consult a physician.

℞ CINA **6C** Common name: wormseed. For patient who is restless, frantic, and irritable. Itchy rectum. May have diarrhea and cramping abdominal pain, better for pressure.

℞ SABADILLA **6C** For chilly and not thirsty person. Itching in the rectum may alternate with itchy nose. Usually considered a hay-fever remedy.

℞ NATRUM PHOSPHORICUM **6C** For greenish diarrhoea and noisy flatus, which can bring some stool with it. Itching anus.
Dosage: one tablet twice daily. Maximum 1 week.

℞ STAPHYSAGRIA For head lice, dilute mother tincture (which is available at homeopathic pharmacies) in a ratio of 1:10 with baby shampoo. Shampoo the hair, then leave on for 10 minutes, rinse and comb hair through. Repeat next night if there are further signs of lice. Repeat again 1 week later.

AROMATHERAPY

℞ ROSEMARY
Rosmarinus officinalis
℞ LAVENDER
Lavandula angustifolia
℞ ROMAN CHAMOMILE
Chamaemelum nobile
℞ NIAOULI
Melaleuca viridiflora
℞ EUCALYPTUS
Eucalyptus radiata
℞ TEA TREE
Melaleuca alternifolia
These oils are calming and soothing and will help to fight infection.

Application:
For threadworm, the oils can be used to massage the abdomen. This should be accompanied by treatment from your physician or pharmacist. To deter or treat head lice, add 1–2 drops of the oils to the final rinse water; or mix 2–3 drops with some warm vegetable oil (about 1tsp/5ml), then massage into the hair, wrap the hair in plastic wrap, and a warm towel, and leave overnight. In the morning comb through, then wash out the hair; repeat if necessary.

PREVENTATIVE *measures*

TRAVELERS' TIPS: *most worms and their eggs survive only in raw or undercooked food. The fish tapeworm—found in pickled, raw, or undercooked fish—is a risk in Scandinavia, parts of Switzerland, the Baltic countries, and the Far East (especially Japan). The beef worm is found throughout the Middle East, Africa, and South America—rare burgers and steak are a real danger. The pork worm is most common in Eastern Europe, Africa, and Southeast Asia—and it represents a much more serious risk than the other worms, as the larvae can migrate to the eye (where they cause blindness) or the brain (epilepsy).*

Mouse droppings may carry the eggs of the dwarf tapeworm, which contaminate food stores, but cause very few symptoms. This parasite is common in Egypt, parts of the Mediterranean, Sudan, and areas of South America.

In Holland and Scandinavia, where raw herrings are a popular delicacy, there is the risk of acquiring roundworm, though modern production techniques of freezing the herring for a few days kill the worms.

LICE: *the only way to protect yourself against head lice is never to let your hair come into direct contact with anyone else's. Pubic lice can only be caught in someone else's bed.*

OUTSIDE HELP

REFLEXOLOGY: as part of a more complete cleansing program, work the reflexes of the digestive tract on the soles and palms. Begin beneath the knuckles or the balls of the feet and work down firmly and thoroughly to the wrists or heels, especially over the liver and colon reflexes.

RIGHT *Peptic ulcers are an inflamed break in the mucous membrane lining the stomach. Like mouth ulcers, they are very painful and are aggravated by certain foods.*

DIAGNOSING PEPTIC ULCERS

- Pain in the upper part of the abdomen, often in a specific place and that can be pointed out with one finger
- Pain is often worse at night
- May be worse when hungry and associated with nausea, flatulence, and heartburn

DIGESTIVE SYSTEM

peptic ulcers

Peptic ulcers are caused by erosion of the lining of the stomach by excessive amounts of gastric acid. While stress frequently plays a part in this condition, we now know that the balance between the acid digestive juices and the protective mucus produced by the stomach lining is also upset. The latest research has shown that bacteria called Helicobacter pylori may cause some ulcers. These bacteria are very widespread and are common in cats, which may pass them on to their human owners, some of whom may develop an ulcer. There are still those who recommend bland diets of boiled rice and steamed fish for people with peptic ulcers, but simple home remedies and good healthy eating can often overcome this problem permanently.

CALL THE PHYSICIAN

■ If you have specific pain in the upper abdomen and have lost weight unintentionally.

■ If it is the first time you have had these symptoms and you are over 40 years old.

CAUTION

Nonsteroidal anti-inflammatory drugs can make the symptoms worse.

Antacids usually contain magnesium or aluminum salts: the former (e.g. Milk of Magnesia) tend to cause diarrhea; the latter (e.g. Aluminum hydroxide) may cause constipation.

CONVENTIONAL MEDICINE

Avoid spicy foods, hot drinks, alcohol, and smoking. Do not take any nonsteroidal anti-inflammatory drugs, which are often used for pain relief. Eating frequent, regular small meals of bland food may relieve the symptoms. Antacids can also be helpful—try them if symptoms persist for more than a week. Your physician may refer you to have further tests or may recommend a trial of an H2 antagonist first. If you have *Helicobacter pylori* infection, you may need a course of antibiotics.

Dosage information ~

Adults and children over 16

■ Many types of antacid are available as tablets or in liquid form; see package for details.

EXERCISE

IF STRESS is a factor, then regular exercise can help to dissipate the build-up of adrenalin and promote the release of the "feel-good" and relaxing hormones known as endorphins. Obviously the amount and type of exercise taken should be commensurate with your age and the state of your physical health.

HERBAL REMEDIES

 Herbal antibacterials, such as blue flag, echinacea, red clover, thyme, and wild indigo, are worth taking in capsules or teas to combat the underlying cause. Symptomatic relief from peptic ulcers comes from soothing demulcents, like slippery elm or marshmallow, meadowsweet or Irish moss, taken as teas, liquid extracts, or tinctures.

■ **Use and Dosage:**
Make 2tsp/10ml of slippery-elm powder into a gruel with a cup of hot milk for relief from the symptoms.

Licorice extracts have been used in orthodox medicine for treating ulceration: make a decoction of the root, or dissolve licorice-juice sticks in water and take in 2tsp/10ml doses or add to teas.

HOMEOPATHIC REMEDIES

A consultation with a homeopath is recommended, after seeing your physician.

❧ ARSENICUM ALBUM **6C** For raw, burning feeling in stomach. Worse for food and drink. Better for milk. Food feels as if it sticks in gullet, with nothing going through. Person is frightened and restless.

❧ GRAPHITES **6C** For burning or constricting pain in stomach. Better temporarily for eating and warm milk. Vomits food immediately after eating.

❧ PHOSPHORUS **6C** For burning pain. Worse for eating, better for cold food. Thirst for ice-cold water, but vomits soon afterwards. May vomit "coffee grounds." **Dosage:** one tablet twice daily. Maximum 2 weeks.

ABOVE *Arsenicum is prepared from white oxide of arsenic.*

KITCHEN MEDICINE
■ Scientists in New Zealand have shown that manuka honey (from the tea tree) has the ability to kill the particular bug responsible for ulcers. 2tsp/10ml with each meal and another at bedtime will normally produce results within a few weeks.
■ In European natural medicine, raw cabbage and potato juice are known to be effective in the treatment and cure of peptic ulcers. A small wine glass before each meal, on a daily alternating basis, is known to work.

OUTSIDE HELP

REFLEXOLOGY: the mid-section of the soles of the feet contains the reflexes of the stomach and duodenum. Make several passes over this area, pausing to compress tender points gently. Complete reflexology treatment may be given regularly to reduce stress levels.

YOGA: see Stress (*p.60*), which is often linked to ulcers. Practice with great awareness to discover what helps. Use Shitali or Sitkari with long exhalation. Lie in the Relaxation Posture, hands resting lightly over your abdomen, and make the sound "aah" as you breathe out.

NUTRITION

 In order to promote healing of the gastric lining, it is important to eat foods that are rich in zinc, so **eat plenty of** whole grains, pumpkin seeds, oysters, and most shellfish; broccoli, red and green bell peppers, kiwis, apricots, and the sweeter citrus fruit for their vitamin C and beta-carotene. These nutrients promote healing of the ulcer. Oily fish is also important, as its omega-3 fatty acids protect the whole gastric lining.

Contrary to traditional dietary advice, a diet that is rich in fiber is also protective, but **avoid** spoonfuls of uncooked bran. Oats, brown rice, and most root vegetables contain soluble fiber, which is more soothing.

AROMATHERAPY

The aim of aromatherapy here would be to reduce stress levels, rather than treat the ulcer, so look up the oils for stress (*see p.60*) and use them in the way that is most relevant to you, applying your sense of smell to find the oils that you like best. Do make sure you have good diagnosis and that you do truly have a peptic ulcer.

PREVENTATIVE *measures*

DIET: *ulcers can be prevented by sensible eating. Food should be taken at regular intervals and in moderate quantities to avoid overloading the stomach and stimulating excessive production of gastric juices. Long periods without food can be a causative factor, and chewing gum may encourage the production of gastric juices, which is a bad thing if there is no food for them to work on, for they are then more likely to attack the stomach lining. Cut down your salt intake, avoid excessive amounts of alcohol (especially spirits), and do not eat large quantities of smoked or pickled foods. If you have had peptic ulcers in the past, it is probably best to avoid hot chilis and very strong curries. Large amounts of coffee (especially instant) may also irritate the stomach lining and cause a recurrence of your ulcer.*

BELOW *Take measures to reduce the amount of stress in your life. Many physicians now offer courses in stress management. Set aside time for periods of complete relaxation within the day.*

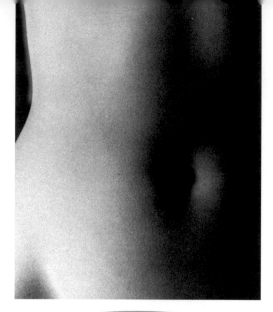

DIAGNOSING IRRITABLE BOWEL SYNDROME

- Recurrent episodes of abdominal pain with constipation or diarrhea
- Pain is often relieved by passing wind or a bowel movement

DIGESTIVE SYSTEM

irritable bowel syndrome *IBS*

Irritable bowel syndrome has in recent years graduated from a relatively obscure condition, known as spastic colon, to epidemic proportions throughout the US and Britain. Though it can be the sequel to a severe bout of food poisoning or gastroenteritis, it is far more likely to be the result of an over-consumption of bran fiber and under-consumption of the soluble fiber found in fruit and vegetables. Contrary to the opinion of some practitioners of alternative medicine, it is not caused by the yeast infection Candida and equally it is not, as many physicians believe, a symptom of depression or other psychological illness. Stress, however, can play a major part and it is hardly surprising that, after years of uncomfortable IBS symptoms, many sufferers do become stressed or depressed. But IBS is a prime example of home remedies offering the best treatment.

KITCHEN MEDICINE

■ Oats are particularly beneficial in the relief of IBS, as they contain both soluble fiber and mucilage, a substance that lubricates the bowel. In addition to eating a bowl of porridge or muesli every day, make sure that you also have 2½ cups/600ml of thin porridge gruel. To make this, add 2 heaped tbsp/40ml of oatmeal to 2½ cups/600ml of boiling water and stir continuously until it comes back to the boil. Simmer the gruel for 20 minutes, still stirring occasionally, then strain through a fine sieve, add 1 tsp/5ml of honey and 1 tbsp/15ml of light cream.

CONVENTIONAL MEDICINE

Keeping a food diary can help to establish links between symptoms and particular foods. Many people find that dietary fiber makes the symptoms worse, although it can be helpful in some cases. Relaxation techniques may be beneficial, as irritable bowel syndrome is often associated with stress. If the symptoms persist, your physician may recommend trying medication to relax the muscle in the digestive tract.

HERBAL REMEDIES

 Herbs can help regulate digestive function as well as ease the discomfort of IBS.

■ **Use and Dosage:**
Make an infusion from equal amounts of agrimony, hops, meadowsweet, and peppermint and drink a cup before meals.

Fenugreek tea can also help—simmer 2tsp/10ml of seeds with a pinch of cinnamon in a cup of water for 10–15 minutes.

Herbs like wild yam and cramp bark can ease painful gut spasms and cramps: use them either in decoctions or as tinctures (10 drops taken on the tongue at 30-minute intervals).

HOMEOPATHIC REMEDIES

 IBS responds well to homeopathic treatment. If the following remedies do not help, then consult a homeopath.

☙ LYCOPODIUM 6C For bloating that is better for passing wind. Rumbling in stomach. Eating little gives a sense of fullness. Craves candies and warm food and drink. Hard stool, then changes to liquid. Constipation away from home.

☙ NUX VOMICA 6C For cramping abdominal pains. Worse for eating. Better after bowels open and for warm drinks. Constipation: small amounts of stool. Constant feeling need to go to bathroom. Diarrhea alternates with constipation.

☙ PULSATILLA 6C For changeable stool, no two alike. Bloating. Indigestion from fatty and rich foods. Little or no thirst.
Dosage: one tablet twice daily. Maximum 1 week.

OUTSIDE HELP

 ACUPRESSURE: regular use of point 4 will help to keep the large bowel functioning efficiently.

REFLEXOLOGY: work the reflexes of the digestive tract daily, especially below the spleen on the left foot. Start working beneath the finger knuckles or toe joints and continue down to the wrist or heel on the palms and soles.

YOGA: see Stress (p.60). When affected, practice gently, with great awareness, and stop if any movement feels wrong. Lie in the Relaxation Posture with your hands over your stomach.

AROMATHERAPY

☙ NEROLI
Citrus aurantium

☙ ROMAN CHAMOMILE
Chamaemelum nobile

☙ ROSE
Rosa damascena/Rosa centifolia
These oils are calming and soothing, not only on a physical level but on an emotional one.
Application:
Use in abdominal massage, with either an aqueous cream or oil. The oils can also be used in a warm compress or in the bath.

NUTRITION

 If alternating bouts of constipation, diarrhea, flatulence, and stomach distension, with almost constant pain, have been with you for years, do not despair. Changing your eating habits can—and does—restore your life to normal. Do not expect instant success, as this is a process of trial and error. Do keep detailed records of what you eat and its consequences, so that you know which foods are okay and which ones you should avoid.

Eat plenty of food that contains soluble fiber—fruit, vegetables, oats, and beans. Cereals contain a mixture of soluble and insoluble fiber; but wheat bran is not only an irritant, but can also interfere with the way in which the body absorbs vital nutrients like iron and calcium. You must drink at least 3pt/1.5l of water every day and ensure that you eat proper meals at regular intervals. And it is important to make generous use of all the culinary herbs that help the digestive process—rosemary, sage, thyme, mint, dill, caraway, garlic, and ginger.

The idea that IBS is an allergic response is erroneous, but for some people it is an adverse reaction to specific foods. These (in descending order of likelihood) are: meat and meat products, dairy produce, and wheat products. Try excluding them in groups—one at a time, for at least 2 weeks. Even if you do not notice a significant improvement, you might find that the symptoms get worse when you reintroduce these foods. This is a clue that you should continue to avoid them. Get professional help before excluding any complete group of food from your diet for any length of time.

PREVENTATIVE *measures*

Simple herbal remedies like hypericum have no side-effects, are not habit-forming, and will help with depression while you experiment with your diet.

EXERCISE

ANY REGULAR exercise will help improve general digestive function, but abdominal exercises are really important here. Take care, though, for many of the traditional stomach exercises can put a strain on your back. Do the following exercises 5 times each night and morning, building up to 20 repetitions once your muscles get stronger.

1. Lie on your back and bend one knee, keeping that foot flat on the floor. Raise the other leg straight until it is level with the knee. Hold for 5 seconds, then lower slowly. Change legs and repeat.

2. Starting in the same position as in 1, with the left leg bent, stretch your right hand toward your left knee, lifting only your head and right shoulder off the floor. Hold for 5 seconds, then relax. Change legs and repeat, stretching left hand toward right knee.

3. Sit with both knees bent and hands grasping the back of the thighs. Using your arm muscles, allow yourself to lean gradually back, then pull up with the arms to the upright position. Do not let your trunk go all the way down to the floor. In time, as your abdominal muscles strengthen, you will gradually get farther and farther back, until you can eventually change from "sit-downs" to sit-ups.

4. Lie flat on the floor, with both heels on a stool or chair about 12in/30cm high. Raise one straight leg and lower slowly. Repeat with the other leg. After 3 weeks, raise both legs together. To protect your back, never do straight-leg raises starting with your feet on the floor, or, worse still, with them wedged under a piece of furniture or held down by somebody else.

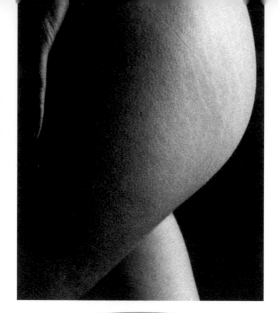

RIGHT *If feces is retained for several days, it dries out and becomes harder to pass. Occasionally, straining will cause an anal fissure. Help it to heal by applying a soothing ointment.*

DIAGNOSING CONSTIPATION

- Straining to defecate
- Hard feces, sometimes painful to pass
- Stomach pain
- Bloating
- Wind
- General feeling of malaise

DIGESTIVE SYSTEM

constipation

Constipation is one of the most common of all digestive problems, and at the same time the one most suited to home treatment. People vary as to how often they open their bowels: some normally go irregularly, maybe no more than every 2 or 3 days; others go two or three times a day, or more. Children, the elderly, and pregnant women are more prone to constipation, but it can occur in either sex at any age. A lack of the right sort of soluble fiber, insufficient fluid, and bad toilet habits are the prime causes, and these are all easily remedied.

KITCHEN MEDICINE

■ Pour 2½pt/1l of boiling water over 2lb/1kg of pitted prunes and a few pieces of bruised licorice stick. Leave to stand overnight. Remove the licorice, drain off the liquid, and purée in a blender. Keep in the refrigerator and take 4tsp/20ml with breakfast and 2tsp/10ml with a warm drink at bedtime.

EXERCISE

ALL EXERCISE is good, but activities that work the abdominal muscles are particularly so. Swimming, rowing (boats or machines), and sit-up exercises all help to tone the abdominal muscles and get rid of constipation. But abdominal exercises can stress the lower back (see *Back Pain* on p.100).

CONVENTIONAL MEDICINE

If the bowel has become stretched and full of feces, it needs to be retrained to respond to the urge to go to the bathroom, by sitting regularly on the lavatory, without being hurried and without straining. The best time to do this is after a meal. Hard feces may need softening by changing the diet and increasing your fluid intake, although this may take a day or two to take effect. In the meantime, a laxative, together with some suppositories, can be helpful. If you suspect that prescribed medicines may be causing your constipation, consult your physician for advice before reducing the dose. If constipation persists seek medical help.

Dosage information ~

Adults

■ Natural or vegetable laxatives are safe and nonaddictive, so ask your pharmacist for advice in choosing one. Consult package for dosage information. A short course will usually restore a regular bowel habit, and the laxative can then be reduced over a week, before stopping. One or two glycerol suppositories, moistened before use, will stimulate bowel movement. Usually once a day is sufficient. Adult and child sizes are usually available.

Children

■ Consult a physician for medical advice before starting laxatives.

HERBAL REMEDIES

Drastic herbal purgatives—like senna and cascara sagrada—were once household standbys, but should be used in moderation, as long-term use can damage the digestive system.

■ **Use and Dosage:**
Each morning, take a decoction of equal amounts of dandelion, yellow dock and licorice roots (2tsp/10ml to 1½ cups/350ml of water, simmered for 10 minutes) with a dash of anise or fennel seeds to ease griping.

Help lubricate the bowel with ispaghula seeds—add 1tsp/5ml to a cup of boiling water, cool, then drink the entire mix; orange juice instead of water improves flavor.

HOMEOPATHIC REMEDIES

 Increase your intake of fluids and fiber, and make sure that you take regular exercise. A teaspoon of linseeds taken daily may help. Sudden changes in bowel habit require medical attention.

☘ ALUMINA **6C** For soft, sticky or hard, dry stools that are difficult to pass, even when soft. Constipation in the elderly, from inactivity. No urge to open bowels.

☘ BRYONIA **6C** For hard, dry, large crumbly stools. May have diarrhea after taking cold drinks. Thirsty for large quantities of fluids.

☘ OPIUM **6C** For stools that are hard black balls. No urge to open bowels. Constipation from fright and in newborn babies. Opium may require a prescription in some countries.

Dosage: one tablet three times daily. Maximum 1 week.

NUTRITION

 In almost all cases constipation is the result of faulty nutrition—insufficient daily liquid and a shortfall in the amount of fiber required. Constipation is aggravated—and may even be caused by—irregular toilet habits. Psychological factors can play a major part, too. Drink at least 4pt/2l of water each day and eat regular portions of unpeeled apples, pears, root vegetables, oats, beans, and all green vegetables; at least one container of live natural yogurt daily; and plenty of real whole wheat bread. Brown rice, whole wheat pasta, porridge, and muesli are great providers of soluble fiber—smoothage, rather than roughage. Do not use uncooked bran or high-bran cereals.

PREVENTATIVE *measures*

Follow the nutritional advice to protect yourself from constipation. Watch out for medicines that can sometimes cause constipation as a sideeffect, including pain-reliever containing codeine and also iron tablets. Children may become constipated following the change from formula or breast milk to cow's milk.

REGULAR TOILET HABITS: *never ignore the essential call of nature (this does not mean going to the bathroom with a cigarette, a cup of tea, and the morning papers). Avoid the regular use of irritant laxatives and excessive straining, which is a certain guarantee of getting hemorrhoids (see p.176).*

OUTSIDE HELP

ACUPRESSURE: points 4, 23, 28, and 29 are all helpful for constipation.

REFLEXOLOGY: the reflex for the colon can be found on the lower half of the hands and feet, but to relieve this condition, work the entire soles and palms in order to stimulate the functioning of the digestive system.

YOGA: emphasize twisting postures and forward bends, contracting the lower abdomen each time you exhale, releasing it as you inhale. Try: standing—Forward Bend, Twisted Triangle, Squat; lying—Relax, Twist, Knees-over-Chest; sitting—Twist, Forward Bend. Finish with Two-Foot Support and relaxation.

The Twist. ① Sit with your left arm around your right knee, palm resting on your thigh, right hand on the floor behind you.

② Exhaling, slowly turn to look over right shoulder. Hold for two breaths, then repeat on the opposite side.

Forward Bend. ① Sit erect, with your feet out in front of you. Inhale and raise your arms.

② Bend forward from the hips whilst exhaling and reaching toward your feet. Hold your feet, lower your head, and stay for several breaths. Come out of the position in reverse.

AROMATHERAPY

 ☘ BLACK PEPPER
Piper nigrum
☘ GINGER
Zingiber officinale
☘ MARJORAM
Origanum majorana

These oils are warming and stimulating to the digestive system.

Application:
Use these oils for abdominal massage—mix the essential oil with either a lotion or a carrier oil and massage in a clockwise direction. This stimulates peristalsis, which is the muscular movement of the digestive tract. Check your stress levels (*see Stress on p.60*).

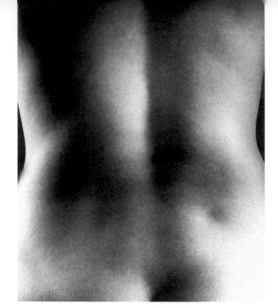

RIGHT *Diarrhea has many possible causes, but an acute attack is usually due to gastroenteritis and should not last for more than a few days. Exercise particular caution about the food you eat when traveling abroad.*

DIAGNOSING DIARRHEA

- Passing of feces more frequently, which are often soft or watery, or may be more bulky than usual
- May also be symptoms reflecting the underlying cause of the diarrhea, including fever, vomiting, and cramp-like abdominal pain

DIGESTIVE SYSTEM

diarrhea

Diarrhea *is a symptom, not an illness. The passing of frequent, loose, or even liquid stool (sometimes uncontrollable) is the result of irritation or inflammation of the gut. It is often accompanied by severe vomiting and may be caused by overindulgence, too much alcohol, or bacterial infection from food poisoning. Most minor bouts of diarrhea can be dealt with adequately in your own home, but prolonged diarrhea may be the result of a more serious underlying illness and can cause severe dehydration, particularly in small children and the elderly.*

CONVENTIONAL MEDICINE

Water, salts and minerals lost through diarrhea need to be replaced. Drinking extra water will help, but after a while, you will feel tired and ill if you do not also replace the salts and minerals. This is particularly important in children and frail adults. Special oral rehydration fluid preparations are available, which taste like strong mineral water. They can be flavored or made into ice cubes to make them more palatable. Prolonged diarrhea may require medical treatment.

Dosage information ~

Adults and children

■ Dissolve the contents of an oral rehydration packet in water and drink after each episode of diarrhea. See package for details.

KITCHEN MEDICINE

■ Garlic comes to the rescue yet again. Crush four cloves of garlic and stir into a 1lb/450g jar of honey. Dissolve 2tsp/10ml of this mixture in a tumbler of hot water and sip slowly, repeating three times daily.

HERBAL REMEDIES

 One household standby to soothe an inflamed digestive tract is simply to drink cups of unsweetened black tea: the high tannin content has an astringent effect, soothing and repairing sore tissues. Herbs to use in teas for all sorts of diarrhea include agrimony, bistort, lady's mantle, meadowsweet, raspberry leaves, and tormentil.

■ **Use and Dosage:**
Use 2tsp/10ml of herb per cup of boiling water.

Package a small bottle of tincture of any of these herbs to combat vacation diarrhea (take 1tsp/5ml in water up to six times a day), or eat papaw—a traditional tropical remedy for diarrhea.

HOMEOPATHIC REMEDIES

Usually self-limiting, diarrhea requires the same general measures as for gastroenteritis. Persistent diarrhea needs medical investigation.

꽃 PODOPHYLLUM **6C** Gushing, watery diarrhea; flatus sometimes causes stool to pass. Stool offensive, may be pasty or yellow. Colic pains before stool better for lying on abdomen.

꽃 CHINA **6C** For painless diarrhea of undigested food, flatulence, and colic. Worse after eating fruit. Patient feels weak.

꽃 COLOCYNTHIS **6C** For jelly-like stool immediately after food or drink. Cutting abdominal pain, relieved by bending double and by pressure.

Dosage: one tablet hourly until improved, then every 4 hours. Maximum 5 days.

OUTSIDE HELP

ACUPRESSURE: points 23, 29, and 39 are helpful.

REFLEXOLOGY: for regulation of the intestines and colon, work the soles of the feet and the palms of the hands. Try rolling a golf ball firmly between your two palms, with the fingers linked.

NUTRITION

Diarrhea is nature's way of getting rid of poisonous or irritating material, so unless absolutely essential, do not take anti-diarrhea drugs for the first 24 hours and do not eat, either. You must replace fluids and electrolytes, so make up 2pt/1l of freshly boiled water with a mixture of 8tsp/45g of sugar and 1tsp/5ml of salt, and drink the whole amount at least twice a day—if necessary, two or three spoonfuls every few minutes.

After 24 hours use the BRAT diet: ripe Bananas, boiled Rice, Apples and dry whole wheat Toast. Eat little and often for the next 48 hours, after which add boiled or jacket potatoes, cooked carrots with any other mixed vegetables, and an egg. Then gradually get back to normal eating, saving all dairy products until last.

RIGHT *The BRAT diet is the safest course to follow after an attack.*

AROMATHERAPY

꽃 ROMAN CHAMOMILE
Chamaemelum nobile
꽃 NEROLI
Citrus aurantium
꽃 LAVENDER
Lavandula angustifolia
꽃 PEPPERMINT
Mentha piperita
These oils are antispasmodic, so they will help griping stomach

pains. They are also calming and soothing, not only to the digestive tract, but also to the nervous system (and stress may play a part). Chamomile is an anti-allergen, useful if the diarrhea is an allergic reaction.

Application:
Apply gentle abdominal massage with any of these oils.

PREVENTATIVE *measures*

HYGIENE: *good kitchen hygiene is a must, as food poisoning in the home is a very common occurrence. Keep all raw meats and poultry totally separate from other foods, in the bottom compartment of the refrigerator. Use separate boards for preparing raw meat, poultry, and fish, and other foods. Wash your hands thoroughly after handling raw meat or poultry and before touching any other food or utensil.*

TRAVELERS' TIPS: *travelers' diarrhea affects vast numbers of vacationers and business travelers, so be extra cautious anywhere outside North America and northern Europe. Do not eat salads; beware the cold buffet standing in the hot sun; and remember the maxim "Cook it, peel it or forget it." Do not eat undercooked meat, poultry or shellfish. And it is no good cleaning your teeth with bottled water, then putting ice cubes in your cocktail. When traveling in Asia or Africa, ignore the normal rules of healthy eating and stick to fried and char-grilled foods—preferably cooked in front of you.*

Eat plenty of garlic, or take garlic capsules when you travel, as this is a powerful antibacterial. And avoid eating in any establishments that look obviously dirty and unhygienic: this includes most burger stalls, hot-dog stands, and ice-cream vendors.

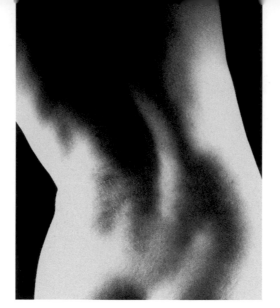

DIAGNOSING WEIGHT PROBLEMS

- Difficulty in maintaining the recommended weight for your height and build
- You may weigh more or less than your ideal weight, or it may fluctuate from one extreme to the other

DIGESTIVE SYSTEM

weight problems

The Western world has become obsessed with being overweight. Every newspaper and magazine, together with countless books, now offer special "diets" that will magically remove the surplus pounds from your body. Many of these diets are based on extreme regimes, pseudoscience, and hocus pocus, and the real truth is that diets often do not work in the long term. At the other end of the scale, there are many thousands of people desperate to gain weight, but for them there is little help or advice. On the contrary, they are usually regarded with envy by the massed ranks of the dieting brigade.

Both groups suffer emotionally as well as physically. Being severely overweight increases the risk of heart disease, diabetes, respiratory problems, arthritis, and some forms of cancer; being painfully thin increases the risk of osteoporosis, menstrual problems in women, and is often linked to reduced life expectancy. Neither group feels comfortable on the beach, at the swimming pool or gym. The overweight will only achieve long-term success by changing the way they eat and increasing the amount of physical activity they do. You might lose 10lb/4.5kg in 10 days on a drastic diet, but low-calorie eating simply leads to exhaustion, irritability, sleep disturbance, and eventually to an eating binge that puts back 12lb/5.5kg in 3 or 4 days. The skinnies end up stuffing in vast quantities of fatty foods to increase their calorie consumption, which puts them at risk of raised cholesterol and heart disease.

CAUTION

Appetite-suppressants are not recommended.

HERBAL REMEDIES

Herbal remedies are no real substitute for calorie control, healthy eating, and exercise, and any proprietary "slimming" tea should be regarded with suspicion: many are mixtures of strong laxatives and diuretics, which will have only a short-term effect on weight problems. Kelp can be useful, if the weight problem is associated with a sluggish metabolism or an underactive thyroid, although professional help is generally advisable in such cases. Malabar tamarind is sometimes recommended for short-term use, as it affects carbohydrate metabolism and can therefore help prevent overeating.

EXERCISE

EXERCISE IS a key factor in both weight loss and weight gain. Long, slow exercise, like cycling, walking, and swimming, helps to burn up surplus calories, stimulate the metabolism, and make a weight-loss plan much more effective. Circuit training in a gym and weight lifting will both help to build bigger muscles, improve body shape, and add more bulk to those who are over-skinny. Both the overweight and underweight will have to overcome their initial embarrassment about exercising in front of others, but the benefits are enormous and the rapid change in shape for both groups will be gratifying.

ABOVE *Most people can benefit from going to the gym, but check with your physician if you have not exercised for some time.*

HOMEOPATHIC REMEDIES

These are best treated with a remedy specific to the individual, which will help weight loss, together with a sensible diet. Consult a qualified homeopath. The following information illustrates how remedies differ.

SULPHUR **30**C For plump, hearty person with red cheeks. Lazy, untidy, does not feel the cold, and is worse for heat. Very sweaty, with hot feet, which they have to put out of bed at night.

CALCAREA CARBONICA **30**C For flabby person, who puts on weight easily. Soft face, pale complexion. Sweaty head at night. Chilly, cold. Cold feet at night in bed and wants to wear socks, which are removed after a while as feet get too hot.

Dosage: 1 tablet twice daily. Maximum 1 week.

CONVENTIONAL MEDICINE

To lose weight, eat smaller portions of everything, avoiding fatty and sugary food and excessive amounts of alcohol. In order to gain weight, do the reverse, but do not increase the amount of alcohol or food containing high amounts of fat or sugar. Treating a serious weight problem may require qualified dietary advice. Psychological help is beneficial in some severe cases.

AROMATHERAPY

If people are overweight, they often have a very poor self-image, for which useful essential oils would be jasmine (for confidence) and frankincense and sandalwood (for insecurity). Any of the citrus or floral oils will help the depression that may accompany weight problems. Again, it is a question of using the oils you like most in a way that supports you—whether that is in the bath; by having regular massage; by using the oil as a perfume; as a lotion for your face/body, or just your hands; or simply by wearing a drop of essential oil on the collar of your jacket.

RIGHT *Lotions perfumed with essential oils lift the spirits with their enveloping fragrance. You can use them as often as you like.*

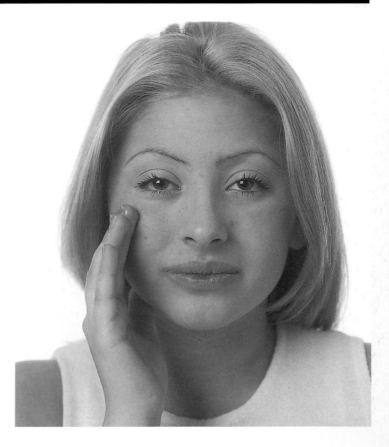

weight problems

NUTRITION

 Weight loss: there is only one successful route to weight control and that is to change your eating patterns and habits. Naturally these have to fit in with your lifestyle, job, and other commitments, but you need to follow a regime that ends up being the way you want to eat, if you are going to achieve permanent success and never have to worry about another diet. Meal replacements, "diet foods," ready-made low-calorie meals and appetite-reducing cookies are all the path to misery and failure. Balanced consumption of real food, eaten at proper intervals, is the only remedy that works and keeps you healthy and happy.

The suggestions in the following 7-day menu plan will provide all the nutrients you need without having to count a single calorie. Combined with some exercise, this way of eating will help you achieve a sensible weight loss of around 1–2lb/450g–1kg a week, without making you a social outcast who is living on celery and carrot sticks. Remember: it is what you do most of the time that matters—if you have one bad meal, or a bad day (or even a whole bad week), don't quit; just get yourself back on the plan as soon as you can.

MONDAY

BREAKFAST: sliced blood oranges and pink grapefruit; a helping of creamy yogurt, with nuts and honey, if liked

LIGHT MEAL OR SNACK: scrambled eggs and mushrooms with a green salad; dried fruit compote (make enough for two meals)

MAIN MEAL: bell peppers stuffed with rice, served with peas and stalks of celery; dates and figs

TUESDAY

BREAKFAST: dried fruit compote; an orange; yogurt

LIGHT MEAL OR SNACK: gratin of mushrooms and potatoes, with a lettuce and watercress salad; a ripe sweet pear

MAIN MEAL: mustard-marinated salmon with puréed spinach; apricot and almond crumble

WEDNESDAY

BREAKFAST: hot whole wheat rolls with butter; a banana

LIGHT MEAL OR SNACK: risotto of marinated vegetables, with a green salad; raisins and nuts

MAIN MEAL: baked eggplant with crudités (carrot, celery, cucumber, fennel, sprigs of cauliflower); meatballs in tomato sauce with green beans and stalks of celery

THURSDAY

BREAKFAST: an orange; half a pink grapefruit; yogurt with honey and nuts

LIGHT MEAL OR SNACK: baked potato with butter or sour cream, and plenty of chopped fresh herbs, served with red salad (tomatoes, red bell pepper, radishes, radicchio) on lettuce leaves; a ripe sweet pear

MAIN MEAL: rabbit with prunes, served with young cabbage; dried fruit compote (make enough for two meals)

FRIDAY

BREAKFAST: dried fruit compote with yogurt or a little light cream

LIGHT MEAL OR SNACK: half an avocado, sliced, with cress, tomatoes, and cucumber, on lettuce with a little oil and a drop or two of lemon dressing; crusty whole wheat roll and a little butter

MAIN MEAL: beet and apple soup; fish in chili sauce with steamed broccoli

SATURDAY

BREAKFAST: an orange; an apple; a banana; yogurt

LIGHT MEAL OR SNACK: salad Niçoise, with stalks of celery and rye crispbread with a little cream cheese

MAIN MEAL: chicken and onion casserole with steamed spring greens and a green salad; spiced apricots (make enough for two meals)

SUNDAY

BREAKFAST: orange or grapefruit juice; cold spiced apricots; yogurt

LIGHT MEAL OR SNACK: zucchini pasta, or black olive paté with toasted rye bread; cucumber, lettuce, and watercress salad

MAIN MEAL: crudités; lamb chop with tarragon and cucumber; orange soufflé omelette

NUTRITION

Weight gain: those of you desperately trying to gain weight have the problem of increasing your calorie consumption without relying on high-fat dairy products—like cream, cheese, and butter—and high-fat meat products. Good carbohydrates, such as whole wheat bread, brown rice, pasta, potatoes, and all the dried beans, are excellent sources of calories, but they are bulky, so the amount you can consume is limited. Make sure that you eat modest amounts of food, but at more frequent intervals—at least every 2 to 3 hours. Get extra calories from fresh unsalted nuts, seeds, unsalted peanut butter, tahini, avocados, olive oil, and plenty of dried fruit as nibbles. And give yourself a real calorie boost with a high-energy but very healthy milkshake (such as one made from a banana, molasses, honey, tahini, wheatgerm, brewer's yeast powder, and dried apricots blended together). Remember: this should be in addition to, not instead of, other meals.

RIGHT *Fibroids are benign uterine growths, which a woman may not even be aware of. They cannot be prevented, and will only be removed surgically if they are causing annoying symptoms.*

DIAGNOSING FIBROIDS

Most women with fibroids have no symptoms, but:

- Commonest symptom is heavy menstrual bleeding
- Some women notice the lower part of their abdomen is swollen
- Urge to pass urine frequently may be caused because fibroids are pressing on the surrounding organs, such as the bladder

REPRODUCTIVE SYSTEM

fibroids

These benign tumors develop in the smooth muscle of the uterus and around 20 percent of women over the age of 35 will be affected. They are more common in Afro-Caribbean women. They are probably the most common reason for a hysterectomy, but unless the symptoms are extreme, less invasive medical techniques can now be used; and self-help, with simple home remedies, may contain the growth of these estrogen-dependent tumors until menopause is reached. After this time the decline in the body's production of estrogen results in a gradual reduction in fibroid size.

KITCHEN MEDICINE

■ For menstrual pain due to fibroids, apply alternate hot and cold compresses to the lower abdomen and the small of the back, adding 5 drops of lavender oil per 2½ cups/600ml of hot and cold water.

AROMATHERAPY

❦ ROSE
Rosa damascena/Rosa centifolia
❦ LAVENDER
Lavandula angustifolia
❦ ROMAN CHAMOMILE
Chamaemelum nobile

Aromatherapy is not going to cure fibroids, but these oils can help to relieve some of the symptoms. If women feel that they are losing their femininity, rose can be beneficial in this respect.

Application:
Apply any of these oils as massage oils for the abdominal area or lower back.

CONVENTIONAL MEDICINE

✚ Most fibroids do not need any treatment, but if the menopause is a long way off and symptoms are troublesome, seek expert medical advice. Treatments include medication, but if this is unsuccessful, then surgery may be required to remove the fibroids or the whole womb.

EXERCISE

ANY FORM of regular but sensible exercise improves the blood flow and stimulates the production of small amounts of testosterone, which can counteract the effects of estrogen. Women with troublesome fibroids should not lift heavy weights or do strenuous high-impact exercise, such as long-distance jogging or intensive aerobics.

LEFT *Walking is good, gentle exercise.*

HERBAL REMEDIES

Herbal treatment should really be left to professionals, although simple remedies can be used to ease symptoms and support other treatments.

■ **Use and Dosage:**
Cramp bark or black haw, in decoction or tinctures, can ease pain, while shepherd's purse infusion (1tsp/5ml per cup) can help stop bleeding.

As a general supportive tea, combine equal amounts of violet leaves, shepherd's purse and motherwort (2tsp/10ml per cup, take three times a day).

Professional practitioners add herbs like blue cohosh, helonias root, agnus-castus, goldenseal, and life root.

NUTRITION

Eat plenty of iron-rich foods, such as liver (but not if you are pregnant), other organ meat, dates, watercress, eggs, dark green leafy vegetables, and sardines, because fibroids frequently cause heavy menstrual bleeding and therefore loss of iron. Cabbage in all its forms is protective against the hormone-mediated tumors, so it should be your number-one vegetable.

In general, your diet should contain a large proportion of foods like oily fish for their essential fatty acids; olive oil, nuts, seeds, and avocados for their vitamin E; shellfish and pumpkin seeds for extra zinc.

Avoid all added salt, both when cooking and at the table. Salt causes fluid retention, which aggravates the pain and discomfort of fibroids.

Cabbage

Avocado

Oily fish

HOMEOPATHIC REMEDIES

Fibroids are best treated using a remedy based on the individual, so you should consult a qualified homeopath. The following remedies may however be a guide.

✿ USTILAGO 6C For left-sided ovarian pain, which may extend to

ABOVE Ustilago maydis, *source of the remedy, is a corn fungus.*

the legs. Fibroids with heavy periods and clots, especially when approaching the menopause.

✿ FRAXINUS AMERICANA 6C For fibroids with heavy feeling in vagina. Watery vaginal discharge.

✿ CALCAREA CARBONICA 6C For use when the person is overweight, chilly, and sweaty. Fibroids associated with heavy periods, which last a long time.
Dosage: one tablet daily. Maximum 2 weeks.

OUTSIDE HELP

ACUPRESSURE: points 34 and 44 can help relieve severe period pain.

REFLEXOLOGY: work the reflexes of the ovaries, uterus, and

endocrine glands (*see charts on pp.214–15*). Regular reflexology sessions on the entire feet and/or hands may help to check further growth of fibroids.

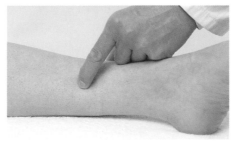

LEFT *Point 34 is on the Liver meridian, and helps period pain.*

PREVENTATIVE *measures*

FASTING: *naturopaths have had considerable success in controlling the growth of fibroids by instituting regular periods of short fasts. Initially this should be done for one 24-hour period each week for 2 months. The fast day should comprise consumption every 2 hours of at least 1¼ cups/300ml of liquid, alternating between herbal teas with honey, freshly pressed unsweetened fruit juices diluted 50:50 with water, and fresh or bottled organic vegetable juices – 3½pt/1.7l in total. An additional 1½pt/900ml of water should also be consumed. During the third month, repeat every 2 weeks and thereafter once a month.*

ORGANIC FOODS: *with the ever-increasing amount of growth hormones (both legal and illegal) being used in the production of meat, poultry, and milk cattle, it is really important for women with fibroids to try to eat only organic produce. For those without fibroids, this is a good idea too, as I am convinced that the increased use of these chemicals is a factor in the large number of women now suffering from this distressing problem, which sadly often leads to infertility followed by major surgery.*

RIGHT *Women are especially prone to an attack of thrush after a course of antibiotics, which destroys even the helpful bacteria in the body, so allowing the thrush fungus to multiply. Beneficial bacteria can be replaced by eating live yogurt.*

DIAGNOSING THRUSH

- Creamy-white vaginal discharge
- Sore, itchy vagina
- Painful intercourse

REPRODUCTIVE SYSTEM

thrush *Candida*

KITCHEN MEDICINE

■ Live yogurt is one of the most effective treatments for this distressing condition. A small amount of yogurt should be placed into the vagina each night, using a tampon inserter. The beneficial bacteria in the yogurt then attack the *Candida* cells and destroy them, helping to restore the normal balance of bacteria that colonize not only the vagina but other warm dark places in the body.

EXERCISE

VAGINAL **thrush can be aggravated by excessive sweating, so it is best to avoid energetic exercise if you have an acute attack.**

Thrush is a common infection that is caused by the yeast organism Candida albicans. "Thrush" usually means vaginal infection, however, as opposed to the other common sites of Candida infection, which are in the mouth and throat and around the anus or areas of damaged skin. Vaginal thrush may be accompanied by pain and burning when passing urine, together with a thick discharge and severe itching and discomfort along the lips of the vagina. For many years the home remedies of complementary practitioners have offered effective treatment.

CONVENTIONAL MEDICINE

✚ Conventional treatment is usually with antifungal medicines. These can be inserted into the vagina as a cream or suppository, or taken by mouth as a single tablet. When a woman has recurrent yeast infections, her partner may need treatment.

Dosage information ~
Adults
■ Follow medical advice on the use of cream or suppositories. Or a single tablet can be taken by mouth.
  All treatment may be combined with an antifungal cream for external use.

ABOVE *Eat plenty of live yogurt to help combat the spread of the Candida infection.*

HERBAL REMEDIES

 Antifungal and antiseptic herbs—such as echinacea, garlic, chamomile, lemon balm, thyme, and marigold—as well as immune stimulants like astragalus and reishi (suitable even though it is itself a type of fungus) can all be helpful for candidiasis. The Amazonian herb pau d'arco is also popular and is widely available in tablet form.

■ **Use and Dosage:**

Try an infusion of marigold, lemon balm, chamomile and elderflowers (2tsp/10ml per cup, four times daily).

For vaginal thrush, try tea-tree or thyme oil pessaries, or put 2 drops of tea-tree oil onto a moistened tampon, insert and leave for up to 4 hours.

AROMATHERAPY

 ❧ LAVENDER
Lavandula angustifolia
❧ TEA TREE
Melaleuca alternifolia
❧ MYRRH
Commiphora molmol
❧ PALMAROSA
Cymbopogon martinii

Lavender eases the pain and promotes healing. Tea tree and myrrh both act against the organism that causes thrush (but use tea tree in a low dilution, as it can be a mucous-membrane irritant). Another useful oil is palmarosa, which helps to balance the intestinal flora, which are out of balance at this point in time. The treatment needs to be long-term, so that you regain the body's balance of intestinal flora—if you stop too soon, thrush may recur.

Application:

Use in the bath or as a compress on the outer areas. Palmarosa can also be used as a massage oil for the abdominal area.

HOMEOPATHIC REMEDIES

 A consultation with a qualified homeopath is recommended.

❧ BORAX 6C For itchy vulva. Discharge thick or like the white of egg, makes vulva sore. Discharge before and after period.

❧ SEPIA 6C For dry vulva and vagina. White or yellow discharge that burns. May have a feeling that the uterus has prolapsed or a bearing-down feeling.

❧ HELONIAS 6C For creamy white discharge, which may recur with itching and soreness of vulva.
Dosage: one tablet twice daily. Maximum two weeks.

❧ CANDIDA ALBICANS 30C
For recurrent thrush.
Dosage: one tablet 12-hourly. Maximum three doses.

NUTRITION

 Garlic is a powerful antifungal and should be used in very generous amounts—at least two whole cloves a day, added to recipes, chopped into salads, or just eaten in a sandwich, are essential.

It also helps to eat a good portion of live yogurt daily, to maintain the balance of beneficial probiotic bacteria in the gut, which may help to prevent the spread of the *Candida* infection.

All the B vitamins are important too, so **eat plenty of** complex carbohydrates, like whole wheat bread, pasta, and brown rice; and eat extra muesli, sunflower seeds, lentils, and white fish for their rich vitamin B_6 content.

Zinc is an important factor in maintaining the good health of the mucous membranes and you can obtain it from eggs, sardines, oysters, most other shellfish, and pumpkin seeds.

ABOVE *Babies often get thrush in the mouth, or in deep folds of skin subject to dampness. Sterilize dummies, and keep baby as clean and dry as possible.*

OUTSIDE HELP

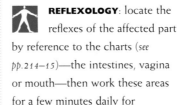 **REFLEXOLOGY**: locate the reflexes of the affected part by reference to the charts (*see pp.214–15*)—the intestines, vagina or mouth—then work these areas for a few minutes daily for symptomatic relief.

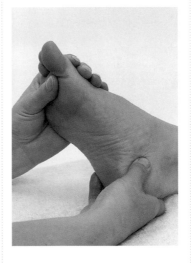

ABOVE *Working the reflex to the vagina helps relieve the irritating itching and soreness that make the sufferer miserable.*

PREVENTATIVE *measures*

HYGIENE: *it is best to avoid wearing synthetic panties, and pantyhose should have a cotton gusset—or, better still, wear stockings. Avoid very hot baths, antiseptic soaps, excessive washing, and all the highly perfumed and foaming bath additives. Vaginal thrush may be sexually transmitted and both partners should receive treatment, although men are frequently symptom-free. Women taking the contraceptive pill are more likely to suffer from episodes of thrush.*

DIAPER-RASH AND ASTHMA SUFFERERS: *thrush is quite a common secondary infection with diaper rash, but lots of exposure to fresh air and a light film of live yogurt once a day usually does the trick. Asthmatics using steroid inhalers may get oral thrush, but this can be avoided by rinsing the mouth with water after using the inhaler and changing your toothbrush every month.*

DIET: *some complementary practitioners advise very extreme yeast-excluding diets, but there is no scientific basis for these. It is, however, advisable to reduce your sugar consumption to the barest minimum, as a high sugar intake can encourage the growth of Candida.*

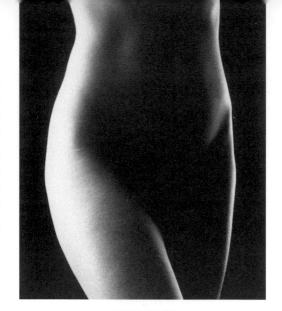

RIGHT *Menstrual problems can make life difficult every month, whether they cause severe pain and heavy bleeding, which are incapacitating, or the uncertainty of irregular periods. Menstrual problems often settle down as a woman gets older.*

DIAGNOSING MENSTRUAL PROBLEMS

- Too frequent, irregular, or absent periods
- Painful periods
- Periods that last a long time
- Heavy bleeding, possibly with clots

REPRODUCTIVE SYSTEM

menstrual problems

The menstrual cycle is controlled by your body's production of hormones and anything that interferes with this mechanism will affect your periods. Significant loss or gain of weight, stress, anxiety, or depression can all upset the natural balance of hormones and thus interfere with the smooth running of your menstrual cycle. The underlying causes of menstrual disorder may be simple and medically unimportant, or complex and carry serious medical implications, but remember that home remedies can play an important part in resolving many of them. The four main period problems are: irregular periods, heavy periods (menorrhagia), painful periods (dysmenorrhea) and lack of periods (amenorrhea). (See also Osteoporosis p.108, Menopause p.172, Fibroids p.164, and PMS p.170).

CALL THE PHYSICIAN

◼ If you are having long-term or very uncomfortable menstrual problems.

HOMEOPATHIC REMEDIES

 It is useful to consult a qualified homeopath.

❧ VIBURNUM **30**C For cramp-like pains in back, which radiate to uterus and down thighs. Periods may be very short.

❧ MAGNESIUM PHOSPHATE **30**C For colicky abdominal pains, eased by hot-water bottle and pressing firmly on abdomen. Better when period is flowing.

❧ CIMICIFUGA RACEMOSA **30**C For labor-like pains from hip to hip. Worse for movement. Pains worse, the heavier the period. Better for bending double. Person is chilly and thirsty.

❧ SEPIA **30**C For cramping, heavy pains in uterus. Better for sitting with crossed legs. Tired.
Dosage: one tablet 2–4 hourly. Maximum 12 doses.

CONVENTIONAL MEDICINE

✚ Most changes in the menstrual cycle are transient, but if there has been a sustained change for more than 6 months, your physician may wish to investigate. Painful periods may need further investigation, but can often be treated with prescribed pain-relievers containing mefenamic acid, which also helps to reduce the amount of blood. The commonest reason for a missed period is pregnancy, and this can be confirmed using an "over-the-counter" pregnancy testing kit. Excessive weight loss and over-strenuous exercise can both stop periods occurring.

EXERCISE

BEING PHYSICALLY active is of great importance in the regulation of the whole hormone system, and a half hour or so of brisk physical activity three times a week will help. Choose something you enjoy—and make sure that you do it energetically enough to get slightly out of breath and sweat a little.

HERBAL REMEDIES

 Warming herbal teas are ideal for soothing period pain *(and see also Fibroids and PMS on pp.164 and 170)*.

■ **Use and Dosage:**
Mix equal amounts of St. John's wort, raspberry leaves and skullcap (2tsp/10ml of the mix per cup).

Black haw is an excellent relaxant for cramping pains: take 4tsp/20ml of the tincture as a single dose in warm water and repeat after 4 hours if necessary.

For heavy periods use of lady's mantle, shepherd's purse, and marigold (2tsp/10ml of each per cup).

Agnus-castus is a hormone regulator—use 20 drops of tincture in water each morning.

OUTSIDE HELP

 ACUPRESSURE: points 34 and 44 will help relieve menstrual pain.

REFLEXOLOGY: the reflexes of the uterus are best located in the area beneath the medial (inside) ankle bone on both feet; of the ovaries, beneath the lateral (outside) ankle bones. Join these two areas over the top of the foot for the Fallopian tube. Work the endocrine gland reflexes.

YOGA: before and during your period, practice more gently, with fewer postures and more relaxation and breathing exercises. Avoid inversion and Bandhas. Cobra, Cobbler Pose, and Maha Mudra are often particularly recommended at this time.

KITCHEN MEDICINE

■ Many of the uncomfortable symptoms of menopausal problems are the result of fluid retention and consequent swelling. So eat lots of parsley, celery, and dandelion leaves, which are all mild diuretics.

■ Inflammation of the lining of the uterus is another common cause of menstrual pain. Eating fresh pineapple and drinking pineapple juice are both very soothing, due to the enzymes in this tropical fruit.

■ Along with the other herbs you grow, you should also include some borage. A few of the flowers (fresh or dried) added to a salad helps relieve many of the discomforts of menstrual problems.

AROMATHERAPY

❀ **ROSE**
Rosa damascena/Rosa centifolia
❀ **GERANIUM**
Pelargonium graveolens
❀ **CLARY SAGE**
Salvia sclarea
These oils relate to the feminine aspect—this is very important with menstrual problems, so that women do not lose their femininity and feel that they are in control of their own bodies.

Application:
Use in the bath, in massage oil or lotion, or as a compress, for excessive bleeding, irregular and painful periods *(see also PMS on p.170)*.

RIGHT *Dried fruit and nuts are a good source of iron to fight anemia.*

NUTRITION

What you eat and drink plays a vital part in the solution of all menstrual problems.

Eat plenty of whole grain cereals, yeast extracts, wheatgerm, dried fruit, nuts, bananas, and oats for abundant amounts of vitamin B. The health-giving essential fatty acids are also important, so get these from oily fish. Vitamin E is crucial—you will find it in good, cold-pressed oils (especially extra-virgin olive, sunflower, and safflower oils), wheatgerm, avocados, and all edible seeds. You need lots of zinc (from shellfish, sardines, pumpkin seeds, and peas) and selenium (from whole wheat bread, Brazil nuts, almonds, and soy products).

Eating disorders can play a major part in menstrual disturbance. If you are constantly dieting (or just not eating), if your weight is going down, and your periods are becoming scant and irregular, you could be heading for anorexia and an artificially induced menopause, with all the long-term problems that accompany it *(see Menopause and Osteoporosis on pp.172 and 108)*.

Heavy periods increase the risk of iron deficiency and anemia, so eat more of the foods rich in iron, including liver (but not if you are pregnant), dark green leafy vegetables, raisins, dates, watercress, and eggs.

ABOVE *Reduce your salt intake: salt encourages fluid retention and bloating.*

PREVENTATIVE *measures*

AVOIDING CONSTIPATION:
constipation can cause pressure in the lower abdomen, which in turn causes and aggravates menstrual problems. Make sure you eat lots of fiber, most of which should be the soluble kind (from oats, apples, pears, and most vegetables). You also need whole wheat bread and cereals, which contain a mixture of soluble and insoluble fiber, but avoid bran and foods with added bran, which can interfere with your absorption of calcium and iron and could lead to Irritable Bowel Syndrome. Most women do not drink enough fluid—a common cause of constipation. You should drink about 6pt/2.75l of liquid a day.

DIET: *modest amounts of alcohol and caffeine are not normally a problem, but an excess of either may interfere with blood flow to the uterus and lead to menstrual difficulties. Salt can be a major hazard—and the average consumption in the US and Britain is well over twice the safe recommended maximum of 1 level tsp/5ml a day. You should stop adding salt to all cooking and banish the salt cellar from your table. Apart from being the prime factor in the cause of high blood pressure, it also leads to fluid retention, which is the last thing you need when you are having a period.*

DIAGNOSING PREMENSTRUAL SYNDROME

- Recurrent symptoms starting from midcycle onward, or in the week before your period, and stopping when the bleeding ends
- Symptoms may include back ache, headache, bloated abdomen, cramps, breast tenderness, irrational behavior, anxiety, depression, and poor concentration

REPRODUCTIVE SYSTEM

premenstrual syndrome *PMS*

Premenstrual syndrome is the most common of all menstrual problems (see p.168) and around 70 percent of women who are still having a menstrual cycle will suffer from it to some extent. The physical and mental changes may begin just after mid-cycle, but usually occur in the seven days preceding menstruation and vanish as soon as the period starts. Sadly, PMS is still a much underrated and often ignored problem, from a medical standpoint, but even in mild cases it can be distressing and uncomfortable. However, the solution can be found in your weekly shopping basket—the ultimate home remedy.

CALL THE PHYSICIAN

■ If your symptoms are significantly interfering with your life.

KITCHEN MEDICINE

■ The calming herbs should be used in cooking—rosemary and basil are very effective—and anything that promotes fluid excretion will relieve discomfort.

■ Dandelion leaves are highly effective—their country name is "wet the bed;" and in France you can buy *pissenlit* salad in any street market. So mix a few of the young leaves with your salad every day. They will help prevent bloating and are a great source of iron.

CONVENTIONAL MEDICINE

Keep a chart that shows when the symptoms occur in relation to menstruation—perhaps grading symptoms on a scale of one to ten. It may then be possible to change or rearrange schedules to avoid particularly difficult days. A chart can also help to determine whether remedies are of benefit. Talking about symptoms can also help, perhaps with other women with similar problems. Try to eat regular meals and avoid sugary foods. Take regular exercise and avoid excessive caffeine. Breast pain may be helped by products containing gamolenic acid (otherwise known as evening primrose oil). If PMS is severe, your physician may recommend hormonal treatments and possibly even some counseling.

Dosage information ~
Adults and children over 16
■ Take three to four capsules of gamolenic acid twice a day, usually for 2–3 months; see package for details.

HERBAL REMEDIES

Agnus-castus—which stimulates production of the hormones associated with the menstrual cycle—is often effective for PMS. It is best taken in the morning when the pituitary gland's hormonal activity is highest.

■ **Use and Dosage:**
Take 10–20 drops of tincture each morning, increasing to 20–40 drops in the 10 days before the period is due.

Helonias, an ovarian stimulant, is available in capsules and tablets, and Dang Gui is also becoming more readily obtainable.

You can make a simple herbal tea from equal amounts of St. John's wort, raspberry leaf, and vervain for daily use.

HOMEOPATHIC REMEDIES

A prescription based on the individual is usually most successful, so consult a qualified homeopath.

❧ LILIUM TIGRINUM 30C For snappy, irritable person. Worse for sympathy. Must keep busy. Heavy period pains, uterus feels as though congested.

❧ PULSATILLA 30C For weepy person, who feels unloved and wants sympathy. PMS starts at puberty. Changeable in mood and symptom. Chilly, but dislikes stuffy room. Likes butter, cream.

❧ LACHESIS 30C Particularly for PMS around menopause. Intense talkative person. PMS improves when period starts. Hot and dislikes tight collars.

Dosage: one tablet twice daily until improved. Maximum 1 week. May be repeated at the next period.

AROMATHERAPY

❧ GERANIUM
Pelargonium graveolens
❧ FENNEL
Foeniculum vulgare
❧ CLARY SAGE
Salvia sclarea
❧ ROSE
Rosa damascena/Rosa centifolia
❧ YLANG YLANG
Cananga odorata
❧ LAVENDER
Lavandula angustifolia
❧ NEROLI
Citrus aurantium
❧ SANDALWOOD
Santalum album
❧ VETIVERT
Vetiveria zizanoides
❧ JASMINE
Jasminum officinale
❧ ROMAN CHAMOMILE
Chamaemelum nobile

ABOVE *Jasmine essential oil benefits the nervous system.*

❧ BERGAMOT
Citrus bergamia
You will have to decide, by trial and error, which of these oils best suits your own range of symptoms.
Application:
Find the oils that you like most and use them in a way that suits you and your particular condition.

NUTRITION

It is not just what you eat that is important in treating PMS, but what you *don't* eat and *when* you eat.

Women with PMS can effect an enormous reduction in their symptoms simply by eating little and often (never going more than 2 hours without food) and eating plenty of complex carbohydrates—whole wheat bread, rice, pasta, potatoes, root vegetables, beans—with sensible protein like fish, eggs, cheese, poultry, and lean meat. Sweet cravings can be satisfied by fruit, which contains an abundance of nutrients, as well as natural sugars.

Vitamins B_6 and E, plus the minerals zinc and magnesium, play an enormous part in controlling the pattern of PMS. **Eat plenty of** spinach and other dark green leafy vegetables, and whole wheat bread, for their vitamin B_6 and magnesium; lean red meat, poultry and all organ meat for their B_6 as well as iron; extra-virgin olive oil, eggs, nuts, and seeds for their vitamin E; shellfish, oysters, and pumpkin seeds for their zinc; all the oily fish for their omega-3 fatty acids. **Avoid** excessive salt, caffeine and alcohol.

EXERCISE

EXERCISE CAN be hugely helpful in the reduction of symptoms and regulation of the cycle. It not only encourages the body to manufacture the feel-good hormones known as endorphins, but stimulates all the other hormones, too—including those that affect the menstrual cycle.

PREVENTATIVE
measures

SUPPLEMENTS: *a daily dose of 50mg of vitamin B_6 should be taken on a long-term basis. This should be supplemented with a combination of evening primrose oil and fish oil (2–3g of a combined capsule daily), starting 10 days before the likely onset of menstruation until the day after the period begins. As the severity of symptoms declines and you get some totally symptom-free months, the dose can be reduced to 25mg of B_6 and 1g of the combined oil pills. Eventually your improved eating habits should supply all the nutrients you require without supplementation.*

OUTSIDE HELP

ACUPRESSURE: pain and discomfort can be relieved by using points 34 and 44, but professional acupuncture treatment will be even more useful.

REFLEXOLOGY: the reflexes of the uterus are best located in the area beneath the medial (inside) ankle bone on both feet; of the ovaries, beneath the lateral (outside) ankle bones. Join these two areas over the top of the foot for the Fallopian tube. Work the endocrine gland reflexes. Work the abdominal and pelvic areas. Treatment should be given weekly throughout the cycle.

YOGA: accept that things are different at this time: pressure builds up. Therefore it is a good time for reflection and stillness, rather than action. Use closing postures like Knees-over-Chest, Head-to-Knee and Seated Forward Bend, Maha Mudra, Pranayama, and meditation.

DIAGNOSING MENOPAUSE

- No periods for more than one year
- Sudden attacks of feeling hot and sweaty, known as hot flushes
- Dry vagina, sometimes causing pain during intercourse
- Urinary problems, including incontinence
- May be associated with depression and anxiety

REPRODUCTIVE SYSTEM

menopause

KITCHEN MEDICINE

■ Two great treats for your skin are found in the kitchen rather than at the expensive cosmetics counter. Once a week make an invigorating facial scrub and cleanser from a container of live yogurt mixed with 1 tsp of coarse sea salt. Massage well into the face and neck, leave on as a mask for 15 minutes, then wash off with lots of cold water.

■ For skin nourishment, pulverize or blend the flesh of half an avocado with 1 tsp/5ml of rosewater, 2 tsp/10ml of olive oil, and the juice of half a lemon. Massage into the face sparingly at night. Covered with plastic wrap and kept in the refrigerator, this cream will last several days.

*S*ome women sail through menopause without batting an eyelid. For others it represents months, and sometimes years, of discomfort and misery. It is my experience that women who regard menopause as an illness are those who suffer most. It is not a disease; it is in fact, for many women, the beginning of their golden years, free from the monthly discomfort of difficult periods and contraception. To be sure, there are medical consequences of menopause, but it is here that home remedies come into their own. They can strengthen the bones, protect against heart disease, and keep your skin glowing and healthy. When your periods stop, no matter at what age or for what reason, menopause begins. Anorexia, overexercising—especially in young, élite athletes like gymnasts and runners—and simply being too thin can all affect your hormone production and cause artificial menopause. Having both ovaries removed produces the same result.

CONVENTIONAL MEDICINE

Not all women need treatment during menopause, either because they do not have symptoms or because their symptoms are not troublesome. Hormone replacement therapy (HRT) can help to alleviate difficult or embarrassing symptoms, and can also help to reduce the risk of osteoporosis and heart disease in later life. It is recommended for women who are at particular risk, including those with early menopause or a family history of osteoporosis.

HRT is given in the form of tablets, patches, gels, or cream, and may cause a regular bleed. Consult your physician for further details.

HERBAL REMEDIES

 Menopausal discomfort can include night sweats, hot flushes, and palpitations, which may be eased by herbal remedies.

■ **Use and Dosage:**
A useful herbal mix to ease the worst of these is a tea made from equal amounts of vervain, sage, mugwort, and motherwort (2tsp/10ml per cup). Sage is rich in hormonal compounds, so a regular daily cup can be helpful throughout menopausal years.

One widely used Chinese herbal tonic for this time is He Shou Wu (also called Fo Ti), now available in many health-food stores.

HOMEOPATHIC REMEDIES

Homeopathy can be used to treat the symptoms of menopause, although there is no evidence that it actually prevents osteoporosis.
♨ LACHESIS **30**C For person who may be talkative, jealous, worse for any sleep or alcohol. Palpitations and flushes. Probably the remedy used most often.
♨ PULSATILLA **30**C For weepy, emotional person, who needs sympathy and reassurance. Changeable, flushes. Upset by rich or fatty foods. Better for air.
♨ SEPIA **30**C For lack of emotions, indifference to own family, loss of sexual drive. Weeping and feelings of guilt. Flushes with fainting. Better for being alone.
Dosage: one tablet twice daily. Maximum 1 week.

AROMATHERAPY

♨ GERANIUM
Pelargonium graveolens
♨ ROSE
Rosa damascena/Rosa centifolia
♨ FENNEL
Foeniculum vulgare
Geranium helps to balance the hormones, fennel produces a plant estrogen, and rose regulates the menstrual cycle. Other oils that you might like to look up are any of the antidepressant oils or those for symptomatic conditions, such as constipation *(see p.156).*

RIGHT *Fennel oil is extracted from the seeds, collected in the fall.*

Application:
Use in baths or in creams (body lotion, hand lotion or a facial cream). The oils could also be used in foot spas—whatever method is most convenient and most pleasant to you. Supplementation with starflower may also help.

OUTSIDE HELP

REFLEXOLOGY: all reflexes may be worked to help to alleviate menopausal symptoms. This can help reduce hot flushes, mood swings, loss of confidence, and the sleep problems commonly associated with menopause.
YOGA: allow the steadiness that yoga brings, help you to accept and cope with this period of change. Practice more Pranayama and meditation. Take time to look at your life and see what you need to change, then decide on small, achievable goals.

EXERCISE

WEIGHT-BEARING exercise is vital if you want to keep your bones in good shape—you should have been doing this all along anyway. Although cycling and swimming are great for the cardiovascular system, they will not strengthen your bones. For this you must be on your own two feet doing any exercise, at least three times a week.

NUTRITION

Your risk of suffering from post-menopausal complications depends to a large extent on your genetic inheritance, but good nutrition is the easiest, safest way of reducing those risks. If your decision has been not to take HRT, you must pay special attention to your diet for the rest of your life; even if you swear by HRT, your chances of avoiding osteoporosis, heart disease, and premature ageing will be greatly enhanced by eating well, too.

Plan your daily eating to include the specific nutrients your body now needs in greater abundance than ever. To protect your bones, you need calcium and vitamin D —so **eat plenty of** low-fat dairy products, sardines and other oily fish (with their bones whenever possible), dark green leafy vegetables, and garbanzo beans.

To protect your heart and circulation, and your skin, you need vitamins A, C, and E, lots of beta-carotene, abundant soluble fiber, and essential fatty acids—so eat plenty of avocados, olive oil, nuts and seeds, oats, brown rice, whole grain cereals, apricots, carrots, and broccoli (in fact, most vegetables), liver at least once a week, and lots of oily fish.

To protect yourself against breast cancer, you need all of the above foods, plus copious quantities of cabbage and its relatives (brussels sprouts, curly kale, spring greens, and Chinese cabbage). You should also eat regular quantities of soy bean products: tofu and soy sauce are readily available.

This is one time in your life when taking regular vitamin and mineral supplements can be a real bonus. I normally advise a daily multivitamin and mineral supplement, calcium with vitamin D supplement, and 1g of evening primrose oil. To help with hot flushes, a combination of vitamin B_6, magnesium, and zinc can be added.

DIAGNOSING BEDWETTING

- Uncontrollable urge to pass urine in a child who is learning to use a lavatory

EXCRETORY SYSTEM

bedwetting *enuresis*

CALL THE PHYSICIAN

■ If bedwetting does not improve after trying the remedies suggested here.

Bedwetting is much more common in boys than girls, and most children grow out of it by the age of four or five. It is seldom the result of underlying disease or physical problems, although occasionally it may be, so medical advice should be sought. It can be the result of stress, anxiety, or other behavioral disturbances, but in most instances is one of those things that "just happen."

CONVENTIONAL MEDICINE

There is no fixed age at which a child should be dry at night, but bedwetting is often treated by physicians in children from the age of seven. A child who has previously been dry may wet the bed during a time of stress, such as starting a new school, or because of a urinary infection. However, there may be no apparent reason. Avoid scolding a child who has wet the bed—reassurance and encouragement to try to use the lavatory next time are more effective. Do not withhold drinks before bedtime, and use protective mattress covers to enable quick bedding changes. Reward a dry night with lots of approval; consider trying a system of rewards for dry nights.

LEFT *Starting a new school, with the attendant uncertainties, may cause your child to resume bedwetting.*

HERBAL REMEDIES

During the day, children can be given dilute herbal teas to help strengthen the bladder and soothe any emotional distress.

■ **Use and Dosage:**
Mix 1tsp/5ml each of cornsilk, shepherd's purse and skullcap and infuse in 1 cup/250ml of water. Give children under three half a cup, sweetened with 1tsp/5ml of pasteurized honey, two to three times daily.

One hour before bedtime give 10 drops of sweet sumach tincture, diluted in 1tsp/5ml of water.

HOMEOPATHIC REMEDIES

ABOVE *Equisetum is made from a plant called horsetail (Equisetum arvense). It is a toning and astringent agent for the urinary system, good for bedwetting and incontinence.*

Ensure that there is no medical cause for this condition.

🌿 CAUSTICUM 6C For sensitive person, who wets bed during early part of sleep. May wet during daytime when sneezing or coughing. Unaware of passing urine.

🌿 EQUISETUM 6C For person who has dreams or nightmares when passing urine. Bedwetting in children and elderly women.

🌿 KREOSOTUM 6C For person who wets bed during first part of sleep, difficult to wake up. Cannot get out of bed quickly enough. Has dreams of urinating.

🌿 PLANTAGO 6C For person who wets bed, lots of urine, during later part of night.
Dosage: one tablet before bed until condition improves. Maximum 2 weeks.

ABOVE *Gently massage your child's lower back before bedtime. This is reassuring and comforting, and will help dispel anxiety. Try making this ritual part of nightly routine.*

PREVENTATIVE *measures*

Avoid giving the child any caffeine-containing drinks—chocolate, coffee, tea, cola—after midday. Make sure the child passes urine just before bedtime and, if the problem is severe, it is worth waking the child to pass urine again just before you go to bed.

EXERCISE: *simple relaxation exercises can be of great help, while gentle massage to the lower part of the back also helps to relieve tension and anxiety.*

OUTSIDE HELP

ACUPRESSURE: points 16, 17, 33, and 34 can all be extremely useful, especially if used just before bedtime on children.
REFLEXOLOGY: all the pelvic reflexes around and beneath the ankles should be worked, as well as

the kidney, ureter, and bladder reflexes. Treat the entire feet or hands, to relieve tension and stimulate nerve response.
YOGA: examine the possibility of psychological causes. Physiologically, you can

strengthen your sphincter muscles by tightening and releasing them, many times a day. When practicing yoga postures and breathing exercises, tighten these muscles gradually on every exhalation, releasing them as you inhale.

AROMATHERAPY

There are no specific oils for this condition, but since it can be stress-related, look up the oils for stress (*see p.60*); for small children, chamomile and lavender are particularly good, being both calming and soothing.
Application:
Whichever oil you choose, use it in the way that is most pleasing to the child—in the bath, in a massage lotion or in a vaporizer.

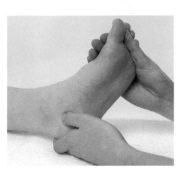

The bladder reflex is the area to the right of the left thumb here, and often appears pink, raised, and slightly polished.

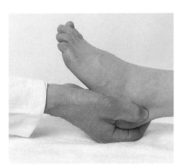

Point 17 is located on the Bladder meridian, in the hollow behind the ankle bone on the outside surface.

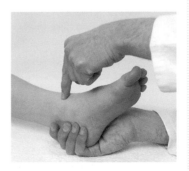

Point 16, on the Spleen meridian, is just above and in front of the inside ankle bone.

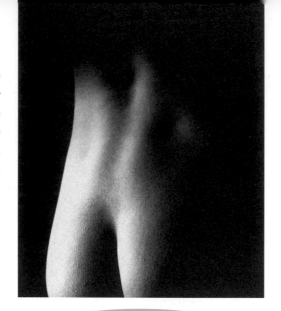

RIGHT *Hemorrhoids are varicose veins outside or inside the anus, often caused by straining to defecate. They are painful, itchy, and may bleed.*

DIAGNOSING HEMORRHOIDS
- Bleeding, often a bright red streak on the bathroom tissue or on the surface of the feces
- Part of the bowel may prolapse (stick out) when feces are passed, and may return or stay out

EXCRETORY SYSTEM

hemorrhoids

CALL THE PHYSICIAN
■ If you have had any bleeding from the anus, to rule out a more serious cause.

If you have had children, suffer from constipation, stand a lot at work, or are seriously overweight, the chances are that you will suffer from hemorrhoids (or piles, as they are more colloquially known). If severe, hemorrhoids—which are varicose veins in the soft lining of the anus—may require surgical treatment, but home remedies can provide great relief for most people.

KITCHEN MEDICINE
■ An acute attack of piles can be excruciatingly painful and cause such itching and irritation that it can drive the poor sufferer to distraction. Instant relief is available in every kitchen, in the form of ice cubes in your refrigerator. Put two or three in a plastic bag and apply it directly onto the piles. The pain may well be worse for the first moment or two, but this will be followed by relief from both pain and irritation.

CONVENTIONAL MEDICINE
✚ Eat plenty of high-fiber foods, such as apples, pears, beans, oats, whole wheat bread, and brown rice. Drink plenty of water. This will help to keep the feces soft and avoid straining to pass a bowel motion. Your physician may prescribe suppositories together with cream containing anti-inflammatory drugs.

ABOVE *Pears, especially when eaten with their skin, provide lots of fiber. Choose organically grown fruit.*

ABOVE *People whose careers demand a lot of standing are at particular risk of hemorrhoids.*

HERBAL REMEDIES

 One traditional—but effective—herb for hemorrhoids is pilewort, so called in the Middle Ages because its roots actually resemble piles. It is extremely astringent and heals the damaged tissues.

■ **Use and Dosage:** Ointments made from both pilewort leaves and root are readily available, or the dried herb can be taken internally in capsules.

Infusions of yarrow, lime flowers, or melilot will help the circulation and blood vessels, while fresh *Aloe vera* leaves, distilled witch hazel, chickweed cream, or borage juice can relieve itching.

HOMEOPATHIC REMEDIES

 Unexplained or persistent rectal bleeding requires medical attention. Paeonia ointment may help to relieve the itching of haemorrhoids.

🌿 AESCULUS 6C For sensation of splinters in rectum. Pain extends to hips. Large, painful, protruding, purple piles. Anus dry and itchy.

🌿 ALOE 6C For hemorrhoids like bunches of grapes. Purple color, better for cold bathing. Itching in rectum. Diarrhea.

🌿 HAMAMELIS 6C For hemorrhoids in pregnancy, profuse bleeding with soreness. **Dosage:** one tablet twice daily. Maximum 2 weeks.

AROMATHERAPY

 🌿 CYPRESS
Cupressus sempervirens
🌿 GERANIUM
Pelargonium graveolens
🌿 JUNIPER
Juniperus communis
🌿 MYRRH
Commiphora molmol
These essential oils will help to increase the circulation. Cypress is also a natural astringent, which can have the effect of actually shrinking the piles.
Application:
Use either alternate hot and cold sitz baths or 3–4 drops of your chosen oil in a warm compress

(a simple facecloth will do), held on the anus or against the hemorrhoid. The oils can also be added to some KY Jelly and then applied: add about 10 drops of geranium and 10 drops of cypress to a whole tube of jelly, mix together and store in a small jar.

CAUTION

Do not apply essential oils without diluting, as this will make things more uncomfortable. If there is any bleeding, seek medical advice before using essential oils.

ABOVE *Dried fruit, especially that old standby, prunes, help to keep the bowels moving.*

NUTRITION

During an episode of painful hemorrhoids it is important to keep the stool as soft as possible. Dried fruit, especially prunes and apricots, and a regular intake of prune juice will help. You must avoid the temptation not to pass stools, however painful it might be, as further constipation will only make the piles worse— and the pain even worse when you eventually go.

If you are constantly losing even small amounts of blood from your piles, there is a risk of anemia, so you must take nutritional steps to prevent this *(see Anemia on p.118)*. This is particularly important for women, especially during pregnancy.

Avoid foods with lots of irritating small seeds, such as tomatoes, gooseberries, raspberries, blackberries, and kiwis, until your condition has settled down, because these can cause further irritation.

PREVENTATIVE *measures*

FIBER INTAKE: *above all, avoid constipation (see p.156), as straining on the lavatory will inevitably cause piles. Plenty of fluid and foods rich in soluble fiber, like oats, apples, pears, and nearly all vegetables, will do the trick for most people. Daily consumption of some dried fruit—prunes, apricots and figs are the best—is recommended.*

CONTRAST BATHING: to prevent hemorrhoids from developing, it is important to stimulate blood flow to the rectum area. The best way to do this is by daily contrast bathing with alternate hot and cold water.

EXERCISE

REGULAR exercise helps improve the circulation in general and is very important in both the treatment and prevention of piles.

OUTSIDE HELP

 ACUPRESSURE: point 4 prevents constipation.
REFLEXOLOGY: work the soles and palms to stimulate the functioning of the digestive tract. For chronic conditions, you can massage and

squeeze gently down the back of the lower leg.
YOGA: if constipation is the cause, *see p.156*. Shoulderstand and/or Headstand positions may help, if you already practice them

regularly. For stress relief, lie in relaxation, or with your legs up against the wall, and focus on long, slow exhalations of the breath.

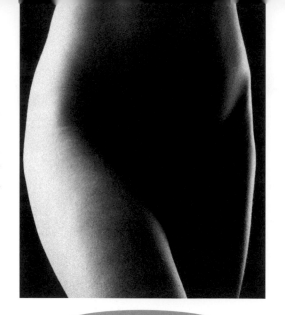

RIGHT *Cystitis is much more common in women than men because their urethra is closer to the anus. Germs living in the bowel are therefore easily transferred to the urethra, and journey up to the bladder.*

DIAGNOSING CYSTITIS

- Painful, burning sensation when passing urine, often worse at the end of the stream
- Urine may be pink, due to the presence of a small amount of blood; sometimes there may be small blood clots
- Frequent need to go to the bathroom, perhaps only passing a small amount each time
- Fever

EXCRETORY SYSTEM

cystitis

*C*ystitis can be an isolated acute problem or a recurring chronic nightmare, which affects millions of women but few men. It is frequently impossible to trace the specific bacteria that trigger an episode of cystitis, which is often linked to concurrent attacks of thrush (see p.166). Recurrent episodes of cystitis may be treated with prophylactic antibiotics. Self-help, on the other hand, and natural home remedies can be of considerable benefit if you have been a martyr to cystitis for years on end.

CALL THE PHYSICIAN

- If you have a high fever with cystitis and/or vomiting.
- If you have cystitis with back pain.
- If your symptoms persist.

CONVENTIONAL MEDICINE

 "Over-the-counter" remedies can usually relieve the symptoms of cystitis by neutralizing the acid in the urine. If symptoms remain, then antibiotics are usually required to prevent the infection spreading to the kidneys.

LEFT *Cranberry juice helps to prevent bacteria from collecting in the bladder.*

Dosage information ~
Adults
- Take antibiotics up to two or four times a day for 3–7 days; follow medical advice.

Children
- Give antibiotic syrup up to four times a day. Dose depends on age and weight of the child; follow medical advice and remember to complete the course. Bottles often contain more than is required to allow for spillages.

NUTRITION

Drink at least 5–6pt/2.25–2.75l of water each day and make sure you **eat plenty of** the diuretic foods, such as celery, parsley, and dandelion leaves. Making sure that plenty of fluid goes in and out of the system reduces the risk of infection.

Avoid caffeine; drink little alcohol and only weak tea.

KITCHEN MEDICINE

■ The traditional kitchen treatment for cystitis is lemon barley water. The combination of citric acid and the soothing demulcents in the barley help relieve the burning discomfort and control the growth of bacteria. Pour 3¾cups/900ml of boiling water over ¼cup/50g of washed barley and the grated rind and juice of an unwaxed lemon. Add ½tsp of sugar, stir thoroughly and drink one glass three times a day.

■ Modern scientific research has now proved that a traditional Native North American remedy—cranberry juice—is even more effective. Chemicals in the juice form a barrier lining on the inside of the bladder and on the tubes that carry urine to and from it, which seems to prevent the cystitis-causing bacteria from making their home in the bladder tissue. Drink at least 2½ cups/600ml a day of a 50:50 dilution of cranberry juice with water. This should be both a treatment during an attack of cystitis and long-term protection, so continue drinking the mixture even when you do not actually have the symptoms.

HERBAL REMEDIES

 Many herbs act as urinary antiseptics and can therefore be helpful in combating infections and inflammation, while drinking herbal teas provides a necessary increase in fluid intake.

Use and Dosage:
Take up to 2pts/1l daily of a tea made from 1 part each of buchu, couchgrass, bearberry and cornsilk, (2tsp/10ml per cup of water). Add 2 parts shepherd's purse to the mix if blood is in the urine; seek professional advice if symptoms persist. Avoid spicy foods and those producing acid residues, such as meat and shellfish.

ABOVE *Bearberry is a urinary antiseptic, soothing, and healing for infections and inflammations.*

OUTSIDE HELP

ACUPRESSURE: points 22, 33, 34, and 37 help to relieve the discomfort of cystitis.

REFLEXOLOGY: work the reflexes of the urethra, bladder, ureter, and kidneys, for immediate relief. On the hand, the large muscle beneath the thumb contains most of these reflexes and is easily accessible.

AROMATHERAPY

🌿 MYRRH
Commiphora molmol
🌿 TEA TREE
Melaleuca alternifolia
🌿 ROMAN CHAMOMILE
Chamaemelum nobile
🌿 LAVENDER
Lavandula angustifolia

These essential oils are calming, soothing, and anti-inflammatory; tea tree is antiviral, antifungal, and antibacterial.

Application:
Use in a warm compress over the lower back, in sitz baths or in ordinary baths.

CAUTION

If blood or pus appears in the urine, contact your physician immediately. If antibiotics are prescribed, continue with the aromatherapy treatment, as they will work side-by-side.

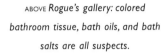

ABOVE *Rogue's gallery: colored bathroom tissue, bath oils, and bath salts are all suspects.*

PREVENTATIVE *measures*

Eat some live natural yogurt every day.

HYGIENE: *after going to the bathroom always wipe yourself from front to back, once only with each piece of paper— daughters should be taught this from the earliest possible age. Only use white bathroom tissue, as colored inks can be an irritant. Always pass urine as soon as decently possible after intercourse, and always pass it as soon as you need to, to prevent the risk of back pressure carrying bacteria into the kidneys. Avoid very hot baths, foaming bath oils, bath salts, and frequent washing of the vaginal area.*

HOMEOPATHIC REMEDIES

Drink lots of fluids. Symptoms in males or worsening symptoms, back pain, or chills require medical help.
🌿 CANTHARIS **30**C For "peeing red hot needles." Constantly wanting to urinate, passing just a few drops. Urine may be bloody.

🌿 SARSAPARILLA **30**C When passing lots of urine and frequently. Pressure felt on bladder, with last drop of urine painful to pass.
🌿 STAPHYSAGRIA **30**C For "honeymoon cystitis." Burning pain after intercourse or after

having had a catheter inserted. Recurrent cystitis related to intercourse.
Dosage: one tablet every 4 hours until condition improves. Maximum 5 days.

cuts

Minor cuts do not usually require medical attention, because blood clots should quickly form and seal them, but they should be carefully cleaned and dressed. For minor cuts and scrapes, a heaped teaspoon of salt in 2½ cups/600ml of warm water makes a good emergency disinfectant; and in desperation the juice of a lemon squeezed over the affected area also works, but this remedy will not be too popular with the patient, as it is likely to sting.

CONVENTIONAL MEDICINE

Apply direct pressure over the cut for 10 minutes with a clean, dry cloth. If something is stuck in the wound, such as glass, do not remove it, but apply pressure around it and seek medical advice. Raise the affected part of the body above chest level.

Remove the pressure after 10 minutes—if the cut is still bleeding, reapply the dressing for 10 minutes more. If the bleeding continues, apply pressure again and seek medical advice. When the bleeding stops, cover with a bandaid or clean dressing.

HERBAL REMEDIES

After cleaning the cut with marigold infusion, apply creams or ointments containing marigold, chickweed, St. John's wort, echinacea, or chamomile.

Emergency poultices for cuts and scrapes away from home can be made from crushed self-heal, woundwort, cranesbill, herb robert, agrimony, or shepherd's purse.

AROMATHERAPY

The most relevant oils are lavender and tea tree. Clean the cut area with a bowl of warm water containing 5 drops of either oil.

BELOW *St. John's wort is the source for hypericum. It is a good wound-healer.*

HOMEOPATHIC REMEDIES

Cuts should be cleaned with water. Check that you are immunized against tetanus, particularly with puncture wounds from nails or needles. Hypercal solution can be used to clean the wound, or hypercal ointment used under a clean dressing.

HYPERICUM **30c** When injury is a puncture wound or injury to a fingertip that is rich in nerves. Pains often sharp and shooting. **Dosage:** one tablet every 4 hours. Maximum 3 days.

KITCHEN MEDICINE

■ A compress made from a clean cloth soaked in 2½ cups/600ml of cold water and 2tsp/10ml of cider vinegar (or any vinegar) is effective for minor cuts.

■ To encourage healing, the old-fashioned remedy of ① crushed garlic ② mixed with honey makes a wonderful salve. ③ Spread it thinly on a piece of clean gauze or lint-free cotton and use it to cover the damaged area.

bruises

Bruises are the visible sign of bleeding beneath the skin, resulting from pressure or a blow. They generally change color over a period of days.

CONVENTIONAL MEDICINE

Apply an ice package as soon as possible after the injury to reduce the swelling and bruising. Take a pain-reliever such as acetaminophen or ibuprofen.

HERBAL REMEDIES

Apply comfrey, chickweed, or arnica creams or lotions (but do not use arnica if the skin is broken); a cold compress soaked in sanicle, rue or St. John's wort infusion; a crushed cabbage leaf (hold in place with a bandaid if necessary).

HOMEOPATHIC REMEDIES

ARNICA 30C This is the main remedy for bruises and is also helpful in treating muscle aches after sport. Probably the first remedy to try. Very useful if the person does not want help and says they are okay, even when it is obvious they are not. Also good after surgery.

BELLIS PERENNIS 30C For bruising that is a little deeper and for very sore muscles.

LEDUM 30C For very dark bruising. Area feels cold and is better for a cold compress. **Dosage:** one tablet every 2 hours for six doses, then three times daily. Maximum 5 days.

KITCHEN MEDICINE

■ Pineapple juice and ice packs (see Black Eyes) are the best kitchen medicine there is for bruises.

■ Massaging the bruised area with a little extra-virgin olive oil will disperse the bruise, and the vitamin E that penetrates the skin is an additional aid to healing.

AROMATHERAPY

Put 4 drops of lavender and chamomile (2 drops of each) into a bowl of hot water and 2 drops of each into a bowl of cold water. Soak a facecloth in each bowl, then apply alternately to the bruised area—in other words, put the hot cloth on and, when that is cool, replace with the cold one; when that has warmed up, repeat the process.

black eyes

A black eye is the result of severe bruising of the eye socket and lids. It is internal bleeding that results in the swelling and the skin turning black or dark blue. Sadly, most black eyes are sustained through accident or anger.

CONVENTIONAL MEDICINE

Apply an ice pack as soon as possible after the injury to reduce the swelling and bruising. Take a pain-reliever such as acetaminophen or ibuprofen.

CAUTION

Two black eyes after a blow to the head may be the sign of a skull fracture—seek urgent medical advice.

HERBAL REMEDIES

Apply fresh *Aloe vera* sap or mashed plantain leaves; a cold compress soaked in rue or comfrey infusion.

AROMATHERAPY

Put 1 drop of chamomile into 2tsp/10ml of ice-cold water, soak a cottonwool pad, then apply to the affected area.

HOMEOPATHIC REMEDIES

ACONITE 30C Give immediately for the "shock" of the blow (can also be given for any sudden injury). One or two doses only, over 15 minutes.

LEDUM 30C For a black eye that is generally better for cold compresses.

Skin around the eye is swollen. **Dosage:** one tablet every 30 minutes for six doses, then every 2–4 hours. Maximum 12 doses.

LEDUM

KITCHEN MEDICINE

■ These days, the old-fashioned remedy of a raw steak as a treatment for black eyes may not be too popular. In fact, the best kitchen remedy for a black eye is to drink copious amounts of pineapple juice—preferably before the injury (if you're a boxer), but even after the event the enzymes in pineapple juice speed up the rate at which the blood causing the black eye dissolves, so that it will heal much more quickly.

■ A clean dish towel filled with crushed ice and applied over the affected area will hasten the healing even further.

bites

If the skin is punctured—whether by an animal or human bite—you will certainly need to check your antitetanus vaccination, and bites should always be seen by a physician as soon as possible. Turn on the kitchen faucet and rinse the bitten area with copious amounts of water. If practical, wash with soap, then rinse again for at least another 5 minutes.

CONVENTIONAL MEDICINE

A bite from any animal (including a human bite) is susceptible to infection, as all animals have germs in their mouths. After cleaning the wound carefully with soap and water, dry and then cover it with a plaster or a small sterile dressing, then seek medical attention.

HOMEOPATHIC REMEDIES

Hypercal tincture or lotion can be applied to the skin and may be soothing.

LEDUM 30c For insect bites where there is a lot of swelling. Discomfort eased when bathing in cold water or a cold compress applied. Has a reputation for preventing mosquito bites in people who are often bitten (for prevention: one tablet daily for a maximum of 14 days). Also useful in animal bites.

APIS 30c For burning of surrounding area. Swelling often marked. Worse for heat.

Dosage: one tablet taken every 30 minutes (every 15 minutes for a severe reaction). Maximum six doses.

AROMATHERAPY

Put a neat drop of lavender directly onto the area of skin affected by the bite.

HERBAL REMEDIES

For insect bites, apply fresh *Aloe vera* sap; diluted lavender or tea-tree oil (5 drops in 1tsp/5ml of water); fresh lemon balm or plantain leaves.

Bathe with marigold or echinacea tea, if the bite becomes infected.

ABOVE *The sap obtained from the leaves of the* Aloe vera *plant can be applied to the skin to relieve insect bites.*

KITCHEN MEDICINE

■ A real old wives' remedy if you are out in the countryside is to chew up a mouthful of plantain leaves and apply the resulting paste to the wound.

■ Flea bites should be rubbed with a slice of raw onion, and mosquito bites with the cut end of a clove of garlic.

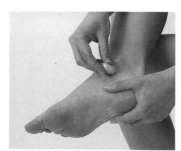

ABOVE *Rub the cut end of a clove of garlic on the skin for relief from mosquito bites.*

FIRST AID

stings

*S*tings, by insects and marine animals, vary in strength and seriousness, but often result in localized pain, reddening, and swelling, and sometimes in nausea, fainting and breathing problems.

CONVENTIONAL MEDICINE

If the stinger is visible, remove it with tweezers. Apply a cold compress. Use calamine or antihistamine to reduce the itching, and apply insect-repellent to prevent further bites.

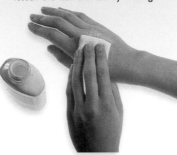

BELOW *Calamine lotion can help lessen the itch created by a sting.*

KITCHEN MEDICINE

■ For wasp stings, make a paste of salt and vinegar and spread the paste over the affected area.

■ For bee stings, use baking powder or sodium bicarbonate, mixed to a paste in the same way— making sure that you remove the sting with a pair of tweezers.

■ A mixture of honey and crushed garlic makes a soothing ointment to apply to the skin after most insect stings and bites.

■ The traditional remedy for stinging-nettle burns is the dock leaf, but, based on homeopathic principles, a cup of nettle tea can be equally soothing; as can the application of an ordinary, used teabag that has been dipped in ice water.

■ Jellyfish stings can be neutralized by sitting in a hot bath for 20 minutes.

CAUTION

Wasps are the most likely to sting the inside of your mouth or throat. Sucking ice cubes will relieve the swelling and discomfort, but at the slightest sign of breathing difficulties, rush to your nearest hospital.

HERBAL REMEDIES

Apply a fresh slice of onion to both bee and wasp stings; sage or marigold cream; crushed plantain leaves.

Bathe the area with sage or marigold infusions, after removing any remaining stinger. (*See also Bites on p.182.*)

ABOVE *The homeopathic remedy Apis is made from the honey bee and helps soothe the bright red, inflamed area caused by a bee or wasp sting.*

AROMATHERAPY

Remove the stinger if possible, then put 1 drop of neat lavender on the affected area. If it is a plant sting (e.g. a nettle), again put 1 drop of neat lavender on the area, repeating if necessary.

HOMEOPATHIC REMEDIES

❧ LEDUM **30**C For insect stings where there is a lot of swelling. Discomfort eased when bathing in cold water or a cold compress applied.

❧ APIS **30**C For burning and stinging of surrounding area.

Swelling often marked. Worse for heat. Good for both bee stings and wasp stings.

Dosage: one tablet taken every 30 minutes (every 15 minutes for a severe reaction). Maximum six doses.

ABOVE *A used teabag dipped in ice water can provide relief from stinging-nettle irritations.*

burns

Burns may be caused by dry heat, such as fire, friction, sun, chemicals, or electricity, and are often accompanied by shock. Never, never use the old kitchen remedy of butter or oil. For small areas, run the affected part under cold water or fill a bowl and immerse the burned area. Cold water should be applied until the pain diminishes—usually for at least 10 to 15 minutes. If the skin is broken or severely blistered, fill a plastic bag with ice, put it inside at least two more plastic bags, then apply to the affected area, removing every 15 minutes to prevent freezing of the tissue.

CONVENTIONAL MEDICINE

Run cold water onto the burned skin until the burning sensation stops. Gently remove any rings if the fingers are burned. Remove burned clothing, unless it is stuck to the burn. Cover the burn with clean, non-fluffy material, such as a clean pillow case. A plastic bag or plastic wrap makes a good temporary covering. If the burn is extensive, on the face, or near the mouth, seek immediate medical advice.

BELOW *Put cold water on a burn right away.*

HOMEOPATHIC REMEDIES

Severe burns require medical attention. For minor burns, cool the area with cold water. Chemical burns need specialist treatment.

ARNICA **30C** Initial remedy to take after any trauma.

Dosage: one tablet every 15 minutes for four doses. Then consider one of the following:

URTICA URENS **30C** For stinging or burning pains. Skin is red and may look like nettle rash.

CANTHARIS **30C** For burn that feels as if it is raw, with severe pains. Better for cold being applied. May have blistering.

Dosage: one tablet every 15 minutes for six doses, then every 4 hours. Maximum 12 doses.

HERBAL REMEDIES

For minor burns, apply a compress soaked in cool chickweed, St. John's wort, marigold, or plantain infusion; a little infused oil of St. John's wort, after cooling the area under a running tap; fresh sap from an *Aloe vera* plant; slippery-elm powder mixed with a little milk or water to form a paste.

NUTRITION

Anyone who has suffered sunburn or serious burns to an area greater than your hand can readily cover, should be given plenty of fluids to drink in order to prevent dehydration.

KITCHEN MEDICINE

■ Mild to moderate sunburn can be relieved by putting three or four chamomile teabags into a tepid bath and soaking for **15 minutes** (*see also Sunburn on p.185*).

AROMATHERAPY

First run the burn under freezing cold water, then immediately put some neat lavender oil on it.

CAUTION

Severe burns need urgent hospital treatment.

FIRST AID

sunburn

*S*unburn is caused by ultraviolet rays and you are at greatest risk when the sun is at its highest. Your susceptibility depends on your coloring and the amount of pigment in your skin. Those with red hair and freckles always burn and never tan; blue-eyed blondes always burn but may tan lightly; and everyone else may burn after too much exposure.

It is difficult to believe that there is anyone unaware of the links between excessive sun exposure and skin cancer. Tanned can never mean healthy, because the tanning process is the result of skin damage (this is equally true of artificial tans acquired from tanning beds). Even one episode of severe sunburn increases your chances of getting skin cancer. Prevention by avoidance is the only sane behavior.

CONVENTIONAL MEDICINE

Find some shade and drink plenty of cold water. Cool the sunburned skin by sponging it with cold water or soaking it in a cold bath. Mild burns can be soothed with calamine or an after-sun preparation.

ABOVE *The best protection against sunburn is to wear light, loose clothing and a hat, even when engaged in watersports, where reflected rays are an added hazard.*

AROMATHERAPY

Add peppermint or lavender to a cool bath or, if the sunburn is quite bad, drip lavender oil on neat after a cool bath, repeating every 2–3 hours if necessary. If the sunburned area is too tender to touch, put the oils into a water spray, then spray on. If you have had just a little too much sun, the oils could be added to your aftersun lotion, to be put on in the evening. Avoid getting too much sun for the next 2–3 days if you have to give yourself treatment for sunburn.

KITCHEN MEDICINE

■ Serious sunburn will certainly require medical attention but a mixture of one part olive oil and two parts cider vinegar, rubbed gently into affected skin, will help to relieve the irritation of mild sunburn.

RIGHT **Belladonna,** *or deadly nightshade, is good for inflammation.*

HERBAL REMEDIES

Apply infused St. John's wort oil with a few drops of lavender oil added; fresh *Aloe vera* sap or ointment; evening primrose or borage cream to help the skin repair when the burn starts to heal.

Drink an infusion of lime flowers, elderflowers, and yarrow to encourage sweating and lower the body's temperature.

HOMEOPATHIC REMEDIES

Sunstroke often accompanies sunburn, so drink plenty of fluids. (*See also Burns on p.184.*)

🍃 BELLADONNA **6C** For red face, very hot to touch, "could fry an egg on it." Throbbing headache, worse for light and noise. May have high fever and dilated pupils.

🍃 GLONOINE **6C** For headaches from sun. Bursting headache with waves of pulsating pain. Worse during hours of sun, even if not directly exposed to it. Worse for moving. Face may be flushed or, if there is sunstroke, pale.

Dosage: one tablet every half-hour for six doses, then every 4 hours. Maximum 4 days.

sprains

A sprain occurs when the ligaments surrounding and supporting a joint are either overstretched or torn, most commonly in the ankle or wrist.

CONVENTIONAL MEDICINE

Apply an ice pack or a cold compress as soon as possible after the injury in order to reduce swelling and bruising. Put on a bandage or ace wrap to provide gentle, even pressure over the sprain. Avoid using or walking on the sprained joint, and raise it in a sling or on a footstool. Take a pain-reliever such as acetaminophen or ibuprofen.

HERBAL REMEDIES

Use crushed comfrey or cabbage leaves as an effective poultice.

Apply arnica, comfrey, or marigold creams, ideally with a few drops of lavender or thyme oil added; alternatively, use a compress soaked in the relevant infusion or diluted tincture.

Soak the affected area with an ice pack and a hot rosemary infusion: use either a foot bath or compress as appropriate.

OUTSIDE HELP

YOGA: sprains need time in order to heal. In your Asana practice, be very careful not to overwork an affected area too early.

HOMEOPATHIC REMEDIES

 ARNICA **30c** Take for the initial bruising.

Dosage: one tablet every 15 minutes for four doses. Continue if bruising is the main problem, at a dose of one tablet twice daily. Maximum 5 days.

LEDUM **6c** For sprains, particularly of the ankle, when the ankle looks black with bruising and is better for cold compresses.

RHUS TOXICODENDRON **6c** Pain worse on initial movement, improves as the joint is "warmed up" by movement. Worse in the morning when the joint seems stiff. Better during the day and for warm weather. Person may be restless.

Dosage: one tablet three times daily. Maximum 2 weeks.

AROMATHERAPY

First ice the sprain to reduce any swelling, then the whole area can be massaged using ginger, lavender, and chamomile. Keep the sprained area elevated and rest it as much as possible. If it does not improve, seek professional advice.

KITCHEN MEDICINE

■ An ice pack applied to the injury is again the most beneficial remedy that is available from your kitchen (*see Nosebleeds on p.188*). Combined with rest, a good compress, and elevation of the affected area, an ice pack will bring speedy healing to any sprained or strained muscle or tendon.

■ The large outer leaves of a green cabbage make an excellent compress (*see below*).

■ Soothing baths bring great relief for all strains and sprains, and a quick hunt round the kitchen cupboard can provide suitable additions—a heaped tablespoon of mustard powder or a cup of Epsom salt. If you live near the sea, a bucket of seawater added to a hot bath, or a handful of seaweed, can be extremely healing.

① Remove the central stalk, and bruise the leaf all over with a rolling pin or knife handle.

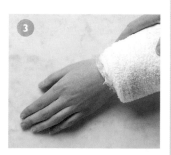

② Heat the leaf gently in a steamer or microwave.

③ Wrap around the affected area and cover with a towel. Leave for at least 15 minutes.

fractures

■ If you suspect that someone has a fracture.

A fracture is a broken or cracked bone, which is caused either by direct force (such as a blow or kick) or by indirect force, when the bone breaks at some distance from the point of force.

CONVENTIONAL MEDICINE

✚ Keep the fractured bone still. Discourage the injured person from drinking or eating anything, in case surgery is necessary. Support the injured part with your hands without moving it. If possible, make a sling to hold a broken arm against the body (see below); a broken leg can be strapped to the other leg for support. Seek urgent medical attention.

① To make a sling, lay a triangular bandage with the point beyond the elbow of the injured arm.

② Lift the lower end of the bandage over the injured arm while the patient supports it.

③ Tie the end to the neck end by the collarbone. Tuck in (or pin) the bandage by the elbow.

KITCHEN MEDICINE

■ The only kitchen medicine of any value in the treatment of fractures is comfrey tea—the traditional name of comfrey is knitbone. No more than two cups a day should be taken for the first couple of weeks after a fracture, to promote rapid healing of the break.

HOMEOPATHIC REMEDIES

❧ Homeopathic remedies may assist orthodox medical treatment, but should not interfere with medication prescribed by your physician.
❧ ARNICA 30C Take this remedy first, for the bruising associated with the injury.
Dosage: one tablet every 2 hours for six doses.

❧ SYMPHYTUM 6C This is also called boneset or boneknit and may help with the joining up of the broken bones. Also used when the fracture is slow to mend or shows signs of not mending.
❧ CALCAREA PHOSPHORICA 6C Use if symphytum does not help.
Dosage: one tablet twice daily. Maximum 14 days.

AROMATHERAPY

With fractures, it is quite difficult to use aromatherapy, as the affected area is going to be encased in plaster; what you can do is work on the corresponding area (i.e. if the wrist is fractured, work the ankle on the same side; if it is the shoulder, work the hip on that side, or work any area that is under stress). You cannot actually treat the fracture itself. Choose an essential oil that is soothing and calming (see Stress on p.60).

HERBAL REMEDIES

Freshly pulped comfrey leaves used as a poultice will be beneficial for minor cracks or broken toes.
Drink an infusion of horsetail, alfalfa, and comfrey to encourage healing of the fracture.

ABOVE *Alfafa is rich in nutrients and will help to rebuild bones and teeth, and encourage healing.*

nosebleeds

Nosebleeds may be caused by illness, a blow, by rupturing the nasal blood vessels, or may occur for no apparent reason.

HOMEOPATHIC REMEDIES

 For persistent nosebleeds, consult your physician.

❀ ARNICA **30C** For nosebleeds resulting from a blow to the nose. This helps stop the bleeding.

❀ PHOSPHORUS **30C** Often used in children. For nosebleeds for no apparent reason. Bright red blood, and nosebleeds when blowing the nose.

Dosage: one tablet every 15 minutes. Maximum six doses.

LEFT *If other methods fail, try a little cider vinegar in water in the nostrils.*

CONVENTIONAL MEDICINE

Sit down, leaning forward. Breathing through the mouth, pinch the soft part of the nose below the bridge. Avoid sniffing, swallowing, coughing, or spitting, which might provoke further bleeding. Use a handkerchief or cloth to mop up the blood. Release the pressure after 10 minutes. If bleeding continues, reapply pressure for another 10 minutes. After 30 minutes, if the bleeding has not stopped, seek medical advice.

If the bleeding does stop, you should rest quietly for several hours, and avoid sniffing or blowing.

KITCHEN MEDICINE

■ The best remedy is in your refrigerator—crush a few cubes of ice and wrap them in a clean handkerchief. Place this ice pack over the top of the nose and apply pressure with the thumb and forefinger on each side for at least 5–6 minutes. If the bleeding persists, put 2tsp/10ml of cider vinegar into a glass of tepid water, tip the head back and use a dropper to trickle the mixture into each nostril.

HERBAL REMEDIES

A traditional and effective remedy is simply to insert a yarrow leaf in the nostril and then to pinch the nose gently until a clot forms.

Insert a small cotton swab soaked in shepherd's purse, witch hazel, lady's mantle, agrimony, or yarrow tincture into the nostril.

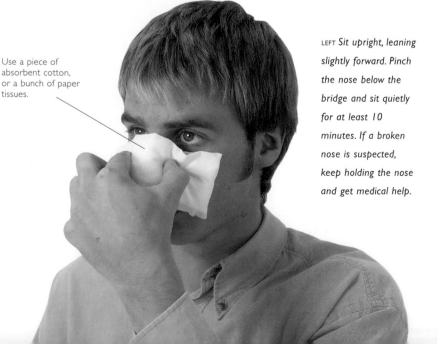

Use a piece of absorbent cotton, or a bunch of paper tissues.

LEFT *Sit upright, leaning slightly forward. Pinch the nose below the bridge and sit quietly for at least 10 minutes. If a broken nose is suspected, keep holding the nose and get medical help.*

FIRST AID

splinters

Splinters are generally small pieces of wood or thorn that become embedded in the skin and may cause infection if they are not removed. Soak the affected area in comfortably hot, very soapy water, before attempting to squeeze the splinter out or remove it with a sterilized needle or tweezers.

CONVENTIONAL MEDICINE

If possible, remove the splinter with tweezers. If the splinter is deeply embedded or difficult to remove, seek medical advice.

Clean the area around the splinter with soap and warm water. Check that your tetanus immunization is up to date.

KITCHEN MEDICINE

■ For stubborn and difficult splinters, cover the area with a hot bread poultice, which will help to draw the splinter to the surface.

① Make the poultice by putting three or four slices of bread (white, brown, whole wheat—it makes no real difference) into a strainer.

② Pour over boiling water. Mash with a wooden spoon until you have a thick, hot paste. Make sure that the temperature is not too hot before applying. For really stubborn splinters, especially underneath finger- or toenails, you may need several applications.

HOMEOPATHIC REMEDIES

Remove the splinter if at all possible. Watch for signs of infection.

❧ SILICEA **6c** Reputed to expel foreign material from the body. Care should be taken, as it may

also aid expulsion of pins or screws used to keep a fracture in place! Has been known to irritate dental fillings. If this occurs, stop.
Dosage: one tablet twice daily. Maximum 14 days.

HERBAL REMEDIES

Use a little chickweed, marshmallow, or slippery-elm ointment to help draw stubborn splinters: apply the ointment, cover with a small bandage, and leave for a few hours before extracting the splinter with tweezers or a clean needle.

AROMATHERAPY

Remove the splinter with tweezers or a sterile needle, then apply 1 neat drop of lavender oil to the site.

ABOVE *Lavender oil is one of the few essential oils that may be applied undiluted to the skin. It is analgesic and antiseptic.*

ABOVE *Silica comes from flint and promotes the expulsion of the splinter.*

motion sickness

Any form of motion can cause the nausea, vomiting, headache, and dizziness that we know as motion or travel sickness. Buses, cars, aeroplanes, boats, even fairground rides can turn a pleasant outing into a nightmare. This condition is much more common in children, though adults too can suffer. But, surprisingly, those who cannot travel a mile as a passenger in a car without being ill are often perfectly all right when driving themselves. Home remedies work effectively, without turning you into a zombie. And it is worth noting that there is a link between severe motion sickness in children and migraine in later life (see Migraine on p.52).

HERBAL REMEDIES

Drink a cup of any of the following as teas, or use 2–3 drops of tincture on the tongue at regular intervals during the journey to provide relief: chamomile, black horehound, lemon balm, or meadowsweet.

CONVENTIONAL MEDICINE

Symptoms can be prevented by lying flat with closed eyes. Try to avoid reading while moving. If possible, get out of the vehicle or take a break from traveling.

KITCHEN MEDICINE

■ Ginger is the king of kitchen remedies, but for maximum benefit you need to administer it before the sickness starts, as once the unfortunate victim begins to vomit, it is not always possible to keep the medicine down long enough for it to be absorbed and become effective. For long journeys fill a thermos flask with ginger tea and, after your pre-travel mugful, sip a small cup every hour. Children, who suffer most, may not accept ginger tea. For them, buy crystallized ginger, cut into small cubes, dust liberally with confectioner's sugar and keep in a small tin, so that the youngster can nibble a piece or two every half-hour during the journey.

The best way to take ginger is as tea.

1 Peel and grate 1in/2.5cm of fresh ginger root into a mug, then add boiling water.

2 Add 2tsp/10ml of honey, cover, then leave for 10 minutes. Strain and sip at least half an hour before traveling.

AROMATHERAPY

Put a couple of drops of ginger or peppermint on a handkerchief; rub a lotion containing them into the hands; or massage the upper abdomen with the essential oils.

HOMEOPATHIC REMEDIES

Homeopathic motion-sickness pills, which are a combination of remedies, are available from some pharmacies.

❦ COCCULUS 30C For nausea and giddiness at even the thought of food. Lots of saliva. Giddiness better for lying down. Worse for watching moving objects (out of car window), for loss of sleep, light, and noise.

❦ TABACUM 30C For person convinced they will die with nausea. Pale with cold sweats. Worse for opening eyes and smell of tobacco. Better in fresh cold air (on deck).

❦ PETROLEUM 30C For nausea that is worse for sitting up, noise. Better for eating. Lots of saliva.

Dosage: one tablet every 30 minutes until improved. Maximum six doses.

OUTSIDE HELP

ACUPRESSURE: point 38, used continuously throughout the journey, will nearly always prevent motion sickness. Elasticated wristbands that apply pressure exactly on this point are available at many pharmacies and health-food stores.

Pressure applied to point 38

fainting

*F*ainting is caused by a temporary reduction in the supply of blood to the brain. It may be due to a shock, fear or exhaustion, missed meals, an over-hot atmosphere, or standing still for too long.

CONVENTIONAL MEDICINE

Encourage the person to lie down with their legs raised about 6in/15cm, until they feel completely better. Check for injuries, such as bruising or cuts.

Make a note of the events that occurred before, during and after the faint (such as how suddenly it occurred; whether the sufferer was pale and sweaty; how their pulse felt) and encourage them to have a medical check-up. The information gathered will be useful for the physician who has to confirm the diagnosis.

HOMEOPATHIC REMEDIES

CARBO VEGETABILIS 6C For chilly person, who collapses with cold sweats. Wants air and to be fanned. Fainting from too much food.

PHOSPHORUS 6C For open, lively, and artistic person. Sympathetic and sensitive to external impressions. Fainting from hunger.

IGNATIA 6C For fainting from emotional shock. Person is grief-stricken, sighing. Intolerant of tobacco. Lump in throat, as if about to cry.

Dosage: one tablet every 10 minutes. Maximum 12 tablets. Crush a tablet and place some powder on the tongue.

KITCHEN MEDICINE

■ A cup of hot green or Indian tea sweetened with honey should be sipped once the fainting has passed.
■ Inhaling the aroma from a small piece of crushed horseradish is a good substitute for old-fashioned smelling salts.

AROMATHERAPY

Loosen all clothing, make sure that the person is comfortable, then waft under their nose some rosemary, peppermint, or basil oil.

HERBAL REMEDIES

Sniff camphor, rosemary, or tea-tree oils.

Drink chamomile or betony tea to help recovery, once consciousness is regained.

ABOVE *The delicious fragrance of basil is quite pungent, and will gently ease a person back into consciousness.*

RIGHT *Sniffing an essential oil with stimulant properties, such as camphor, rosemary, or tea tree, may stave off a faint.*

Part Three

A PRACTICAL
HOME
PHARMACY

Herbal remedies

BASIC METHODS

Although it is now possible to buy many herbal remedies commercially,

it is often cheaper (and a lot more satisfying) to make your own at home.

That way you can make just the amount you need.

HOW TO MAKE A COMPRESS

A compress—used either hot or cold—is an effective way of applying a herbal remedy directly to the site of an inflammation or skin wound to speed up the healing process. Heat enhances the action of the herbs, but a cold compress may be preferable for treating some headaches and fever.

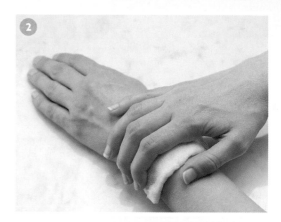

(|) Soak a clean linen or cotton cloth, or a pad of cotton gauze, in a hot infusion or decoction (see p.195).

(2) Apply to the affected skin as hot as is bearable, changing it for a fresh compress as it cools down or covering it with plastic or waxed paper, then with a hot-water bottle, to maintain its temperature for as long as possible. Prepare a cold compress in the same way, but let it cool before applying to the skin.

HOW TO MAKE A POULTICE

A poultice consists of a pulp or paste made directly of herbs. It is often used to draw pus out of the skin.

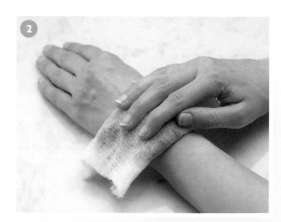

NOTE: all quantities given throughout the herbal sections refer to dried herbs, rather than fresh.

(|) Mix dried herbs into a pulp with a little hot water until you have the right consistency for a paste. Alternatively, use the mushy herbs left over from a hot infusion or decoction (see p.195); or process fresh herbs in a food mixer.

(2) Sandwich the paste between two layers of gauze, then apply to the affected skin as hot as is bearable, changing it or placing a hot-water bottle on top as for a compress.

HOW TO MAKE AN INFUSION

Infusions represent the simplest and most versatile method of taking herbal remedies, since you can drink them as teas or tisanes (sweetened with a little honey, as desired, and drunk either hot or cold); use them as a mouthwash, gargle, or as an eyebath (simmered to sterilize, then cooled); and even add them to the bath. They are made from the aerial parts—flowers or leaves—of the plant, which readily release their active ingredients.

(1) Warm a china or glass teapot, then add the dried herb, breaking it into small pieces if necessary.

(2) Cover with near-boiling water. Allow 1–2tsp/5–10ml of the herb for each cup of water. Steep for 5–10 minutes, then strain and drink. Alternatively, use 1–1¼ cups/25–30g of herb per 1pt/500ml of water, which will be enough for one day's dosage. Make a fresh infusion each day.

HOW TO MAKE A DECOCTION

Decoctions are similar to infusions, and may be used in much the same way, but involve boiling the herb in water to release its active ingredients. This enables woody stems, roots, bark, berries, and seeds to be used.

(1) Chop or crush the herb, to let it to break down more easily, into an enamel, stainless-steel, or glass-lidded pan (never use aluminum).

(2) Cover with cold water. Allow 1½ cups/350ml of water to ½–1tsp/2.5–5ml of herb (or 3 cups/750ml to 1–¼ cups/25–30g of herb, if you want to make enough for the whole day). Bring to a boil and simmer for 10 to 15 minutes or until the volume is reduced by one-third.

(3) Strain and use while still hot. It is preferable to make fresh decoctions daily.

Tinctures are alcohol preparations. The alcohol dissolves most of the herb's useful ingredients and preserves the preparation for a long time. Tinctures are stronger, volume for volume, than infusions or decoctions and are best diluted with a little water.

① Place 1½ cups/40g chopped or powdered herb in a container with a tightly fitting lid. Use a ratio of 1 part herb to 5 parts liquid (e.g. 1lb to 5pt, or 200g to 1l.)

② Pour over a 25% water/alcohol mix. (Dilute a bottle of vodka [25fl oz/75cl] by adding 12½fl oz/37.5cl of water to get the right water/alcohol concentration.)

③ Leave for 2 weeks, shaking the mixture regularly.

④ Strain the mixture through cheesecloth, squeezing the cloth well to extract as much liquid as possible.

List of herbs mentioned,

Common name	Botanical name
AGNUS-CASTUS	Vitex agnus-castus
AGRIMONY	Agrimonia eupatoria
ALEXANDRIAN SENNA see SENNA	
ALFALFA	Medicago sativa
ALOE VERA	Aloe vera
AMERICAN ARBOVITAE see THUJA	
AMERICAN CRANESBILL see CRANESBILL	
AMERICAN GINSENG	Panax quinquefolius
ANGELICA	Angelica archangelica
ANISE	Pimpinella anisum
ARABIAN COFFEE see COFFEE	
ARNICA	Arnica montana
ASTRAGALUS	Astragalus membranaceus
BASIL	Ocimum basilicum
BAYBERRY	Myrica cerifera
BEARBERRY	Arctostaphylos uva-ursi
BENZOIN—FRIAR'S BALSAM	Styrax benzoin
(COMPOUND TINCTURE OF BENZOIN)	
BETONY	Stachys officinalis
BILBERRY	Vaccinium myrtillus
BIRCH	Betula pendula
BISTORT	Polygonum bistorta
BITTER ORANGE	Citrus aurantium
BLACK COHOSH	Cimicifuga racemosa
BLACK HAW	Viburnum prunifolium
BLACK HOREHOUND	Ballota nigra
BLESSED THISTLE see HOLY THISTLE	
BLUE COHOSH	Caulophyllum thalictroides
BLUE FLAG	Iris versicolor
BONNET BELLFLOWER see CODONOPSIS	
BOGBEAN	Menyanthes trifoliata
BONESET	Eupatorium perfoliatum
BORAGE	Borago officinalis
BROAD-LEAVED DOCK see DOCK	
BUCHU	Agathosma crenulata
BUCKWHEAT	Fagopyrum esculentum
	(now known as Polygonum fagopyrum)
BURDOCK	Arctium lappa
CABBAGE	Brassica oleracea
CADE OIL	Eucalyptus globulus
CALIFORNIAN POPPY	Eschscholzia californica

CARAWAY	Carum carvi
CARDAMOM	Elettaria cardamomum
CASCARA SAGRADA	Rhamnus purshianus
CATMINT	Nepeta cataria
CATNIP see CATMINT	
CAYENNE	Capsicum frutescens
CENTAURY	Centaurium erythraea
CEYLON CINNAMON see CINNAMON	
CHAMOMILE	Matricaria recutita
CHASTE TREE see AGNUS-CASTUS	
CHICKWEED	Stellaria media
CHILLI	Capsicum annuum
CHILI PEPPER see CHILLI	
CHINESE FIGWORT (Xuan Shen)	Scrophularia ningpoensis
CINNAMON	Cinnamomum zeylanicum
CLEAVERS	Galium aparine
CLOVE	Syzygium aromaticum
CODONOPSIS	Codonopsis tangstien
COFFEE	Coffea arabica
COLA	Cola nitida
COLTSFOOT	Tussilago farfara
COMFREY	Symphytum officinale
COMMON BALM see LEMON BALM	
COMMON BASIL see BASIL	
COMMON BEARBERRY see BEARBERRY	
COMMON CENTAURY see CENTAURY	
COMMON COMFREY see COMFREY	
COMMON DANDELION see DANDELION	
COMMON FUMITORY see FUMITORY	
COMMON GINGER see GINGER	
COMMON HOP see HOP	
COMMON HORSE CHESTNUT see HORSE CHESTNUT	
COMMON HOREHOUND see WHITE HOREHOUND	
COMMON HORSETAIL see HORSETAIL	
COMMON HOUSE LEEK see HOUSE LEEK	
COMMON JUNIPER see JUNIPER	
COMMON MULLEIN see MULLEIN	
COMMON PLANTAIN	Plantago major
COMMON SAGE see SAGE	
COMMON TANSY see TANSY	
COMMON THYME see THYME	
COMMON VALERIAN see VALERIAN	

COMMON WORMWOOD see WORMWOOD	
COMMON YARROW see YARROW	
CORIANDER	Coriandrum sativum
CORNSILK	Zea mays
COUCHGRASS	Elymus repens
COWSLIP	Primula veris
CRAMP BARK	Viburnum opulus
CRANBERRY	Vaccinium oxycoccos
CRANESBILL	Geranium spp.
CURLED DOCK see YELLOW DOCK	
CYPRESS	Cupressus sempervirens
DAMIANA	Turnera diffusa
DANDELION	Taraxacum officinale
DANG GUI	Angelica polyphorma var. sinensis
DEVIL'S CLAW	Harpagophytum procumbens
DILL	Anethum graveolens
DOCK	Rumex obtusifolius
ECHINACEA	Echinacea spp.
ELDER	Sambucus nigra
ELECAMPANE	Inula helenium
ENGLISH LAVENDER see LAVENDER	
ENGLISH OAK see OAK	
EPHEDRA	Ephedra distachya
EUCALYPTUS	Eucalyptus globulus
EUROPEAN ELDER see ELDER	
EUROPEAN WHITE BIRCH see BIRCH	
EUROPEAN WILD PANSY see HEARTSEASE	
EVENING PRIMROSE	Oenothera biennis
EYEBRIGHT	Euphrasia officinalis
FALSE UNICORN ROOT see HELONIAS	
FENNEL	Foeniculum vulgare
FENUGREEK	Trigonella foenum-graecum
FEVERFEW	Tanacetum parthenium
FORSYTHIA	Forsythia suspensa
FRAGRANT SUMACH see SWEET SUMACH	
FRINGE TREE	Chionanthus virginicus
FUMITORY	Fumaria officinalis
GALANGAL	Alpinia officinarum
GARLIC	Allium sativum
GENTIAN	Gentiana lutea
GINGER	Zingiber officinale
GINKGO	Ginkgo biloba

HOW TO MAKE A SUGAR SYRUP

⑤

⑤ Pour into dark glass bottles and keep well stoppered. Store in a cool, dark place. The dosage is generally 1tsp/5ml three times a day.

Syrups are concentrated sugar preparations, which help preserve infusions and decoctions and also mask the unpalatable taste of some herbs. They are the traditional way of making cough mixtures and herbal brews more acceptable to children.

① Bring some of your selected infusion or decoction to a boil with honey or sugar, using the ratio 1pt liquid to 1lb honey or sugar (500ml to 500g).

② When the mixture turns syrupy, store until required in a corked bottle (not a screwtop one).

with botanical names

GINSENG .... Panax ginseng
GOLDEN GROUNSEL see LIFE ROOT
GOLDEN SEAL .... Hydrastis canadensis
GOTU KOLA .... Centella asiatica
GREATER CELANDINE .... Chelidonium majus
GROUND IVY .... Glechoma hederacea
GUARANA .... Paullinia cupana
GUM BENZOIN see BENZOIN
HEARTSEASE .... Viola tricolor
HELONIAS .... Chamaelirium luteum
HERB ROBERT .... Geranium robertianum
HE SHOU WU/FO TI .... Polygonum multiflorum
HOLY THISTLE .... Cnicus benedictus
HOPS .... Humulus lupulus
HORSE CHESTNUT .... Aesculus hippocastanum
HORSERADISH .... Armoracia rusticana
HORSETAIL .... Equisetum arvense
HOUSE LEEK .... Sempervivum tectorum
HYSSOP .... Hyssopus officinalis
INDIAN TOBACCO see LOBELIA
IRISH MOSS .... Chondrus crispus
ISPAGHULA .... Plantago psyllium
ITALIAN CYPRESS see CYPRESS
KELP .... Fucus versiculosis
KING'S CLOVER see MELILOT
KOREAN GINSENG .... see Ginseng
LADY'S MANTLE .... Alchemilla vulgaris
LARGE CRANBERRY see CRANBERRY
LAVENDER .... Lavandula angustifolia
LEMON BALM .... Melissa officinalis
LESSER CELANDINE see PILEWORT
LICORICE .... Glycyrrhiza glabra
LIFE ROOT .... Senecio aureus
LIME FLOWERS .... Tilia cordata
LOBELIA .... Lobelia inflata
LOVAGE .... Levisticum officinale
MAD-DOG SKULLCAP see SKULLCAP
MALABAR TAMARIND .... Garcinia cambogia
MARIGOLD .... Calendula officinalis
MARJORAM .... Origanum majorana
MARSH CUDWEED .... Gnaphthalium uliginosum
MARSHMALLOW .... Althaea officinalis

MEADOWSWEET .... Filipendula ulmaria
MELILOT .... Melilotus officinalis
MILK THISTLE .... Silybum marianum (previously Carduus marianus)
MOTHERWORT .... Leonurus cardiaca
MUGWORT .... Artemisia vulgaris
MULLEIN .... Verbascum thapsus
MYRRH .... Commiphora molmol
NARROW-LEAVED PLANTAIN see RIBWORT/PLANTAIN
NORTHERN PRICKLY ASH see PRICKLY ASH
NUTMEG .... Myristica fragrans
OAK .... Quercus robur
OATS .... Avena sativa
ONION .... Allium cepa
PAPAW .... Carica papaya
PARSLEY .... Petroselinum crispum
PARSLEY PIERT .... Aphanes arvensis
PASSIONFLOWER .... Passiflora incarnata
PAU D'ARCO .... Tabebuia impetiginosa
PEPPERMINT .... Mentha x piperita
PILEWORT .... Ranunculus ficaria
PINE .... Pinus sylvestris
POET'S JESSAMINE see JASMINE
POPLAR .... Populus alba
POT MARIGOLD see MARIGOLD
PRICKLY ASH .... Zanthoxylum americanum
PURPLE CONE FLOWER see ECHINACEA
RASPBERRY .... Rubus idaeus
RED CLOVER .... Trifolium pratense
RED RASPBERRY see RASPBERRY
REISHI .... Ganoderma lucidum
RIBWORT PLANTAIN .... Plantago lanceolata
ROSE .... Rosa spp.
ROSE GERANIUM see GERANIUM
ROSEMARY .... Rosmarinus officinalis
SAGE .... Salvia officinalis
SANDALWOOD .... Santalum album
SANICLE .... Sanicula europaea
SCOTS PINE see PINE
SELF-HEAL .... Prunella vulgaris
SENNA .... Senna alexandrina
SHEPHERD'S PURSE .... Capsella bursa-pastoris
SHIITAKE MUSHROOM .... Lentinus edodes

SIBERIAN GINSENG .... Eleutherococcus senticosus
SILVERWEED .... Potentilla anserina
SKULLCAP .... Scutellaria lateriflora
SLIPPERY ELM .... Ulmus rubra
SOAPWORT .... Saponaria oficinalis
ST.-JOHN'S-WORT .... Hypericum perforatum
STINGING NETTLE .... Urtica dioica
SWEET MARJORAM see MARJORAM
SWEET SUMACH .... Rhus aromatica
SWEET VIOLET see VIOLET
TABASCO PEPPER see CAYENNE
TANGERINE .... Citrus reticulata
TANSY .... Tanacetum vulgare
TEA .... Camellia sinensis
TEA TREE .... Melaleuca alternifolia
THUJA .... Thuja occidentalis
THYME .... Thymus vulgaris
TORMENTIL .... Potentilla erecta
TURNIP .... Brassica 'Rapifero Group'
VALERIAN .... Valeriana officinalis
VERVAIN .... Verbena officinalis
VIOLET .... Viola odorata
WHITE HOREHOUND .... Marrubium vulgare
WHITE POPLAR see POPLAR
WHITE SANDALWOOD see SANDALWOOD
WHITE WILLOW/BLACK WILLOW .... Salix alba/S. nigra
WILD BLACK CHERRY see WILD CHERRY
WILD CHERRY .... Prunus serotina
WILD INDIGO .... Baptisia tinctoria
WILD LETTUCE .... Lactuca virosa
WILD PASSIONFLOWER see PASSIONFLOWER
WILD YAM .... Dioscorea villosa
WINTERGREEN .... Gaultheria procumbens
WITCH HAZEL .... Hamamelis virginiana
WORMWOOD .... Artemisia absintheum
WOUNDWORT .... Stachys palustris
YARROW .... Achillea millefolium
YELLOW GENTIAN see GENTIAN

The 20 most useful herbal remedies
and the ailments they can help

1 AGRIMONY: *soothes digestive problems (including diarrhea and food intolerance), cuts and scrapes, skin problems, minor eye problems (e.g. conjunctivitis), sore throats, catarrh.*

2 ALOE VERA: *effective for skin problems, minor cuts and burns, insect bites, digestive problems; acts as an appetite stimulant and tonic.*

3 BETONY: *relaxing nervine for anxiety and stress, headaches, cuts and bruises, mouth and gum disorders, sore throats; encourages contractions in childbirth; acts as a digestive stimulant and circulatory tonic.*

4 CHAMOMILE: *beneficial for digestive problems (including irritable bowel syndrome and indigestion), poor appetite, insomnia, nervous tension and anxiety, mouth inflammations and sore throats, minor eye problems, nasal catarrh, eczema and skin problems, asthma, and hay fever; homeopathic dilutions for colic, restlessness, and teething problems in babies and toddlers.*

5 COMMON PLANTAIN: *wound herb for cuts, insect bites, stings, sores, etc., and skin disorders (including eczema); antibacterial, soothing for digestive-tract problems (including irritable bowel*

syndrome); good for cystitis, heavy menstrual bleeding, thrush, vaginal discharges, gum diseases; cooling in fevers.

6 ECHINACEA: *antibacterial, antiviral, and antifungal for a wide range of infections (including colds and flu), and for skin problems such as athlete's foot and acne, sore throats, kidney infections.*

7 ELDER: *flowers are useful for catarrh, colds, flu, hay fever, fevers, and inflammation; leaves can be used in ointments for bruises and sores.*

8 GARLIC: *antibacterial, antifungal, and antiseptic; lowers blood cholesterol levels and useful to combat candidiasis and respiratory infections; strengthens the immune system.*

9 GINGER: *warming for chills and colds; combats nausea and vomiting; calming for the digestive system (especially indigestion and flatulence); acts as a circulatory stimulant.*

10 LAVENDER: *sedative and cooling for migraines, headaches, insomnia, and stress; good for digestive upsets (including indigestion); use externally on burns, scrapes, and sunburn.*

Herb gardens are a delight for the senses, as well as a source of exotic flavorings for the kitchen, and a living medicine cabinet. The term "herb" encompasses a range of different plants—from annuals and perennials to woody shrubs—requiring a variety of growing conditions. There are a great many medicinal herbs to choose from, so allow plenty of space when planning your herb garden. It also needs to be easily accessible.

Start giving consideration to your garden practices. Medicinal and culinary herbs should not be contaminated by chemicals, so avoid excessive spraying against pests and diseases. This may be the time to turn to organic gardening! Use soap solution to combat aphids, or marigold infusion for mildew and fungal problems. Try and ensure that the herb garden is not sited where it is subjected to car fumes or agricultural chemicals. Prepare and enrich the soil, and get planting...

11 LEMON BALM: ✿ *calming for digestive upsets and nervous problems; antidepressive; antibacterial—useful for infections and fevers; use externally for wounds, on insect bites and as an insect repellent.*

12 MARIGOLD: ✿ *good in creams for cuts, scrapes, fungal infections, eczema, and many other skin problems; acts as a digestive stimulant, menstrual regulator; cooling in fevers; beneficial for gum disease and swollen glands.*

13 MARSHMALLOW: ✿ *soothing for digestive inflammations and ulceration, urinary inflammations, coughs, catarrh; use externally for skin sores, boils, abscesses, and for drawing splinters and pus.*

14 MEADOWSWEET: ✿ *calming and antacid for digestive upsets (including gastritis and ulceration); good for arthritic and rheumatic disorders; antiseptic and cooling.*

15 ROSEMARY: ✿ *stimulating and restorative for nervous exhaustion and depression; beneficial for headaches, migraine, digestive problems (including gallbladder problems, indigestion, etc.); use externally for arthritic and rheumatic pains.*

16 ST. JOHN'S WORT: ✿ *antidepressive, sedative, restorative for the nervous system; useful in anxiety, nervous tension, depression, neuralgia, post-operative pain, period pain; antiseptic and soothing, so useful topically for burns, skin sores, cuts, and scrapes.*

17 TEA TREE: ✿ *antiseptic, antifungal; useful for all infections, including thrush, athlete's foot, ringworm, septicemia, tooth and gum infections and abscesses, warts, cold sores, acne, insect stings, and bites.*

18 THYME: ✿ *respiratory antiseptic and expectorant for coughs and bronchitis; acts as a digestive stimulant—warming for chills and diarrhea; the oil is antiseptic, for use as a wound herb and in infections.*

19 VERVAIN: ✿ *relaxing nervine for depression and tension; acts as a digestive and liver stimulant; used in childbirth to ease labor pains; use topically for nerve pains (neuralgia).*

20 YARROW: ✿ *used in fevers and to dilate peripheral blood vessels; acts as a wound herb, digestive tonic, and helpful for urinary and menstrual irregularities.*

Kitchen medicine

Medicine started in the kitchen and now, centuries later, it is going back to its origins. While no sane person would ignore the life-saving benefits of the modern pharmaceutical industry, millions of people are becoming increasingly concerned about using powerful drugs, with all their side-effects, in the treatment of minor ailments and simple first-aid situations.

The use of all medicines is based on the balance between risk and benefit—and in many household situations the risks are simply not justified. As public awareness grows, there is a great revival in the craft of the "wise woman" and in the value of simple home remedies prepared in your own kitchen. With the help of this book you will find a safe remedy to suit most situations of minor illness or accident.

Every cookbook published before World War II contained whole chapters related to health: recipes for convalescent foods, instructions for making poultices, fomentations, and curative baths, and even detailed information on the preparation of plant-based creams, lotions, and potions. Cooking writers—from the Roman epicure Marcus Gabius Apicius to Britain's renowned Mrs Beeton— used the kitchen as a dispensary and described the healing properties of foods and how they should be prepared. More than 400 years ago European books were detailing the therapeutic value of vegetable juices and how they should be used to heal the sick.

In modern times the naturopath's use of fasting and special diets has become the twentieth-century

ABOVE *The heart of the home, and also of the healthy body. A return to more traditional remedies counters our over-reliance on manmade drugs.*

version of kitchen medicine, and what we see in the health spas of today is the heritage of those kitchen pioneers. But it is not only the value of medicinal preparations that we consider in this book; it is the whole concept, described by Hippocrates 2,000 years ago, when he said that man's food should be his medicine, and his medicine his food.

Throughout this book you will find not only advice on preparing and using specific treatments for individual ailments. In almost every

entry there is information about the healing foods that should be eaten so that the body can speedily be returned to health and vitality.

It is this combination of natural remedies with the ideal food regime that represents the true spirit and practice of kitchen medicine.

POULTICES

Bread poultices are the most effective way of treating boils. Put a few slices of bread in a strainer and pour boiling water over them.

Then use a wooden spoon to squeeze out the excess water and mash the bread into a paste. Wrap the paste in a piece of clean cloth, apply as hot as is bearable over the site of the boil—or a stubborn splinter—and leave until cold. Repeat as necessary until the boil comes to a head or the splinter emerges.

ICE PACKS

Ice packs for the treatment of nosebleeds, sports injuries, and damaged muscles or tendons can be made by putting ice cubes in a plastic bag, wrapping them in a cold, wet cloth, then applying them to the affected area. Never apply ice cubes directly to the skin as this can cause severe damage. For information on how to prepare a hot (or cold) compress, *see p.194.*

GARGLES AND MOUTHWASHES

For sore throats or mouth ulcers, make a gargle/mouthwash by adding a teaspoonful of fresh chopped sage leaves (red sage is best) to a cup of boiling water. Cover and leave to stand for 10 minutes, strain, then use as gargle or mouthwash. For gingivitis, or boils or abscesses in the mouth, follow the same method with a glass of hot water containing a heaped teaspoonful of sea-salt. Rinse the mouth thoroughly several times and repeat every 3 hours.

SPICES

Everybody thinks of spices as flavorings that you add to curries, chilis, tacos, and apple pie, but although spices all taste great, they also have important medicinal value:

BLACK PEPPER: ✳ *stimulates the circulation and the digestion.*

CAYENNE: ✳ *added to any dish will help relieve the itching and discomfort of chilblains.*

GINGER: ✳ *is the best of all remedies for morning sickness, travel sickness, and nausea after anesthesia. It also relieves the pain of arthritic joints.*

NUTMEG: ✳ *in excessive quantities can be hallucinogenic, but a sprinkle in rice pudding, over a salad or cooked greens such as spinach is very calming.*

SAFFRON: ✳ *has an ancient history in the treatment of depression, menstrual pain, and menopausal problems—though costly, it is effective.*

TURMERIC: ✳ *is a traditional ingredient in Indian food and has a history of use for all liver complaints. Modern research shows that it is also anti-inflammatory (as effective as cortisone), antibacterial, and a powerfully protective antioxidant.*

WATER TREATMENTS

Since Roman times, and even earlier, water has been used as a healing remedy and, since it is on tap in your home, it is certainly the cheapest medicine of all. Many of the ailments described in this book will benefit from increased consumption of water, and simply turning on the bathtub faucet can create your own private spa.

Start by experiencing a cold bath: quite the opposite to what you might expect, this is not a variation of an ancient form of torture, but is highly invigorating. When you apply cold water to any part of the body there is an initial chilling effect, followed by dilation of the small blood vessels in the skin. The

increased blood flow suffuses the whole area with a ruddy, warming, healthy glow. Sit in a cold bath with 6in/15cm of water and give your body a good splash for a minute. Stand up, add another 6in/15cm of water and repeat the splashing. Keep on until the water is up to your navel, then finish with a quick lie down. (This treatment is not for the elderly, infirm, small children, or those of a nervous disposition.)

Hot baths are relaxing, lower the body's energy, stimulate sweating, and increase the elimination of toxins. For backache or chest problems, add 2tbsp/30ml of bath mustard to a hot bath; use rosemary for the circulation; chamomile for the skin; and hops for stress and insomnia (fresh herbs or essential oils will do). Adding Epsom salt to the bath helps arthritis and rheumatism; seaweed or peat extracts improves the skin; and sea salt promotes healing, reduces inflammation and prevents infection.

For circulatory problems, such as varicose veins, piles, and chilblains, and for muscle, joint, or ligament injuries, use alternate hot and cold water: hot water for 3 minutes, then cold for 30 seconds, five times twice a day, ending with cold water.

If the world has wound you up, just throw three lime-blossom tea bags into a hot bath.

Early civilizations knew the value of honey as a healing remedy. Traces of honey have survived in Egyptian tombs for 2,000 years.

HONEY

Never dismiss honey as nothing more than a substitute for sugar. It has been used as a healer since time immemorial. For sore throats, coughs, and colds, honey with hot water and lemon is just as effective as—and in many cases more so than—all the expensive, proprietary medicines.

As a dressing, honey speeds the healing of varicose ulcers and is favored by many plastic surgeons to prevent postoperative scars. Local honey can help hay-fever sufferers, as the bees feed on plants that are likely to trigger attacks and the offending pollens end up in concentrations in the honey. Honey contains a natural antibiotic produced by the bees, which prevents it going off or growing mold spores—small residues of edible honey have even been found in the pharaohs' tombs.

ABOVE *Only organic honey contains the healing ingredients.*

The 20 most useful
conventional medicine remedies
and the ailments they can help

1 ACETAMINOPHEN: ✿ (*e.g. Panadol, Tylenol*): *provides pain relief; useful for treating headaches and sprains, and for reducing a fever. Many other tablets contain paracetamol in combination with other drugs, such as codeine phosphate and caffeine, to enhance their effect. Be aware that codeine phosphate tends to cause constipation. Avoid paracetamol if you have liver problems.*

2 ANTACIDS: ✿ *relieve indigestion; usually contain magnesium or aluminum salts. Aluminum salts (Aluminum hydroxide, Alu-Cap) may cause constipation, whereas magnesium-containing antacids (e.g. Milk of Magnesia) tend to cause diarrhea. Some preparations contain both aluminum and magnesium (e.g. Gaviscon, Maalox). Other mixtures contain dimethicone to relieve wind (e.g. Alka-Seltzer, Gas-X).*

3 ANTIHISTAMINE: ✿ *prescription tablets such as loratadine (Claritin) or citirizine (Zyrtec): help to relieve the symptoms of hay fever without causing drowsiness.*

4 BECLOMETHASONE DIPROPRIONATE: ✿ (*Beconase*): *a nasal spray that relieves a long-standing problem with a blocked or dripping nose, such as in hay fever. If the spray causes dryness and crusting, seek medical advice for an alternative.*

5 BENZOCAINE: ✿ (*e.g. Chloraseptic*): *a local anesthetic found in lozenges or sprays, which relieves the pain of sore throats.*

6 CALAMINE: ✿ *found in many preparations used to treat itching skin.*

7 CHLORPHENIRAMINE MALEATE TABLETS: ✿ (*e.g. Chlortrimetron*): *useful to prevent itching at night. It is not so useful during the day as it causes drowsiness. Also used to prevent jet lag and motion sickness, and for hay fever.*

8 CIMETIDINE: ✿ (*Tagamet*) or RANITIDINE: ✿ (*Zantac*): *may be helpful in cases of indigestion that do not respond to an antacid.*

9 CLOTRIMAZOLE: ✿ (*Gyne-lotrimin-Mycelex*): *an antifungal treatment available as a cream or suppositories; provides relief for yeast infections, although occasionally it can cause stinging (if this occurs, seek medical advice).*

RIGHT *Conventional medicines should not be rejected out of hand: sometimes they are the best solution to a problem.*

10 EMOLLIENTS: ✿ (*e.g. Euceria*): *may alleviate dry skin; can be added to bath water or applied directly to the skin, and used for babies. Almond oil can help to soften ear wax prior to syringing.*

11 FLUCONAZOLE: ✿ (*Diflucan*): *available as a single tablet, as an alternative to creams to treat vaginal yeast infections.*

12 HYDROCORTISONE ACETATE 0.5–1%: ✿ *a mild steroid cream, particularly useful for treating minor skin irritation, such as mild cases of eczema; can be used to stop itchy ears, by gently applying to the ear canal using the little finger.*

13 IBUPROFEN: ✿ (*e.g. Advil, Motrin*): *a painkiller that is particularly helpful where there is inflammation—for example, sprains, backache, or swollen joints. Avoid ibuprofen if you have asthma or stomach ulcers.*

14 METHOL SALICYLATE: ✿ (*e.g. Icy Hot, Bengay*): *sprayed or rubbed onto the skin, it produces heat or cold and can ease the pain of a sprained joint or muscle ache.*

15 MICONAZOLE: ✿ (*e.g. Micotin*): *available as a spray for easy treatment of fungal skin infections, such as athlete's foot. Miconazole gel is available for treating oral thrush.*

16 POTASSIUM CITRATE: ✿ (*e.g. Cymalon*): *can be used to relieve the symptoms of a mild urinary infection.*

17 PSYLLIUM: ✿ (*e.g. Metamucil*): *useful for constipation that does not respond to dietary change and exercise. Children may prefer the taste of lactulose, which softens the feces and takes a couple of days to work.*

CHILDREN'S REMEDIES

18 CHLORPHENIRAMINE MALEATE LIQUID: ✿ (*e.g. Chlortrimetron*): *treating itchy skin, particularly at night.*

19 DIMETHICONE: ✿ (*e.g. Mylicon*): *used for infantile colic.*

20 MINERAL OIL: ✿ *softens cradle cap.*

Also IBUPROFEN (*e.g. Motrin*) *and* ACETAMINOPHEN (*e.g. Panadol, Tylerol*) *as above.*

Doses for adults, children, and pregnant women

NOTE: *check all doses with the information given on the package and by your pharmacist or physician. If symptoms persist, seek medical advice.*

ACETAMINOPHEN

Not known to be harmful in pregnancy. Usually take four times a day, but not more frequently than every 4 hours. Not to be given to babies under 3 months except under medical supervision.

Adults: formulations may come as tablets, capsules, or may be dispersible. Liquid acetominophen is also available. Take 1g every 4–6 hours. Maximum: 4g in 24 hours.

Children: available either as a liquid containing 100mg acetominophen in 1ml, or a liquid containing 120mg acetominophen in 1tsp/5ml. Use a measuring pipette, four times a day, to provide the correct dosage, or pharmacists can provide a syringe (without the needle).

BECLOMETHASONE DIPROPRIONATE

Not known to be harmful in pregnancy.
Adults/children over 6 years: 2 doses per nostril twice a day.

CALAMINE

Not known to be harmful in pregnancy. Apply as often as required.

CHLORPHENIRAMINE MALEATE

Not known to be harmful in pregnancy. To prevent itching at night and to avoid excessive drowsiness, restrict to one nighttime dose only. The following are the total daily doses possible.
Adults: 4mg every 4–6 hours. Maximum: 24mg daily.

Children: not recommended for children under 1.
1–2 years: 1mg twice a day.
2–5 years: 1mg every 4–6 hours. Maximum: 6mg daily.
6–12 years: 2mg every 4–6 hours. Maximum 12mg daily.

CIMETIDINE

Avoid in pregnancy.
Adults/children over 16: for heartburn and indigestion take 200mg when the symptoms appear, then repeat after 1 hour if symptoms persist. Maximum daily dose: 800mg, but not more than 400mg in any period of 4 hours. If symptoms continue after 2 weeks, seek medical advice. To prevent nighttime heartburn take 200–400mg 1 hour before bedtime.

CLOTRIMAZOLE

Not known to be harmful in pregnancy. Take as a vaginal tablet containing 500mg inserted into the vagina at night; as vaginal cream containing 5g of 10% clotrimazole inserted using an applicator at night; or as a cream containing 1% clotrimazole applied two or three times a day.

FLUCONAZOLE

Avoid in pregnancy. Otherwise, take a single dose of 150mg.

HYDROCORTISONE

Topical treatments not known to be harmful in pregnancy. Apply cream twice a day.

IBUPROFEN

Most manufacturers recommend avoiding use in pregnancy.
Adults: initially take 400mg, repeated every 4 hours if necessary. Maximum: 1.2g in 24 hours.
Children: give liquid containing 100mg ibuprofen in 1tsp/5ml, three or four times a day. Not recommended for children under 1 year old or weighing less than 16lb/7kg.
1–2 years: ½tsp/2.5ml.
3–7 years: 1tsp/5ml.
8–12 years: 2tsp/10ml.

MICONAZOLE

Avoid oral treatment in pregnancy. For athlete's foot, apply a spray twice a day for 10 days after the fungal infection has cleared. For thrush infection in the mouth:
Adults: 1–2tsp/5–10ml held in the mouth after food four times a day.
Children:
0–2 years: ½tsp/2.5ml twice daily.
2–6 years: 1tsp/5ml twice daily.

over 6 years: 1tsp/5ml, four times a day.

POTASSIUM CITRATE

Not known to be harmful in pregnancy.
Adults: 1 sachet dissolved in water three times a day for 48 hours. If symptoms persist, seek medical advice.

RANITIDINE

Avoid in pregnancy.
Adults/children over 16: take 75mg with water when the symptoms appear. If symptoms persist for more than 1 hour, or return, another tablet can be taken. Maximum: 300mg in 24 hours. If symptoms continue after 2 weeks, seek medical advice.

SYMPTOMS THAT REQUIRE URGENT MEDICAL ATTENTION

- Temperature of more than 104°F/40°C
- Vomiting for more than 24 hours
- Difficulty rousing someone/unconsciousness for more than 2 minutes
- Unexplained confused behavior
- Not specifically unwell child, but possibly lethargic and floppy
- Difficulty in breathing
- Vomiting with blood
- Painful urination with back pain
- Severe headache, if associated with a fever and possibly with a rash
- Severe headache that develops very suddenly
- Difficulty in swallowing saliva
- Central, crushing chest pain in an adult
- Nosebleed for more than 30 minutes, despite first-aid measures
- An object, such as a bead, up the nose of a child (but not if in the ear)
- Bee sting near or in the mouth
- Swallowed detergents or poisons
- Chemicals in the eye

Homeopathy

Homeopathy was established by a German physician, Samuel Hahnemann, nearly 200 years ago. He found that a medicine that causes symptoms in a healthy person could, in small doses, be used to cure those same symptoms in a sick person (the principle of "like cures like"). It is therefore important to match the symptoms of the condition with those associated with the remedy. Whatever makes the pain better or worse, whether you feel weepy or irritable, whether or not you are thirsty, etc., offers a useful pointer to individualize the symptom picture and so select the correct remedy.

There are too many symptoms associated with each remedy to list them in full throughout the book, but a few important ones are given under each ailment to act as guides. It is always best to consult a qualified homeopath, who will be able to prescribe a remedy based on you as an individual. Try the remedy that appears to match your symptoms. It is not necessary to continue taking the remedy once improvement occurs, although another one or two doses may be taken if the improvement slows or stops. Once all the symptoms have gone, there is no need to take any more of the remedy "just in case." If the symptoms change, consult the remedy pictures again.

Homeopathic remedies are prepared by serial dilutions of a solution of the remedy in alcohol. Those remedies that are not soluble in alcohol are mixed with lactose until they become soluble. Two scales are commonly used: the decimal (x) scale and the

ABOVE *The bark of the white ash,* Froxinus americana, *is used to produce a remedy that is beneficial for painful heavy periods.*

centesimal (c) scale, used throughout this book. In the c-scale, one drop of the remedy solution in alcohol is added to 99 drops of alcohol and shaken vigorously to produce a 1c potency; one drop of the 1c is then added to 99 drops of alcohol and shaken to make a 2c potency, etc. Remedies are usually sold over the counter in 6c or 30c potency. The higher the dilution, the greater its strength. (The x-scale is serial dilution in the ratio 1:10.)

When the required strength is obtained, a few drops of the solution are placed on lactose tablets, powders, granules, or pillules. The choice of preparation is a personal one—powders can be dissolved in water to give to babies, or tablets crushed. A small amount of the liquid or crushed tablet comprises one dose. Remedies can also be bought as creams or solutions to put on the skin.

All remedies should be stored in a cool, dry place, well away from strong-smelling substances. Tablets should never be handled—instead, tip one onto the lid of the bottle and then straight into your mouth. Remedies are absorbed from the mouth and should be sucked, not swallowed. You should have nothing strong-tasting in your mouth before taking the remedy, nothing to eat or drink for 10 minutes beforehand or immediately after taking the remedy.

ABOVE *Cuttlefish produce ink, which is used to make the remedy Sepia. Sepia is often used for treating women's problems.*

The 20 most useful homeopathic remedies
and the ailments they can help

1 ARGENTUM NITRICUM: ✹ for anxiety, chronic fatigue syndrome, depression, gastritis, irritable bowel syndrome, laryngitis.

2 ARSENICUM ALBUM: ✹ for diarrhea and vomiting, food poisoning, gastritis, peptic ulcers, eczema, psoriasis, hay fever, asthma.

3 BELLADONNA: ✹ for earache, fever, tonsillitis, arthritis, German measles, scarlet fever.

4 BRYONIA: ✹ for gastritis, indigestion, chest infections, sciatica, headache.

5 CHAMOMILLA: ✹ for earache, teething, colic, cough, painful periods, toothache.

6 GELSEMIUM: ✹ for fear of dentist or of driving test, anxiety symptoms generally, flu, diarrhea, chronic fatigue syndrome.

7 HEPAR SULPHURIS: ✹ for abscesses, acne, sore throat, coughs and bronchitis, earache.

8 IGNATIA: ✹ for grief, cough, depression, headache.

9 IPECACUANHA: ✹ for asthma, cough, nausea in pregnancy.

LEFT *The remedy Belladonna comes from deadly nightshade. It is prescribed for sudden-onset complaints such as fevers and immobilizing headaches.*

10 LACHESIS: ✹ for asthma, flushes and menopausal problems, heavy periods, sore throats.

11 LYCOPODIUM: ✹ for bowel problems, bloating, irritable bowel syndrome, heartburn, migraine, urinary tract infection, premature baldness.

12 MERCURIUS: ✹ for mouth ulcers, colds, sore throat, colitis, ear infections, ulcerative colitis.

13 NATRUM MURIATICUM: ✹ for mouth ulcers, cold sores, asthma, eczema, psoriasis, irritable bowel syndrome, headaches, premenstrual syndrome.

14 NUX VOMICA: ✹ for stress, overwork, fatigue, insomnia, hay fever, asthma, colic, irritable bowel syndrome, headaches, peptic ulcers.

15 PHOSPHORUS: ✹ for peptic ulcers, gastritis, colitis, coughs and bronchitis, nosebleeds.

16 PULSATILLA: ✹ for pregnancy sickness, breech presentations during pregnancy, cystitis, postnatal depression, period problems, hay fever, conjunctivitis, recurrent ear infections, irritable bowel syndrome, bedwetting.

17 RHUS TOXICODENDRON: ✹ for chicken pox, shingles, arthritis, rheumatism, eczema, sprains.

18 SEPIA: ✹ for depression, fatigue, cystitis, premenstrual syndrome, back pain, nausea in pregnancy, warts, ringworm.

19 STAPHYSAGRIA: ✹ for depression, cystitis related to intercourse, premenstrual syndrome, psoriasis (particularly after grief), warts, pain in surgical wounds.

20 SULFUR: ✹ for abscesses, acne, eczema, asthma, dandruff, menopausal flushes, migraine, arthritis, tonsillitis.

LEFT *Homeopathic remedies are often stored in dark glass bottles. Your first consultation with a homeopath is likely to last for an hour, while he or she builds up a detailed picture of you.*

Aromatherapy

ESSENTIAL OILS

Essential oils are extracted from various parts of plants and trees—the leaves, fruit, flowers, bark, roots and wood—and are absorbed by the body in aromatherapy, either through inhalation or through the pores of the skin. Numerous chemical components in each essential oil react with the mind and with the body's chemistry to help the healing process. Each oil has both a dominant characteristic and a unique smell, and much of the benefit of aromatherapy lies not only in selecting an oil that will treat your particular ailment, but in selecting one whose aroma appeals to you personally. Essential oils may be used in numerous ways, including massage, steam inhalations, baths, vaporizers, compresses, and sprays.

CAUTION

Essential oils should never be ingested, or applied undiluted to the skin (unless specifically suggested in the text), as they can cause irritation.

BASE, OR CARRIER, OILS

For direct skin application, essential oils should always be mixed with a base, or carrier, oil. This enables them to penetrate the skin without causing irritation or burning. Any of the light vegetable-based oils—grapeseed, soy, sunflower, safflower, or groundnut—can be used. Whatever you put in your mouth you can put on your skin.

MASSAGE OILS

To make a massage oil, add 2 drops of essential oil to every 1tsp/5ml of carrier oil. Alternatively, add 2 drops of oil to 1tsp/5ml of aqueous cream or lotion (available from pharmacies). For a child, add 1 drop of essential oil to 2tsp/10ml of carrier oil or cream.

STEAM INHALATIONS

Add 4 to 6 drops of essential oil to a bowl of hot water. Bend over the bowl, cover your head and the bowl with a towel, and inhale the steam. This treatment is not suitable for asthmatics or small children. Alternatively, you can put 1 or 2 drops of essential oil on a handkerchief, coat or shirt collar, or on your pillow or the corner of your sheet at night, and inhale its aroma.

BATHING WITH OILS

Fill the bath, then add your chosen essential oils: 4 to 6 drops for adults and 1 or 2 drops for children. Alternatively, mix the essential oils with a carrier oil or with milk before adding to the bath water. Then agitate the water to disperse the oils. Keep the bathroom door and windows shut to obtain maximum benefit from the vapors. Soak in the bath for at least 20 minutes. You can follow the same process, using a smaller receptacle, for foot and hand baths; and if a bidet is not available, a bowl of warm water will do just as well for a sitz bath.

VAPORIZERS

There are many varieties of essential-oil burners on the market, and some are much better than others: make sure that the water container is not situated too close to the candle and that the candle has a good supply of oxygen. Never let your burner run dry or leave it unattended, as some essential oils are highly flammable. There are also electric diffusers, vaporizers for the car that plug into the cigarette-lighter socket, and light-bulb rings, which simply fit on top of the light bulb before you switch the lamp on. They all follow the same principle of vaporizing the oil into the air, so releasing its aroma.

Whichever system you choose, put 1 or 2 drops of your selected essential oil in the vaporizer and let it heat up for 15–20 minutes. Then turn the vaporizer off, or blow out the candle. The effects will last for at least 4 to 6 hours, depending on the flow of fresh air through the area, without the need to repeat the process. If you do not have any special vaporizing equipment, then a piece of material prepared as for a compress (see right) and hung on a warm radiator will be quite effective, as will be a piece of cotton soaked in 1 or 2 drops of essential oil and then tucked down behind a warm radiator.

COMPRESSES

The size of the area to be treated will determine the size of the compress you need to cover it: for instance, a facecloth or cotton pad. Add 4 to 6 drops of essential oil to a bowl of warm water and mix well. Soak the compress, then squeeze out the excess water (but do not wring the compress). Apply to the affected area. If possible, cover in plastic wrap followed by a warm towel. Keep covered for a minimum of 2 hours, and preferably overnight.

SPRAYS

Put 10–15 drops of essential oil into 2pt/1l of water, then spray lightly over the affected part of the body. This treatment is particularly useful if the area is too painful to be touched.

ABOVE *Orange-blossom essential oil is an antidepressant, helps the circulation, and is reputed to be an aphrodisiac!*

The 20 most useful aromatherapeutic oils
and the ailments they can help

1 BASIL: *mind-clearing and focusing—useful to help studying, or for switching off at the end of a busy day; clearing to the sinus.*

2 CLOVE: *good for toothache; pleasing in a burner at Christmastime and on other occasions, used with orange, pine, and/or cinnamon.*

3 EUCALYPTUS: *beneficial for upper respiratory tract problems, including cold and flu symptoms and sinus problems; good as a massage medium or in the bath for muscular aches and pains.*

4 FRANKINCENSE: *calming and soothing to the emotions; slows and deepens the breathing; good for asthmatics in a vaporizer or on a handkerchief.*

Lavender (Lavandula angustifolia)

ABOVE *Jasmine* (Jasminum officinale)

5 GERANIUM: *for all women's problems, especially those concerned with hormonal imbalance, including PMS and menopause.*

6 GINGER: *warming to the muscles; beneficial for digestive disorders; good for nausea (both morning and motion sickness).*

7 JASMINE: *eases labor pains; useful for postnatal blues.*

8 JUNIPER: *detoxifying, both mentally and physically.*

9 LAVENDER: *calming, soothing, relaxing, de-stressing; useful for burns and insomnia.*

10 LEMON: *an alternative to tea tree; good for treating warts and verrucae.*

11 LEMON GRASS: *builds the body's resistance to fatigue; good in a foot bath for tired, aching, restless legs; an effective insect-repellent.*

12 MANDARIN: *safe and gentle, relaxing and calming for everyone, from babies to the elderly; a valuable general oil.*

13 NEROLI: *the best oil for stress-related problems.*

14 ORANGE: *a bright, sunny, cheering oil—uplifting and joyful.*

15 PETITGRAIN: *the poor person's neroli—good for stress conditions, where neroli is indicated but is unaffordable.*

16 ROMAN CHAMOMILE: *the children's oil—1 drop in a bath will soothe a fractious child at bedtime; soothing for skin irritations and inflammations; good in a tea for digestive disorders.*

17 ROSE: *the ultimate feminine oil for menstrual disruption; beneficial for emotional stress and grief.*

18 SANDALWOOD: *soothing to the skin and the emotions; sore throats respond well to being massaged with sandalwood (mixed with a carrier oil or lotion) in the throat area.*

19 TEA TREE: *antiviral, antifungal, and antibacterial; good for warts, verrucae, athlete's foot and other conditions where the body's immune system needs a boost.*

20 YLANG YLANG: *antidepressant—a heady, perfumed oil whose name means "flower of flowers." purportedly an aphrodisiac.*

Roman chamomile
(Chamaemelum nobilis)

Additional remedies

HANGOVERS	INSECT REPELLANT	A QUICK BOOST	GRIEF
Put 2 drops of fennel and juniper in a warm bath to detoxify the system. **Caution:** avoid fennel oil if you suffer from epilepsy or kidney problems.	If you get eaten alive by mosquitoes, try adding 3 drops of lemon grass, and 3 drops of basil to 2tbsp/30ml of aqueous cream and using it in the evenings and at bedtime. Use in a burner during the summer to deter flies.	To wake you up, or prior to an evening out, put 3 drops of lemon grass and 3 drops of rosemary in a bath to give you a physical and mental boost. **Caution:** avoid rosemary oil if you suffer from epilepsy or high blood pressure.	For those experiencing grief the following combination acts like a great hug: put 3 drops of rose and 3 drops of benzoin in the bath, or in 2tbsp/30ml of carrier oil or lotion to use as a massage treatment.

The 20 most useful healing foods
and the ailments they can help

1 APPLES: ❧ *if you only have room for one tree in your garden, plant an apple tree. Apples are good for the heart; protective against pollution; lower cholesterol; good for food poisoning and gastroenteritis; antibacterial and antiviral; their fiber helps digestion.*

2 ARTICHOKES: ❧ *Globe artichokes are good for all liver complaints, biliousness, hepatitis, and gallstones; lower cholesterol; relieve fluid retention; are excellent for rheumatism, arthritis, and gout.*

3 AVOCADOS: ❧ *are ideal convalescing food; good for stress and sexual problems; excellent for skin conditions; powerfully antioxidant and protective against heart disease and cancers; contain a valuable antibacterial and antifungal chemical.*

4 BANANAS: ❧ *are nature's magic fast food—full of potassium, so excellent for the physically active and for anyone taking diuretics; good for PMS because of their vitamin B_6 and zinc content; very healing for the whole digestive tract; good for both constipation and diarrhea.*

5 CABBAGE: ❧ *Cabbages are the medicine of the poor—use cabbage juice for peptic ulcers; cabbage leaves as compresses for painful joints; cabbage soup for chest infections; the dark green leaves for anemia. Cabbage and all its relatives are powerful protectors against a whole range of cancers.*

6 CARROTS: ❧ *are rich in beta-carotene, which the body converts to vitamin A; good for the eyes; useful puréed for the treatment of infant diarrhea; excellent for liver problems; great for healthy skin; another antioxidant vegetable that protects against heart disease and specifically lung cancer.*

7 GARLIC: ❧ *the king of healing plants—antibacterial, antifungal, and good for everything from bronchitis to athlete's foot; protective against food poisoning; lowers cholesterol and blood pressure; improves the circulation.*

8 KIWI FRUIT: ❧ *Kiwis are very rich in vitamin C, fiber, and vitamin E; contain lots of potassium, so are good for blood pressure, digestive problems, chronic fatigue, and heart problems.*

9 LEEKS: ❧ *have been cultivated for at least 4,000 years and were highly prized by the ancient Egyptians, Greeks, and Romans. They are beneficial for all breathing problems; are cleansing and diuretic; and excellent for gout, arthritis, and rheumatism.*

10 LEMONS, ORANGES, AND GRAPEFRUIT: ❧ *Citrus fruit are extremely rich in vitamin C and the protective bioflavonoids; valuable in the treatment of coughs, colds, and flu, and in the strengthening of natural immunity.*

11 NUTS: ❧ *these are the healing plants and trees of tomorrow, and are densely full of nutrients—minerals like selenium, zinc, iron, lots of protein, healthy oils, and the B vitamins. Fresh, unsalted nuts should form a daily part of everyone's diet.*

12 OATS: ❧ *are rich in proteins, healthy fats, vitamins E and B, and minerals, making the humble oat a cornucopia of nutrients. The best anticonstipation food, they also lower cholesterol, control blood pressure, have a calming effect on the mind, and a healing effect on the stomach.*

13 OLIVE OIL: ✢ *extra-virgin olive oil is a remarkable food/medicine. It lowers cholesterol; is rich in vitamin E, which protects against cell damage; increases the level of the healthy blood fats that scavenge bad fats from the arteries; is good for liver and gallbladder problems; protective against arthritis, senility, and some cancers.*

14 ONIONS: ✢ *from the same family as leeks and garlic, onions are important in the treatment of all chest infections; should be eaten by anyone with high blood pressure, raised cholesterol, or heart disease; and are an excellent food for anemia, asthma, urinary infections—and even hangovers.*

15 PINEAPPLES: ✢ *together with the other tropical fruits, like mangoes and papaws, the health benefits of pineapples are much under-rated. Healing enzymes and valuable anti-inflammatory and antibiotic chemicals make these foods ideal for sore throats, joint diseases, digestive problems, and all muscular injuries.*

16 LEGUMES: ✢ *dried peas, beans, and lentils are complex carbohydrates with high amounts of fiber, protein, vitamins, and minerals. They are protective against heart disease and cancers (especially of the bowel); excellent for constipation, fatigue, chronic fatigue syndrome, and diabetes.*

17 RICE: ✢ *is a perfect food for convalescents, those with digestive problems, stress, and exhaustion. Brown rice is also important in the treatment of all circulatory disorders. Plain boiled rice lowers cholesterol and is ideal as a treatment for diarrhea.*

18 WHEAT: ✢ *this amazing grain is used in breadmaking, and a good whole wheat loaf is not only nourishing but highly protective against bowel disease, high blood pressure, constipation and stress-related illnesses. Sprouted wheat seeds help in the fight against cancer. Bread can also be used as a hot poultice for boils, abscesses, and splinters.*

19 WATERCRESS: ✢ *like its relatives—cabbage, broccoli, sprouts, turnips, and horseradish— watercress is a great protector against cancer; rich in potassium and a type of mustard oil, it is powerfully antibiotic, without killing off the natural bacteria; helps with urinary infections; is also a good stimulant of the thyroid gland.*

20 YOGURT: ✢ *live yogurt, which is rich in natural bacteria, protects against stomach infections, food poisoning, and constipation. The beneficial bacteria boost the immune system and should be eaten by those with viral or bacterial illnesses, as well as to protect against fungal infections like thrush.*

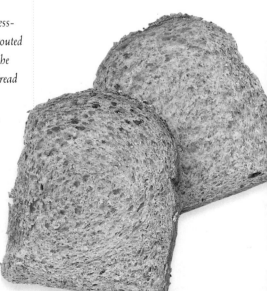

Food combining (the Hay diet)

There are many misconceptions and much pseudoscientific nonsense surrounding the food combining, or Hay, diet. It is not the panacea for all ills, nor is it "the only way to eat to be healthy." It is, though, a way of eating that can be highly beneficial for people suffering from digestive complaints. Try it for a couple of weeks and see if it suits you—the added bonus is that anyone who is overweight will certainly lose a few pounds.

The only rule that matters is not combining starch foods and protein foods in the same meal. For example: no fish (protein) and french fries (starch); no meat (protein) and potatoes (starch); no cheese (protein) and crackers (starch). Allow 3 hours between each meal and if you want to snack, choose from the neutral list. All foods in the neutral group can be eaten either with starch or with protein.

LEFT *Protein and neutral foods: there's a wide choice to concoct interesting meals from.*

PROTEIN FOODS	NEUTRAL FOODS		STARCH FOODS
MEAT	ALL VEGETABLES *(except those listed in the starch group)*	OLIVE, SESAME, AND SUNFLOWER OILS	POTATOES
POULTRY		LENTILS	YAMS
GAME			CORN
FISH	ALL NUTS *(except peanuts)*	SPLIT PEAS	BREAD
SHELLFISH		BEANS	FLOUR
EGGS	BUTTER	GARBANZO BEANS *(but not soybeans)*	OATS
FRUIT *(except those listed in the starch group)*	CREAM		WHEAT
	CREAM CHEESE	ALL SEEDS AND SPROUTED SEEDS	BARLEY
PEANUTS	RICOTTA		RICE
SOYBEANS	EGG YOLK	HERBS	MILLET
TOFU	YOGURT AND MILK *have a very low protein content, so they can be used in tiny amounts with starchy foods*	SPICES	RYE
MILK		RAISINS	BUCKWHEAT
YOGURT		GOLDEN RAISINS	PASTA
ALL CHEESE *(except cream cheese and ricotta)*		HONEY	VERY SWEET FRUIT SUCH AS RIPE PEARS
WINE AND CIDER		MAPLE SYRUP	BANANAS
			PAPAYA
			MANGOES
			SWEET GRAPES
			BEER

LEFT *Starchy and neutral foods: some of the most filling meals can be made from these.*

The exclusion diet

You will certainly know if you have any real food allergies, but many people are unaware that they may be suffering from "food intolerance"—a very different kettle of fish—to dairy products, coffee, strawberries, lettuce leaves, or in fact any food imaginable. Irritable bowel syndrome, bloating, flatulence, headaches, nausea, exhaustion, and skin problems are just some of the conditions that may be triggered by intolerance to one or more foods.

Follow this exclusion diet for a couple of weeks and see if it makes a difference. If it does not, then you need professional help. If it does, start adding foods back one at a time to see which, if any, causes your symptoms. Culprit foods should then be excluded for a few months, then tried again. Often you will be able to consume small amounts of them with no problems, as long as you do not do so every day.

The following are foods you may and may not eat during the first 2 weeks of the exclusion diet:

	NOT ALLOWED	ALLOWED
MEAT	preserved meats, bacon, sausages, all processed meat products	all other meats
FISH	smoked fish, shellfish	white fish
VEGETABLES	potatoes, onions, corn, eggplants, bell peppers, chilis, tomatoes	all other vegetables, salads, legumes, rutabaga, parsnips
FRUIT	citrus fruit (e.g. oranges, grapefruit)	all other fruit (e.g. apples, bananas, pears)
CEREALS	wheat, oats, barley, rye, corn	rice, ground rice, rice flakes, rice flour, sago, rice breakfast cereals, tapioca, millet, buckwheat, rice cakes
COOKING OILS	corn oil, vegetable oil	sunflower oil, soy oil, safflower oil, olive oil
DAIRY PRODUCTS	cow's milk, butter, most margarines, cow's milk yogurt and cheese, eggs	goat, sheep, and soy milk and products made from them, dairy and trans fat-free margarines
BEVERAGES	tea, coffee (beans, instant, and decaffeinated), fruit squashes, orange juice, grapefruit juice, alcohol, and tap water	herbal teas (e.g. chamomile), fresh fruit juices (e.g. apple, pineapple), pure tomato juice (without additives), mineral, distilled, or de-ionized water
MISCELLANEOUS	chocolates, yeast, yeast extracts, artificial preservatives, colorings, and flavorings, monosodium glutamate, all artificial sweeteners	carob, sea salt, herbs, spices, and small amounts of sugar or honey

AFTER TWO WEEKS introduce other foods in this order: tap water, potatoes, cow's milk, yeast, tea, rye, butter, onions, eggs, porridge oats, coffee, chocolate, barley, citrus fruit, corn, cow's cheese, white wine, shellfish, natural cow's milk yogurt, vinegar, wheat, and nuts.

Any diet that is very restricted puts your health at risk and, although it is all right to experiment on your own for a few weeks, any long-term removal of major food groups should only be done under professional guidance.

ABOVE AND BELOW *Grapes and mangoes are good sources of vitamin C.*

Outside help

This section gives brief descriptions of the four therapies—acupressure, the Alexander Technique, reflexology, and yoga—grouped under the heading "Outside help," since you may already be practicing them with a teacher. Charts depict the relevant acupressure and reflexology points mentioned throughout the text.

ACUPRESSURE

The acupressure described in this book (which uses pressure points rather than the needles used in acupuncture) is a highly simplified treatment, designed to provide effective first aid by the lay person in terms of pain relief and the resolution of symptoms. This is not a substitute for acupuncture treatment from a qualified professional, but even qualified acupuncturists will sometimes use acupressure rather than needles, and it can be of enormous help in all the situations described.

Ideally the treatment should be done with the patient lying or relaxing in a comfortable chair. Pressure should be applied to the indicated points (see the charts opposite), either with a finger—the little or fourth finger is usually the

easiest—or with the end of a ballpoint-pen cap, which is more precise. Apply the pressure firmly, but never severely, for anything up to 10 minutes, releasing and reapplying the pressure every 15 seconds. The length and strength of the treatment should take into account the age and general health of the patient. In pregnancy all points on the abdomen should be avoided during the first 3 months—and thereafter only light pressure should be applied. Do not treat anyone who has consumed alcohol or drugs.

In China acupressure is widely used for relieving acute symptoms in children, and you will find this an effective supplement to any other home remedies that you are using.

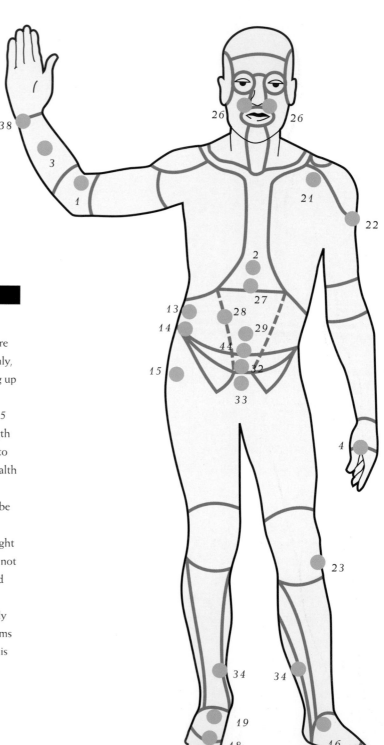

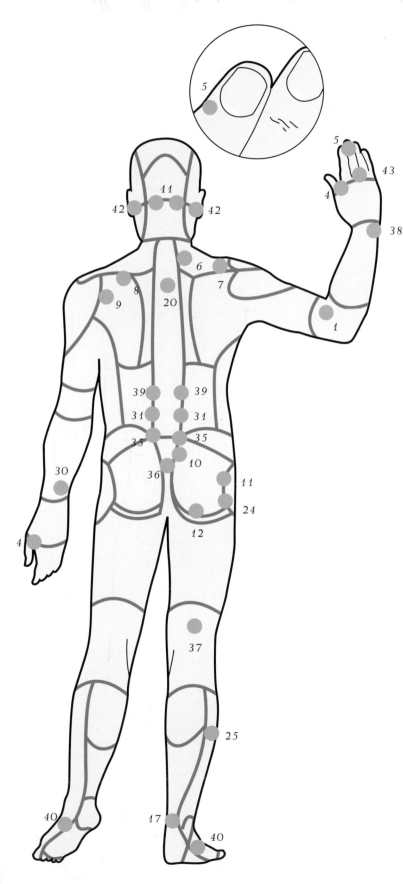

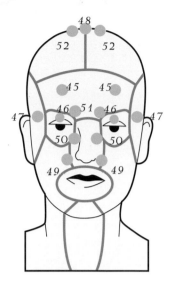

Acupressure points are positioned along the meridians, or energy pathways, of the body. These points are found on the front (far left) and back (left) of the body, as well as the head (right). Applying pressure to these specific points will help relieve ailments relating to those meridians. Throughout the Outside Help sections of this book specific acupressure points relating to various conditions are listed by number. Consult the charts opposite and right to identify the numbered point(s) that you need to massage.

THE ALEXANDER TECHNIQUE

The Alexander Technique is not a therapy, but a method of mental and physical re-education, which helps reduce tension in all human activities. Improving the way we use our body addresses an underlying cause of many medical conditions, where psychophysical misuse and loss of poise are contributory factors.

Alexander lessons are taught individually and last for 30–40 minutes. The pupil learns to appreciate the practical implications of thought and its effect on muscular activity. The teacher's hands help to release unnecessary tension and, through manual guidance, the pupil is given a new experience. Usually people discover, fairly early on in their course of lessons, a new-found sense of lightness and ease, as well as relief from some of their specific ailments.

It takes an average of 20–30 lessons for pupils to begin on their own to re-create reliably experiences gained in lessons. The Alexander Technique does not treat any specific medical condition, but if you are already practicing the Technique, it could well be beneficial to certain conditions mentioned throughout this book.

In 1973, after undergoing a course of lessons in the Alexander Technique for himself and·his family, the winner of the Nobel Prize for Medicine, Nicholas Tinbergen, observed the following in *Science* magazine: "A very striking improvement in such diverse things as high blood pressure, breathing, depth of sleep, overall cheerfulness, mental alertness, resilience against outside pressure, and also in such a refined skill as playing a stringed instrument."

REFLEXOLOGY

Reflexology is the application of finger or thumb pressure to the hands and feet. Reflexologists believe that specific points and areas in the hand and feet (see the charts opposite) relate to specific organs, systems, and functions, and that palpation can detect and locate imbalances. Various corrective techniques are applied to reduce symptoms and stimulate the healing processes.

The most popular method of pressure application is alternating pressure, or the "thumb walk." The tip and edge of a flexed thumb (or finger) are used to apply "on/off" pressure, while at the same time traveling forward in tiny steps and with a rhythmical movement, maintaining contact with the skin. For pain relief, 10–15 seconds (10 for children and the elderly) of continued pressure is applied to the reflex of the affected part, and repeated three times. Reflex points are often tender, one of the indicators of imbalance, and tolerance levels should be noted and respected.

It is not unusual to show some reaction to the treatment—perhaps a headache, runny nose, frequent urination, tiredness, or, on the positive side, more energy. These reactions should not last more than 24 hours and indicate self-cleansing by the body.

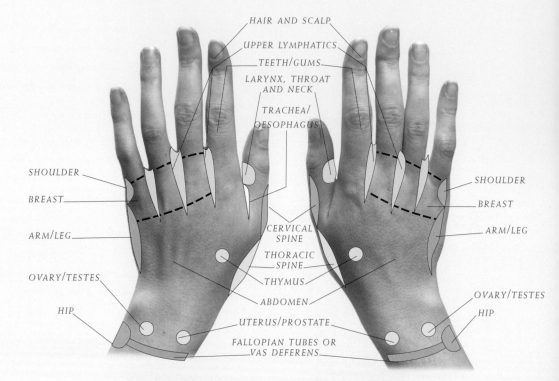

REFLEXOLOGY POINTS FOR BACKS OF HANDS

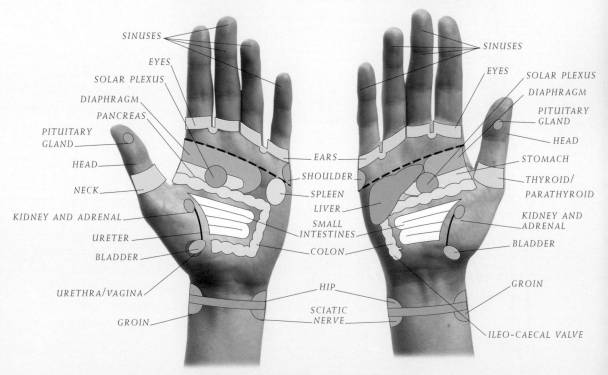

PALMS OF HANDS

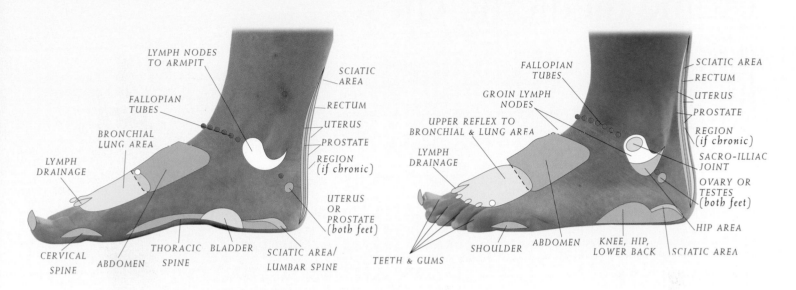

RIGHT FOOT

ABOVE AND BELOW *Reflexology areas on the feet, and their related areas of the body.*

LEFT FOOT

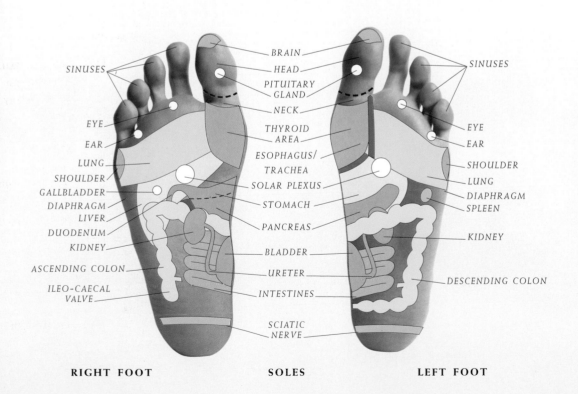

RIGHT FOOT   **SOLES**   **LEFT FOOT**

Yoga has a vast range of techniques to help its practitioners in their quest for health, healing, and the meaning of existence. The suggestions in this book give a mere hint of its possibilities, but it is hoped that they may help you if you already have some experience, or may perhaps inspire you to find a teacher.

Home medicine chest

Every medicine chest needs the normal range of bandages, plasters, dressings, safety pins, antiseptics, tweezers, and scissors, together with a supply of proprietary pain-relievers, antidiarrheals, and whatever is "Mom's magic ointment." But the home medicine chest recommended here also includes many other natural ingredients that will benefit you and your family: essential oils such as lavender and tea tree; herbs such as chamomile and slippery elm; a range of homeopathic medicines such as arnica, belladonna, and urtica; kitchen remedies such as garlic, ginger, and mustard. Throughout the book you will find ways to use these gifts from nature, as powerful aids to safe and effective treatment of most minor ailments.

KITCHEN REMEDIES FOR THE HOME MEDICINE CHEST

1. Cider vinegar
2. Cinnamon
3. Cloves
4. Epsom salt
5. Garlic (fresh)
6. Ginger root
7. Horseradish
8. Mustard powder
9. Organic honey
10. Sage (either a plant or dried)
11. Sodium bicarbonate
12. Wheat germ

Cider vinegar

Epsom salt

Sage

Horseradish

Garlic

Cloves

Mustard

Lavender

Cinnamon

Ginger

Sodium bicarbonate

Wheat germ

CONVENTIONAL REMEDIES
FOR THE
HOME MEDICINE CHEST

1. Acetaminophen
2. Bacitracin ointment
3. Calamine lotion
4. Chlorpheniramine maleate
5. Clotrimazole cream
6. Dextramethorpan cough syrup
7. Hydrocortisone 1% cream
8. Ibuprofen
9. Oral rehydration powder sachets (for reconstitution in case of diarrhea)

HERBAL REMEDIES
FOR THE
HOME MEDICINE CHEST

1. A potted *Aloe vera* plant to grow on a sunny windowsill
2. Arnica cream
3. Chamomile flowers—loose or in teabags
4. Chickweed cream
5. Echinacea tablets
6. Lavender oil
7. Marigold cream
8. Meadowsweet tincture
9. Myrrh tincture
10. Slippery-elm tablets
11. Tea-tree oil
12. Distilled witch hazel (or witch-hazel tincture)

HOMEOPATHIC REMEDIES
FOR THE
HOME MEDICINE CHEST

All at 6c potency and 30c potency.

1. Aconite
2. Arnica
3. Apis
4. Belladonna
5. Bellis perennis
6. Cantharis
7. Hypercal ointment
8. Hypericum
9. Ledum
10. Rhus toxicodendrum
11. Silica
12. Symphytum
13. Urtica urens

AROMATHERAPY OILS
FOR THE
HOME MEDICINE CHEST

It is not worth storing large quantities of essential oils, as they have a shelf-life of only 1 to 2 years, so unless you are going to use them regularly, do not keep a large stock of them in your medicine chest. Buy oils that have a multitude of uses for you and your family, such as the ones listed below, or oils to help specific ailments, as suggested throughout the book.

1. Eucalyptus
2. Lavender
3. Tea tree

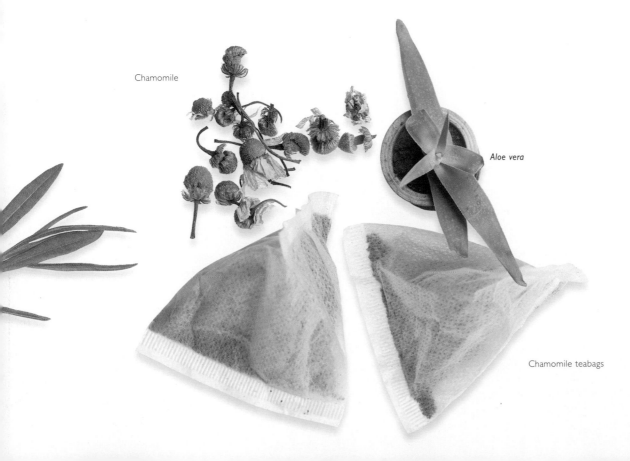

Chamomile

Aloe vera

Chamomile teabags

USEFUL ADDRESSES

ACUPRESSURE

Australasia

Australian Traditional Medicine Society Limited
ATMS
PO Box 1027 (mailing)/12/27 Bank Street (office)
Meadowbank
New South Wales 2114
Australia
Tel: 61 2 809 6800

New Zealand Register of Acupuncturists Inc.
PO Box 9950
Wellington 1
New Zealand
Tel/Fax: 64 4 476 8578

Europe

British Acupuncture Council
Park House
206–8 Latimer Road
London W10 6RE
Great Britain
Tel: 44 181 964 0222
Fax: 44 181 964 0333

College of Integrated Chinese Medicine
19 Castle Street
Reading
Berks RG1 7SB
Great Britain
Tel: 44 1734 508880
Fax: 44 1734 508890

North America

American Association for Acupuncture and Oriental Medicine
4101 Lake Boone Trail
Suite 201
Raleigh
North Carolina 27607
USA
Tel: 1 919 787 5181

American Association of Oriental Medicine (AAOM)
433 Front Street
Catasauqua
Pennsylvania 18032
USA
Tel: 1 610 266 1433
Fax: 1 610 264 2768

National Acupuncture and Oriental Medicine Alliance
PO Box 77511
Seattle
Washington 98177-0531
USA
Tel: 1 206 524 3511

National Acupuncture and Oriental Medicine Alliance (National Alliance)
14637 Starr Road, SE
Olalla
Washington 98359
USA
Tel: 1 206 851 6896
Fax: 1 206 851 6883

ALEXANDER TECHNIQUE

Australasia

Australian Society of Teachers of the Alexander Technique (AUSTAT)
PO Box 716
Darlinghurst
New South Wales 2010
Australia
Tel: 61 8 339 571

Europe

Society of Teachers of the Alexander Technique (STAT)
20 London House
266 Fulham Road
London SW10 9EL
Great Britain
Tel: 44 171 351 0828
Fax: 44 171 352 1556
STAT can provide information about affiliated societies elsewhere in Europe.

North America

Canadian Society of Teachers of the Alexander Technique
PO Box 47025
No.19-555 West 12th Avenue
Vancouver
British Columbia V5Z 3XO
Canada

North American Society of Teachers of the Alexander Technique (NASTAT)
PO Box 517
Urbana
Illinois 61801-0517
USA
Tel: 1 217 367 6956

AROMATHERAPY

Europe

Academy of Aromatherapy and Massage
50 Cow Wynd
Falkirk
Stirlingshire FK1 1PU
Great Britain
Tel: 44 1324 612658

International Federation of Aromatherapists
Stamford House
2–4 Chiswick High Road
London W4 1TH
Great Britain
Tel: 44 181 742 2605
Fax: 44 181 742 2606

International Society of Professional Aromatherapists
ISPA House
82 Ashby Road
Hinckley
Leics OE10 1SN
Great Britain
Tel: 44 1455 637987
Fax: 44 1455 890956

International Therapy Examination Council (ITEC)
James House
Oakelbrook Mill
Newent
Glos
Great Britain
Tel: 44 1531 822425

Tisserand Institute
65 Church Road
Hove
East Sussex BN3 2BD
Great Britain
Tel: 44 1273 206640
Fax: 44 1273 329811

North America

American Alliance of Aroma Therapy
PO Box 750428
Petaluma
California 94975-0428
USA
Tel: 1 707 778 6762
Fax: 1 707 769 0868

American Aromatherapy Association
PO Box 3679
South Pasadena
California 91031
USA
Tel: 1 818 457 1742

National Association of Holistic Aromatherapy
PO Box 17622
Boulder
Colorado 80308-0622
USA
Tel: 1 303 258 3791

CONVENTIONAL MEDICINE

Australasia

Skin and Psoriasis Foundation of Victoria
PO Box 228
Collins Street
PO 3000
Melbourne 671962
Victoria
Australia

Europe

Arthritis and Rheumatism Council for Research
Copeman House
St Mary's Court
St Mary's Gate
Chesterfield S41 7TD
Great Britain
Tel: 44 1246 558033

British Association of Counselling (BACS)
1 Regent Place
Rugby
Warwickshire CV21 2PL
Great Britain
Tel: 44 1788 578328

British Migraine Association
178a High Road
Byfleet
West Byfleet
Surrey KT14 7ED
Great Britain
Tel: 44 1932 352468

Enuresis Resource and Information Centre
65 St Michael's Hill
Bristol BS2 8DZ
Great Britain
Tel: 44 117 9264920

Hairline International: The Alopecia Patients' Society
Lyon's Court
1668 High Street
Knowle
West Midlands B93 0LY
Great Britain
Tel: 44 1564 775281

Herpes Association
41 North Road
London N7 9DP
Great Britain
Tel: 44 171 607 9661
(Helpline: 44 171 609 9061)

Medic Alert Foundation
12 Bridge Wharf
156 Caldeonian Road
London N1 9UU
Great Britain
Tel: 44 171 833 3034

National Asthma Campaign
Providence House
Providence Place
London N1 0NT
Great Britain
Tel: 44 171 226 2260

National Back Pain Association
16 Elmtree Road
Teddington
Middlesex TW11 8ST
Great Britain
Tel: 44 181 977 5474

National Eczema Society
4 Tavistock Place
London WC1H 9RA
Great Britain
Tel: 44 171 388 4097

National Osteoporosis Society
PO Box 10
Radstock
Bath BA3 3YB
Great Britain
Tel: 44 1761 432472

Patients' Association
PO Box 935
Harrow
Middlesex HAI 3YJ
Great Britain
Helpline: 44 181 423 8999

Psoriasis Association
7 Milton Street
Northampton NN2 7JG
Great Britain
Tel: 44 1604 711129

Seasonal Affective Disorder Association
PO Box 989
London SW7 2PZ
Great Britain
Tel: 44 181 969 7028

Sense National Deafblind and Rubella Association
11–13 Clifton Terrace
Finsbury Park
London N4 3SRI
Great Britain
Tel: 44 171 272 7774

Society of Chiropodists
53 Welbeck Street
London W1M 7HE
Great Britain
Tel: 44 171 486 3381

Women's Health Concern
83 Earls Court Road
London W8 6EF
Great Britain
Tel: 44 171 938 3932

North America

American Counseling Association
5999 Stevenson Avenue
Alexandria
Virginia 22304-9800
USA
Tel: 1 703 823 0988

National Psoriasis Foundation
Suite 200
6415 South West Canyon Court
Portland
Oregon 97221
USA
Tel: 1 503 297 1545

HERBALISM

Australasia

National Herbalists Association of Australia
Suite 305
BST House
3 Smail Street
Broadway
New South Wales 2007
Australia
Tel: 61 2 211 6437
Fax: 61 2 211 6452

Europe

British Herbal Medicine Association
1 Wickham Road
Boscombe
Bournemouth
Dorset BH7 6JX
Great Britain
Tel: 44 1202 433691

The Herb Society
Deddington Hill Farm
Warmington
Banbury
Oxon OX171XB
Great Britain
Tel: 44 1295 692900

National Institute of Medical Herbalists
56 Longbrook Street
Exeter
Devon EX4 6AH
Great Britain
Tel: 44 1392 426022

School of Herbal Medicine/Phytotherapy
Bucksteep Manor
Bodle Street Green
Near Hailsham
Sussex BN27 4RJ
Great Britain
Tel: 44 1323 833 812/4
Fax: 44 1323 833 869

North America

American Botanical Council
PO Box 201660
Austin
Texas 78720-1660
USA
Tel: 1 512 331 1924

American Herbalists Guild
PO Box 1683
Soquel
California 95073
USA

HOMEOPATHY

Australasia

Australian Homeopathic Association
11 Landsborough Terrace
Toowong 4006
Australia
Tel/Fax: 61 7 3371 7245
e-mail: vikiwill@powerup.com.au

Australian Institute of Homeopathy
21 Bulah Heights
Berdwra Heights
New South Wales 2082
Australia

New Zealand Institute of Classical Homeopathy
PO Box 7232
Wellesley Street
Auckland
New Zealand
e-mail: jwinston@actrix.gen.nz

Europe

British Homoeopathic Association
27A Devonshire Street
London W1N 1RJ
Great Britain
Tel: 44 171 935 2163

Centre d'Etudes Homéopathiques de France
228 Boulevard Raspail
75014 Paris
France
Tel: 33 143 20 7896

Faculty of Homeopathy
Hahnemann House
2 Powis Place
London WC1N 3HT
Great Britain
Tel: 44 171 837 9469

Helios Homeopathic Pharmacy
97 Camden Road
Tunbridge Wells
Kent TN1 2QR
Great Britain
Tel: 44 1892 537254

Nelsons Homeopathic Pharmacy
73 Duke Street
Grosvenor Square
London W1M 6BY
Great Britain
Tel: 44 171 495 2404

Société Médical de Biothérapie
62 rue Beaubourg
75003 Paris
France
Tel: 33 143 346000

Society of Homoeopaths
2 Artisan Road
Northampton NN1 4HU
Great Britain
Tel: 44 1604 21400
Fax: 44 1604 22622

Weleda Homeopathic Pharmacy
Heanor Road
Ilkeston
Derbyshire DE7 8DR
Great Britain
Tel: 44 115 944 8200

North America

Council for Homeopathic Certification
1709 Seabright Avenue
Santa Cruz
California 95062
USA
Tel: 1 408 421 0565
Website: www.healthy.net/che

Homeopathic Association of Naturopathic Physicians
(HANP)
PO Box 69565
Portland
Oregon 97201
USA
Tel: 1 503 795 0579

National Center for Homeopathy
801 North Fairfax Street
Suite 306
Alexandria
Virginia 22314
USA
Tel: 1 703 548 7790
Fax: 1 703 548 7792
e-mail: nch@igc.org

North American Society of Homeopaths (NASH)
2024 S. Dearborn Street
Seattle
Washington 98144-2912
USA
Tel: 1 206 720 7000
Fax: 1 206 329 5684
e-mail: NashInfo@aol.com
Website: www.homeopathy.org

NUTRITION

Europe

The British Naturopathic Association
Frazer House
6 Netherhall Gardens
London NW3 5RR
Great Britain
Tel: 44 171 435 7830

Eating Disorders Association
Sackville Place
44 Magdalen Street
Norwich NR3 1JU
Great Britain
Helpline: 44 1603 621414
Fax: 44 1603 664915
Website: www.gurney.org.uk/eda/

Vegetarian Society
Parkdale
Dunham Road
Altrincham
Cheshire WA14 4QG
Great Britain
Tel: 44 161 928 4QG
Fax: 44 161 926 9182

North America

American Association of Nutrition Consultants
1641 East Sunset Road, Apt B-117
Las Vegas
Nevada 89119
USA
Tel: 1 709 361 1132

American Dietetics Association
216 West Jackson Boulevard
Apt 800
Chicago
Illinois 60606-6995
USA
Tel: 1 800 877 1600

Eating Disorders Awareness and Prevention
603 Steward Street
Suite 8013
Seattle
Washington 98101
USA
Tel: 1 206 382 3587

International Association of Professional Natural
Hygienists (fasting)
104 Stambaugh Building
Youngstown
Ohio 44503
USA
Tel: 1 216 746 5000
Fax: 1 216 746 1836

National Nutritional Foods Association
150 East Paularino Avenue
Apt 285
Costa Mesa
California 92626
USA
Tel: 1 714 966 6632
Fax: 1 714 641 7005

North American Vegetarian Society
PO Box 72
Dolgeville
New York
NY 13329
USA
Tel: 1 518 568 7970

REFLEXOLOGY

Australasia

Australian School of Reflexology
15 Kedumba Crescent
Turramurra 2074
New South Wales
Australia
Tel: 61 299 883881

New Zealand Institute of Reflexologists Inc.
253 Mt Albert Road
Mt Roskill
Auckland
New Zealand

New Zealand Reflexology Association
PO Box 31 084
Auckland 4
New Zealand
Tel: 64 9486 3447

Europe

Association of Reflexologists
27 Old Gloucester Street
London WC1N 3XX
Great Britain
Tel: 44 990 673320

British School of Reflexology and Holistic Association
of Reflexologists
92 Sheering Road
Old Harlow
Essex CM17 0JW
Great Britain
Tel: 44 1279 429060
Fax: 44 1279 445234

International Institute of Reflexology
15 Hartfield Close
Tonbridge
Kent
Great Britain
Tel/Fax: 44 1732 350629

Irish Reflexologists Institute
3 Blackglen Court
Lambs Cross
Sandyford
Dublin
Republic of Ireland

Scottish Institute of Reflexology
Secretary: Mrs Ann McCaig
15 Hazel Park
Hamilton
Lanarkshire ML3 7HH
Great Britain
Tel: 44 1698 427962
Fax: 44 1698 427962

North America

International Council of Reflexologists
PO Box 621963
Littleton
Colorado
USA

International Institute of Reflexology
PO Box 12642
Saint Petersburg
Florida 33733
USA
Tel: 1 813 343 4811

Reflexology Association of America
4012 S. Rainbow Boulevard
Box K585
Las Vegas
Nevada 89103-2509
USA

Reflexology Association of Canada (RAC)
11 Glen Cameron Road
Unit 4
Thornhill
Ontario L8T 4NB
Canada
Tel: 1 905 889 5900

YOGA

Australasia

BKS Iyengar Association of Australia
1 Rickman Avenue
Mosman
New South Wales 2088
Australia

International Yoga Teachers' Association
c/o 14/15 Huddart Avenue
Normanhurst
New South Wales 2076
Australia
Tel: 61 2 9484 9848

Europe

British Wheel of Yoga
1 Hamilton Place
Boston Road
Sleaford
Lincs NG34 7ES
Great Britain
Tel: 44 1529 306851

Viniyoga Britain
105 Gales Drive
Three Bridges
Crawley
West Sussex RH10 1QD
Great Britain

North America

BKS Iyengar Yoga National Association of the US
8223 West Third Street
Los Angeles
California 90088
USA
Tel: 1 213 653 0357

International Association of Yoga Therapists
109 Hillside Avenue
Mill Valley
California 94941
USA
Tel: 1 415 383 4587
Fax: 1 415 381 0876

FURTHER READING

(All books on this list have been published in the UK, unless otherwise noted)

ACUPRESSURE

Acupressure for Common Ailments, by Chris Jarmey & John Tindall (Gaia Books, 1991)

Acupressure Techniques, by Julian Kenyon (Thorsons, 1987)

ALEXANDER TECHNIQUE

The Alexander Principle, by Wilfred Barlow (Arrow, 1983)

The Alexander Technique, by Chris Stevens (Vermilion, 1992)

The Alexander Technique: The Essential Writings of F. Matthias Alexander, ed. by Edward Maisel (Thames & Hudson, 1974)

The Alexander Technique: Natural Poise for Health, by Richard Brennan (Element Books, 1991)

The Alexander Technique Workbook: Your Personal Programme for Health, Poise and Fitness, by Richard Brennan (Element Books, 1992)

Body Learning, by Michael Gelb (Aurum Press, 1987)

The Complete Illustrated Guide to the Alexander Technique, by Glynn Macdonald (Element Books, 1998)

Freedom to Change: The Development and Science of the Alexander Technique, by Frank Pierce-Jones (Mouritz, 1997)

AROMATHERAPY

Aromatherapy: An A–Z, by Patricia David (C.W. Daniel, 1988)

Aromatherapy for Common Ailments, by Shirley Price (Gaia, 1991)

Aromatherapy for Home Use, by Christine Westwood (Amberwood, 1991)

Aromatherapy for Pregnancy and Childbirth, by Margaret Fawcett (Element Books, 1993)

The Complete Illustrated Guide to Aromatherapy, by Julia Lawless (Element Books, 1997)

GENERAL

A–Z of Natural Healthcare, by Belinda Grant (Optima, 1993)

All Day Energy, by Kathryn Marsden (Bantam Books, 1995)

The Alternative Dictionary of Symptoms and Cures, by Dr Caroline Shreeve (Century, 1987)

The Alternative Health Guide, by Brian Inglis and Ruth West (Michael Joseph, 1983)

Arthritis & Rheumatism: A Comprehensive Guide to Effective Treatment, by Pat Young (Element Books, 1995)

Better Health through Natural Healing, by Ross Tratler (McGraw-Hill, USA, 1987)

Choices in Healing, by Michael Lerner (MIT Press, USA/UK, 1994)

The Complete Guide to Food Allergy and Environmental Illnesses, by Dr Keith Mumby (Thorsons, 1993)

The Complete Natural Health Consultant, by Michael van Straten (Ebury, 1987)

The Complete Relaxation Book by James Hewitt (Rider, 1987)

The Encyclopaedia of Alternative Health Care, by Kristen Olsen (Piatkus, 1989)

Encyclopaedia of Natural Medicine, by Brian Inglis and Ruth West (Michael Joseph, 1983)

Encyclopaedia of Natural Medicine, by Michael Murray and Joseph Pizzorno (Macdonald Optima, 1990)

The Fountain of Health: An A–Z of Traditional Chinese Medicine, by Dr Charles Windrige/Dr Wu Xiaochun (Mainstream Publishing, 1994)

Gentle Medicine, by Angela Smyth (Thorsons, 1994)

Guide to Complementary Medicine and Therapies, by Anne Woodham (Health Education Authority, 1994)

The Handbook of Complementary Medicine, by Stephen Fulder (Oxford Medical Publications, 1988)

Headaches, by Dr John Lockie with Karen Sullivan (Bloomsbury, 1992)

How to Live Longer and Feel Better, by Linus Pauling (W. H. Freeman, USA, 1986)

The Illustrated Encyclopaedia of Essential Oils, by Julia Lawless (Element Books, 1995)

Life, Health and Longevity, by Kenneth Seaton (Scientific Hygiene, USA, 1994)

Massage: A Practical Introduction, by Stewart Mitchell (Element Books, 1992)

Maximum Immunity, by Michael Wiener (Gateway Books, 1986)

Medicine and Culture, by Lynn Payer (Gollancz, 1990)

Migraine: A Comprehensive Guide to Effective Treatment, by Eileen Herzberg (Element Books, 1994)

Reader's Digest Family Guide to Alternative Medicine, by ed. Dr Patrick Pietroni (The Reader's Digest Association, 1991)

Teach Yourself Meditation, by James Hewitt (Hodder and Stoughton, 1978)

The Which Guide to Women's Health, by Dr Anne Robinson (Which Consumer Guides, 1996)

You Can Heal Your Life, by Louise Hay (Eden Grove, USA, 1988)

You Don't Have To Die, by Leon Chaitow (Future Medicine Publishing, USA, 1994)

You Don't Have to Feel Unwell, by Robin Needes (Gateway Books, 1994)

HERBALISM

The Complete Floral Healer, by Anne McIntyre (Gaia, 1996)

The Complete Herb Book, by Jekka McVicar (Kyle Cathie, 1994)

The Complete Illustrated Holistic Herbal, by David Hoffman (Element Books, 1996)

The Complete New Herbal, ed. Richard Mabey (Penguin Books, 1991)

Encyclopaedia of Herbal Medicine, by T. Bartram (Grace Publishers, 1995)

Encyclopaedia of Herbs and Their Uses, by D. Brown (Dorling Kindersley, 1995)

Evening Primrose, by Kathryn Marsden (Vermilion, 1993)

Herbal First Aid, by A. Chevallier (Amberwood Publishing, 1993)

Herbal Medicine, by R.F. Weiss (Beaconsfield Publishers, 1988)

Herbal Medicines, by C.A. Newell, L.A. Anderson and J.D. Phillipson (Pharmaceutical Press, 1996)

The Herbal for Mother and Child, by Anne McIntyre (Element Books, 1992)

Herbs for Common Ailments, by Anne McIntyre (Gaia, 1992)

The Herb Society's Complete Medicinal Herbal, by Penelope Ody (Dorling Kindersley, 1993)

The Herb Society's Home Herbal, by Penelope Ody (Dorling Kindersley, 1995)

The Home Herbal, by Barbara Griggs (Pan Books, 1995)

The Illustrated Herbal Handbook for Everyone, by Juliette de Bairacli Levy (Faber & Faber, 1991)

100 Great Natural Remedies, by Penelope Ody (Kyle Cathie, 1997)

Out of the Earth, by S.Y. Mills (Viking, 1991)

Potter's New Cyclopaedia of Botanical Drugs and Preparations, by R.C. Wren (C.W. Daniels, 1988)

HOMEOPATHY

The Complete Family Guide to Homeopathy, by Dr Christopher Hammond (Element Books, 1996)

Emotional Healing with Homoeopathy: A Self-Help Manual, by Peter Chappell (Element Books, 1994)

The Family Guide to Homoeopathy, by Andrew Lockie (Hamish Hamilton, 1990)

The Family Health Guide to Homoeopathy, by Dr Barry Rose (Dragon's World, 1992)

Homoeopathy: The Family Handbook, British Homoeopathic Association (Thorsons, 1992)

Homeopathy: The Principles & Practice of Treatment, by Dr Andrew Lockie & Dr Nicola Geddes (Dorling Kindersley, 1995)

The New Concise Guide to Homeopathy, by Nigel and Susan Garion-Hutchings (Element Books, 1993)

The Women's Guide to Homoeopathy, by Andrew Lockie and Nicola Geddes (Hamish Hamilton, 1992)

NUTRITION

The Amino Revolution, by Robert Erdmann & Meirion Jones (Century, 1987)

Anorexia and Bulimia, by Julia Buckroyd (Element Books, 1996)

The Complete Guide to Vitamins and Minerals, by Leonard Mervyn (Thorsons, 1986)

The Complete Illustrated Guide to Nutritional Healing, by Denise Mortimore (Element Books, 1998)

Food: Your Miracle Medicine, by Jean Carper (Simon & Schuster, 1993)

Foods for Mind and Body, by Michael van Straten (HarperCollins, 1997)

Foods that Harm, Foods that Heal, (The Reader's Digest Association, 1996)

The Healing Foods, by Patricia Hausmann & Judith Benn Hurley (MJF Books, USA, 1989)

The Healing Foods Cookbook, by Jane Sen (Thorsons, 1996)

Healing Nutrients, by Patrick Quillen (Contemporary Books, USA/Beaverbooks, Can, 1987, Penguin, 1989)

Jekka's Complete Herb Book, by Jekka McVicar (Kyle Cathie, 1994)

Minerals: What They Are and Why We Need Them, by Miriam Polunin (Thorsons, 1979)

Nutritional Medicine, by Stephen Davies and Alan Stewart (Pan Books, 1987)

Prescription for Nutritional Healing, by James & Phyllis Balch (Avery Press, USA, 1990)

Raw Energy, by Leslie & Susannah Kenton (Arrow Books, 1985)

Superfoods: Superfoods Diet Book and Superfast Foods, by Michael van Straten and Barbara Griggs (Dorling Kindersley, 1994)

The Vitamin Bible, by Earl Mindell (Arrow, 1993)

Vitamin C, The Common Cold and Flu, by Linus Pauling (Berkeley, USA, 1970)

Vitamin C: The Master Nutrient, by Sandra Goodman (Keats, USA, 1991)

What the Label Doesn't Tell You, by Sue Dibb (Thorsons, 1998)

REFLEXOLOGY

The Complete Illustrated Guide to Reflexology, by Inge Dougans (Element Books, 1996)

Hand Reflexology: a textbook for students, by Kristine Walker (Quay Books, 1996)

In a Nutshell: Reflexology: A Step-by-Step Guide, by Nicola Hall (Element, 1997)

Reflexology, by Chris Stormer (Headway/Hodder & Stoughton, 1992)

Reflexology: A Practical Approach, by Vicki Pitman with Kay Mackenzie (Stanley Thornes, 1997)

Reflexology: A Step-by-Step Guide, by Ann Gillanders (Gaia, 1995)

YOGA

The Heart of Yoga, by T.K.V. Desckachar (Inner Traditions International, 1995)

Yoga for Common Ailments, by R. Nagarathna, H. R. Nagendram and Robin Monro (Gaia Books, 1990)

Yoga for the Disabled, by Howard Kent (Thorsons, 1985)

Yoga for Your Life, by Pierce and Pierce (Rudra Press, 1996)

INDEX

*Page numbers in italics indicate the
main entry on a subject.*

A

abdominal pain 10, *140–1*
acetaminophen 202, 203
acid indigestion *134–5*
acne 10, *64–5*
aconite 25, 49, 85, 125, 181
aesculus 177
agaricus 113
agnus-castus 169, 171
agrimony 23, 198
alfalfa 187
allergies 10, *22–3*
allium cepa 125, 129
aloe 177
Aloe vera 45, 149, 181, 182, 185,
  198
alumina 157
anemia 10, *118–19*
anise 157
antacids 202
antihistamines 22, 76, 128, 183,
  202
antimonium crudum 41, 68
antimonium tartaricum 39, 41
apis 22, 77, 86, 182, 183
apples 208
argentum nitricum 86, 205
arnica 99, 181, 184, 186, 187,
  188
arsenicum album 63, 74, 133,
  149, 153, 205
arsenicum iodatum 79
arthritis 10, *104–5*
artichokes 208
aspirin 77, 136
asthma 10, *132–3*, 167
astragalus 56
aurum 59
avocados 172, 208

B

back pain 10, *100–3*
bacteria *see* infections
bad breath 10, *88–9*
bicarbonate of soda 137, 147
baldness 82
bananas 208
base oils 206
basil 123, 207
  fainting 191
  fatigue 55
  hay fever 129
  headaches 51
  insomnia 63
  PMS 170
  psoriasis 79
  SAD 58

sinusitis 131
baths 201, 206
beclomethasone diproprionate
  202, 203
bedwetting 10, *174–5*
beet juice 122
belladonna 25, 36, 45, 66, 85,
  185, 205
bellis perennis 181
benzocaine 202
benzoin 109, 111, 123, 127
berberis 145
bergamot 21
  acne 65
  boils 66
  chicken pox 41
  PMS 171
  psoriasis 79
  shingles 43
betony 53, 191, 198
birch sap 105
bismuth 147
bites 11, *182*
black eyes 11, *181*
black haw 97, 165, 169
black horehound 139
black pepper 201
  chilblains 113
  constipation 157
  heartburn 135
  indigestion 137
  osteoarthritis 107
  osteoporosis 109
boils 11, *66*
borage 73, 169, 185
borax 91, 167
bran 84, 101
brazil nuts 20
bread 62, 66, 189, 200
bronchitis 12, *126–7*
bruises 11, *181*
bryonia 26, 31, 51, 205
  arthritis 105
  back pain 102
  constipation 157
  coughs 127
buckwheat 115
burns 11, *184*

C

cabbage 101, 104, 107, 151,
  153, 186, 208
caffeine 63
cajup 121
calamine 183, 185, 202, 203
calcarea carbonica 57, 107, 161,
  165
calcarea phosphorica 119, 187
calcarea sulphuricum 65
calendula 69

Californian poppy 63
calluses 12, *68–9*
camphor 191
candida 17, *166–7*
candida albicans 167
cantharis 179, 184
capsicum 135, 147
caraway *seeds* 88, 140, 142
carbo vegetabilis 137, 143, 191
carbolic acid 57
carrier oils 206
carrots 151, 208
catarrh 11, *122–3*
causticum 45, 49, 67, 99, 116,
  175
cayenne 49, 201
cedarwood 75, 83
celery 110, 169, 178
cellulite 11, *70–1*
chamomile 123, 198
  asthma 132, 133
  baths 201
  bruises 181
  earache 85
  fainting 191
  rheumatism 111
  rubella 32
  sprains 186
  sunburn 184
  tea 32, 62
chamomilla 85, 95, 141, 205
chelidonium 145
chicken pox 11, *40–1*, 42
chickweed 66, 181, 189
chilblains 11, *112–13*
children 202, 203
chili 117
china 119, 159
Chinese angelica 109, 119
chlorpheniramine maleate 202,
  203
chronic fatigue syndrome 11, 54,
  56–7
cider vinegar 81, 180, 185, 188
cimetidine 136, 202, 203
cimicifuga racemosa 168
cina 151
clary sage 57, 63, 169, 171
cleavers 79
clematis 74
clotrimazole 202, 203
clove 94, 95, 207
cocculus 190
coffea 63, 95
coffee beans 88
colchicum 111
cold sores 14, *28–9*
colds 11, *124–5*
colocynthis 141, 159
comfrey 107, 181, 187

common cold 11, *124–5*
compresses 195, 206
conjunctivitis 11, *86*
constipation 11, 89, 143, *156–7*,
  169
corns 12, *68–9*
coughs 12, *126–7*
cowslip 63
cradle cap 83
cramp 12, *96–7*
cramp-bark 97, 117, 155, 165
cranberry juice 179
cucumber 86
cuprum metallicum 39, 97
cuts 12, *180*
cyclamen 121
cypress 97, 115, 177
cystitis 12, *178–9*

D

dandelion 67, 118, 119, 157,
  169, 170, 178
dandruff 82, 83
decoctions 195
dehydration 139, 184
dermatitis 12, *72–3*
devil's claw 101, 105, 107
diarrhea 12, *158–9*
dill 120, 140, 142, 147
dimethicone 202
dioscorea 141
dosage 203
drosera 39
dulcamara 67, 111, 125
dys. co.(Bach) 61

E

earache 12, *84–5*
echinacea 21, 29, 66, 119, 125,
  198
  bites 182
  gastroenteritis 149
  ME 56
  mumps 35
  scarlet fever 37
  shingles 43
  sore throats 45
  whooping cough 39
eczema 12, *74–5*, 83
elder 198
elecampane 132
emollients 202
enuresis 10, *174–5*
ephedra 23
Epsom salts 107, 186, 201
equisetum 175
eucalyptus 29, 31, 207
  arthritis 105
  bites 182
  catarrh 123

INDEX

eucalyptus (**cont.**)
  chicken pox 41
  colds 125
  coughs 127
  German measles 33
  headaches 51
  infections 21
  infestations 151
  shingles 43
  sinusitis 131
eupatorium perfoliatum 26
euphrasia 31, 86, 129
evening primrose 56, 75, 170, 185
exclusion diet 76, 211
eyebright 87

F

fainting 12, *191*
fatigue 12, *54–5*
fennel 71, 147
  constipation 157
  flatulence 142, 143
  gingivitis 93
  heartburn 135
  indigestion 137
  menopause 173
  osteoporosis 109
  PMS 171
fenugreek tea 155
ferrum metallicum 114, 119
ferrum phosphoricum 25
ferrum picricum 68
fever 12, *24–5*
feverfew 52, 53
fibroids 13, *164–5*
fish oils 105, 106
flatulence 13, *142–3*
flea bites 182
flu *see* influenza
fluconazole 202, 203
fluoricum acidum 114
food combining 210
food poisoning *148–9*
fractures 13, *187*
frankincense 39, 121, 127, 133, 161, 207
fraxinus americana 165
frostbite *see* chilblains
frozen shoulder 110, 111

G

gallbladder problems 13, *144–5*
gallstones 139, 144–5
gargles 200
garlic 21, 31, 66, 125, 151, 198, 208
  allergies 23
  bites 182

corns 69
coughs 127
cuts 180
dermatitis 73
diarrhea 158
mouth ulcers 90, 91
ringworm 81
sinusitis 130
stings 183
thrush 167
tonsillitis 47
warts 67
whooping cough 38
gastritis 13, *146–7*
gastroenteritis 13, *148–9*
gelsemium 25, 26, 51, 205
gentian 119
geranium 113, 169, 207
  cramp 97
  eczema 75
  hemorrhoids 177
  menopause 173
  PMS 171
  varicose veins 115
German measles 13, *32–3*
ginger 117, 198, 201, 207
  arthritis 104, 105
  back pain 102
  constipation 157
  cramp 97
  flatulence 143
  heartburn 135
  indigestion 137
  migraine 52
  motion sickness 190
  nausea 139
  osteoarthritis 107
  rheumatism 111
  RSI 99
  sprains 186
gingivitis 13, *92–3*
ginseng 55, 58, 61
globe artichokes 144
glonoine 53, 185
glossypium 139
gnaphalium 102
goldenseal 29
gout 105
grapefruit 83, 208
graphites 68, 74, 83, 153
grief 207
gruel 54, 154
guaiacum 105

H

hair problems 13, *82–3*
halitosis 10, *88–9*
hamamelis 114, 177
hangovers 207
Hay diet 210

hay fever 13, *128–9*
He Shou Wu 173
headaches 13, *50–1*, *52–3*
head lice 150, 151
heartburn 14, *134–5*
helleborus 59
helonias 167, 171
hemorrhoids 13, *176–7*
hepar sulphuris 205
hepar sulphuris calcareum 66, 131
herpes simplex 14, *28–9*
hiatus hernia 134
hiccups 14, *120–1*
hives 14, *76–7*
honey 114, 191, 201
  colds and flu 27, 124
  cuts 180
  gastritis 147
  hay fever 128
  indigestion 137
  insomnia 62
  peptic ulcers 153
  sore throats 45
  stings 183
  tonsillitis 47
  whooping cough 38
hops 201
hormone replacement therapy (HRT) 172, 173
horseradish 117, 130, 191
horsetail 187
HRT *see* hormone replacement therapy
hydrastis 131, 145
hydrocortisone 203
hydrocortisone acetate 202
hyoscyamus 121
hypericum 180

I

IBS *see* irritable bowel syndrome
ibuprofen 202, 203
ice packages 98, 110, 176, 181, 186, 188, 200
ignatia 121, 191, 205
Indian tonic water 96
indigestion 14, *136–7*
infections 14, *20–1*
infestation 14, *150–1*
influenza 14, *26–7*
infusions 194
insect bites 182
insomnia 14, 57, *62–3*
ipecacuanha 39, 133, 139, 205
iris 53
irritable bowel syndrome (IBS) 14, *154–5*
ispaghula 157

J

jasmine 161, 171, 207
jellyfish stings 183
juniper 25, 71, 207
  arthritis 105
  boils 66
  eczema 75
  hemorrhoids 177
  osteoarthritis 107
  rheumatism 111
  RSI 99

K

kali arsenicosum 73
kali bichromicum 89, 123, 131
kali bromatum 65
kali phosphoricum 55
kali sulphuricum 83
kelp 161
kiwi fruit 208
Korean ginseng 55
kreosotum 73, 93, 175

L

lachesis 35, 45, 47, 171, 173, 205
laryngitis *see* sore throat
lavender 39, 198, 207
  abdominal pain 141
  acne 65
  allergies 23
  arthritis 105
  back pain 102
  bites 182
  boils 66
  bruises 181
  burns 184
  chicken pox 41
  chilblains 113
  corns/calluses 69
  cuts 180
  cystitis 179
  dermatitis 73
  diarrhea 159
  earache 85
  eczema 75
  fever 25
  fibroids 164
  gallbladder 145
  gastritis 146
  gastroenteritis 149
  German measles 33
  headaches 51
  hiccups 121
  hives 77
  infections 21
  infestations 151
  insomnia 63
  ME 57

INDEX

measles 31
migraine 53
mumps 35
nausea 139
neuralgia 49
osteoarthritis 107
osteoporosis 109
PMS 171
psoriasis 79
rheumatism 111
ringworm 81
RSI 99
shingles 43
splinters 189
sprains 186
stings 183
sunburn 185
thrush 167
tonsillitis 47
ledum 181, 182, 183, 186
leeks 31, 42, 130, 208
lemon 207, 208
  bad breath 89
  chilblains 112
  cold sores 28
  colds and flu 27, 124
  gallbladder 145
  hair problems 82, 83
  mumps 35
  neuralgia 49
  skin nourishment 172
  sore throats 45
  warts 67
lemon balm 29, 31, 35, 58, 198
lemon barley water 179
lemon grass 55, 57, 117, 207
lettuce, insomnia 62
licorice 142, 147, 153, 156, 157
lilium tigrinum 171
lime-blossom tea 27, 62, 201
lycopodium 137, 143, 155, 205

M

magnesium carbonicum 95
magnesium phosphate 168
magnesium phosphoricum 97,
  141
Malabar tamarind 161
male-pattern baldness 82, 83
mandarin 207
manuka honey 147, 153
marigold 66, 81, 87, 182, 183,
  198
marjoram
  back pain 102
  constipation 157
  flatulence 143
  insomnia 63
  ME 57
  neuralgia 49

osteoarthritis 107
osteoporosis 109
rheumatism 111
RSI 99
marshmallow 135, 147, 189, 199
massage oils 206
ME see myalgic encephalomyelitis
meadowsweet 199
measles 14, 30–1
medicine chest 216–17
melissa
  allergies 23
  gastritis 146
  gastroenteritis 149
  hay fever 129
  hives 77
  migraine 53
Ménière's disease 139
menopause 15, 172–3
menstrual problems 15, 168–9
mercurius 35, 47, 89, 91, 205
mercurius solubilis 93
methol salicylate 202
mezereum 43
miconazole 202, 203
migraine 15, 52–3
milk 62, 75, 131
mineral oil 202
mint 88, 137, 140, 142
morbillinum 31
morning sickness 139
mosquito bites 182
motherwort 165
motion sickness 15, 190
mouth ulcers 15, 90–1
mouthwashes 200
mullein 85
mumps 15, 34–5
mustard 101, 186, 201
myalgic encephalomyelitis (ME)
  11, 54, 56–7
myrrh
  cystitis 179
  gingivitis 93
  hemorrhoids 177
  mouth ulcers 91
  ringworm 81
  sore throats 45
  thrush 167

N

nappy rash 167
nasal congestion see catarrh
natrum muriaticum 29, 91, 125,
  205
natrum phosphoricum 151
natrum sulphuricum 133
nausea 15, 138–9
neroli 207
  diarrhea 159

IBS 155
ME 57
PMS 171
nettle soup 118
neuralgia 15, 48–9
niaouli 35
  bad breath 89
  infections 21
  infestations 151
nitric acid 67, 91, 93
nosebleeds 15, 188
nutmeg 201
nuts 208
nux vomica 51, 55, 205
  cramp 97
  gastritis 147
  hiccups 121
  IBS 155
  indigestion 137
  insomnia 63
  stress 61

O

oats 72, 74, 154, 208
oleander 83
olive oil 82, 145, 181, 185,
  209
onions 31, 125, 130, 182,
  183, 209
opium 157
orange essential oil 63, 207
oranges 208
orchitis 34
osteoarthritis 15, 104, 106–7
osteoporosis 15, 108–9

P

palmarosa 167
papaw juice 37
parasites 14, 150–1
parsley 119, 142, 169, 178
passiflora 63
peppermint 147
  bad breath 89
  diarrhea 159
  fainting 191
  fatigue 55
  fever 25
  flatulence 143
  headaches 51
  heartburn 135
  indigestion 137
  migraine 53
  motion sickness 190
  nausea 139
  sunburn 185
peptic ulcers 15, 152–3
petitgrain 207
petroleum 73, 79, 113, 190
pharyngitis 44

phosphorus 45, 93, 153, 188,
  191, 205
phytolacca 45, 47
picric acid 57
piles see hemorrhoids
pilewort 177
pine 125
pineapple juice 27, 31, 35, 37,
  169
  black eyes 181
  bruises 181
  chicken pox 41
  sinusitis 130
  tonsillitis 47
pineapples 209
pinworms 150, 151
plantago 95, 113, 175
plantain 181, 182, 183, 199
PMS see premenstrual syndrome
podophyllum 159
post-herpetic neuralgia 42–3, 48
potassium citrate 202, 203
potato juice 153
poultices 194, 200
pregnancy 177
pregnant women 203
premenstrual syndrome (PMS) 16,
  170–1
prunes 156
psoriasis 16, 78–9, 83
pulsatilla 31, 35, 205
  bad breath 89
  catarrh 123
  chilblains 113
  conjunctivitis 86
  earache 85
  IBS 155
  menopause 173
  osteoarthritis 107
  PMS 171
  styes 87
  varicose veins 114
pulses 209
pumpkin seeds 20, 151

R

ranitidine 136, 202
ranunculus bulbosus 43, 111, 121
raphanus 143
repetitive strain injury (RSI) 16,
  98–9
restless legs 16, 116–17
rheumatism 16, 110–11
rheumatoid arthritis 104
rhinitis 45
rhododendron 105
rhus toxicodendron 29, 41, 43,
  205
  dermatitis 73
  osteoarthritis 107

Index

rhus toxicodendron (cont.)
  restless legs 116
  sprains 186
rice 209
ringworm 16, 80–1
robina 135
Roman chamomile 33, 207
  abdominal pain 141
  allergies 23
  arthritis 105
  back pain 102
  chicken pox 41
  corns/calluses 69
  cystitis 179
  dermatitis 73
  diarrhea 159
  earache 85
  eczema 75
  fever 25
  fibroids 164
  flatulence 143
  gallbladder 145
  gastritis 146
  gastroenteritis 149
  hair problems 83
  hay fever 129
  heartburn 135
  hives 77
  IBS 155
  indigestion 137
  infestations 151
  ME 57
  measles 31
  mumps 35
  nausea 139
  neuralgia 49
  osteoarthritis 107
  osteoporosis 109
  PMS 171
  rheumatism 111
  RSI 99
  shingles 43
  toothache 95
rose 207
  eczema 75
  fibroids 164
  IBS 155
  ME 57
  menopause 173
  menstrual problems 169
  PMS 171
rosemary 199
  baths 201
  cellulite 71
  fainting 191
  fatigue 55
  hair problems 83
  infestations 151
  neuralgia 49
  osteoarthritis 107

osteoporosis 109
PMS 170
rheumatism 111
RSI 99
rosewater 172
RSI see repetitive strain injury
rubella 13, 32–3
rubella 30C 33
rue 181
rumex 127

S

sabadilla 129, 151
SAD see seasonal affective
  disorder
saffron 201
sage 37, 91, 125, 173, 183, 200
salt 92, 172, 183, 201
sambucus nigra 123
sandalwood 39, 207
  coughs 127
  PMS 171
  sore throats 45
  weight problems 161
sanguinaria 53
sarsaparilla 179
scabies 150
scarlet fever 16, 36–7
seasonal affective disorder (SAD)
  16, 58–9
seaweed 201
selenium 20
sepia 55, 59, 139, 167, 205
  menopause 173
  menstrual problems 168
  psoriasis 79
  ringworm 80
serotonin 61
shepherd's purse 165
shingles 16, 42–3, 49
shiitake mushrooms 56
Siberian ginseng 55, 58, 61, 87
silicea 189
sinusitis 16, 130–1
skin nourishment 172
slippery elm 66, 135, 147, 153,189
sodium bicarbonate 87, 183
sore throat 16, 37, 44–5, 125
spices 200–1
spigelia 49
splinters 16, 189
sprains 16, 186
sprays 206
St. John's wort 199
  earache 85
  mumps 35
  rheumatism 111
  SAD 58
  shingles 43
  sunburn 185

stannum 127
staphysagria 87, 99, 151, 179,
  205
stinging nettles 119, 183
stings 17, 183
stomach ache 10, 140–1
stress 17, 60–1
styes 17, 87
sugar syrup 197
sulphur 65, 66, 74, 135, 161,
  205
sunburn 17, 184, 185
symphytum 187

T

tabacum 190
tarantula 116
TAT see tired all the time
  syndrome
tea tree 27, 29, 199, 207
  acne 65
  bad breath 89
  bites 182
  boils 66
  colds 125
  coughs 127
  cuts 180
  cystitis 179
  dermatitis 73
  fainting 191
  fever 25
  gastroenteritis 149
  gingivitis 93
  infections 21
  infestations 151
  measles 31
  mumps 35
  ringworm 81
  rubella 33
  shingles 43
  sinusitis 131
  sore throats 45
  thrush 167
  tonsillitis 47
  warts 67
teabags 86, 87
tellurium 80, 102
temperature 24–5
tendonitis 110
tennis elbow 110, 111
thrush 17, 166–7
thuja 67
thyme 47, 123, 199
  bad breath 88, 89
  gingivitis 92, 93
  infections 21
  infestations 151
  ME 57
  ringworm 81
tinctures 196–7

tinea 80–1
tired all the time syndrome (TAT)
  54
tonsillitis 17, 46–7
tooth care 89, 93
toothache 17, 94–5
travel sickness 138, 190
trigeminal neuralgia 48
tryptophan 61
turmeric 201
tymol 92

U

ulcers, mouth 90–1
urtica urens 77, 184
urticaria 14, 76–7
ustilago 165

V

vaginal yeast infection see thrush
valerian 53, 57, 61
vaporizers 206
varicose veins 17, 114–15
vegetable oil 69
veratrum album 149
vervain 199
vetivert 79, 171
viburnum 168
vinegar 82, 183
violet 165
vipera 114
viruses see infections

W

wake-up remedy 207
warts 17, 67
water treatments 201
watercress 209
weight loss 71
weight problems 17, 160–1
wheat 209
wheatgerm 74, 78
whooping cough 17, 38–9
worms 14, 150–1
wormwood 151

Y

yarrow 188, 199
yellow dock 157
ylang ylang 171, 207
yogurt 21, 37, 43, 149, 166,
  167, 172, 209

Z

zinc 20, 167
zincum 116